Feminism's Progress

SUNY series in Feminist Criticism and Theory

Michelle A. Massé, editor

Feminism's Progress

Gender Politics in British and American Literature and Television since 1830

Carol Colatrella

Cover image of Miss Louise Hall with brush and Miss Susan Fitzgerald assisting bill posting in Cincinnati (from the Library of Congress).

Published by State University of New York Press, Albany

© 2023 State University of New York

For information, contact State University of New York Press, Albany, NY
www.sunypress.edu

Library of Congress Cataloging-in-Publication Data

Name: Colatrella, Carol, author.
Title: Feminism's progress : gender politics in British and American
  literature and television since 1830 / Carol Colatrella.
Description: Albany, NY : State University of New York Press, [2023] |
  Series: SUNY series in feminist criticism and theory | Includes
  bibliographical references and index.
Identifiers: LCCN 2022049711 | ISBN 9781438493930 (hardcover : alk. paper) |
  ISBN 9781438493954 (ebook)
Subjects: LCSH: Feminism—History—21 century. | Equality. | Women—Social
  conditions—21st century. | Sex discrimination against women. |
  Television and women. | Women in literature.
Classification: LCC HQ1155 .C65 2023 | DDC 305.42—dc23/eng/20221028
LC record available at https://lccn.loc.gov/2022049711

10 9 8 7 6 5 4 3 2 1

To Rick, Charlie, and Lena

"Hope" is the thing with feathers -
That perches in the soul -
And sings the tune without the words -
And never stops - at all -

And sweetest - in the Gale - is heard -
And sore must be the storm -
That could abash the little Bird
That kept so many warm -

I've heard it in the chillest land -
And on the strangest Sea -
Yet - never - in Extremity,
It asked a crumb - of me.

—Emily Dickinson

Contents

Contents

Acknowledgments

I thank individuals and publishers allowing me to include previously published material in this book. Chapter 1 incorporates revised passages from Carol Colatrella, "Review of Christopher F. Karpowitz and Tali Mendelberg, *The Silent Sex: Gender, Deliberation, and Institutions*," published in *International Journal of Gender, Science, and Technology* 8, no. 2 (2016): 313-16. An earlier version of part of chapter 1 was published in Carol Colatrella, "The Innocent Convict: Character, Reader Sympathy, and the Nineteenth-Century Prison in *Little Dorrit*," in *In the Grip of the Law: Prisons, Trials, and the Space in Between*, edited by Monika Fludernik and Greta Olson (Frankfurt am Main: Peter Lang, 2004): 185-204. An earlier version of chapter 1 appears in Carol Colatrella, "Information in the Novel and the Novel as Information System: Charles Dickens's *Little Dorrit* and Margaret Drabble's *The Radiant Way* Trilogy," published in *Information and Culture: A Journal of History* 50, no. 3 (2015): 339-71; I appreciate the University of Texas permitting publication. A section of chapter 2 was published as Carol Colatrella, "The Evils of Slavery and Their Legacy in American Literature," in *Evil in American Popular Culture*, vol. 2, edited by Jody Pennington and Sharon Packer (Santa Barbara, CA: Praeger, 2014): 45-61. I have adapted portions of chapters 4 and 6 from chapters 3 and 4 in Carol Colatrella, *Toys and Tools in Pink* (Columbus: Ohio State University Press, 2011); I thank the copyright holder the Ohio State University for their permission to incorporate passages from that book. An earlier version of chapter 4 was published as Carol Colatrella, "When the Scientist Is a Woman: Novels and Feminist Science Studies," in *Science under the Literary Microscope*, edited by Susan Gaines, Roslynn Haynes, and Sina Farzin (Harrisburg: Pennsylvania State University Press, 2021); I thank the editors and the press for allowing publication. Part of chapter

6 is a revision of Carol Colatrella, "Narrative Complexity, Character, and Action: Reconfiguring Gender Norms and Genre Conventions in a Police Procedural," published in *Signs & Media* 11 (Autumn 2015): 17–39; I appreciate the journal's allowing publication. I thank Janine DeBaise for allowing me to use as an epigraph to chapter 6 some lines from her poem "What We Learn," published in *Body Language* (Charlotte, NC: Main Street Rag, 2019), 15.

I am grateful to organizers of and audiences at various conferences where I presented drafts of chapters. Groups include the Modern Language Association; the International Society for the Study of Narrative; and the Society for Literature, Science, and the Arts. I thank the organizers of 2015 PopSci, the International Conference on Science, Research and Popular Culture, in Klagenfurt, Austria, who encouraged me to present on *Call the Midwife* and *The Bletchley Circle.* Lecturing on gender studies, STEM, and media to audiences at Aarhus University, Tianjin University, Louisiana State University, Lafayette College, the University of South Carolina-Upstate, and Emory University also helped me develop the book's argument. I appreciate the generous responses of hosts and attendees at these events.

Colleagues and friends, including Fulbright collaborators Nelly P. Stromquist, Elizabeth Balbachevsky, Manuel Gil-Antón, Reitumetse Obakeng Mabokela, Anna Smolentseva, and Heather Eggins provided encouragement and support in the form of congenial collaboration on related publications, as did the late Kirsten Gomard, who was my coauthor on one essay and an adviser on others. I value significant advice offered by Jamie Barlowe, Mita Choudhury, Ellen Esrock, Deborah Johnson, Ellen McCallum, Michelle Massé, Alan Nadel, Peter Rabinowitz, and Priscilla Walton, and by Atlanta colleagues, especially Deepika Bahri, Nihad Farooq, Narin Hassan, Janet Murray, Nassim Parvin, Anne Pollock, Mary Lynn Realff, Carol Senf, and Joycelyn Wilson. Celeste Goodridge and Shirley Gorenstein also advised on this project and much more; I miss their wise counsel. My ideas have benefited from conversations with friends Kathy Buck, Beth Gibson, Marjorie Hutter, Megan Missett, Carol Plaut, and V. P. and Becky Loggins. I thank my students for sharing their insights, and I am grateful to Georgia Tech library and information technology staff for helping me access materials and employ technologies to continue research and teaching despite challenges. Thanks are also due to the editing and production staff of SUNY Press, particularly Rebecca Colesworthy, and to the generous advice offered by the manuscript reviewers.

Since March 2020 I have depended on the company and support of Lena, Charlie, and Rick Denton. Rick deserves special thanks for so many reasons, including that he is always willing to read and offer incisive comments about my writing. During the pandemic my family walked our newly adopted dog in nearby parks and neighborhoods on our breaks from study and work, made delicious meals, watched a lot of media, and enjoyed entertaining, enlightening conversations at the end of each day. I will always be grateful for their insights and patience in a difficult time.

Prologue

And it is important to note that identity continues to be a site of resistance for members of different subordinated groups. . . . At this point in history, a strong case can be made that the most critical resistance strategy for disempowered groups is to occupy and defend a politics of social location rather than to vacate and destroy it.

—Kimberlé Williams Crenshaw, "Mapping the Margins: Intersectionality, Identity Politics, and Violence against Women of Color" (1994)[1]

Rather than echoing the rhythms of fashion, where ephemeral image constellations and shiny surfaces pop up as "new and improved" attractions and then pop out with the regulated and unmemorable cycles of the clock, the backstory of feminist discursive engagements animates the deep structures of feminist thought and politics in future time.

—Robin Truth Goodman, "Introduction," *The Bloomsbury Handbook of Feminist Theory* (2019)[2]

Setting the stage for contemporary views of gender and society, many fictional narratives produced from 1830 to the present reference feminist ideas in conveying messages about gender inequities and needed reforms. This book serves as a basic introduction to the history of women's social roles as represented in literature and media from different periods, looking at the ways in which these texts present feminist ideas and considering how their narrative elements operate and appeal to audiences. My account traces a trajectory of optimism in these fictions by looking at expressions of resistance to sexism and racism and at suggested reforms that could eliminate discrimination and promote equity. In this way, the study of past feminist representations enables us to follow the varying fortunes of gender equity over time and to advocate for further feminist efforts. British and American fictions build a case for the benefits of developing a feminist society, largely by describing constraints experienced by women, recommending social and political reforms, and speculating about future actions and attitudes to foster progress. Fictional narratives that explicate the ways in which past feminisms stumbled or prospered illustrate historical developments that encourage gender equity. In short, readers' ideas of feminism and desires for a gender equitable society have been shaped by representations of women's problems and prospects in historical and contemporary literature and media.

Since March 2020, there has been a pandemic-related shift in the political landscape to recognize that care, compassion, and community, values that feminism supports, ought to be prioritized by individuals and institutions. Fictional narratives reference oppressive social and political structures and point to reforms founded on feminist ideas. Tracing those ideas in literature and media reveals gradual acceptance of progressive attitudes toward gender, women's political power, and intersectionality that replace a rigid patriarchal sex/gender system and that question gender and racial hierarchies.[3] This book applies concepts and insights from feminist and other critical theories in various disciplines to the study of literary and televisual narratives. By focusing on structural features of narrative representations—characterizations, plots, settings associated with women and feminism—in specific works, readers understand the ways in which these elements develop feminist critiques of gender bias and discrimination and recommend gender equity reforms.

The narratives discussed in these pages represent an optimistic politics promoting social justice and thereby constitute an underrecognized subgenre of post-Romantic fictions that argue for women's empowerment. Lauren Berlant reminds us in *Cruel Optimism* that

> History hurts, but not only. It also engenders optimism in response to the oppressive presence of what dominates or is taken for granted. Political emotions are responses to prospects for change: fidelity to those responses is optimistic, even if the affects are dark. . . . But the compulsion to repeat optimism . . . is a condition of possibility that also risks having to survive, once again, disappointment and depression, the

protracted sense that nothing will change and that no-one, especially oneself, is teachable after all. . . . To be teachable is to be open for change.[4]

Berlant's book elaborates the misguided premises of cruel optimism, ideas encouraged by a capitalist myth of social mobility that is difficult, if not impossible, to effect in practice. She recognizes critical negligence ("Dreams are seen as easy optimism, while failures seem complex"), and, in doing so, acknowledges the work of Eve Sedgwick, who "writes against the hermeneutics of suspicion on the grounds that it always finds the mirages and failures for which it looks: she finds critics overdedicated to a self-confirming scene of disappointment."[5] Taking a turn, I present in this book a dimension of feminism focusing on optimism in examples of literature and media that inspire rather than disappoint. These realist feminist fictions outline challenges and imagine prospects for access, opportunity, and equity for women, and, to a certain extent, minorities.[6] While narratives discussed in these pages primarily reference gender equity, some notice social inequalities related to race, ethnicity, class, and sexual orientation that continue to bedevil society.

My focus here on literature and media is a deliberate attempt to recognize the cultural influences of print and televisual fictional texts in shaping ideas about gender and its intersections with race, ethnicity, and class. Martin Eve asks about the political influence of literature: "what type of influence literature has . . . how do . . . political elements of short stories, novels and poetry, amid other hybrid forms, translate into action? Is it enough . . . for a text to present an ethical worldview? . . . There is clearly a persistent and widespread social anxiety about the potential political power of literature and its translation into action."[7] I include analyses of televisual media in thinking about textual influence because cable television and streaming services enable widespread consumption of fictional narratives influencing public opinion and action.

Two historical examples related to race and gender demonstrate the power of representations to affect attitudes in ways that lead to enhanced social equity: television news coverage of 1960s civil rights advocates that captured abuse of Black citizens by police and others and contemporary narrative accounts of transsexuality. William G. Thomas III notes, "Dedicated segregationists and committed civil rights proponents both recognized the potential of television news to upset the inertia of segregated society. . . . Whether it changed minds may never be known, but there is evidence television inspired some to act forcefully in the streets and others to try desperately to control the media."[8] The mission statement of *Trans Book Review* asserts that fictional and nonfictional accounts help readers understand transsexuality: "We need stories to help our cisgender brothers and sisters understand us and support us in carving out our places in the world. We need stories to bring us together and bridge the gap between us and them."[9] Reading or viewing realist narratives encourages engagement with social justice issues as readers unpack representations that reproduce and reconfigure elements in the world, often forecasting social change. Print and televisual narratives explore social and political solutions to eliminate inequities via characters, narrators, settings, and plots constituting a realistic fictional world. Information in texts develops political arguments by describing oppressions to be eliminated and affirming long-standing hopes of characters to overturn sex/gender hierarchies and, in some instances, racial and/or sexual oppression. In this way, the feminist imagination expressed in fictional narratives proposes ways to enact justice for those lacking power.

Print and visual narratives that contain messages promoting equity and objecting to oppression operate via structures associated with feminism and/or enact communication processes reflecting feminist ways of reading. Basic definitions of feminism identify it as practices and ideologies opposing inequities based on gender identity and expression and sexual orientation. Feminisms of different waves explain how identity, power, and knowledge intersect with social characteristics such as sex/gender, race/ethnicity, and class. Realist fictions characterized as feminist notice disparate treatments of persons based on gender, class, and ethnicity; texts describe individual and social barriers and facilitators affecting attitudes and conduct. In this way, feminist texts speculate about how problems of social inequality will be corrected in a deferred future. I note definitions of critical terms I employ, as follows:

- Feminism: a system that recognizes the marginalization of the feminine and that resists the imposition of gender- and sex-based norms and conventions constraining and oppressing individuals.

- Woman: the Other in patriarchy, which opposes it to man/masculine; a cultural concept rather than a biological one.

- Intersectionality: an important concept in contemporary social theory developed by Black feminists that recognizes the multidimensional social characteristics of a person or persons.

- Antiracism: action against racist practices and systems.

- Realism: a genre of writing that attempts to represent things as they are; also, a stylistic mode of establishing authenticity.

These definitions incorporate principles recognized by other critics. Asserting "the usefulness of seeing all representations of identity as simultaneously possible and impossible," Diana Fuss questions whether it is "legitimate to call oneself anti-essentialist feminist, when feminism seems to take for granted among its members a shared identity, some essential point of commonality?"[10] Ellen Rooney argues for retaining the category "woman" as a useful term in framing the political aims of feminism, "Feminism contests the meaning of femininity and women's place in society; it cannot take seriously Kristeva's (in)famous assertion that 'woman does not exist.' Without the grounding provided by the category woman, it is not possible to pursue any political program whatsoever, within the academy or elsewhere. The alternative—'to tear down the "identity" woman' or 'to seek some other identity altogether'—is not an alternative politics. It is a retreat from the political as such."[11] Rooney cites Parveen Adams, who "reasserts the 'political fact' that systems of representation produce sexual differences, differences that are not a reflection of already existing, static, and knowable sexual divisions, masculine and feminine, differences that cannot be known in advance, that must be read and reread as they emerge."[12] Judith Lorber acknowledges issues of the identity groups "insiders" and "outsiders," citing Sylvia Waldby's preference for recognizing "politics across difference" and noting Dale Bauer's and Priscilla Wald's understanding that "coalition politics does not offer a united front of feminism. . . . A coalition comes together to get some work done, not to nurture."[13] Feminists connect around issues to leverage change, doing so for certain purposes in particular contexts that will be discussed later in this book.

My literary and media analyses build on these feminist critical principles in recognizing dimensions of intersectionality in discussing print and visual texts. Black feminists developed the term *intersectionality* as a concept acknowledging multiple aspects of identity that affect one's circumstances and outcomes. The writers who produced *Combahee River Collective Statement* (1978) understood "that the major systems of oppression are interlocking," pointing out that "white male rule" "determined" their "membership in two oppressed racial and sexual castes."[14] Intersections of gender and race are significant in novels by Frances Ellen Watkins Harper, Ann Patchett, Catherine Chung, and Toni Morrison, as noted in chapters 2, 4, and 6, while chapters 1, 3, 5, and 7 track intersections of gender and class.

Feminist analyses consider how concepts of empowerment and collectivity describe new attitudes toward gender equity and sketch new social arrangements resisting those identified as normative, which narratives represent as insufficient. Judith Fetterley argues that "the first act of the feminist critic must be to become a resisting rather than an assenting reader and, by this refusal to assent, to begin the process of exorcising the male mind that has been implanted in us"; she aligns the resisting reader with change, remarking on what "Adrienne Rich describes as revision—'the act of looking back, of seeing with fresh eyes, of entering an old text from a new critical direction.'"[15] My interpretations adopt such principles of second-wave feminism to analyze fictions illustrating social structures, political ideas, and individual situations related to sex differences, gender roles, and the political rights of women and racial minorities. Fictional representations persuade audiences to understand the urgency of enacting reforms aimed at increasing women's opportunities, agency, and autonomy and expanding their political power. Ellen Messer Davidow points to how applying feminist critical practices in disciplines leads to advocacy.

> The feminist criticisms proceeding in these traditional disciplines and in women's studies constitute a single inquiry. The story they are piecing together is how the sex/gender system organizes every aspect of our lives, why, and what we might do to change this unwholesome situation. . . . We see the sex/gender system because we belong to a social movement that aims to redistribute power and privilege and because we find that available theories fail to account for the problems that concern us.[16]

While there is growing public interest in dismantling systemic and structural inequalities, more reforms related to gender, race, ethnicity, and class equity are needed in the United States, Britain, and other nations. Reading the texts discussed here offers opportunities for audiences to reflect on problems and prospects affecting women and minorities as a dimension of pursuing action; the act of reading becomes one step toward implementing progressive changes.

Completing this book in 2022 has been complicated as attitudes toward feminism are multiple and evolving in a period stressed by a pandemic, inflation, and violent conflicts. Pressing inequality issues highlighted in news and social media include police profiling and police violence against Blacks and other persons of color; disparate sentencing guidelines for offenders, and the growth of the private prison-industrial complex; the lack of affordable, accessible health treatment, including mental health treatment and rehabilitation facilities for alcohol and drug abusers; the uncertain legal status of persons displaced because of gangs, wars, or other conflicts; discrimination against immigrants; disparities in political and economic opportunities related to religion, race, class, and gender; intimidating, harassing sexist behaviors and speech, including by leaders; hostile personal and virtual interactions in the workforce and in public discourses; the weakening of women's legal reproductive rights; and acts of violence directed against women, trans individuals, and those expressing non-hetero-normative sexual orientations. Many citizens in the US and Great Britain are interested in dismantling structural inequalities, while some pursue conservative goals of deregulation, shoring up existing economic interests, controlling reproduction, and repressing minority and progressive votes and voices. Conservatives fear that ensuring equity for the disadvantaged and dismantling hierarchies threatens the privileged.

The desired outcomes of feminism promise to address bias and barriers affecting women and other marginalized groups and to develop equitable conditions to improve their circumstances. Many realist fictions identify social discrimination while looking toward the future and sketching reforms that could improve civil rights and socioeconomic opportunities for those currently disadvantaged. Fictions persuade by noting plausible, necessary individual, economic, and legal reforms to improve gender equity and by utilizing the affordances of print and visual media to convey and advance feminist claims. Narrative plots describe sympathetic, worthy female protagonists who suffer structural and/or individual inequities. These characters navigate bias and barriers so they can survive, and in many cases thrive, even under extraordinary circumstances. Fictional settings delineate characteristics of oppression, including rigid social conventions, economic constraints, and laws and public policies limiting the capacities of narrators and characters. Immersed in realistic fictional worlds, audiences experience challenges ranging from lack of access to education and jobs to violent, even deadly attacks. Narrators and characters notice or imagine reforms offering better prospects, providing audiences with lessons to apply to life.

We can posit that narratives form a fictional ecology, offering landscapes in which characters interact and imagine opportunities for friendship, collaboration, and solidarity that overcome discriminatory practices to create a just society. Yet Darwinistic terminology has limited applicability, for, in the biological world changing physical conditions affect diverse outcomes of species, which evolve, either to survive and reproduce or to die without issue; however, fictional feminist narratives look forward to a future in which mutually beneficial conditions prevail rather than ensuring privileges for one group. In this way, fictions provide insight into the nonhierarchical world imagined by R. W. Connell in *Masculinities*: "I think a fresh politics of masculinity will develop in new arenas. . . . And in some sense it must be a politics above interests, a politics of pure possibility. Though that is, perhaps, another way of expressing the interest all people on this planet share in social justice, peace and balance with the natural world."[17] Reading a story or a novel or viewing a television show or film that incorporates an optimistic, radical message anticipating a feminist future prompts readers to press forward to consider how an individual can contribute to social progress. Narrative fictions outline hierarchies of gender, race, and class and sketch ways to overturn rigid social systems inhibiting change and mobility. In this way, fictions inspire advocacy and help us imagine how to unbuild and reconfigure the world.

Contextualizing my reading of canonical and paracanonical works, the book's introduction summarizes relevant key concepts in feminist literary criticism.[18] Subsequent chapters analyze narratives arguing for increasing women's rights and designing legal and social improvements to enhance individual lives, families, and communities. Each chapter considers a cluster of texts addressing a social institution or social dimension, identifying political actions that could improve conditions. Following Elizabeth Freeman's example in *Time Binds*, I have selected "a small number of imaginative texts rather than amass[ing] a weighty archive of or around texts."[19] Narratives variously note social and legal barriers that are difficult for characters, particularly women, to navigate. Post-Romantic British and

American fictions discussed in these chapters detail cultural factors contributing to oppression and identify obstacles that should be eliminated to promote opportunities for those who lack access to education, work, and housing. Textual messages encourage optimism, referencing a better future for all and encouraging readers and viewers to speculate about the possibilities of eliminating gender discrimination and promoting gender equality.

Narrative elements of fictions—voice, characterization, plots, and settings—work together to persuade readers to support initiatives enabling equity. Authors of realist fictions promoting a cultural politics of feminism employ accessible language and resist avant-garde stylistic innovations while developing relatable characters and situations to influence how audiences respond to the political content within fiction. My analyses explicate the ways in which reader and viewer sympathies respond to characters' temperaments and their actions within plots touching on issues of citizenship, including enfranchisement, civil rights, and political agency. The threads woven through chapters include discussions of ways to eliminate economic disparities, social and legal discrimination, and political inequities affecting women and minorities, and to introduce mechanisms developing collaborations and communities across social categories to redistribute power.

Literature and media discussed in these pages attempt to persuade audiences that the future should be and must be feminist by illustrating examples of positive (equity-oriented) and negative (sexist, racist, classist) attitudes and behavior within plausibly realistic fictional worlds. Fictions identify problems and they also recommend opportunities, especially in suggesting strategies, tactics, and ideas worth pursuing in the name of equity, morality, and social progress. Each chapter traces contours of "the feminist imagination" and includes the ways that feminist fictions propose role models, acknowledge biases and barriers for women and others in marginal groups, and identify characters' strategies of leveraging personal and social resources.[20] Texts describe ways of organizing social and institutional relations to improve women's prospects and to eliminate biases against gender, gender identity, and sexual orientation in educational institutions, the workforce, romantic relationships, and marriages. Because negative stereotypes about women, minorities, and nonbinary individuals persist in our time, it is not surprising that stories about overcoming bias and discrimination and hinting at an equitable future appeal to audiences. Whether narratives include historical or contemporary plots, they constitute a subgenre of realist fiction, for audiences recognize similar circumstances in the era of #MeToo and #TimesUp and value the ways in which narratives promote optimism and collective action in working toward equity.

Introduction

Feminist Literary Criticism, Liberation, and Social Change

Carlyle, hearing from Emerson that Margaret Fuller had agreed to accept the universe, pounded out "By God, she'd better!" But now our minds work against Carlyle in the anecdote. Why should Margaret Fuller accept the universe? And why should Carlyle insist upon her doing so?

—Mary Ellmann, *Thinking about Women* (1968)[1]

And of course I am afraid, because the transformation of silence into language and action is an act of self-revelation, and that always seems fraught with danger.

—Audre Lorde, "The Transformation of Silence into Language and Action" (1978)[2]

Because the counterstance stems from a problem with authority—outer as well as inner—it's a step towards liberation from cultural domination. But it is not a way of life. At some point, on our way to a new consciousness, we will have to leave the opposite bank, the split between the two mortal combatants somehow healed so that we are on both shores at once and, at once, see through serpent and eagle eyes. Or perhaps we will decide to disengage from the dominant culture, write it off altogether as a lost cause, and cross the border into a wholly new and separate territory. Or we might go another route. The possibilities are numerous once we decide to act and not react.

—Gloria Anzaldúa, "Borderlands/La Frontera" (1987)[3]

1

How can we eliminate the inequities affecting women, nonbinary individuals, and minorities who live in a world limiting their opportunities and oppressing them in violent ways? The epigraphs provide three, not wholly distinct, feminist responses to the problem of gender-based and other social inequalities, responses formed during an age that witnessed the US civil rights movement and the emergence of a women's liberation movement. Mary Ellmann questions male authority that represses women, Audre Lorde understands the dangers of those speaking out against established authority, and Gloria Anzaldúa acknowledges that liberation could include reconciliation, estrangement, or moving to a new "territory" to escape from cultural domination. These statements appeared in critical works addressed to general audiences and to scholars who observed cultural factors shaping attitudes toward women and minorities in literature, media, and culture. While supporters of women's rights in the United States and Great Britain helped many women gain voting, property, marital, and other legal rights, advocates in the 1960s and later, as the epigraphs demonstrate, continued to press for equality, concentrating their efforts on raising women's consciousness, inspiring collective action, and aiming to achieve legally sanctioned equal rights. In a period that also witnessed the strengthening of the US civil rights movement, the authors of these epigraphs, and many others, developed feminist criticism targeted at moving the sex/gender system toward equality.

Tracing how feminism fares in fiction, *Feminism's Progress* looks at fictional information—plots, characters, settings, and voice—in selected narratives that incorporate discussions and illustrations of women's empowerment, social collectivity, equality, resistance, and other issues important to supporters of women's rights and feminists of different waves. Fictional texts from the nineteenth century to the present—novels, stories, television shows, and films—identify social problems such as bias, discrimination, and violence, and explore feminist arguments promoting gender equity in marriage, education, careers, and politics. My subject includes representations of suffrage movements and women politicians in discussing fictions that recommend reconfiguring the sex/gender system and encouraging individuals to act collectively and cooperatively with others to ensure an equitable future for all.

Many theoretical accounts of gender, literature, and culture and fictional texts have helped shape my understanding of feminism—how to define it, ways to evaluate its appearance in literature and media, and its application as a reading strategy. Moira Ferguson explains in the preface to her anthology of British women writers: "By feminist I mean those ideas and actions that advocate women's just demands and rights, or that counter or offset, at any level, the socio-cultural, sexual and psychological oppression and exploitation of women."[4] Rachel Blau Duplessis offered a dynamic account of feminism in a 2015 interview: "For me feminism is sex-gender justice intertwined with social and economic justice, and it involves female co-equality with males amid female differences, the positions working in endless dialectical movement. Women's gains in agency, co-equality, and legal redress should not come at the expense of others who endure social wrongs, although there is undoubtedly some cost to people's claims of power-over-others and to their claims of interpretive hierarchies of importance where women rank as lesser."[5] Sharing a core belief in feminism's focus on advocacy, equality, and opposition to inequity, these definitions align with the succinct one provided by bell hooks: "feminism is a movement to end sexism, sexist exploitation, and oppression."[6] Identifying problems and recommending solutions, print and televisual fictions assert feminism's potential to eliminate sexism and overcome gender inequities.

Referencing critical disparities between women and men in private and public spheres, many realist fictions produced in the United States and Great Britain advocate for women's rights and point to social marginalization by class, race, and other social characteristics such as sexual orientation, sexual identity, age, and disability status. Narratives inspire hope in a feminist future by noticing barriers and positing facilitators affecting women's empowerment and gender equity. Fictional texts identify the possibility of cultural change over time, largely by encouraging women's participation in education, work, and governance. Narratives illustrate inequities and identify social capacities to effect political change, noting the ways in which reforms related to equality and equity are proposed, if not instantiated within the texts. Fictions nevertheless provide readers with hope for the success of feminist ideas, despite deferring their development to the future.

Some critics and scholars subsume various forms of feminism as living under one banner, while others recognize types of feminism, with differences pertaining to cultural contexts or political principles. The perspectives of early feminist scholars who addressed gender issues in literature remain salient, although we now recognize that diverse social dimensions combine to oppress individuals and that all women are not the same. Catherine Belsey acknowledges, "Women as a group in our society are both produced and inhibited by contradictory discourses."[7] Recognizing that not all women are similarly situated and that earlier feminists sometimes exploited and/or marginalized women of color, scholars writing since 1989 incorporate Kimberlé Williams Crenshaw's term *intersectionality* to consider the "layers of oppression" caused by gender, race, ethnicity, class, immigration status, and sexual orientation and to acknowledge multidimensional social characteristics of a person or persons.[8] Third-wave feminism includes supporting more recently developed principles: recuperating dimensions of femininity, stopping demonizing pornography, democratizing sex work as a viable occupation, and appreciating the fluid aspects of gender identity.

Readers assess fictional information in analyzing representations of political ideas and actions; more specifically, they evaluate characters that serve as role models, understand point of view in conveying strategies to navigate society and institutions, and regard plots as situated case studies exploring problems and prospects for women. Additionally, many fictions suggest improvements to establish gender equality. My argument links discussion of cultural practices, reform attitudes, and texts in ways similar to the connections Laura Fisher makes in *Reading for Reform*, which examines "the rich interplay of reform institutions and US literature" that "brimmed with oppositional energy" and inspired progressive reforms in the period between 1890 and World War I: "Reformers of the Progressive Era . . . rushed to devise new institutional forms for ameliorating the social ills that ailed the nation and that had transformed their cities and towns."[9] She contrasts earlier nineteenth-century reform efforts as sentimental and focused on individuals, while in the 1880s and 1890s "activist energies shifted both rhetorically and practically from individual victims to the health of the whole civic body."[10] Citing the Occupy Wall Street movement, she allows that "recent events point to the enduring cultural afterlife of uplift institutions and reform literature."[11] Fisher builds on chapters detailing the connections between literary texts and reform practices in the late nineteenth and early twentieth centuries with a "Coda" describing the Tenement Museum and other contemporary cultural initiatives.

A key element of fictional narratives promoting progressive cultural reforms involves representing circumstances influencing historical inequities so that readers and viewers can recognize cultural forces shaping individuals and the need for social groups to shift attitudes and develop opportunities. Simone de Beauvoir remarks in *The Second Sex*, "One is not born, but rather becomes, a woman. No biological, psychological, or economic fate determines the figure that the human female presents in society; it is civilization as a whole that produces this creature, intermediate between male and eunuch, which is described as feminine."[12] Fictional representations identify biases that should be eliminated and structural improvements to be adopted so that woman is no longer treated as the Other. Supporting Beauvoir, Rosi Braidotti characterizes the work of women's and gender studies in changing cultural assumptions: "The feminist position ever since the eighteenth century has consisted in attacking the naturalistic assumptions about the mental inferiority of women, shifting the grounds of the debate towards the social and cultural construction of women as being different."[13] Fictions explore the ways that reconfiguring social and economic opportunities for women could adjust cultural attitudes about women and minorities to establish an equitable society.

Texts advocating political and social reforms prompt audiences to act on feminist principles to overturn traditional sex/gender hierarchies. Many feminist literary critics have advanced such arguments over the past fifty years. In 1979, Annette Kolodny acknowledged the "pace of inquiry" in feminist literary studies from 1969 to 1979 as "fast and furious," noting "the diversity of that inquiry easily outstripped all efforts to define feminist literature criticism as either a coherent system or a unified set of methodologies," and understanding that under feminism's "wide umbrella, everything has been thrown into question: our established canons, our aesthetic criteria, our interpretative strategies, our reading habits, and most of all, ourselves as critics and as teachers. To delineate its full scope would require nothing less than a book—a book that would be outdated even as it was being composed."[14] Kolodny thus affirmed the capacious, evolving nature of feminisms that influence texts, interpretation, reading practices, and individuals, acknowledging that the dynamic dimensions of feminisms make it difficult to form a coherent, comprehensive account.

By interrogating the status quo and representing imaginary, even radical, possibilities for individuals and society, feminist literature inspires readers to think beyond existing attitudes and conditions and to develop an ethics of equity. In 1988, Barbara Christian pointed to playfulness: "writers/artists have a tendency to refuse to give up their way of seeing the world and of playing with possibilities; in fact, their very expression relies on that insistence. Perhaps that is why creative literature, even when written by politically reactionary people, can be so freeing, for in having to embody ideas and recreate the world, writers cannot merely produce one way."[15] Laurie Finke recommended in 2018 that feminists should build on Donna Haraway's recommendation to reconstruct knowledge: "I believe it is important for feminists to go beyond simply showing the myriad ways in which the sciences and other institutions have oppressed women; the more difficult task is to rethink the boundaries separating different cultural practices, to examine how structures of knowledge function as strategies of oppression, and to explore how feminism might help restructure larger cultural institutions."[16] Realist narratives supply information revealing oppression and proposing equity, providing readers with opportunities to contemplate social changes in fiction and to enact them in life by restructuring social systems.

Representations and Social Change

Feminist scholars in literature and cultural studies acknowledge that the key means of creating social change requires influencing individuals' thoughts about sex and gender, particularly in being attentive to culture and language. Judith Butler considers the cultural shaping of gender as demanding "a compulsory performance of sex" that is related to language and to cultural ideologies, as she concludes in "Imitation and Gender Insubordination" (1991).

> If a regime of sexuality mandates a compulsory performance of sex, then it may be only through that performance that the binary system of gender and the binary system of sex come to have intelligibility at all. It may be that the very categories of sex, of sexual identity, of gender are produced or maintained in the *effects* of this compulsory performance, effects which are disingenuously renamed as causes, origins, disingenuously lined up within a causal or expressive sequence that the heterosexual norm produces to legitimate itself as the origin of all sex.[17]

In regarding sexuality as a cultural performance, Butler helps us recognize the arbitrariness of heterosexuality, of assigning gendered roles for women and men, and of assuming a binary system of sex/gender as biologically determined. Thirty years after Butler wrote about gender insubordination, concepts of gender variance and gender fluidity are widely accepted.[18] The complexities of gender expression produced a cultural shift from a binary system to a spectrum of gender diversity recognizing human attributes such as transgender, nonbinary gender identity, and gender nonconforming.[19] In objecting to rigid sex/gender roles, feminist ideas helped eradicate cultural prohibitions, doing so by informing theories, practices, and literature to validate difference, diversity, equity, and inclusion.[20]

As universities and governments decrease financial support for the humanities, it has become difficult to persuade individuals that literature and media provide critical knowledge, useful information, and designs for the future.[21] The first decades of the twenty-first century have been dominated by economic (recession and inflation), environmental (climate change), and health (pandemic) challenges along with violent internal and international conflicts, concerns that elevate the importance of scientific and technical knowledge making. Defending humanities study as an equally valid and relevant pursuit, Butler in a spring 2020 *Academe* article argues that teaching literature develops students' critical inquiry skills and refines their moral sensibilities.

> Sometimes only imaginary worlds can shed light on history or modes of life, on moral dilemmas and emotional realities, including, for instance, the animate and vocal traces of the history of subjugation in novels by Toni Morrison. They chart human longing and aspiration and constitute modes of linguistic or representational experimentation that depart from established schools and methods and make their mark by doing so. They leave reality behind on purpose in order to bring to the fore the possibilities of the materials and media through which we generally represent reality.[22]

Asserting the power of imaginative literature to explore human emotions and ethical ideas in nuanced ways that disciplines dominated by facts do not pursue, Butler credits fiction for teaching and persuading by resonating with the audience's experiences, emotions, and observations. One can also add "desires" to this list of audience expectations, following Ann Ardis who references Roland Barthes's discussion of "classic" nineteenth-century realism in distinguishing between representation and figuration: "To figure something is to give up the pose of objectivity to acknowledge that you are not simply reproducing something that exists in the 'real' world. Figuration means acknowledging the subjective desires that inform your textual constructions of the world."[23]

Realist literary and media fictions incorporate feminist principles and values within stories about sympathetic characters navigating social inequities that readers recognize. For example, *This Is How It Always Is* by Laurie Frankel combines a dramatic story about a family, contemporary medical and cultural information, and advice about bringing up a transgender child. The 2017 novel focuses on well-meaning heterosexual, progressive parents raising five children, one of whom transitions and has difficulty managing interactions in elementary school. In an interview, Frankel explains her aim: "So one of the things that I hope is that people who read this book will read it and forget about the transgender issues and just be in the embrace of this family and realize that this family is like all families: They love and they keep secrets from one another and they protect one another and they struggle with how to do that and they have these challenges. And it's hard, but it isn't scary and it isn't abnormal at all."[24] Characters in the book include an American social worker and a Thai medical caregiver whose informed perspectives about biology and culture are represented in conversations with the parents who struggle to manage their preconceptions and preferences while striving to protect their child's interests.

Frankel's progressive parents resist traditional gender roles and encourage their children's creativity. The physician-mother and writer-father have different perspectives on Claude becoming Poppy. After ten-year-old Poppy is outed as having a penis when she is in fourth-grade, Rosie and Penn debate how they should help their child grow up mentally and physically healthy. A practicing physician, Rosie recognizes that gender dysphoria "is a medical issue, but mostly it's a cultural issue. It's a social issue and an emotional issue and a family dynamic issue and a community issue. Maybe we need to medically intervene so Poppy doesn't grow a beard. Or maybe the world needs to learn to love a person with a beard who goes by 'she' and wears a skirt."[25] Rosie's husband Penn looks for information about vaginoplasties, assuming the world is unlikely to change anytime soon; he ends the conversation about whether surgery is necessary with this question: "How do we learn to live in that world and be happy anyway?" The deus ex machina in the novel involves a trip to Thailand, during which Rosie works as the doctor in a clinic aided by a Thai caregiver, the amazingly adept in all things K, who is a kathoey.[26] K informs Rosie that Thai culture offers Poppy another way, a middle way that allows being transgender or embracing both genders. The novel teaches readers about a transgender child's emotions and about parents' caring for an offspring who transitions, arguing that societies should evolve to be more accepting of varied gender identities and expressions.

Representations of Oppression

While Western philosophy and religion have long identified paths of righteous action with the possibility of creating "the beloved community," some fictions that focus on women's oppression emphasize social and political divisions without supplying solutions to eliminate gender inequities.[27] Alexandra Alter reviews a number of books constituting a "new canon of feminist dystopian literature" that "reflects a growing preoccupation among writers with the tenuous status of women's rights, and the ambient fear that progress toward equality between the sexes has stalled or may be reversed," and she notices "a growing wave of female-centered dystopian fiction, futuristic works that raise uncomfortable questions about pervasive gender inequality, misogyny and violence against women, the erosion of reproductive rights and the extreme consequences of institutionalized sexism."[28] Many science fiction novels highlight the elimination of women's rights and contribute to the genre of dystopian narratives about women's disempowerment.

Fictional representations identify women's oppression in the past, present, and future. Margaret Atwood's speculative fiction *The Handmaid's Tale* (1985) represents plausible circumstances repressing women in Gilead, a totalitarian, theocratic state understood as a future version of the US.[29] This book provides a classic study of how "power operates and how it deforms or shapes the people who are living within that kind of regime" by outlining how religious fundamentalism could enslave many women by forbidding them access to money, work, and romance.[30] The novel concludes with the handmaid Offred's escape from being a breeder to an uncertain end; however, the 1990 film adaptation (Dir. Volker Schlöndorff), starring Natasha Richardson, depicts Offred's escape. Atwood's fiction has also been transformed into an opera, radio play, ballet, and stage play, and most recently inspired a popular streamed series, which tracks the novel's plot in the first year of the series and enters new territory in later seasons. The popularity of the Hulu adaptation of *The Handmaid's Tale*—first streamed in 2017 and with season five released in fall 2022—emblematizes for many viewers and critics the backlash against women taking place in political discourse and legislative actions.

Referencing fall 2018 Washington, DC, protests following Brett Kavanaugh's nomination to the Supreme Court that took place around the US Capitol, Sophie Gilbert acknowledges, "for the most part, women connected with *The Handmaid's Tale* in this moment because the path of history seemed to be suddenly pointing the wrong way. That's why protesters in white bonnets and crimson gowns have become the uncanny visual motif of women demonstrating in the Trump era."[31] Protesters wearing the distinctive costuming of Atwood's fictional female characters embody fears of a nation dominated by elite, white male rulers enshrining gender discrimination into law as legislatures attenuate or eliminate reproductive and other rights. In May 2022, after *Politico* published the leaked Supreme Court draft memo by Justice Samuel Alito who argued for overturning *Roe v. Wade*, protesters wearing white bonnets and crimson gowns appeared in front of Justice Amy Coney Barrett's home.[32]

In her introduction to the 2017 edition of the novel, Atwood acknowledges that the possibility of a future theocratic, antiwoman state, seemed "fairly outrageous" in 1984 when she conceived the premise of the book in observing efforts in the US to control women's reproduction. Nevertheless, she resists the notion that the book offered a prediction: "No, it isn't a prediction because predicting the future isn't really possible: there are too many variables and unforeseen possibilities. Let's say it's an anti-prediction: if this future can be described in detail, maybe it won't happen, but such wishful thinking cannot be depended on either."[33] Future oppression of women is not inevitable, for, as the epilogue to the novel *The Handmaid's Tale* suggests, individual effort, collective action, and the formation of resistance groups offer protection and enable political changes to effect gender equity. Atwood's 2019 novel *The Testaments* provides both a prequel and a sequel to *The Handmaid's Tale* describing Gilead's early days during which women were imprisoned or executed in presenting three intertwined first-person testimonies of how corruption in Gilead and its continuing domination of women inspire rebellion. Both novels embed personal accounts of women's oppression within frameworks of legal testimony and academic discourses from a later period during which women have achieved equality and are once again able to become social, academic, and political leaders. As Michelle Goldberg asserts, "Rather than a warning, it reads, in 2019, like wish fulfillment. Instead of a new glimpse of hell, it's a riveting and deeply satisfying escapist fantasy. . . . 'The Testaments,' it turns out, isn't a dystopian work at all. It's utopian."[34] Atwood's fictions, like others considered in this book, hold out hope that society could eliminate present-day repressions of women and marginalized minorities to enable a future state based on equity.

Rollback of Rights

Even readers dispirited by legal decisions that limit women's reproductive choices and empowerment can hope for gender equity and fight against the further diminution of women's and minority rights. In her October 9, 2018, *New York Times* column titled "How Do I Explain Justice Kavanaugh to My Daughters?," Jennifer Weiner argues that "The spectacle of this confirmation has reminded us that to many people, women's suffering is a joke." Yet Weiner concluded her column, published after Kavanaugh's swearing-in as a Supreme Court Justice on October 6, 2018, an event that took place one month before the much-anticipated November 6, 2018, US midterm elections, by recalling details from the Congressional testimony of Christine Blasey Ford, who accused Kavanaugh of attacking her: "Speak up, even if those in power do not want to listen. Speak your truth, even if men laugh. Be loud, even though power prefers girls quiet. Speak up, even if they call you strident or shrill. Don't let anyone put a hand—real or metaphorical—over your mouth. March, demonstrate, chant, shout, vote. And maybe someday, you, or your daughters, or your daughter's daughters will be the ones with the last laugh."[35] Encouraging women to look forward and to engage in collective action, Weiner hopes that justice long denied will eventually prevail.

Similar encouragement to persist and resist patriarchal domination appears in fictions that identify the social and legal limits that women have confronted and continue to face, as literary and media scholars publishing after 1968 acknowledge. Peter Rabinowitz explains, "It is not exactly that women's lives are inappropriate to narrative fiction. We have canonical plot structures that deal with women who ruin themselves in adultery (*Madame Bovary, Anna Karenina*) or who remain self-sacrificially steadfast even under extreme adversity (Southworth's *Changed Brides/The Bride's Fate*). But the potential roles for women in such plots are restricted." Rabinowitz quotes Alice Jardine: "If the author is male, one finds that the female destiny (at least in the novel) rarely deviates from one or two seemingly irreversible, dualistic teleologies: monster and/or angel, she is condemned to death (or sexual mutilation or disappearance) and/or to happy-ever-after marriage. Her plot is not her own."[36] Rita

Felski makes the related point that "It is not very difficult to show that complaining about the sexism of the Western canon is not an especially sophisticated or fruitful idea. . . . No writing is immune to criticism, but a serious engagement with feminist scholarship requires more than bluster and invective."[37] Clearly, the limited possibilities and expectations for women in many fictional narratives reveal historical restrictions, but these limitations are often supplemented with visions of possibility.[38] Complementing the observations of Rabinowitz, Jardine, and Felski that many fictions detail women's oppression, and noticing the rise of dystopian fictions speculating about the dismal future of women, this book examines narratives that point to the future success of feminism in producing progressive social change.

I argue that there is an underrecognized category of realist narratives that describe improvements to enhance gender equity and that suggest if certain reforms are enacted, there will be positive outcomes for society. A narrative of this type illustrates a sympathetic protagonist, usually a woman, navigating a difficult environment and confronting bias and discrimination, while acknowledging that greater opportunities could be available if reforms such as abolition, enfranchisement, educational and work opportunities, and reproductive freedoms are established and prompt a shift in social attitudes. While dystopian fictions show society in retrograde, other fictional narratives depict women's opportunities, rights, and responsibilities to persuade readers there will be a feminist future. Historian Christine Stansell begins her book *The Feminist Promise* by recognizing that "Feminism is one of the great and substantial democratic movements, a tradition of thought and action spanning more than two hundred years. Its reach is huge, because it addresses the claims and needs of half the population. At its best, feminism incorporates men as well, to make it a politics of universal aspiration."[39] Referencing barriers and injustices that individuals confront, fictional literary and televisual narratives endorse women's aspirations and outline reforms that make gender equity a plausible prospect.

Yet while feminism appears as a promising development in many fictions, its fulfillment is often denied in the timelines of narratives. Rebecca Coleman and Debra Ferreday acknowledge Angela McRobbie's account of "a double entanglement" that affects feminism's fortunes in culture.

> In Western post-industrial countries, feminism is involved in a
> "double entanglement," where it is at once "taken into account"

and "repudiated." Focusing particularly on media representations of gender, femininity and sexuality, McRobbie suggests that certain aspects of feminist critique (including, but not restricted to, critiques of heteronormativity, the standardization of a beauty ideal and restricted access to public spheres of education and work) have been so widely incorporated into mainstream culture that they are seen as arguments that have been won.[40]

Thus, feminism appears as both accepted and dangerous according to this account. Despite general familiarity with feminism, defined as a restructuring of society according to gender equitable, nonhierarchical, and inclusive norms, it has not yet developed to its full capacities, and we await the social changes it will foster in its mature state.

Feminism in Society

Pointing to historical disparities between women's and men's lives, realist fictions identify role models and acknowledge critical strategies to establish gender equity, including implementing material and attitudinal changes to enhance the lives of women and underrepresented minorities. Janet Todd points out that "Feminist literary history is not a study of women as nature or of a natural woman, but of women intervening in culture, making culture, and being naturalized by culture in subtly different ways at different times; it is the study of codes that intervene between subjectivity and history and help to fashion both."[41] Literary criticism recuperating submerged feminist narratives contributes to activism by deciphering these codes and pressing for social, cultural, and political reforms. I originally considered titling this book "Feminism's Long Arc," adapting the civil rights leader Dr. Martin Luther King Jr.'s well-known statement, which is based on a passage from a sermon by nineteenth-century abolitionist and Unitarian minister Theodore Parker. King claimed in several speeches: "The arc of the moral universe is long, but it bends toward justice."[42] In 1853 Parker published "Ten Sermons of Religion"; his third sermon "Of Justice and the Conscience" mentions the arc of the moral universe: "Look at the facts of the world. You see a continual and progressive triumph of the right. I do not pretend to understand the moral universe, the arc is a long one, my eye reaches but little ways. I cannot calculate the curve and complete the figure by the experience of sight; I can divine it by conscience. But from what I see I am sure it bends towards justice."[43] Feminist narratives considered in this book take a long view, identifying the necessity for reforms and forecasting the inevitability of prospective changes that enable gender equity.

Today many people accept that individuals should have equal opportunities in education and at home and work as well as equality before the law, although feminism and its ideological principles are not always well understood or supported.[44] There is not one feminist ideology or movement, as centuries of arguments addressing social inequality and gender equity continue to combine with diverse religious, political, and cultural values to produce a variety of feminisms and an understanding of intersectional and global feminisms. Roxane Gay acknowledges that feminists should know that their goals may not appeal to all while understanding that feminist principles and practices should be inclusive and should respect diversity.

> Feminism is a choice, and if a woman does not want to be a feminist, that is her right, but it is still my responsibility to fight for her rights. I believe feminism is grounded in supporting the choices of women even if we wouldn't make certain choices for ourselves. I believe women not just in the United States but throughout the world deserve equality and freedom but know that I am in no position to tell women of other cultures what that equality and freedom should look like.[45]

In short, feminist ideas adapt to individual situations and social contexts, depending on specific values that endorse enhancing gender equity and increasing opportunities for women of all ethnicities, classes, gender identities, and sexual orientations. Benefits would accrue to all, for under the rubric of feminism, gender equity should also include releasing individuals, regardless of gender, from the constraints of sex and gender stereotypes and upturning other social hierarchies that oppress or marginalize individuals and groups.

The history of feminisms is intertwined with past cultural and political discriminations, including those related to race and ethnicity. Although suffragists in the United States and Britain began their reform efforts as dedicated abolitionists, many white women later advocating for enfranchisement objected that they could not cast ballots while Black men could. During the Reconstruction period in the US, instead of working collectively with underrepresented minorities, some suffragists applied ideologies of Social Darwinism and eugenics to support discriminatory attitudes toward immigrants and persons of color.[46] Arguing against such discrimination, Anna Julia Cooper's *A Voice from the South* (1892) explains that Black women suffer doubly based on race and gender.[47] The nineteenth US constitutional amendment enacted in 1920 granted women the right to vote, a right that white women exercised more easily than other women. Similar measures passed in 1918 and 1928 ensured the vote for some women in Great Britain. Yet enfranchisement did not resolve all inequalities based on sex, and many restrictions continue to hinder women of color, disabled women, and lesbian and trans women.

Inequalities appear magnified in the digital age as we are enabled and constrained by a plethora of information sources, including social media used by individuals and groups publishing sometimes fake or questionable views without editorial review.[48] Given that human beings are political, as Aristotle recognized long ago, our social media communications and "like" preferences reveal our political inclinations, which tend to be partisan and polarized.[49] The United States and Britain are divided nations, with the latter also experiencing a generational split on many political issues, including gender equity, given a growing Labour movement attracting younger citizens and a definitive split among voters about Brexit, Britain's exit from the European Union.[50] A similar generational divide in the United States affects choice of political party, revealing increased frustration with two-party dominance and the structural limitations of the electoral college.[51]

Contemporary public discourse includes a range of presentations, publications, and compositions endorsing feminist principles. Speeches such as Emma Watson's at the United Nations in 2014, Chimamanda Ngozi Adichie's Ted Talk and 2012 book *We Should All Be Feminists*, and Facebook/Meta board member Sheryl Sandberg's 2014 *Lean In* book, website, and original Ted talk are available to anyone with a device and internet access and are widely influential, particularly with young people.[52] Popular music also reflects and refracts social, economic, and political concerns related to gender, incorporating elements from others' works. As one reviewer explains, Beyonce's 2016 video album *Lemonade* has "underlying themes of modern feminism, monogamy, and the numerous pleasures of sex"; "the daring 'Flawless' opens with a portion of the previously-previewed and already-confrontational 'Bow Down' before seguing into a TEDxEuston talk by Chimamanda Ngozi Adichie, placing a boldly feminist credo right in the middle of one of the most important pop albums of the past five years."[53] News stories about the May 2018 royal wedding between Great Britain's Prince Harry and American television actress Meghan Markle (now Duchess of Sussex) often mentioned the latter's feminism and sometimes noted her 2015 speech in which she honored her role as United Nations Women's advocate and declared her feminism.[54] In this way, celebrity endorsements of feminist principles inspire audiences and have extensive cultural reach during a period in which "Every single day there's a new instance of gender trouble," as Roxane Gay acknowledges.[55]

The 2015-2016 political campaign of Hillary Clinton, the first woman to run for president as a standard bearer of a major United States political party, and the subsequent election of Donald J. Trump, an avowed nonfeminist, misogynist, and sexual predator, to that office focused public attention on questions of gender and power, including "how can we improve the representation of women in government and enhance gender equity in the public sphere?" After the election, news stories detailed sexual assaults and sexual discrimination affecting women (and men) of different ethnicities and classes working in various fields. Employing the hashtag #MeToo, news articles, Tweets, or blog posts relevant to the discussion of gender equity, sexual discrimination, and sexual harassment regularly appear. But reading accounts of nondisclosure agreements, abuses, settlements, and punishments for malefactors may not offer satisfactory conclusions for survivors or lead to specific reforms increasing women's political power. Eliminating abuse and discrimination and creating equal social, economic, and political access and opportunities for women remain unreached goals in many places.[56] Realist fictions illustrate problems individuals and institutions should address and outline recommendations offering hope.

Images of Equity

Forecasting progress, print and televisual fictions discussed in this book note prospects for social reform and imagine the inevitability of gender equity in ways that recall King's statement "The arc of the moral universe is long, but it bends toward justice." His statement was on my mind while I reviewed media coverage of various Women's Marches held on January 21, 2017, the day after Donald J. Trump's presidential inauguration and one hundred years after suffragists' 1917 protests at the White House.[57] Social-media assisted organizers of and attendees at the 2017 Women's Marches that took place around the world, and television news disseminated photos and video of large, diverse crowds demonstrating for progressive causes opposed to Trump's agenda. Greater numbers of women and men turned out in Washington, DC, for the 2017 Women's March than did for the previous day's presidential inauguration of Trump, indicating significant opposition to the outcome of the 2016 US national election and signaling resistance to his many campaign proposals directed at dismantling or restricting progressive policies, including those related to provisions of the Affordable Care Act, immigration orders, accessible national borders, women's right to equal pay and reproductive choice, climate change controls, banking regulations, and other legislative and executive decisions.[58] Motivated by anger at Trump's politics, discourse, and personal behavior, protesters at the 2017 Women's Marches decried issues of misogyny, sexism, racism, and anti-immigrant sentiments and expressed fears of fascism and authoritarianism.[59] Nevertheless, the Trump administration from its earliest days sought to cancel Obama-era initiatives, including environmental and other regulations, while also changing immigration policies and pressing Congress to fulfill the Trump campaign agenda.

In January 2017, women's marchers followed in the footsteps of approximately 5,000 women who protested Woodrow Wilson's opposition to women's suffrage in a January 1917 parade in front of the White House, a demonstration that took place before that president's inauguration. Eleanor Flexner describes the occasion:

> With that dramatic sense which always characterized her suffrage work, Miss [Alice] Paul chose the day before Woodrow Wilson's inauguration, since Washington would be filled with visitors from all over the country. When Mr. Wilson reached Washington and found the streets bare of any welcoming crowd, he is said to have asked where the people were; he was told they were over on Pennsylvania Avenue, watching the woman suffrage parade.
>
> As it turned out, they were doing more than just watching.[60]

Flexner notes that one newspaper account of the 1917 parade reported, "No inauguration has produced such scenes, which in many instances amounted to nothing less than riots," while another stated, "Many of the women were in tears under the jibes and insults of those who lined the route. . . . Few faltered, though some of the older women were forced to drop out from time to time."[61] In contrast, the January 2017 Women's March in Washington, DC, was less violent and inspired fewer incidents than other protests, perhaps because police were reluctant to arrest women in pink hats.[62]

Not every protest movement develops visual markers, but many use images to galvanize supporters such as the red cloaks and white bonnets donned by feminist protesters emulating signs of oppression in *The Handmaid's Tale*. Early twentieth-century British suffragists encouraged wearing certain colors to promote the cause of votes for women: "The British women's suffrage colors were purple, white, and green. Purple, white, and gold were the colors of the American suffrage movement."[63] US Democratic presidential candidate Hillary Clinton evoked the history of suffrage when she wore a white suit during a critical presidential debate in October 2016, and "the internet goes crazy."[64] Acknowledging the long, difficult history of the suffrage movement, many women in the US Congress wore white on Election Day 2016, on the evening of President Trump's first joint address to Congress in early 2017, and during the inauguration of the 2019 Congress, which included a record number of Democratic women and minority Congressional representatives elected.[65] Continuing the tradition, on November 7, 2020, Kamala Harris, the first Black woman and first person of South Asian descent to be elected as vice president, wore a white pantsuit and pussy bow blouse in introducing the president-elect Joe Biden, who defeated Donald Trump in the 2020 election.[66]

A vibrant political symbol of gender resistance, the pink pussy hat crystallized feminist concerns motivating the March for Women held on January 21, 2017, coming to public attention in the weeks before the demonstration. A bright pink hat designed by a knitting teacher developed into the Pussyhat Project, coordinated by activists Jayna Zweiman and Krista Suh, who shared the design in social media and in news accounts.[67] The hat symbolizes resistance to misogyny, recalling a comment made by Donald Trump about his approach to women: "Grab 'em by the pussy. You can do anything."[68] According to Diana Pearl, "The hope . . . is that the pussy hats will live on as a symbol of feminist activism for far longer than just the day of the march—or even the length of the Trump administration. 'My dream is that a grandmother will give her granddaughter her pussy hat, and say 'I wore this on January 21, 2017,'

Suh said. 'I hope it has an impact for generations and leads to the change that we are all hungry for."[69] Reminding observers of Trump's comment while reclaiming femininity and feminism as pretty in pink and eager to protest, the hat was a practical, powerful symbol; after all, wearing a wool hat helps a marcher cope with winter weather. The hat's adoption in different climates reflects a collective commitment to fight for equity.

The easily imitated and portable pink hat connected protests around the world and through time. Photos from different marches on January 21, 2017, and the anniversary march on January 20, 2018, document the many marchers who wore pink hats and carried posters displaying related progressive images and messages.[70] The hats were in greater abundance in wintry climates than in summer ones, but pops of pink color stand out in many newspaper photographs and television coverage. The pink hats and their representations on protest signs and other graphics objected to Trump's harassment of women, signaling revolution and change. *The Atlantic* magazine reproduced a photograph of the Eiffel Tower as a backdrop for the sign "Women of Paris: Nasty since 1789," while a *New York Times* photo taken in Fairbanks, Alaska, offered an explicit reminder of Trump's Access Hollywood comments: "Women's Rights are not up for grabs."[71] Many protesters drew parts of women's anatomy on their signs to protest control of women's bodies.

Whether one recognizes a pussy hat as having kitten ears or as resembling a uterus is in the eyes of the beholder, the hat became an inspirational symbol protesting misogyny and aiming to promote gender equity. The February 6, 2017, *New Yorker* cover illustrated the pink pussy hat on a woman of color in an image updating the Rosie the Riveter image, which has figured since World War II as a symbol of woman's empowerment. Françoise Mouly, the magazine's art editor, commented about the cover: "Abigail Gray Swartz, who marched in her state capital of Augusta, Maine, was inspired by the spirit of the day to paint 'Rosie the Riveter' as a woman of color wearing a knitted pink cap."[72] *The grio* described Swartz's *New Yorker* cover in a January 28, 2017, post as follows:

> The image is not only significant because of its feminist message but because of the message of intersectionality at a time when feminism is coming up against the problem of how to address the fact that women of color have historically been left out of the movement and even actively pushed out of it. Some critics of the march noted that there needed to be more of a place

for women of color and others, and this image takes that need and puts it on the cover.[73]

Underlining the common cause of women does not mean that all women are the same; instead, connecting women in different circumstances and providing access to resources establishes a larger community fighting various forms of discrimination, bias, and abuse. The imagery utilized to represent intersectional politics grafts a new symbol (the pussy hat) on to a transformed vision of the well-known older representation of Rosie the Riveter, reminding us of women's contributions in times of conflict.

French scholar Maurice Agulhon explains that "Political imagery may be considered a marginal subject but perhaps it would be better to describe it as a frontier zone."[74] Images are especially important in a televisual and social media age, and their employment builds on a convention in realist fictions of representing the visual markers of protest.[75] As a symbol of resistance, the pink pussy hat is akin to the red Phrygian cap denoting liberty, an item from the classical period that was transformed by revolutionaries in late-eighteenth-century France. Representations in art and literature document that the red cap became an important feature recalling revolutionaries' heroic fight for liberty in the 1780s; it was later associated with the Marianne figure depicted in Eugène Delacroix's painting *Liberty Leading the People* (1830).[76]

Contemporary protest marches, including the 2018 Women's Marches held in various cities, carried forward the pussy hat as a symbol along with other messages from the January 2017 Women's March, including "Not My President," "Feminism Is Equality," "A Woman's Place Is in the Revolution," "Women's Rights Are Human Rights," "Trust Women, We Will Not Be Silent," and "Nasty Woman."[77] The last is a phrase that Trump used during the presidential campaign to describe Hillary Clinton, who lost the election although she won the popular vote. Despite Trump's intent to demean Clinton with the epithet, "nasty woman" became a positive label for many because the phrase identified a woman who raised unprecedented sums to run for office and to persist in the race despite being troubled by a complicated history as a first lady and being challenged within her own party by popular progressive US senator Bernie Sanders.[78]

Why don't women speak up more? A 2017 Women's March sign in Cleveland, "Women Want to Be Heard #Just Listen" and the sign "Hear

Our Voice" in Oslo, Norway, indicated frustration concerning women's underrepresentation in politics and lack of participation in public discourse.[79] Christopher F. Karpowitz and Tali Mendelberg in *The Silent Sex: Gender, Deliberation, and Institutions* explain why women don't speak up and why their words are less persuasive. That women's speech lacks authority helps us understand gender disparities in many situations: "this inequality, and injustice, must be understood in light of the gender context and institutional rules within which men and women deliberate."[80] Karpowitz and Mendelberg consider the problem—that women speak less and less assertively than men do in public forums—and offer evidence-based research explaining women's lack of participation. Women have less confidence that their words matter, for they suspect that their contributions to deliberative discussions will not be respected or could be distorted. Women appear more reluctant than men to engage in competition or conflict in political discussions. Lack of participation might also stem from women feeling "more sensitive to social bonds."[81]

The Silent Sex's findings—that women's communitarian, egalitarian arguments in deliberations are often disregarded—provided a context for Bernie Sanders's appeal to women voters in the 2016 Democratic presidential primary race. According to the *Washington Post*, on the eve of the Nevada primary in February 2016, Yvette Williams, chairwoman of the Clark County Black Caucus, shared that she found it easy to endorse Senator Sanders: "His message really resonates when he talks about income inequality, race justice and prison reform."[82] Williams's statement aligns with findings described in *The Silent Sex* and notes specific issues of interest to minority voters as well as women. Sanders's status as a political independent and his communitarian and egalitarian perspective not surprisingly attracted many women who felt marginalized in political discussions and who prioritized caring about others. Thus, Sanders, regardless of his gender, was seen as articulating feminine positions that are often discounted as less authoritative. In contrast, Hillary Clinton found it difficult to establish being identified as an expert endorsed by a masculine establishment while also speaking in an appropriately feminine register (i.e., not too shrilly or aggressively), although she was recognized as a role model for bringing a woman's perspective to politics.[83]

Women have long had reduced access to public discourse and political power in Western civilization. Classics scholar Mary Beard, in *Women and Power: A Manifesto*, demonstrates "how deeply embedded in Western culture are the mechanisms that silence women, that refuse to take them seriously, and that sever them . . . from the centres of power."[84] In discussing Homer's epic *The Odyssey*, Beard points to Telemachus's silencing of his mother Penelope who asked the bard to play a different song, one not referencing the challenges for Greek heroes returning after the war with Troy. Penelope's concern for her husband Odysseus, who is still missing long after the battles, motivates her request, but her son pulls rank as a man to order her to "go back to her quarters, and take up your own work, the loom and the distaff . . . speech will be the business of men, all men, of me most of all; for mine is the power in this household."[85] Telemachus tells his mother to "shut up," because "her voice was not to be heard in public."[86] Beard connects the young man's silencing of his mother with examples from other Western texts to demonstrate how women were kept quiet, sometimes by losing their tongues. Eschewing extensive analysis, she notes compelling examples of cultural proscriptions that silence women in the Bible and European literary works, including Ovid's *Metamorphoses*, Boccaccio's *Decameron*, Shakespeare's *Titus Andronicus*, and Henry James's *The Bostonians*.

Two late comedies by Aristophanes, *Lysistrata* (411 BCE) and *Ecclesiazusae* (391 BCE), depict problems with women's civic authority. In the earlier comedy, Lysistrata, whose name means "releaser of war," coordinates with other women to negotiate peace between Athens and Sparta using two weapons: sex and seizure. She convinces women in these city-states to withhold sex from their husbands until the warriors stop engaging in warfare. The Athenian women also seize the treasury to prevent the men from continuing military actions. Although the comedy ends in peaceful song and dance and seems "respectful" toward Lysistrata in representing her authority over the women, the play mocks women's rights and offers many jokes about sexual desire. *Ecclesiazusae (The Women of the Assembly)* describes the creation of a female communitarian government designed to care for the less fortunate and the ugly before meeting the desires of the fortunate and the attractive. Both comedies portray women as a kinder, gentler, and more naive species than their male counterparts, while demonstrating that feminine mechanisms to provide equity go awry in politics. Aristophanes' suspicions of women's management abilities explain their absence from public roles.

Women in classical Greek society were limited to domestic life, sheltered by the family, and "under the legal protection of its head."[87] In ancient Athens the prospect of women governing and making decisions, at least onstage, must have seemed hilarious when performed by totally male casts of actors hamming up their parts in ridiculous, priapic costumes and playing to male audiences who attended the sex-segregated festivals. Theater scholar Sue-Ellen Case argues, "As a result of the suppression of real women, the culture invented its own representation of the gender, and it was this fictional 'Woman' who appeared on stage in the myths and in the plastic arts, representing the patriarchal values attached to the gender while suppressing the experiences, stories, feelings and fantasies of actual women. . . . 'Woman' was played by male actors in drag, while real women were banned from the stage."[88] Comparative literature scholar Nancy Sorkin Rabinowitz offers additional context: "in Athens the separation of the sexes did coincide with a widespread, if not universal, misogyny and a devaluation of the female realm. This was not only a sex-segregated society but also one in which the accepted virtues of woman and man were radically different in kind: his lay in courageously winning glory in battle, hers in bearing the pain of childbirth and loving her children."[89] Despite the passage of centuries, confining gender roles still influence social behaviors and politics in many places, including in industrialized countries offering suffrage, education, and employment for women.

In the twentieth century, *Lysistrata* was reframed in the United States and Europe within the context of proposed reforms for women's rights, including securing the vote for women, and as a play advocating peace. In 1912, American suffragists performed an English abridgment of a French translation of *Lysistrata* during a benefit attracting adherents to the cause of women's suffrage; Harriot Stanton Blatch, a writer and the daughter of women's rights pioneer Elizabeth Cady Stanton, introduced the play when it was performed on a private Westchester, New York, estate.[90] The Lysistrata Project formed in the early twenty-first century to encourage readings of the play as a pacifist statement.[91] Thus, *Lysistrata*'s messages about the human desire for peace and women's lack of political power to effect change continue to have salience. The comedy's gender politics attract audiences, even today after women's suffrage, affirmative action, Title IX, and other enacted mechanisms have increased the percentages of women in politics, professions, and positions of authority.[92] The topsy-turvy world of women in charge that Aristophanes' comedies depict still appears humorous because gender equity continues to elude us.[93]

Feminism and Realist Fiction

The question of what economic, political, and social rights women should have to conduct their lives and participate in society is a topic intimately connected with the birth and evolution of the novel.[94] Madame de Lafayette's *La Princesse de Clèves* (1678), Samuel Richardson's *Pamela* (1740) and *Clarissa* (1748), Jane Austen's novels, and fictions by late-nineteenth-century British writers such George Gissing and Thomas Hardy highlight constraints and discriminations directed against women to suggest that prevailing norms of sexuality and marriage were injurious to them. The opening of *Pride and Prejudice* (1813) sets up the marital premise animating so many fictions about women's lives: "It is a truth universally acknowledged, that a single man in possession of a good fortune, must be in want of a wife."[95] Highlighting the issue of what makes a good marriage, Austen's *Mansfield Park* (1814) presents perspectives on Fanny Price's stubborn refusal of the rich Henry Crawford's marriage proposal; Fanny's resistance appears perverse to many, including her uncle and her mother, who are among those admiring Henry's income while disregarding the young man's character. Although finding a wealthy husband was the goal of many young women characters, including her female cousins, Fanny quietly insists that she will only marry someone who shares her values, whom readers know is her cousin Edmund, for he has been kind and caring to her. Austen's novels describe constrained marital choices for women: they too often must seek financial security rather than compatibility, as most women were unable to support having independent lives. Well into the modern era, social conventions limited acceptable ways for women to earn money if they wished to maintain social standing, and laws limited their ability to control what they might inherit or earn. Edith Wharton's *The House of Mirth* (1905) outlines few employment possibilities for the orphaned Lily Barth to support herself after she fails to secure a marriage that could be emotionally and financially satisfying for her. Mary Taylor's *Miss Miles: A Tale of Yorkshire Life Sixty Years Ago* (1890) acknowledges that women are constrained by abusive marriages and by limited prospects to earn money; however, the three women who are central characters (Sarah Miles and her friends Maria and Dora) navigate barriers to find acceptable work, and in two cases, marriage.

The limited capacities of women to control their money, possessions, and children contributed to more than two centuries of resistance movements in Anglo-American society. In the opening chapter to her history of women's suffrage, Eleanor Flexner acknowledges the common condition affecting British and American women before 1800: "Whatever their social station, under English common law, which became increasingly predominant in the colonies and among all religious denominations (until the advent of the Quakers), women had many duties, but few rights. Married women in particular suffered 'civil death,' having no right to property and no legal entity or existence apart from their husbands."[96] The limitations placed on women, in fiction and in life, contrasted with men's opportunities to make good or bad, responsible or irresponsible, choices with consequences for them and others.

The consequences of women's limited authority to control their own lives and to resist the constraints of bad marriages had ramifications for society, and nineteenth-century authors pointed to a marriage penalty as causing problems for both men and women. Charles Dickens's *Hard Times* (1854) considers the terrible social outcomes of bad marriages (wealthy Louisa's to the hypocritical bully Bounderby and factory worker Stephen's to his alcoholic wife), relationships that were difficult to escape absent a proper divorce law. George Eliot offers a cynical view of marital relations in *Middlemarch* (1871–1872), as Dorothea's first marriage with the scholar Casaubon and Dr. Lydgate's with the social butterfly Rosamund are painful for all parties, respectively forcing Dorothea into an ancillary, unsatisfying domestic role and wrecking Lydgate's career as a physician. Many fictions depict dismal prospects for women characters whose few choices are tedious, subservient work or uncomfortable, abusive marriages. Jill Rappoport points to the ways British Victorian authors depicted women's gift-giving to reveal "a complex history of bourgeois women's strategies for achieving economic agency during a period when most lacked property rights and professional opportunities."[97] Noting the restrictions on personal liberties, freedom narratives and antislavery fictions produced in the US outline oppressive, deadly conditions for Blacks. Like Frederick Douglass's autobiographical narratives, Harriet Beecher Stowe's *Uncle Tom's Cabin* (1852) and Harriet Wilson's *Our Nig* (1859) point to how white women could be complicit in exploiting and abusing enslaved persons. Wilson describes the dehumanizing, violent aspects of slavery, while Stowe's sentimental account represents another kind of abuse recommending the wholesale return of freed Blacks to Africa.

After higher-education institutions began to prepare women for work outside the home, some fictions published in the nineteenth-century United States and Great Britain represented women pursuing professions.

Elizabeth Stuart Phelps's interest in social reforms prompted her writing of novels with strong female protagonists following unconventional paths. Christine Stansell describes "Phelps' superwomen" as "daring, strong, and competent, in a word, powerful: fit opponents for the powerful male with the feudal view, who insists on treating women like the tassel of his dressing gown."[98] Phelps's *Doctor Zay* (1882) portrays a capable female doctor who resists marriage, while her novel *The Silent Partner* (1871) considers two women, "Sip, a mill worker, and Miss Kelso, the silent partner in the mill after her father's death. The lives of these two women intersect as worker and owner as they both reject marriage proposals in favor of new vocations—underscoring Phelps's vision that, regardless of class, women can be united around their right to work."[99] Work provides one's livelihood while enabling economic independence and autonomy.

Charlotte Perkins Gilman's late-nineteenth- and early-twentieth-century writings, including her nonfictional essays and books, short stories, novels, poems, and songs, contain positive images of strong women empowered by work and sympathetic representations of their feminist principles.[100] Many of her fictional females serve as role models, notably by pursuing work outside the home and developing innovations in housework, childcare, and entrepreneurship.[101] Some essays, stories, and novels by Gilman (1860-1935) illustrate how women in various situations and marital arrangements (single, married, and widowed) access resources that allow them to enjoy careers. Her novel *What Diantha Did* (1909-1910) describes how one young woman defies social conventions to establish businesses revolutionizing housework in a community, while producing enough income to support her, her parents, her husband, and her children. Although Gilman's fictional reforms were ingenious, her status as a feminist heroine is problematic. She thought of her contributions as humanist; however, during her lifetime her ideas about immigration included becoming "increasingly suspicious of some categories of immigrants" in calling for structured assimilation schemes and quotas, revealing her "white feminist investment in biocentric, eugenic, and racial discourses."[102]

Identifying dimensions of sexuality, novels published around the fin-de-siècle and later offer the model of the New Woman, a type "named" in 1894 articles by Sarah Grand and Ouida. Although she was associated with decadence and deemed socially and sexually transgressive, the "figure [of the New Woman was] committed to change and to values of a projected future."[103] Nella Larsen points to ensuing problems for women who assume that freedom has no costs. Her novel *Quicksand* (1928) depicts a biracial young woman unmoored from family and without resources whose sexuality and intellect complicate her life. Helga Crane struggles to find support; however, in different communities she encounters only discriminatory and exploitive circumstances. The novel ends with her passive resignation to the demands of her life as a minister's wife and as a mother of many children. Larsen's characterization of Helga recognizes seemingly intractable social circumstances, primarily racism and sexism, as limiting her prospects.

Women's Liberation on Television

In her introduction to feminist media studies, Alison Harvey acknowledges the diversity of feminist identities, experiences, and "multiple understandings of feminism as a politics," and she "distinguishes feminist media studies from the study of media and gender" in indicating that feminist media studies "entails a commitment to action, transformation, and change."[104] That is, it is not only the visibility of women in media that should concern us but the characterizations they are assigned and the contexts in which they function. For example, considering the representation of women in blockbuster films, she notes that "there are still inequities in terms of speaking parts and the inclusion of multiple nonmale characters in these films (as well as a preponderance of animated rather than live-action female characters).[105] Harvey is careful to explain that we should not assume "an overly simplistic cause and effect relationship between norms of gender portrayal in media and their impact on girls and women."[106] Describing "the process of media-making as collaborative, involving sometimes teams of thousands of people to make blockbuster video games, television series, and films," she asserts that an "imbalance in [the numbers of people contributing] behind-the-screen work may also have an impact on the number of women on the screen."[107] Political messages in fictional media may also affect whether a production survives to have an audience.

Depicting women working collectively to create workplace equity, the 2016 Amazon Prime series *Good Girls Revolt* looks at the impact of the women's liberation movement on employees in the 1969 newsroom of the fictional *News of the Week* magazine for which the women have been relegated to doing uncredited research for men reporters and writers with bylines. The fictional series is based on Lynn Povich's nonfictional account of women's legal actions against their employer *Newsweek*: "On March 16, 1970, the day *Newsweek* published a cover story on the fledging feminist movement titled 'Women in Revolt,' forty-six employees filed the first class-action complaint by female professionals, charging the magazine with discrimination in hiring and promotion."[108] Ten Amazon Prime episodes of *Good Girls Revolt* delve more into fictionalized characters' personal lives and into visual depictions of sixties free love rather than following the intricacies of the women's strategies and their group's legal negotiations that are the main matter of the book.

The only historical figures appearing in the streamed series are Eleanor Holmes Norton, the lawyer advising the female employees, and the writer Nora Ephron, who worked briefly at the magazine, although she left before the lawsuits were filed. Melding an account of late 1960s and early 1970s cultural attitudes toward professional women with stories of women "coming to consciousness," *Good Girls Revolt* offers feminist counterpoint to other televisual shows about the era such as *Mad Men* (2007-2015), which depicts 1960s advertising agencies dominated by competitive, hard-drinking, philandering men with limited patience for women's needs for creative expression and work.[109] *Good Girls Revolt* offered an upbeat message about the power of feminist collective action to redress workplace discrimination, but the series was canceled after one season by Amazon Studios president Roy Price. Rebecca Traister reported later that Price was forced to resign "after being accused of making aggressively lewd comments toward a female producer," remarking that "entertainment executives help to determine whose stories, what kind of stories about women and power audiences receive."[110] Although *Good Girls Revolt* was a timely if retro narrative, it was canceled because it did not have executive support or attract a broad audience, which may be too much to expect of content highlighting feminist activism in an era in which feminism seems to be seen as already accepted while also being regarded by many as dangerous.

Feminist Politics in Narratives

Feminism's Progress builds on fifty years of feminist literary and media criticism considering fictional representations of political rights and realities for women in the US and Great Britain that suggest the future might offer more hope than reason to fear for advocates of gender equity. Rather than developing a theory of feminist fiction, my efforts in this book focus on discerning fictional claims that feminism will improve individuals and society, discussing the oppression of women and minorities, and detailing efforts to overcome injustice. Information about gender problems and equity solutions connects these texts as feminist narratives sharing optimistic attitudes and communitarian strategies to resolve social ills.

Thematically organized chapters consider narrative representations of gender equity related to political rights, education, marriage, reproduction, professional work, violence, and political careers. Chapter 1, "Feminist Information and the Novel as Information System," discusses Charles Dickens's novel *Little Dorrit* (1855–1857) and Margaret Drabble's *The Radiant Way* (1987), the first novel in a trilogy with *A Natural Curiosity* (1989) and *The Gates of Ivory* (1991), as information systems that promote sharing information as a feminist practice to protect women and to resist inequities of class and gender. Dickens and Drabble depict women protagonists as important transmitters of key information improving social relations and binding individuals together in communities.

The next chapter "Liberty and Suffrage in Nineteenth-Century Narratives" looks at nineteenth-century literary works describing the evils of slavery and offering gendered perspectives concerning it and sectional conflict in the United States. Short stories by Rebecca Harding Davis, Louisa May Alcott, and Constance Fenimore Woolson examine painful circumstances of the Civil War that traumatized families. Frances Ellen Watkins Harper's novel *Iola Leroy, or Shadows Uplifted* (1892) illustrates how one family's members became enslaved, suffering abuse and violent separation during the war before reuniting during Reconstruction. The last part of the chapter looks at class divisions and political debates about women's legal rights in Laura Curtis Bullard's *Christine, or Woman's Trials and Triumphs* (1856), Henry James's *The Bostonians* (1885–1886), and George Gissing's *Odd Women* (1893). These fictions explain women's efforts to intercede in public discourse and to increase women's political participation, encouraging readers to advocate for enhancing equity in their families, their communities, and the nation.

As women have gained political rights, the novel genre has developed to include more information reflecting positively on specific possibilities for women to pursue educational and work opportunities previously open only to men. Three British novels discussed in chapter 3 "Feminist Marriage and the Academic Novel"—C. P. Snow's *The Search* (1934), Dorothy

Sayers's *Gaudy Night* (1935), and Penelope Fitzgerald's *The Gate of Angels* (1990)—characterize tensions between women's pursuit of scholarly advancement and their establishment of satisfactory marriages in detailing settings of elite British institutions of higher education. The chapter ends with a discussion of Jeffrey Eugenides's novel *The Marriage Plot* (2011), which tracks the romantic entanglements of three US undergraduates in Brown University's class of 1982 and their fluctuating attitudes about sex roles and education.

Chapter 4 "Feminism Meets Science" considers seven novels and a film reporting the professional outcomes of women navigating barriers and biases as they pursue scientific careers. The novels—*The Signature of All Things* (2013) by Elizabeth Gilbert, *A Whistling Woman* (2002) by A. S. Byatt, *Brazzaville Beach* (1990) by William Boyd, *Carbon Dreams* (2001) by Susan Gaines, *Intuition* (2006) by Allegra Goodman, *State of Wonder* (2011) by Ann Patchett, and *The Tenth Muse* (2019) by Catherine Chung—cover a range of historical periods and scientific disciplines, aligning with feminist critiques of science that describe "gender in the cultures of sciences" and "gender in the substance of science."[111] The chapter ends with discussion of *Hidden Figures*, a film based on Margot Lee Shetterly's 2016 history of African American women who worked for the US space agency. Realist narratives about women in science illustrate professional role models and detail how institutional, economic, and societal constraints combine with personal ambition, romance, and integrity to affect scientists' work and the development and reception of scientific theories in society.

The fifth chapter, "Reproductive Independence and Collectivity," analyzes fictions about pregnancy and reproduction that represent social collectivity and individual concepts of self-reliance and independence. Margaret Drabble's *The Millstone* (1965) and Heather Swain's *Luscious Lemon* (2004) depict two young women's personal feelings about pregnancy and medical aspects of reproduction. John Irving's novel *The Cider House Rules* (1985) describes medical personnel at an orphanage who defend women's reproductive rights, providing refuge to orphans and safe abortions to women. The last part of chapter 5 examines representations of women banding together in the British dramatic series *Call the Midwife* (2012-2022), set in post-World War II London. Adapted from a midwife's memoirs, the television series tracks developments in medicine and public health, while noting how emerging scientific information influences gender equity.

Chapter 6, "Overcoming Violence against Women," discusses narratives about women's subordination by sexual violence, asserting the need for increased collective action by women and for better legal and institutional protections for women. Connecting repression in different historical eras, Toni Morrison's *Paradise* (1997) describes founders of an African American town and their progenitors who maintain its legacy of patriarchy. Flashbacks to scenes of women helping each other follow a violent opening, suggesting that by encouraging women to share information, feminism becomes a resource contributing to women's agency. Set in 1988, Louise Erdrich's novel *The Round House* (2012) illustrates how inhabitants on an Ojibwe reservation endure despite the failure of the law to compensate them for the historical cases of Federal land-grabbing that include violence, racial oppression, and gender discrimination. The long arc television series *The Closer* (TNT 2005–2012) focuses on Chief Brenda Leigh Johnson's excellent police work as well as her abhorrence of and personal vulnerability to sexual violence.[112] Characters in these narratives acknowledge pervasive biases and violence against women; the fictions point to the need for legal and political reforms to supplement personal communications and connections that protect marginalized individuals.

Fictional narratives supply information about examples of inequities as well as identifying feminist principles of equity and equality, offering imaginative possibilities for society to overcome misogyny, discrimination, and abuse. Narratives discussed in chapter 7, "Feminist Politics in Fiction," reveal how conflicts emerge for women leaders who were elected or appointed because of their honesty, integrity, and flexibility—as well as their commitments to social equity and gender equality—when they bend their ethical principles to reach their goals, to help allies, or to stay in power. In this way, readers recognize how realist narratives observe constraints affecting women's lives while leaving open the possibility that feminist principles can inform political and social change in the future. Readers identify optimistic outcomes of feminism, extrapolating from the lesson of *Lysistrata* by envisioning solutions to develop equity in the course of time. The persistence of feminist possibilities hinted at by fictions promises a better future, eventually.

Chapter 1

Feminist Information
and the Novel as Information System

The aim of the poet is to inform or delight, or to combine together, in what he says, both pleasure and applicability to life. In instructing, be brief in what you say in order that your readers may grasp it quickly and retain it faithfully. Superfluous words simply spill out when the mind is already full.

—Horace, *Ars Poetica* (20 BC)[1]

Only connect! That was the whole of her sermon. Only connect the prose and the passion, and both will be exalted, and human love will be seen at its height. Live in fragments no longer. Only connect, and the beast and the monk, robbed of the isolation that is life to either, will die.

—E. M. Forster, *Howard's End* (1910)[2]

Fiction educates readers and offers the promise of reforming the world by presenting a persuasive account of characters interacting and transforming in recognizable settings.[3] Each realist novel collects, interprets, and transmits bits of information about what it means to be human in a particular time and place, often identifying social problems and suggesting improvements. Interest in socially relevant information flourished in the nineteenth century, as Geoffrey Nunberg explains: "Information, in the socially important sense—stuff that is storable, transferable and meaningful independent of context—is neither eternal nor ubiquitous. It was a creation of the modern media and the modern state (Walter Benjamin dated its appearance to the mid-19th century). And it accounts for just a small portion of the flood of bits in circulation."[4] "Storable, transferable and meaningful independent of context" is a description appreciating novels as information and their history as part of information history. Widely published and read in significant numbers in the eighteenth and nineteenth centuries in Europe and America, the realist novel grew up with the modern state and offers a lens on to historical social transformations, particularly those related to gender, race, and class.[5] Commentary in novels complements insights from the social sciences gained via other technologies of the nineteenth century, including affordable newspapers and books, public education, sociological studies, and policing.[6] Narratives come in many formats as we create and access digital and multimodal media, including graphic comic books, reproduced texts in online archives, and downloadable electronic texts and audio files. But all fictional narratives, regardless of genre, mode of deployment, or particulars of character, setting, and plot, are composed of and convey information about the human condition.[7] Offering information and acting as information, novels rely on cognitive capacities of readers to notice inequity and to posit reforms to minimize it.

Lisa Zunshine explains how "fiction builds on and experiments with our other cognitive propensities."[8] In *Why We Read Fiction*, she asserts that readers can understand fictional characters and their behaviors because we assume they are like us, a principle of Theory of Mind or what she terms "mind-reading." She acknowledges that one's interpretation of novelistic information might be subject to misreading: "Literary critics . . . know that the process of attributing thoughts, beliefs, and desires to other people may lead to *misinterpreting* those thoughts, beliefs, and desires."[9] Reader sympathies are important in figuring out what information in a novel signifies. Referencing a passage in Virginia Woolf's *Mrs. Dalloway*, Zunshine notes, "Knowing *whose sentiment it is* constitutes a crucial aspect of our understanding of the psychological dynamics of this particular scene and of the novel as a whole. . . . our tendency to keep track of sources of our representations—to metarepresent them—is a particular cognitive endowment closely related to our mind-reading ability."[10] Reader identification with characters' thoughts and actions is a critical narrative capacity enabling immersive reading and leading to developing a coherent understanding of a text.

Charles Dickens's *Little Dorrit* and Margaret Drabble's *The Radiant Way* trilogy encourage readers to combine information from accounts offered by fictional innocents and malefactors, to increase our sympathies for the former, and to speculate about future reforms to protect the vulnerable from the latter. This interpretive process helps us to recognize the workings of the fictional social world, including its inequities for girls and women, and to sustain hope that the future will incorporate improved prospects for the marginalized. Set within a satire of a government unable to function fairly, Dickens's portrait of the generous Amy Dorrit in *Little Dorrit* illustrates an individual's capacity to overcome social inertia and discrimination; the novel emphasizes her kindness as she connects individuals across socioeconomic classes, thereby allowing her family to come into their inheritance and enabling her to marry Arthur Clennam. Drabble's trilogy of novels looks at female friendship as a protective feminist attribute fueled by the exchange of information during a period of national disinvestment. Although the novels depict different historical phases of feminism, *The Radiant Way*'s female characters share perspectives and information, like Amy Dorrit, as they develop a feminist community through their social practices, including their extensive communications.

Novel Capacities

Fictions are capacious, flexible, and convincing in their capacities to influence audience attitudes and to suggest social reforms. Imaginative narratives represent events and ideas, contain information about real or invented worlds, and adapt real or invented texts, doing so with much less regard for brevity than Horace recommends for poetry. But, like poetry, novels attempt to educate, largely by delving into the psychology of human beings, their actions and initiatives, and the dynamics of their political and social interactions in ways that persuade readers to think differently. These narratives aim for authenticity reimagined: they contain information about material conditions, social customs and values, the organization of institutions, and individual perceptions and identities, often depicting divergent points of view within the same work. Fictions outline individual transgressions, detail consequences of these, and suggest ways to avoid future problems, including changing social attitudes and laws. A novel's elements inevitably enable different interpretations. "Information" in novels is necessarily relayed by author, narrator, and character and parsed by readers, who evaluate characterizations, plot, point of view, tone, and other elements in developing interpretations. Additionally, understanding fictional information and appreciating historical circumstances rely on recognizing literary (and social) codes and conventions.[11]

Each novel includes, constitutes, and transmits information, consisting of facts and opinions contextualized by perspectives within the fictional world and interpreted by readers, who may or may not be familiar with the circumstances represented. Although novels contain facts, they are not reference books; rather they are "information systems" that describe fictional worlds with critical relevance to our understanding of history, politics, social organization, and psychology.[12] Many fictions describing conditions for those in the middle and working classes detail problems affecting women and minorities in a patriarchal society, calling for changed social attitudes and conditions to foster the empowerment of those without autonomy or authority. Readers recognize the ways in which characters' situations and decisions demonstrate how materialism and selfishness doom some while benefiting others, regardless of whether a reader may identify with a character or understand the dilemmas that women and racial minorities faced. In short, each realist novel describes social conditions, criticizes moral deficiencies, and points to social reforms. Offering compelling portraits of fictional personalities that could appear as "real" as people we know, a novel encourages readers to understand other points of view, to appreciate ambiguities, and to consider possibilities for individual and social improvement that might be adopted in the present or future.

Novels describe material conditions, offering information identifying socioeconomic and political conditions and problems; in doing so, they also suggest reforms necessary to establish or enhance equity. Charles Dickens's *Little Dorrit* (1855-1857) and Margaret Drabble's *The Radiant Way* trilogy of novels—*The Radiant Way* (1987), *A Natural Curiosity* (1989), and *The Gates of Ivory* (1991)—identify failing mechanisms of social institutions and notice unjust conditions, especially those harming the poor and women. These works critique social hierarchies and inequities, weaving historical and social information into their thematics of plot, character, and setting and their use of multifocal narratives. *Little Dorrit* describes nineteenth-century English society as institutionalizing unjustified imprisonment, depicting an environment fueled by selfishness and rumor reinforcing masculine privilege, while *The Radiant Way* trilogy describes a shift in social investment, contrasting a period of open access to education in post–World War II Britain with decreased institutionalized opportunities for social mobility for the next generation. Dickens embeds criticism of imperialism, bloated government bureaucracy, capitalist greed, and social hypocrisy in detailing Amy Dorrit's interactions with characters from diverse classes. Drabble's story of feminist friendship links various women's perspectives within a critique of Thatcherism and colonialism. Focusing on overcoming gender inequities through communication, these novels illustrate complex societal webs connecting individuals with partial information and limited opportunities to improve their situations.

Multifocal Narratives

Dickens and Drabble combine different discourses to connect the viewpoints of different characters in ways that demand significant reader attention and rereading, for, as Paula M. L. Moya argues concerning multifocal narratives, "They disrupt the conventional form of the realist novel with digressive and non-linear narratives" that "shift with varying degrees of rapidity, between different characters' perspectives [and] jump in time and space."[13] She recognizes that these fictions advocate for equity by making available the "inner lives" of characters and narrators; such texts "distribute narrative attention and character-space more or less equally among a large number of characters" and aim to "democratize the space of the novels."[14] Moya's argument about contemporary decolonial novels acknowledges that narrative features highlighting multiple perspectives are not new. She notes that "a focus on interiority that is dispersed across a large number of major characters" will "make visible the large number of 'worlds of sense' that make up any one social world."[15] The fictional worlds of the *Little Dorrit* and *The Radiant Way* novels rely on such a structure; they include many characters, combine multiple interior perspectives, and jump in time and space. These features encourage readers to appreciate the capacities and limitations of characters as they manage social conditions by leveraging whatever information they have; readers must also pull together disparate pieces of information to understand what a narrative means and signifies.

In their multifocal narratives, Dickens and Drabble draw attention to the ways that information moves around society, the ways in which it is available to some and not others, and how a surfeit of information is nevertheless insufficient to ameliorate social inequalities, particularly bias and discrimination against women and the poor. *Little Dorrit* describes characters' conversations and movements around London, containing various forms of discourse (song lyrics, letters, posters, testimonies) and elaborating in two sections he calls "Books" ("Poverty" and "Riches") how dozens of characters interact over decades. Planned and chance meetings of characters in Dickens's novel enable information exchanges, as characters, particularly Amy Dorrit, move about among different families and social groups to serve as communication mechanisms. Although subplots in *Little Dorrit* converge to explain injustices, not all characters are able to leverage information to establish financial security or social success. Similarly, characters in the *The Radiant Way* trilogy receive information shared between individuals and among groups in the form of dialogues and conversations and in glimpses of literature, rumor, and print, television, and radio news stories, building a picture of gender, race, class, and ethnic inequities in families, cities, and nations. Drabble's trilogy presents fragmented descriptions of characters and plot events, while highlighting the transmission of information as inspiring individual ambition and social activism. Information in *The Radiant Way* novels loosely connects characters within global networks that fail to protect individuals. Both Dickens and Drabble represent realistic fictional worlds and critique public policies that do not offer sufficient social investment and security. Readers become immersed in novels that function as fictional worlds full of information about inequities, provoking us to question what could be done to save and to protect those less privileged, notably girls and women, and to posit possible individual and institutional solutions.

Novel Information

Information matters to the content, function, and form of the novel, for, as already noted, this protean genre incorporates, reveals, and embodies information. Authors include observations, experiences, and research in fictions, and readers expect novels to communicate details of setting, characterization, and plot that elaborate an understandable fictional world. As Christopher Bode explains, it is "a constitutive part of the conception of the novel: its proximity to reality."[16] Each novel provides information about people, places, and ideas that we may recognize from our own experience or that may be new to us as we follow its plot and respond to characters and their actions. Megan Ward points to "what Georg Lukács calls realism's ability to depict 'the lasting features in people.' In doing so, Lukács argues, realism captures 'man in the whole range of his relations to the real world, above those that outlast mere fashion.' "[17] Characters represent and adapt features of real people, or they may be totally fictional. Events in a novel may be historical, adapted from historical incidents, or created by the author. Settings may represent versions of actual, adapted, or invented places. Information in the novel includes the work's format and style, including the way the story is told, by whom, in what order, and according to what structure or pattern. Fictions represent socioeconomic and political principles and ideas, although they do so in ambiguous and sometimes obscure ways. Each text is subject to reader interpretation that multiplies meanings, as readers have different experiences, values, aims, and contexts that affect the ways they apply information from a fictional narrative.

The history of information offers a promising way of thinking about the appearance, function, and outcome of information as a topic and a thematic device in novels. Donald Case's comprehensive volume surveying "research on information seeking, needs, and behavior" points to "five problematic issues in defining information": utility, physicality, structure/ process, intentionality, and truth.[18] According to Case, the concept of *utility* allows humans to think about the usefulness of information and to question how some information does not reduce uncertainty but may provide "entertainment, emotional uplift, or some other kind of useful stimulation."[19] The concept of *physicality* considers whether "Most information always take on some physical form" and assesses whether information must be directly observable or not.[20] *Structure/process* asks if information must "be composed of elements in fixed relations to one another, or in some ways consist of a complex 'whole' " or "is information a process, some kind of function, a series of steps—a sort of recipe."[21] Under *intentionality* Case questions whether we must "assume that someone (or something) intends to communicate it to another entity" or if there "is some information simply out there in the environment, to be perceived by a sentient organism."[22] *Truth* questions whether untrue information is really information. These concerns acknowledge that information can be stimulating, take physical shape, represent a process, offer communication, and may or may not be untrue, dimensions that can be ascribed to literature.

Novels reveal information through characters and narrators who confront and question information in the fictional world. Employing Case's terminology, we recognize that novels teach as well as entertain (*utility*), that they can be read as print and screen texts in addition to evoking material conditions (*physicality*), that they suggest what an author's intentions might be or if they matter, that they exhibit patterns and processes (*structure/process*), and that they illustrate some sort of *truth*. The question of *intentionality* includes discussions of what a historical author meant and how the author function works in a novel.[23] Some critics believe reading fiction improves our understanding of human thinking and behavior and inspires ethical conduct, often by illustrating positive and negative examples of characters and their actions. According to this approach, novels focus on characters that model or transgress courtesy, good taste, social convention, or laws, according to information in the text.

Fictional Influence

Yet to say that reading a novel is a pleasurable and educational activity with diverse capacities to convey truthful information enters us into disputed terrain. Disagreement over whether literary works bear truth began with Plato, who argued that because literature appeals to our emotions, we should not trust Homer's poetry, which presents misleading illusions rather than truth (*The Republic*, Book II). It is fitting that the third book in Drabble's trilogy, *The Gates of Ivory*, opens with lines from Homer's *Odyssey* that reference deception as a feature of the imagination: "Dreams, said Penelope to the stranger, may puzzle and mislead. They do not always foretell the truth. They come to us through two gates: one is of horn, the other is of ivory. The dreams that come to us through the traitor ivory deceive us with false images of what will never come to pass: but those that appear to us through polished horn speak plainly of what could be and will be."[24] Literary critic Harry Levin quotes the same section (albeit using a different translation) of the *Odyssey* on the title page of *The Gates of Horn*, his work of literary criticism about realist novels by Stendhal, Honoré de Balzac, Gustave Flaubert, Émile Zola, and Marcel Proust. Explicating the Homeric passage, Levin remarks "Truth and fiction seldom, if ever, come to us unadulterated and clearly labeled. . . . As books and readers have multiplied, as we have become more dependent on the printed word and less conscious of its limitations, our heads have all been slightly muddled."[25] Levin's claim prevails in the Information Age:

texts vary in authenticity and accuracy while fostering multiple, conflicting interpretations.

Novels often identify confusions without resolving them. Gustave Flaubert's most famous character, Emma Bovary, suffered unfortunate consequences because her mind was muddled: educated in a convent, she believed that what she read in romances accurately described the real world. In many ways, the novel as a form can be regarded as an archive of ways that individuals in specific circumstances misinterpret what they read in texts and expect in life. Results may be fatal. Readers may sympathize (or not) with characters while deploring their choices. How characters fare under certain circumstances can provide lessons that might be reenacted by readers (such as suicides imitating Goethe's *The Sorrows of Young Werther*, first published in 1774) and the recurrent fears of parents and educational authorities about the effects of fiction on young readers. Recognizing the novel as information includes considering whether a text is false or too dangerous to be shared, although such assessments are often biased.

Narratives outlining consequences of characters' choices provide didactic examples for readers, who respond differently to fictional characters and situations based on their own preferences and experiences. Yet reading a moral text and enacting a moral life may not be causatively or even correlatively connected. Literary theorist Suzanne Keen considers the effects of reading narrative on empathy, "a vicarious, spontaneous sharing of affect," as not yet empirically demonstrated by research on readers.[26] She cites Jèmeljan Hakemulder's conclusion that "direct evidence of such changes is missing and that 'effects of stories are probably marginal compared to other social influences.' "[27] Keen also notes that Hakemulder, who conducted empirical research on reading, found both "good evidence that 'reading stories with positive portrayals of outgroups leads to a reduction of social distance' " and "that a 'narrative presentation causes stronger effects on our beliefs about the emotions and thoughts of others' than nonnarrative presentation of the same content."[28] In short, even if we suspect the claim that reading a novel inspires positive social attitudes and actions, we accept that reading a novel about marginalized characters familiarizes us with attitudes and circumstances far from our own and that information presented in the form of a story that includes elements of character, plot, and narrative voice can more powerfully engage sympathy than similar information presented in expository form.

Providing information through stories, characters, and situations, novels enhance our social understanding of our own world by giving shape to fictional worlds in words. Charles Dickens's *Little Dorrit* and Margaret Drabble's *The Radiant Way* novels elaborate family, social, professional, and random connections that link individuals across diverse classes and throughout a range of social, political, and economic affiliations and organizations to demonstrate the profound disparity of ambitions and outcomes between the rich and the poor and to identify specific constraints and opportunities affecting women. Drabble acknowledges that the broad sweep and moral vision in her trilogy resemble similar characteristics of Victorian novels.[29] Both Dickens and Drabble construct their fictions around emerging family secrets and various degrees of deception exhibited by diverse characters. Their narratives reveal painful socioeconomic outcomes for women, as idealistic characters gather critical information about family histories, while being constrained by legal restrictions and social conventions from pursuing large-scale social reforms. These novels inform readers about circumstances and human behavior that can be compared or contrasted with our own experiences, as we, like the characters, resist limits, struggle to decipher moral truths, apply these to our own lives, and posit individual and social shifts necessary to improve equity.

Dickens on Social Inequality

Little Dorrit suggests that relying on pleasant fiction is suspect, showing that social conventions concerning criminality and poverty employ faulty information to define inequalities without eliminating them. Subplots in the novel reveal that it is possible for the incarcerated debtor Dorrit and the greedy landlord Casby to be celebrated as beneficent patriarchs, the devious fraud Merdle to masquerade as a successful speculator, the dangerous murderer Rigaud to elude capture by acting as a society gentleman, and the hard-hearted Mrs. Clennam to appear a concerned mother. The novel also illustrates how good can be spun as evil when the saintlike Amy Dorrit and the generous Arthur Clennam are at certain points in the novel judged as transgressors against propriety and the law by those with selfish motivations.

Dickens links subplots according to connections of kinship, residence, employment, business dealings, and legal inquiry. *Little Dorrit* includes characterizations of debtors and criminals, descriptions of jail and other prison-like settings, and thematic references to the government's favoring the elite to elucidate Amy as an innocent in a world full of deceit, hypocrisy, moral lapses, and crimes. Each chapter describes a prison, a setting like a prison, a prisoner, a person acting as a prisoner, and/or the inexorably tedious interactions with bureaucracy that make the patriotic, genial citizen ready to riot against government. The relentless presentation of individuals (whether virtuous or vicious) in captive situations produces a social critique directed against legal fraud, social hypocrisy, false gentility, and the ambiguous results of fiction-making that disproportionately harm women and the poor.[30] Recognizing a human propensity to transgress, Dickens's novel advocates for dispossessed populations by encouraging readers to sympathize with the economically downtrodden such as Amy and those beaten down by social institutions such as Daniel Doyce, who is driven to exasperation by a bureaucracy designed to reward officeholders instead of helping him patent his invention. The poor residents of Bleeding Heart Yard are charged excessive rent by their greedy landlord, while the prisoners in the Marshalsea, particularly those jailed for trivial debts, suffer punishments that far exceed the magnitude of their crimes. Privy to information about all characters and able to connect seemingly disparate activities, readers collate sufficient evidence from various quarters and draw conclusions about injustice and inequities that contextualize Amy's biography. The episodic arrangement of bits of information provided by or about individuals in different social classes forces readers to connect pieces of evidence to understand the emerging plot revealing how the powerful oppress women.

Detailing how the unfortunately incarcerated suffer exploitation, *Little Dorrit* reveals a more progressive view of criminality than is represented in many other narratives of the period.[31] Dickens goes so far as to illustrate the ambiguous moral qualities of all characters in his novel, even those not engaging in criminal or unethical behaviors and generally considered law-abiding and respectable. The novel employs oppositions, inversions, and doubles to connect moral integrity and criminality. To take a phrase as an example: the title and nickname *Little Dorrit* simultaneously allude to Amy's slight build and her father's great pretensions to gentility; yet the phrase reinvests the adjective "little" with positive connotations that reference Amy's hard work and great heart. At the same time the title diminishes positive values one might associate with Dorrit, a name suggestive of "Doric," the plainest of the three classical orders of architecture, and of the Dorian mode (now called minor) in music.

The original title page of Dickens's novel emphasizes this contradictory mix of high/low and noble/humble associated with the title in using an unadorned font for both words and wrapping the name Dorrit in chains.[32]

Of all families described in the novel, the Dorrits remain the focus of attention. They are most closely associated with the prison, for residence in the Marshalsea develops their generally deficient moral characters, provides them a common history as family members, and affects their interactions with others. In *Little Dorrit* the prison is a source of contagion in that incarceration demoralizes all prisoners. Dickens knew that nineteenth-century American and European prison reformers worried about convicts sharing information and teaching their trade to fellow prisoners; governments promoted silent and separate systems of incarceration to prevent the spread of criminality.[33] His fictional rendering of the Marshalsea stresses its close conditions and poor sanitation.[34] The Dorrits' jail taint is identified as a moral quality, derived from imprisonment or from associating with those in prison and causing degeneration of the will to work honestly. The taint is an infection that manifests different symptoms in individuals: it causes William Dorrit to lapse into narcissism and false gentility, his son Tip to eschew any honest profession, and his daughter Fanny to seek the highest possible social status at the cost of her happiness and well-being.

The family's tainted condition has the opposite effect on daughter Amy, who was born in the prison and is "inspired" "to be that something, different and laborious, for the sake of the rest."[35] Amy's inspiration and her diligence are linked to her innocence and generosity. Despite "drinking from infancy of a well whose waters had their own peculiar stain," she resists collecting information for selfish purposes and avoids manipulating others to improve her situation.[36] Instead she frequently cautions her siblings against such impulses. Presenting the family as a case study of how punishing poverty encourages criminality in most subjects, *Little Dorrit* indicts society for hypocritical gentility, fraud, and using false information for one's own gain. Amy's innocence and generosity become model attributes for others.

Arthur Clennam admires Amy's integrity as he seeks information to aid him in helping her family because he suspects that his father has injured the Dorrit family. Arthur's estrangement from his mother along with her bizarre household and her cruelty motivate him to learn the truth about his family's connection to the Dorrits and to clear William Dorrit's name. Many novel readers are more sympathetic to romantic passion than religious piety, so Mrs. Clennam's punishing of sin appears worse than the sin she deplores: the past secret amorous relationship between Arthur's father and biological mother, who are both long dead in the present time of the novel. Seen in the context of progressive views of female sexuality, Arthur's birth mother was a victim of the rabidly religious Mrs. Clennam. Dickens's narrative connects this family plot to sociopolitical critique arguing against the hypocrisy of pious propriety and of seemingly upstanding families, for appearances belie both the corrupting force of Mrs. Clennam's vindictive jealousy and its outcomes of repression and fear.

The novel's conclusion informs readers that Arthur's birth mother's relationship with his father initiated a chain of events that could not be stopped until his parents' secret marriage and Arthur's birth could be revealed and understood as innocent rather than transgressive acts. Dickens's novel turns out to be a long plea of innocence for an offstage character—Arthur's biological mother, who only appears in the text as an imagined apparition frightening Affery and as a memory of Mrs. Clennam—whose love motivates the jealous hatred of a powerful rival. Arthur's actions and his adoptive mother's testimony ultimately enable Amy to receive the legacy long denied Arthur's birth mother, who sacrificed her claim on it for the love of Arthur, demonstrating the critical link between Amy (the child born in prison) and the mother in the asylum who is deprived of her child. The outcomes for these two women designate them as innocent convicts, despite their different temperaments and appearances. Arthur's birth mother bends first to Clennam and then his second wife, while Amy appears childlike and acts motherly with a quiet strength. Both Amy and her birth mother are subject to incarcerations, and both sacrifice their claims, to money and to child, for the sake of Arthur.

Dickens offers an enigmatic ending to *Little Dorrit*: after uncovering truths about their families, Amy and Arthur, who are now romantic lovers, eschew an inheritance. They continue to bear the burden of caring for others, showing the younger generation pays for the acts of the elder. The conclusion reveals some social progress as Amy's love improves her life and others', overcoming circumstances Arthur's mother was not able to escape, namely, the deadly forces of social respectability that doomed her liaison and took away her child. Yet Amy continues to pay for family crimes that she did not commit; her story, like that of Arthur's mother, proposes that existing social values are selfish and cruel, that women deserve to live according to their desires, and that the criminal justice system, which causes needless suffering for those who do not deserve to be punished, ought to be reformed.

Narrative Sense

As an information system, *Little Dorrit* describes how individuals and institutions are subject to corruption in familial, romantic, and social relations; philanthropy; investment practices; medical care; legal disputes, and government bureaucracy. Characters' experiences provide source material for developing the novel's related themes of imprisonment, selfish obsessions, and social conventions that owe to hypocritical proprieties rather than morality. Dickens establishes a web of characters and links them chapter-by-chapter within tableaux to reveal the haphazard arrangement of communication in society, the precarious nature of family and social relationships, the likelihood of transgression, and prevailing gender discriminations. As Jonathan Grossman explains, Dickens's novel conveys the ways in which "the density and extensivity of people's interconnections exceeds their capacity to grasp them."[37] Interlocking plots connect characters, while their and reader suspicions about past behavior and criticisms of present actions emerge out of how/when/why odd characters meet and/or hear of each other.

Christopher Bode argues, "To narrate is to claim that something makes sense—and it's this sense that the narration is to bring out. Narration is the endowment of sense against the possibility of the absurd."[38] Dickens's novel circles around the question of social responsibility as chapters make sense of different forms of information to illustrate and to criticize the hardships endured by some at the hands of others. In addition to the explanatory accounts provided by the third-person narrator, characters' dialogues, and internal monologues, interpolated narratives such as the letter in chapter 21: "The History of a Self-Tormentor," and paratexts such as the title page and illustrations contribute to the novel's plot, characterizations, and settings and develop its fictional world. These elements of the realist novel create an information system on the order of what Richard Menke describes: "As a literary attempt to order reality's connections and disjunctions, realism now comes to suggest the limitations and biases of any information system. In aesthetic terms, this could provide a starting point for a modernism that foregrounds the force of representation over its reference to the thing represented."[39] Thus, readers of *Little Dorrit* can regard the novel as focusing on social and transportation mobility (Grossman), narration as rational sense-making (Bode), or the representation of information (Menke), but we are likely to see these dimensions as acting in concert to produce a fictional experience of a world that is both foreign to ours while resembling it in recognizable ways.

Dickens presents this world as a panorama that spans classes, generations, and countries in elaborating the intertwined histories of the Dorrits, Clennams, and other families, and investigating odd corners of society, including the government offices of the Barnacles, the Marshalsea prison, the poverty-stricken Bleeding Heart Yard, the courts, and high-status circles of London and foreign cities. Learning about these different situations, connecting scenarios located in various settings, and tracking characters' movements, readers of *Little Dorrit* make sense out of odd facts to solve the intertwined mysteries of Arthur Clennam's parentage and William Dorrit's incarceration. This storyline exemplifies the broader scope of the novel, exploring how the poor, particularly women, are forced to live without, while the greedy extract as much as they can. To narrate this information is to make sense of what Dickens understood, and what his readers should recognize, as absurd: that some human beings live comfortably while profiting off others' misery.

Drabble's Way

Margaret Drabble originally published *The Radiant Way* as a one-off novel commenting on female friendship, feminism, and changing social conditions in late twentieth-century Britain. This realist fiction and its successor, *A Natural Curiosity*, note the impact of Prime Minister Margaret Thatcher's policies on privatization, trade unions, deregulation, and defunding of social services during her administration (1979–1990), while the third volume in the trilogy, *The Gates of Ivory*, looks at the effects of armed conflict, dictatorships, and expanding capitalism in postcolonial countries in Southeast Asia after the Vietnam War. Katherine Hayles explains that in fictional discourse, "Maximum information is conveyed when there is a mixture of order and surprise, when the message is partly anticipated and partly surprising."[40] *The Radiant Way* novels rely on this principle, presenting familiar historical events with unexpected fictional plot turns. Considered together, *The Radiant Way*, *A Natural Curiosity*, and *The Gates of Ivory* describe characters struggling to understand a plethora of information about their family histories, government policies, and world events. They seek or accidentally encounter historical and historically plausible information that is variously unpredictable, hidden, unknown, confusing, or ambiguous. Drabble's trilogy connects primary female characters who share the same milieux and similar values as they discover new information about their genealogies and about events affecting other families on other continents.

Key features of the trilogy (also sometimes called "the Liz Headleand trilogy") include illustrating women's (and secondarily men's) experiences and emotions related to friendship, education, work, social activism, romance, marriage, divorce, adultery, and the deaths of loved ones and friends; presenting different political perspectives articulated by characters; developing mystery plots related to deception and transgression; and loosely connecting ideas about late-twentieth-century events and cultural transformations filtered through the minds of variously situated characters. *The Radiant Way* thus presents a collage of information revealing the perceptions of characters that are in the process of figuring out what all these details signify, while readers also assess the mix of invention and historical fact to determine meaning. Like many authors of realist fictions, including Dickens, Drabble has authored nonfiction and worked as an editor; her fiction incorporates information drawn from observation and research to examine how fictional humans navigate personal challenges and social ambitions.[41] And, similar to Dickens's *Little Dorrit*, Drabble's trilogy presents various social groups to illustrate that the socioeconomic constraints and discriminations experienced by women can be eliminated in the future if individuals share information and work together to improve social conditions.

Describing historical events and fictional ones, that is, incorporating and devising information, Drabble's trilogy contrasts attitudes of men and women, of citizens in the North and the South regions of England, of those in Eastern and Western countries, and of different generations in the post–World War II and post–Vietnam War eras. Differences, repetitions, and variations emerge from the trilogy's representations of its three primary female (and feminist) protagonists: Liz Ablewhite Headleand, Alix Doddridge Bowen, and Esther Breuer. Like *Little Dorrit*, which sketches individual interactions across diverse social classes while focusing on Amy Dorrit, the novels comprising *The Radiant Way* trilogy describe characters linked to Alix, Esther, and Liz. The long narrative arc of Drabble's trilogy tracks their friendships and their romantic, marital, parental, and employment relationships, while inserting flashbacks to scenes set in the past and incorporating fragmentary information of different types, including literary allusions, political ideas, and historical events.

Drabble's trilogy links the personal to the political by combining mystery subplots set within an account tracing the decline of Britain during Thatcher's administration and the related narrative of capitalism's expansion around the world. The mysteries center on deception and disappearance and include what Liz learns about her parents and siblings in the first two books, the serial murders in London solved in *The Radiant Way*, Alix's search in *A Natural Curiosity* for the murderer Paul Whitmore's parents, Cliff Harper's illness and sudden suicide followed by Shirley Harper's escape from Northam, Esther's romantic relationships throughout the trilogy, the execution of Charles's former colleague Dirk Davis in the Middle East, and the disappearances of Stephen Cox and others in Cambodia. Some mysteries are resolved within the trilogy, while others, notably Stephen's disappearance in *The Gates of Ivory*, are not. The narrative in the trilogy spirals out from the first two volumes' elaboration of family histories to the third volume's consideration of economic and political instabilities in Southeast Asia, so that Stephen's death and the other disappearances and deaths in the novels connect an extraordinary number of characters who receive, disperse, and often remain puzzled by bits of information.

Each novel in the trilogy provides information in content and form, as sociopolitical content appears in a variety of stylistic formats. For example, focusing on Liz, Alix, and Esther—three female friends approaching middle age in the 1980s—allows Drabble to offer political commentary on cultural changes, noting how educational and professional opportunities opened for women. Her novels consider their friendships and their attitudes toward family and work in the context of the 1970s women's movement inspiring women to pursue higher education and to enter professional occupations. Drabble's invented female protagonists come from middle-class backgrounds, but their political perspectives and sexual choices vary, and they make disparate life decisions concerning careers, romantic partners, children, and travel. These focal characters reveal their thoughts about what they read, see, and hear, enabling the novelist to compare their views and experiences with those of generational peers, their parents, and children.

The Radiant Way trilogy presents women and men whose ambitions are constrained and enabled by personal situations (parental attitudes and financial circumstances) and historical conditions (economic and political realities). The trilogy introduces Liz, Alix, and Esther in middle age and offers a flashback to when they met as prospective students visiting Cambridge. They remain friends while completing their educations, developing careers, and managing family relationships. After graduating from Cambridge, enabled by an increase in professional opportunities for women, they pursue careers: Liz Ablewhite completes medical school and becomes a psychiatrist, Alix Doddridge after being married and widowed at a young age works as a teacher in a prison and then as a writer's assistant, and Esther Breuer finishes a graduate degree to work as a freelance art historian. Government policies in postwar Britain that support education as social investment make their degrees and professional success possible and enable their privileged status:

> These three women, it will readily and perhaps with some irritation be perceived, were amongst the *crème de la crème* of their generation. Illustrious educational institutions not merely offered them places, but also attempted to entice them. Narratives, in the past, related the adventures of the famous and the wealthy. Kings, queens, emperors, warlords. In *The Tale of Genji*, which has a claim to be considered the world's first novel, an emperor weeps for a lost love in the opening pages. (Do pages open in a Japanese novel? Probably not.) In Jane Austen, to come nearer home, the protagonists are not, it is true, titled, but they are privileged. By youth, by wit, by beauty, and sometimes by wealth. The princesses of their country villages.[42]

The narrator acknowledges that while "Liz, Alix, and Esther were not princesses," their educational and employment prospects exceeded those available to earlier generations of women. Thus, the trio's successful lives were launched from their 1952 meeting as prospective students at Cambridge. In the 1950s and 1960s, individuals from all classes could benefit if they were ambitious enough to receive prestigious degrees. Liz, Alix, and Esther, and others coming of age in the post-World War II era, appreciated government support of education, labor, transportation infrastructure, and health care. Men in this generation were channeled into educational opportunities through military service. For example, Brian Bowen (who becomes Alix's second husband and a teacher) and his army colleague Stephen Cox (who becomes a writer and is later close to Liz) also received university educations because they tested well while in service. The personal and professional successes enjoyed by these characters because of their educations affirm for readers the necessity of supporting social investment to enable mobility and equity, particularly for women and the working classes.

Socioeconomic circumstances are less positive in the trilogy's present time, the early 1980s, as prospects for ordinary citizens (i.e., the nonaristocratic, the nonrich) diminish after the nation privatizes operations, reduces government expenditures directed toward social investment, and leaves citizens to fend for themselves. The title of the first novel, *The Radiant Way*, is also the title of an educational primer, itself a tool of social mobility. The same phrase is employed ironically by Liz's second husband, Charles Headleand, as the title of a documentary film he produced about class inequalities in Britain.

> The nation smiled as the camera elicited words, accents, attitudes of extraordinary, outmoded quaintness and patronage from Oxford dons, from headmasters and pupils of public schools, from prep school boys in short trousers; then frowned thoughtfully as the camera showed these attitudes to be entrenched within the educational structure itself, and within the very fabric of British society. It was great television: Charles let his people speak for themselves, they condemned themselves in their own words from their own mouths, they won sympathy by the way they stood at a bus stop or fed their rabbits or bought a copy of *Exchange and Mart* at the corner shop: or so, at least, it seemed to the British public, which was still innocent in its response to the television documentary.[43]

Promoted in publications of its day, *The Radiant Way* documentary connected scenes of individuals from diverse backgrounds to illustrate the rigidity of class structure and lack of class mobility. Charles later becomes more conservative but nevertheless argues with his son Jonathan that the *Radiant Way* documentary is a classic in offering information directly from its subjects, whose direct presentation to viewers helps them understand class, race, and gender privileges.

Like Charles's film, Drabble's novels present information in a piecemeal collection of conversations, speculations, and news accounts filtered through the observations of characters. Drabble's main characters live better than most, although Liz (a psychiatrist) and Charles (a television producer) have more money and latitude than Alix (an adjunct teacher) and Brian (teacher) or Esther (art historian). *The Radiant Way* begins on December 31, 1979, with a New Year's Eve party hosted by Liz and Charles for two hundred or so friends, family members, and professional acquaintances in their five-story, meticulously renovated Harley Street house. Partygoers divulge much information in their conversations. During the party, Alix uncomfortably converses with a hostile government official about the Open University ("the inadvisability of wasting money on the education of housewives and taxi drivers"), while

> dozens of other topics floated gaily on the lively, slightly choppy waters, their pennants bobbing and fluttering in the end-of-year, the terminal breeze: the approaching steel strike, the brave new era of threatened privatization, the abuse of North Sea oil resources, the situation in Afghanistan, the Annan report, the prospect of a fourth television channel, the viability of Charles's attempt to conquer the United States, the Cambridge Apostles, the disarray of the Labour party, the deplorable vogue for Buck's Fizz as a party drink, the Yorkshire Ripper, the Harrow Road murderer, the Prince of Wales.[44]

Simultaneous conversations consider "whether or not a television program was a primary product or a service" and "the nature of ancestral voices in schizophrenic patients and the Homeric and Biblical epic, and the portrayal of the Holy Ghost in Anglo-Saxon manuscripts," as well as "talk of broccoli, of death in Kabul, of the phenomenal transatlantic success of Pett Petrie's new novel."[45] Political debates about domestic and foreign policies, rumors, news of crimes, trivial opinions, fads, and scholarly discussions blend together in catalogs, mixing fiction and fact and revealing preoccupations and anxieties as well as hot button issues of the era, including some that persist to our day (Afghanistan, television's function, death in Kabul).

Information conveyed at the party includes personal secrets with devastating consequences: one intrusive guest, Ivan Warner, alerts Liz to an apparently long-standing affair between Charles and Lady Henrietta Latchett. After the party, Liz confronts Charles. The Headlands argue, sleep in the same bed for the first time in years, and then separate. Charles later marries Henrietta, and they move to New York so he can take up an important position heading a section of Independent Broadcasting. After her initial upset, Liz later realizes that she will not suffer financially from the divorce because her practice is quite profitable. As an established doctor, she can manage to maintain a proper household even without her ex-husband, whose own finances are far more precarious. Her concerns recognize political and economic realities of the period. Although the country's national health system has had significant cutbacks, Liz sees a combination of public and private patients and profits from government decisions that push more patients to find private care.

Approximately four years pass after the New Year's Eve party, a gap referenced in the middle of *The Radiant Way*: "during these years, war continued to rage between Iraq and Iran, but the West did not pay much attention."[46] This section of the novel lists personal and professional commitments for the protagonists who pay less attention to politics. Charles and Liz remain amiable after their divorce, which is made easier after he returns from New York, after his poor decisions on the job and his separation from Henrietta. In Northam, Liz's mother suffers from dementia and a stroke and is admitted to hospital on Christmas. During the drive north to see her, Charles brings "Liz up to date on the subject of dish receivers, birds, footprints and NTVROs."[47] She seems "unable to follow a manual for tuning a car radio," thinks Charles while they are traveling, but over Christmas with their children "he had heard her dropping some well-informed comments on information technology, videotext, and videodata and discussing the philosophical implications of this brave new world with Jonathan and Alan."[48] The novel exhibits abundant concern about the transformation and transmission of information, mentioning increasing utilization of numerous formats and pointing to the changing dimensions of communication enabling and constraining human interactions and understanding. A surfeit of information appears to be inversely related to our abilities to reach consensus and to undertake mutually beneficial social programs to reduce inequalities.

In other sections of the trilogy, Liz, Alix, and Esther and their partners split their attention among romantic relationships, jobs, children, and parents. Although allusively referenced, information about national policies provides a context for family matters and women's social outcomes. Soon after her return to London, Alix helps organize the Werners' Twelfth Night party for the besotted Otto. Preparing food for the party, Alix and Otto chat about the government's privatization of gas and telephone, considering that water, trains, hospitals, prisons, law courts, police, sewerage, the post office, schools, the military, and perhaps even the monarchy might also be privatized. Otto kisses Alix, although since they are married to other partners, they will not become more involved. Because Alix arrives late to the party, Otto worries that she has been murdered, a foreshadowing that follows on Esther's dream of a speaking severed head on the canal towpath. Thus, dreams, anxieties, and rumors also contribute to narrative information, changing characters' lives.

Women's Problems

Complementing the trilogy's direct concern with economic reforms that minimize the social obligations of government, *The Radiant Way* mixes mundane and dramatic events to illustrate a degenerating society in which personal finances suffer and women bear increasing burdens of care as national support wanes. Alix and Brian give up their car, Liz's mother Rita Ablewhite remains in the hospital, and Alix's first mother-in-law Deborah Manning dies and leaves her estate to her grandson Nicholas (Alix's first son). Crimes in the trilogy include murders, notably the Harrow Road murders mentioned at the New Year's Eve party and intermittently referenced as the murderer crosses paths with the primary characters. Alix feels sorry for the lonely Jilly Fox, a released prisoner abandoned by her parents, and is enticed to visit her. Alix's automobile is vandalized during the visit, so she abandons it. She returns the next day with a new tire and a coworker to find Jilly's severed head in the car. The police later arrest the Horror of Harrow Road, the serial murderer Paul Whitmore, who lives a floor above Esther, for this and other crimes. The arrest takes place in Paul's apartment after a standoff between the murderer and the police during an evening when the astonished Liz and Alix visit Esther in her flat. The women wonder: How could they have been unaware of how dangerous Paul was?

More secrets emerge as characters' circumstances shift. Soon after Paul's arrest, Alix and Brian Bowen move to Northam, where he takes up a better job in a city that continues to support socialist principles and public infrastructure. Also in Northam, Rita Ablewhite quietly suffers a heart attack and dies in her hospital bed. To settle her mother's estate, Liz helps Shirley clean up the house where they grew up. Liz's vague childhood memories of being molested surface after she finds newspaper clippings that describe men (a man?) being charged with sexual improprieties with minors and committing suicide: "One could rearrange these pieces as one wished, like the jigsaw scraps of an experimental novel. A man had killed himself in Stanhope Wood with a penknife, reported an item in the *Evening Star*. A man had been charged with the murder of a six-year-old girl. Suspicious behaviour on school premises. Claimed to be depressed because of operation. Committed an offense on the railway bridge."[49] Confused by this information, Liz looks around her mother's house and finds a copy of *The Radiant Way*. The children's primer releases more memories as Liz recalls that she learned "to read from this very book" and that it is linked to a memory of her father bouncing and fondling her: "Guilt. Shame. Infantile sexuality."[50] She realizes that her professional interest in helping adults deal with their childhood traumas owes to her own childhood experiences, however buried the memories were in her consciousness. Almost immediately, the narrative turns to another's guilt, as Charles regrets his own appalling behavior regarding his former colleague Dirk Davis and dwells over Dirk's execution in Baldai. Although Liz's recollection of her childhood trauma is prompted by a print text, terrorism is now broadcast on television and disseminated widely, prompting generalized guilt.

Information cannot be contained. Liz prefers to repress memories evoked by her mother's clippings about sexual crimes and does not want to share what she learns with her sister Shirley, but Shirley's youngest child, her daughter Celia, had spent a good deal of time with Rita Ablewhite and already knew about her maternal grandfather. Discussing Celia's knowledge and her keeping quiet about the family secret, Liz and Shirley "pondered the mysteries of heredity"; Rita's solicitor had passed information about their father Alfred Ablewhite to his successor, who tells Liz and her sister that after her father was acquitted of exposing himself to children, he committed suicide: "A sad case. Accidental death. There had been a good claim on the insurance."[51] Liz burns the papers saved by her mother, rationalizing that "she didn't know much about that kind of thing, it was not the kind of sexual deviation with which she associated herself, professionally."[52] The sisters decide to avoid speaking about their father and acknowledge different perspectives about their mother.

Many characters react to information by exhibiting cynicism about the government and their own capacities to improve society, while others imagine a better future. Liz argues that "belief in evil has caused immense suffering" and that she prefers "to believe in suffering, and the alleviation of suffering."[53] The miners' strike ends and diminishes interest in the story of serial murderer Paul Whitmore. Alix begins working for the bard of Northam; she has lost faith in social activism and thinks others are delusional in hoping for positive government policies. Otto Werner is more disillusioned and leaves the country. A few pages later, *The Radiant Way* concludes in June 1985, when Liz, Esther, and Alix enjoy a picnic reunion in Somerset, where Esther lives temporarily before moving to Bologna, to celebrate her fiftieth birthday. Their discussion avoids politics and news of family and friends to focus on their enjoyment of the landscape. The time for information sharing has passed, as Drabble ends the book with a static image: "The sun bleeds, the earth bleeds. The sun stands still."[54]

Throughout the trilogy, Drabble connects personal and political in a chain that moves reader attention from one character's thoughts and problems to another's, and that regards social disinvestment as a problem to be ameliorated by feminist practices of caring for the community. Liz, Alix, and Esther, along with other characters, muddle through various quotidian challenges: faulty cars, accidents, adulterous partners, divorce, sadistic/selfish boyfriends, illnesses, children's and parents' demands, financial concerns, crimes, and deaths. These incidents are focalized through feminist characters and narrators and are associated in the text with larger political events such as the miners' strike and the defunding of social services. Despite her difficult childhood and complicated marriage to Charles, Liz's income provides a cushion. As a single mother and then subsequently as wife to an ill husband, the less-well-off Alix is fascinated by what makes people commit evil action. The second book in the trilogy, *A Natural Curiosity*, which begins on January 2, 1987, details Alix's investigation concerning the motivations and experiences of the serial killer Paul Whitmore. Esther, a freelance writer, pursues two affairs: one with a sadistic man and another with his jealous sister. In *The Gates of Ivory*, she marries a much wealthier fellow connoisseur who raises money for government support of the arts from corporations. The relatively privileged lives of the primary female characters exemplify how their educations provided them with advantages enabling them to enact feminist principles in their relationships and in professions and communities.

Making Connections

Drabble's author statement at the British Council website references her method of composition as looking for elements and hoping for their dynamic interaction.

I walk around, looking for plot, structure, characters, images, trying not to repeat or imitate or listen too much to the wrong voices. This is a dreary time, comfortless, irritable, unsatisfying. When the book begins to move, everything changes, and everything I see or hear or read seems to be part of, to contribute to the new pattern. This is exciting. It's the only time when I forget time. Past the halfway mark, a novel almost writes itself. Events beget events, characters insist on seeing one another again, and I just sit and transcribe. I get quite cheerful and communicative. A strange process.[55]

For Drabble, determining the scope of a novel and organizing its "voices" precedes establishing "plot, narrative structure, characters, images." Her method allows specific voices to compose characters and determine elements of her texts, resulting in a mix of internal monologues, dialogues, and conversations among characters and sometimes with readers.

The Radiant Way begins with Liz's self-satisfied meditation on the joys of her life, while *A Natural Curiosity* starts with Alix's thoughts as she drives to see a man she has come to think of as "her" murderer. The first two novels encourage readers to enter the mind-sets of these two primary characters and offer occasional glimpses into what Esther and the women's romantic partners, children, and friends think. *The Gates of Ivory* opens with a note of thanks, the epigraph about its title from Homer, and a direct address to the reader: "This is a novel—if novel it be—about Good Time and Bad Time. Imagine yourself standing by a bridge over a river on the border between Thailand and Cambodia. . . . Many are drawn to stare across this bridge. . . . They are asking a question, but there is no answer. Here too Stephen Cox will stand."[56] This opening offers an unusual and effective way to entice readers into an international story world that contrasts the pointlessness of masculine heroics with the continuing responsibilities of women to care for others.

The Gates of Ivory reveals only allusive information concerning why Stephen went to Kampuchea and how he died. In London, Stephen's belongings are dispersed among his friends, including Alix and Brian Bowen. Alix finds a note dated June 28, 1951, which was penned by a seventeen-year-old Stephen and inserted in a Palgrave edition of *Golden Treasury of English Songs and Lyrics*. The note tells of the human tendency to search for origins and "simplicity," which reveals "superimposed blindness, an exclusion of truth," because although it is "tempting" "to claim that we once possessed innocence . . . we cannot do it."[57] Alix finds these words familiar but is not sure if Stephen wrote them or copied them; they enigmatically serve as his only direct message.

Near the end of *The Gates of Ivory*, Liz coordinates a memorial service for Stephen. At the chapel, his family, friends, and acquaintances arrive to celebrate his life and at the same time to reconcile with each other. Konstantin Vassiliou returns to England to attend the service and finds his mother in the chapel. The coincidence of disparate characters arriving in the same place is typical of randomness in Drabble's trilogy, in which a particular element from one scene often slides into another or different subplots converge. The Headleands' New Year's Eve party in *The Radiant Way* and Fanny Kettle's party in *A Natural Curiosity* bring disparate persons together in one place to receive surprising news, respectively, Charles's affair and Liz's half-sister Marcia's existence. Drabble's *The Radiant Way* novels do not have chapters or identified sections or parts. Instead, each passage focuses on the experiences, thoughts, and/or actions of a specific character or group. Passages are linked thematically, semantically, and generally chronologically with requisite flashbacks and rare flash forwards. Sometimes the connection between scenes has to do with the transmission of information via media, or personal conversation about the everyday mixed with the significant. Details connecting different subplots turn up in *A Natural Curiosity*, when Liz's television appearance to discuss "teenage sex and suicide" helps prepare us for the teenagers who have sex after the Kettles' party and for the revelations about Liz's father even as these details add to the general narrative thread about gender and power.[58]

In this way, *The Radiant Way* novels piece together information relevant to the three primary female characters and their lives, elements that are drawn from various internal and external sources: characters' interior monologues, dialogues, and conversations; narrative descriptions of quotidian experiences; and paraphrasing of literary and media texts. Updates on economic and social conditions in Britain during the first half of Thatcher's administration appear in the novels as fictional and factual news stories relayed by print, television, and radio reports inserted in the texts or discussed by these primary characters and others. In their communications, Liz, Alix, and Esther comment on changing social and political conditions affecting themselves and their coworkers, neighbors, and families. Their lives illustrate various costs and benefits for women in late-twentieth-century Britain, suggesting that economic success can improve social relations.

The trilogy describes difficulties and losses, while including some examples of redemption in scenes of mourning and forgiveness. Anger about poverty in developing and developed countries must share space with small signs of hope and improvement. The ending of *The Gates of Ivory* links events in a tableau of reconciling characters whose lives intersected with Stephen Cox's at his memorial service and at the gathering following the service at Liz's home. The subplots connect memorializing Stephen and others with the living and the newly born, linking those who mourn for what could have been and what might yet be. The last pages of the novel (and trilogy) point to loss and reconciliation in describing the Vassilious and Mitra Akrun, whose histories identify burdens borne by mothers. Multitudes of young men seeking adventure and participating in political campaigns will always be with us, the novel implies, because Western intervention into conflicts in other places will inevitably provoke resistance and terrorism that lead to further interventions. Disconnected, unverifiable information contributes to confusion and conflict resulting in destruction. Drabble's trilogy combines the trivial and the world historical in detailing the thoughts and experiences of the primary characters. Like other characters, Stephen hopes to know and to affect the course of history; this hope is like Liz's desire to rescue him and Mitra's desire to change the political regime.

In sum, information sharing is the subject and information is the stylistic form of novels by Dickens and Drabble that notice the burdens women carry and explain communication as a collective force to enhance equity. Fiction depends on the cognitive capacities of readers to make connections within and among novels and to recognize the comparability of fictional and nonfictional information. Erich Auerbach explained in the epilogue to *Mimesis: The Representation of Reality in Western Literature* (1953) that he wrote the book as an exile in "Istanbul, where the libraries are not well equipped for European Studies."[59] Without secondary materials, he relied on textual interpretation to develop his accounts of representations of reality in works ranging from Homer's *Odyssey* to Virginia Woolf's *To the Lighthouse*. His chapters on realist novels offer minimal historical explanation in comparing how writers inform readers about socioeconomic inequities while encouraging readers' sympathies for those less fortunate. This chapter follows a similar trajectory in examining novels by Dickens and Drabble, which move from incorporating information about individual cases of misfortune to suggesting the general case for how society fails to protect the innocent, particularly women and the poor. Fictional information enables readers to understand the necessity for social changes to improve their lives and enhance equity.

Critics consider the ways in which readers make sense of novelistic information as dependent on understanding human behavior and narrative structure. Characters in *Little Dorrit* and in the *Radiant Way* trilogy reveal perceptions, realizations, and interpretations that exemplify how information processing takes place and why it matters to form satisfying human relationships and to enable dreams of a better world. Not all characters are successful, but the structural features of the narratives emphasize that information teaches readers to learn from their mistakes as well as from their achievements. Interpretations of novelistic information depend on readers' abilities and circumstances. We know that a novel describes a fictional world with relevance to our own situations and that interpretation forecasts a new future.

Chapter 2

Liberty and Suffrage
in Nineteenth-Century Narratives

Would men but generously snap our chains and be content with
rational fellowship instead of slavish obedience, they would find us
more observant daughters, more affectionate sisters, more faithful
wives, more reasonable mothers—in a word, better citizens.

—Mary Wollstonecraft,
A Vindication of the Rights of Woman (1792)[1]

The war of my life had begun; and though one of God's most
powerless creatures, I resolved never to be conquered.

—Harriet Jacobs, *Incidents in the Life of a Slave Girl* (1861)[2]

"I may never see it," replied Christine, with a sigh; "but it must be;
it will go on, for the truth must succeed, sooner or later."

—Laura J. Curtis Bullard,
Christine, or Woman's Trials and Triumphs (1856)[3]

Influenced by Enlightenment ideas of justice, some eighteenth- and early-
nineteenth-century British and American reformers discussed abolition
in conjunction with women's rights.[4] They understood slavery and the
oppression of women as related types of confinement that constrained the
liberty of persons, limited subjects' civil rights, and threatened subjects

61

with bodily harm. Moira Ferguson allows that Mary Wollstonecraft was "a pioneer" whose "intervention regarding sexually abused female slaves is not surprising," because for her "white women, slaves and oxen become part of a metonymic chain of the tyrannized."[5] "We must remember," Cora Kaplan points out, "to read *A Vindication [of the Rights of Woman]* as its author has instructed us, as a discourse addressed mainly to women of the middle class. Most deeply class-bound is its emphasis on sexuality in its ideological expression, as a mental formation, as the source of woman's oppression."[6] Wollstonecraft noted the injustice of slavery in *A Vindication of the Rights of Men* (1790), but she referenced slavery far more often in *A Vindication of the Rights of Woman* in arguing that women would remain dependent on men if they were always deprived of equality, education, and work. According to Ferguson, Wollstonecraft "favoured a discourse on slavery that highlighted female subjugation. Whereas the *Rights of Men* refers to slavery in a variety of contexts only four or five times, the *Rights of Woman* contains over eighty references; the constituency Wollstonecraft champions—white, middle-class women—is constantly characterized as slaves."[7] Calling the subjugation of women "slavery" helped persuade middle-class readers that an enlightened society demands ending both wrongs: the oppression of women and the enslavement of men and women.

Many fictional and nonfictional narratives produced in the US and the UK that consider injustices employ similar forms. Amanda Claybaugh explains, "Nineteenth-century novelists and reformist writers not only shared a representative project but also borrowed one another's formal techniques."[8] According to her transnational account, novelists "thought of novels not as self-centered aesthetic objects but as active interventions into social and political life" that could "'inculcate' their 'doctrines' and so intervene in the contemporary world."[9] Anglo American fictional representations arguing for increased women's political rights note existing inequities and discrimination while looking forward to future equity. Abolitionist arguments document extreme physical and mental cruelties delivered to those enslaved, detailing the sadistic and sexualized tortures the enslaved endured before achieving liberty.[10] Many of the formerly enslaved escaped brutal captivity and later wrote accounts documenting their sufferings in slavery, for they hoped their testimonies would lead to its abolition. In describing the appalling, unjust conditions of their captivities, many writers developed the genre of the freedom narrative, which, like many earlier captivity narratives, outlined an individual's difficult path to liberty.

Nineteenth-century US reform movements drew inspiration from the American myth of redemption offered by the grace of God. As this chapter explores, abolitionist and women's rights texts encourage temperance and faith while also recommending that citizens exercise strenuous, sometimes risky, bodily interventions to overcome gender and race differences and to guarantee opportunities for all. Troubled by the wrongs of slavery and the anxieties of sectional conflict, Herman Melville, Harriet Beecher Stowe, Rebecca Harding Davis, Louisa May Alcott, and Constance Fenimore Woolson described the painful circumstances of the Civil War as traumatizing individuals and disrupting families and communities. Frances Ellen Harper's Reconstruction-era novel *Iola Leroy, or Shadows Uplifted* (1892) depicts Black soldiers fighting for the North and the experiences of a nurse who attends them, tracking formerly enslaved individuals' postwar struggles as free persons and optimistically describing a future bringing enfranchisement, educational opportunities, and community support. The last part of this chapter looks at political debates about women's suffrage advanced in Laura Curtis Bullard's *Christine, or Woman's Trials and Triumphs* (1856), Louisa May Alcott's *Little Women* (1868–69), Henry James's *The Bostonians* (1886), and George Gissing's *The Odd Women* (1893). Like the abolitionist texts, fictions arguing for women's rights envision legal remedies, including suffrage, as necessary to eliminate gender inequities, particularly those related to work, marriage, and property. Progressive reforms providing equity, even if difficult to effect, are imagined as plausibly implemented in the future.

The Evils of Slavery

Considerations of slavery in American literature include discussions of racial abuse, putative biological differences, discrimination, and identity, topics refracting and reflecting sociopolitical interests regarding personhood. The first published African American writer was an enslaved woman; Phillis Wheatley was encouraged by her owners to pursue her literary talent. Her *Poems on Various Subjects, Religious and Moral* appeared in 1773 as a result of her visit with relatives of her owner to London; her poetry "uses her own experience of oppression" to criticize "racial inequity."[11]

Literary works discuss slavery and race by highlighting issues of identity and social justice and noting the physical and sexual torments inflicted by masters and overseers on those enslaved, their resistance, escaping from these conditions, and the discrimination, torture, and execution that African Americans experienced before and after emancipation. Contemporary US literary, televisual, and cinematic texts continue to explore the tragic history of slavery, with many referencing women's oppression and sexual abuse and arguing for reparations to ensure a better future.

The US outlawed importing individuals into enslavement in 1808, while still allowing ownership, breeding, and trading of persons in many states until President Lincoln's Emancipation Proclamation of January 1, 1863. Slavery expanded in the nation between the American Revolution and the Civil War, as different regional investments in the institution divided the country. Eric Sundquist points to instability in the period between wars that affected literary production: "A time of new revolutions in Europe, it was in America a time during which the national memory of Revolution took on a particularly fragile cast and during which the forces of social and sexual reform, an accelerating market economy, and the crisis over territorial acquisition and the extension of slavery that were to produce the major issues for the writers of the American Renaissance first become tangible."[12] Identifying "the contradiction between liberty and slavery" in the early republic, Sundquist notes that, "Revolutionary pamphlets often cast Americans as slaves of king and parliament, suggesting at times that chattel slavery was but an extreme form of a more pervasive political oppression."[13] As political divisions over slavery persisted in the antebellum era, the rhetorical association of rebels and enslaved persons, the depiction of oppression, and the plea for social justice, especially regarding the sexual abuse of enslaved females and the breaking apart of families, became mainstays of the abolitionist argument against slavery.

Countering abolitionist claims, proslavery arguments made on behalf of owners and traders pressed politicians to protect and expand slavery, falsely claiming that free wage laborers in the north suffered more discrimination and abuse than enslaved Blacks on Southern plantations. The antebellum paradox of whether those enslaved were property or citizens prompted Major General Benjamin Butler to claim fugitives from slavery as contraband in 1861, and some formerly enslaved to enlist in the Union Army. The Emancipation Proclamation in 1863 freed all those persons who had been enslaved, and the Thirteenth Amendment ratified in 1865 abolished slavery except as a punishment for criminal conviction. Lincoln's second inaugural address delivered in March of that year affirmed "American slavery is one of those offenses which in the providence of God, must needs come, but which, having continued through His appointed time, He now wills to remove."[14]

Questions concerning the supposed inferiority of Blacks pervaded sociopolitical arguments about slavery. Many Americans and Europeans voiced opinions about "natural" inferiority aiming to account for the persistence of inequality. Stephen Jay Gould reports in *The Mismeasure of Man* (1981) that "All American culture heroes embraced racial attitudes that would embarrass public-school mythmakers," quoting Benjamin Franklin's desire to exclude "all blacks and tawneys" so as to increase "the lovely white and red" and noting philosophical and moral views expressed by other Americans, including founding father Thomas Jefferson and Abraham Lincoln (in the Douglass debates), who also argued that Blacks were inferior.[15] European visitors seeking to understand democratic reforms in the United States observed persistent socioeconomic inequalities between races that hindered progress in various regions, leading to their criticism of physical abuses and legal inequities heaped on persons of color. Frenchman Alexis de Tocqueville referenced tensions regarding racial difference that he observed during his 1831–1832 visit to the United States. In *Democracy in America* (1835), he predicted that abolishing slavery would not eliminate these challenges: "I plainly see that in some parts of the country the legal barrier between the two races is tending to come down, but not that of mores: I see that slavery is in retreat, but the prejudice from which it arose is immovable."[16] Later in the passage, he wrote, "Race prejudice seems stronger in those states that have abolished slavery than in those where it still exists, and nowhere is it more intolerant than in those states where slavery was never known."[17] Tocqueville presciently recognized the persistent problem of color prejudice in a US society that resisted recognizing Blacks as persons. Gustave de Beaumont, who had accompanied Tocqueville during his tour of the US, wrote *Marie or, Slavery in the United States* (1835), a novel about the love affair of a Frenchman and an American young woman of African ancestry that depicts their persecution by whites. Charles Dickens, in a chapter of *American Notes for General Circulation* (1842), documents the evils of slavery in the US, listing phrases from approximately sixty advertisements seeking return of fugitive slaves and documenting tortures such as "collar with one prong turned down," "iron bar on her right leg," and "much marked with irons" and "iron band about her neck."[18]

Powerful arguments against slavery describe the practice as propped up by violence, greed, and immorality, detailing its injuries to individuals, families, and society. Those escaping from slavery shared their histories in speeches and in narrative accounts, to document injustices and to shore up abolitionist arguments against slavery, and to share their observations and experiences of discrimination harming their descendants and other citizens.[19] Henry Louis Gates argues that the written "narratives provided the basic paradigm for virtually all later fiction and biography by black Americans."[20] The narrative "paradigm" includes torture, violent physical punishments, and sexual abuse; social injustices; economic inequalities; discrimination based on race or color; anxieties over racial identity and mixing; and religious hypocrisy rationalizing slavery and punishments.

Like captivity narratives and accounts of religious transformation, the paradigmatic freedom narrative promises redemption, often linking learning to read and write with the opportunity to escape from captivity. Gates points out that "there is an inextricable link in the Afro-American tradition between literacy and freedom. . . . In literacy lay true freedom."[21] For many of those enslaved, literacy enabled freedom; both are represented as recompense for suffering abuse, oppression, and the destruction of families. Olaudah Equiano's memoir begins with his and his sister's kidnapping, moving from "African freedom, through European enslavement, to Anglican freedom," a transformation that becomes a model for subsequent narratives.[22] Frederick Douglass acknowledges his witnessing of horrific scenes of torture, including his aunt's whipping, and his own later punishments as motivating his desire to escape, which his learning to read made possible. Mary Prince begins her account describing how her master sold Mary (at age twelve) and her sisters to separate owners. She subsequently lists what she learned from her next mistress: "She taught me to do all sorts of household work; to wash and bake, pick cotton and wool, and wash floors and cook. And she taught me (how can I ever forget it!) more things than these: she caused me to know the exact difference between the smart of the rope, the cart-whip, and the cow-skin, when applied to my naked body by her own cruel hand."[23] Prince's narrative, the first by a woman, dwells particularly on sadistic, indecent punishments endured by enslaved females, including those who were sick or pregnant.

Harriet Jacobs's incredible story describes the relentless attentions of Dr. Flint who refused to let her marry a free Black man so that he could continue what the narrator calls his "base proposals," including planning to send her to the family plantation.[24] Linda Brent, as Jacobs styles herself in the narrative, escapes to hide with accommodating friends before sneaking into her grandmother's attic, spending nearly seven years hiding in its close confines. The narrator acknowledges that she was protected from Dr. Flint "by trading sexual favors for the protection of another white man, Mr. Sands, by whom she bears two children."[25] Although many assumed that white abolitionist Lydia Maria Child wrote the book, Jean Fagan Yellin pieced together archival evidence to document Jacobs as the true author.

Sentimental Power

The lack of legal redress for enslaved and free Blacks and the moral damage caused by the institution of slavery to individuals and society became critical topics in fictions. Many narratives emphasize social, political, and economic inequities for those held in slavery, as well as the physical and mental abuses inflicted on those held as chattel. Sentimental fictions particularly explore how women and families, Black and white, suffer from the practices. Inspired by and imitating conventions of freedom narratives, Harriet Beecher Stowe's *Uncle Tom's Cabin, or Life among the Lowly* (1852) contributed to the abolitionist cause by persuasively depicting slavery as a crime against Christianity and motherhood. Stowe's novel was a bestseller and prompted a backlash from Southerners who countered by producing proslavery sentimental novels.[26] Many episodes in *Uncle Tom's Cabin* paint a picture of male greed and selfishness as enemies of women's feelings and caring for others. For many female characters in Stowe's novel, maternal affection and understanding of true Christianity enable respect for the natural rights of all humans, countering (mostly) masculine selfishness and aggression and offering a sentimental rationale to eliminate slavery from the United States. Pitched to white, female, and religious readers, *Uncle Tom's Cabin* claims the power of women to leverage individual and familial bonds to intervene in a national discourse about sectional discord.

Although Stowe argues that the formerly enslaved should leave the US to migrate to Africa, a more positive message in the novel is a sentimental, potent one, hinting that if women ruled the country, slavery might have been recognized as an abhorrent crime and eliminated from the US. Jane Tompkins recognizes "the sentimental novel not as an artifice of eternity answerable to certain formal criteria and to certain psychological and philosophical concerns, but as a political enterprise, halfway between sermon and social theory, that both codifies and attempts to mold the values of its time," including "attitudes toward the family and toward social institutions, a definition of power and its relation to individual human feeling, notions of political and social equality, and above all, a set of religious beliefs which organize and sustain the rest."[27] Characterizations of women from various social groups in antislavery fictions portray objections to slavery on sentimental and religious grounds, while some white female characters represent the evils of slavery. For example, Stowe paints Marie St. Clair as cruel and sadistic, but other characters demonstrate sentimental goodness, as readers appreciate Eliza's maternal anxieties, Mrs. Bird's sympathies, and Eva's love for all around her. Even the northern Ophelia overcomes her initial prejudice against Blacks to love and care for Topsy.

Seeking to explain the poor treatment of Blacks in the north, Harriet E. Wilson's *Our Nig; or, Sketches from the Life of a Free Black* (1859), the first novel by an African American woman, relates the story of Frado, an orphaned mixed-race girl tortured by Southern-inspired members of a Northern family who require her to labor incessantly in their miserable home. Frado survives physical and emotional abuse heaped on her, drawing strength from her religious training and her interest in books; however, she unfortunately married a man who earned a living as a lecturer by falsely claiming to have escaped from slavery. Henry Louis Gates in his preface to *Our Nig* identifies the novel's intermediate status between autobiographical slave narrative and sentimental fiction in that its silences and gaps point to tensions between these genres.[28] Both genres share a concern with protecting women, Black and white, suggesting that their empowerment would be key in eradicating slavery.

Other works rely on personal experiences and careful observation to make the case for the abolition of slavery, for the goals of Reconstruction, and for women's empowerment. Portraying the sincerity of President Lincoln and his aggrieved widow, Elizabeth Keckley's memoir *Behind the Scenes: Or, Thirty Years a Slave and Four Years in the White House* (1868) acknowledges the wrongs of slavery in a chapter that draws a veil over the institution's worst abuses. *Behind the Scenes* describes the author's working as a seamstress for the Lincolns during the period 1861–1865. The author defends Mrs. Lincoln and reports anecdotes of domestic life in the White House, mentioning that Frederick Douglass was not permitted to attend the reception at the second inauguration of President Lincoln in 1865, until "a gentleman, a member of Congress" intervened on behalf of

Douglass.[29] Keckley's memoir relies on personal experience with Lincoln to suggest that sustained effective, compassionate leadership could guide the nation to racial equality and gender equity.

Melville's Civil War

After the outbreak of the Civil War in 1861, many Northern writers set aside concerns about slavery to consider the costs of a war, representing sectional strife as a struggle among family members. Herman Melville's volume *Battle-Pieces and Aspects of the War* (1866) collects poetry and prose that meditate on noteworthy persons, battles, and other events leading up to, during, and after the Civil War; its "Supplement" argues for a form of national reconciliation that accepts emancipation without punishing Southerners.[30] Rebecca Harding Davis's "John Lamar" (1862), Louisa May Alcott's "Contraband" (or "The Brothers") (1863), and Constance Fenimore Woolson's "Crowder's Cove: A Story of the War" (1876) describe men and women living on the border of the conflict and offer domestic accounts of rebellion, trauma, and reconciliation.[31] Referencing the costs of war for Northerners and Southerners, Melville, Davis, Alcott, and Woolson limit arguments focusing on the evils of slavery to instead consider the problems of "fratricidal" disagreement and associated anxieties about disunion and violence. Their texts reveal psychological uncertainty about the war's outcomes, including future socioeconomic prospects for those freed from slavery, while suggesting that women's personal and political interventions could work toward equity and reconciliation.

Not all citizens agreed with the official stances of their governments during the Civil War: some Northerners sympathized with the Confederates' position on states' rights and were opposed to the radical stance of abolitionists, while some Southerners were pained by the division threatening the Union and hoped to see the elimination of slavery. After General Beauregard's troops fired on Fort Sumter on April 12, 1861, and President Lincoln mobilized a Northern army to put down the rebellion, more states joined the Confederacy. Citizens of Maryland and Virginia, the two states bordering the Union capital of Washington, DC, were on opposite sides of the conflict. The designation "Gone South" frequently appeared in records next to the names of men who during the Civil War left Maryland, a Union state with slavery, to join Confederate forces. Residents of "border states" made their own choices, and different loyalties led to bitter family disputes. As the frontline shifted southward, an increasing number of residents in border states were caught between two sides, living in a war zone.[32] Historian Drew Gilpin Faust acknowledges, "Violence invaded everyday life in other parts of the nation as well, especially in locations where political loyalties divided the civilian population. East Tennessee, western North Carolina, southwest Virginia, and the Missouri borderland were among the areas that experienced guerrilla conflict that made few distinctions between combatants and noncombatants."[33] Although women were not drafted into armies, many volunteered as nurses and many families suffered from destructive consequences of wartime battles.

Noting that most Civil War literature does not pay significant attention to slavery or issues of race, Daniel Aaron groups Hawthorne, Whitman, and Melville as supporters of the Union who distanced themselves from slavery; these writers expressed more ambivalence about the war's outcomes than bellicose abolitionists did.[34] Melville's *Battle-Pieces* contains only one poem focusing on an individual held in slavery: "Formerly a Slave," subtitled "An idealized Portrait, by E. Vedder, in the Spring Exhibition of the National Academy, 1865." Describing a painting of a woman, the poem's three short verses represent the subject as illustrating "The sufferance of her race." The iconic female subject is enslaved but recently "deliverance dawns upon" her and "she is not at strife." More significantly,

> Her children's children they shall know,
> The good withheld from her;
> And so her reverie takes prophetic cheer—
> In spirit she sees the stir.

The final verse acknowledges the woman's "dusky face is lit with sober light, Sybilline, yet benign."[35] Melville's poem presents a heroic view of a formerly enslaved woman anticipating her children's future; she becomes a prophet of optimism thinking about the eventual reconciliation of the politically divided country.

Battle-Pieces connects Melville's ideas about the war, which were based on his reading of newspapers and the *Rebellion Record*, and on his observing the military efforts taking place in Washington, DC, and Northern Virginia during his trip in mid-April 1864. His poems include glimpses of Union and Confederate troops meeting on the battlefield and in guerrilla warfare, detailing violence and destruction affecting individuals, communities, and both armies.[36] Melville's equivocation in *Bat-*

tle-Pieces, his unwillingness to blame one side, troubles critics, particularly those who appreciate the support his other works offer for downtrodden sailors, colonized Pacific Islanders, and impoverished veterans.[37] William Dean Howells's 1867 review of *Battle-Pieces* in *The Atlantic Monthly* finds fault with the collection despite praising musicality "in many of the verses" and judging Melville's "eccentric metres" as "gracefully managed." Howells argues that Melville's sympathies for the white Southerner should be regarded as a fantasy. Melville writes of the Confederates surrendering at Appomatox in "Rebel Color-bearers at Shiloh": "Perish their Cause! but mark the men!" but Howells has less sympathy for the Confederates.[38] Melville's request for forgiveness and reconciliation could have been related to his respect for diverse political views held by those in his extended circle of friends and family, including moderate Southerners such as Richard Lathers, who visited the Confederacy in the early days of the war in a "quixotic" attempt to effect peace.[39]

Reconciliation of different views becomes a rhetorical strategy in *Battle-Pieces*. Different languages represented in *The Rebellion Record*, a key source for Melville, illustrate how the rhetoric of *Battle-Pieces* encodes fratricidal conflict. Melville's "suspicions of radical evil" appear as a framework connecting diverse languages in a national rhetoric.[40] His "metrically impossible" rhymes convey the costs of civil war within a structure that "intensifies the sense of historical event as inassimilable into controlled poetic design," for the poet creates a "national" rhetoric based on division, revealing respect for both North and South.[41] Poems in *Battle-Pieces* utilize oppositions to show political division as a moral conflict between two passionate views. "The Conflict of Convictions" sees differences between political viewpoints, emphasizing the tragic nature of the conflict and the anxieties of people witnessing its manifestations, taking "the middle way" to preserve the Union.

Melville's "Supplement" at the end of the volume expresses the author's "patriotism" in closing the gap between enemies and issuing a call for future reconciliation of the divided country, acknowledging "There were excesses which marked the conflict, most of which are perhaps inseparable from a civil strife so intense and prolonged, and involving warfare in some border countries new and imperfectly civilized," and adding "But surely other qualities—exalted ones—courage and fortitude matchless, were likewise displayed, and largely; and justly may these be held the characteristic traits, and not the former."[42] Yet forgiveness toward Southerners should be accompanied by "sympathies" toward "blacks, in their infant pupilage to freedom," "For the future of the freed slaves we may well be concerned; but the future of the whole country, involving the future of the blacks, urges a paramount claim on our anxiety."[43] Melville approved the "downfall" of slavery, which he describes as an "atheistical iniquity," remarking that "emancipation was accomplished not by deliberate legislation; only through agonized violence could so mighty a result be effected."[44] He feared violence, speculating that confirming "the benefit of liberty to the blacks" might "provoke" "exterminating hatred of race toward race."[45] Against slavery and for emancipation, Melville agreed with those who acknowledged that the violence of war was a necessary tool to overcome the political division of secession, and he argued for forgiving Southerners and reconciling the nation. *Battle-Pieces* did not have a wide audience in its own time, but its sentimental argument for forgiveness was aimed at securing the nation's future.

War on the Border

Other writers shared less nuanced political views when pointing to war's brutalities. Rebecca Harding Davis's memoir *Bits of Gossip* recalls her meetings with famous contemporaries, including time spent in the company of Ralph Waldo Emerson and Nathaniel Hawthorne, friends of her *Atlantic* publisher James Fields. Born in 1831 in Alabama, Davis spent her early life in Virginia and Pennsylvania, considered "border states" during the Civil War. Her chapter "Boston in the Sixties" contrasts her experience of the war with the distant view held by these famous men. Davis acknowledges her frustration with the Boston Brahmins who opined on the war to abolish slavery while living far from its battles.

> I had just come up from the border where I had seen the actual war; the filthy spewings of it; the political jobbery in Union and Confederate camps; the malignant personal hatreds wearing patriotic masks and glutted by burning homes and outraged women; the chances in it, well improved on both sides, for brutish men to grow more brutish, and for honorable gentlemen to degenerate into thieves and sots. War may be an armed angel with a mission, but she has the personal habits of the slums. This would-be seer [Bronson Alcott] who was talking of it, and the real seer [Ralph Waldo Emerson] who

listened, knew no more of war as it was, than I had done in my cherry-tree when I dreamed of bannered legions of crusaders debouching in the misty fields.[46]

Davis's short story "John Lamar" mounts strong criticisms against both Southern genteel racism and Northern aggression in describing the last days in the life of the eponymous protagonist, a Georgian imprisoned by Federal troops.[47] Lamar is incarcerated on the West Virginia plantation once owned by his grandfather but now under the authority of his "friend" Charley Dorr, a Union captain who married Lamar's cousin and onetime sweetheart Ruth. Lamar's grandfather was a Rebel sympathizer who was killed by Union soldiers; his property was confiscated to serve as a prison and a graveyard for those killed by brutal Union soldiers. Fearing the "Snake-hunters," a Union guerrilla band who fight the rebel "Bush-whackers," John Lamar conspires with Ben, whom he had enslaved, to obtain a saw and other tools to escape from prison.[48]

At first appearing loyal to his owner Lamar, Ben later wavers. After a Union sentry tells Ben that "the Northern army had come to set the slaves free," Ben overhears Lamar trying to persuade Dorr that anyone enslaved is not capable of taking care of himself and his people and that if the enslaved were freed they could only be uplifted if the South could grow industries to employ them.[49] Ben reacts quickly and violently. Instead of helping his master escape, Ben kills Lamar, whose last thoughts struggle to make sense of this act: "the wrongs of the white man and the black stood clearer to his eyes than ours: the two lives trampled down."[50] A Confederate affirming the repugnant ideology of slavery, Lamar cannot be redeemed, while the man enslaved only finds freedom by killing a man acting as master. Davis's story details Lamar's personal virtues and suffering that accompany his racism, while regretting violence and claiming those enslaved and Union troops are righteous in killing Southern slave owners to end slavery.

Like "John Lamar," Louisa May Alcott's short story "Contraband," sometimes titled "The Brothers," was published in *The Atlantic Monthly*.[51] A first-person narrative of a Northern, abolitionist white nurse called to care for a dying Reb, the story illustrates Alcott's ambivalences.[52] The doctor coordinating medical treatment in the Washington, DC, hospital apologizes as he asks Nurse Dane to provide treatment for the injured Confederate, offering her "a contraband" to help her nurse the wounded man. Signifying Robert's status as property rather than citizen, the word *contraband* acknowledges the uncomfortable role occupied by those formerly enslaved who received Federal government protection before emancipation. A mixed-race man who appreciates Nurse Dane's respectful treatment of him, Robert agrees to care for the Rebel captain, who deliriously speaks of loving "Lucy" and hating "Bob," the man loved by Lucy. One night when the nurse and Robert are in the captain's room, Robert throws away the Reb's medicine and locks the door to prevent the nurse from providing help to the captain. Far from caring for the captain, Robert tries to kill him. Robert explains to the nurse that he is the half-brother of the captain, a vicious master who interfered with Robert's marriage to the enslaved Lucy. The captain "took" Lucy for his own and sold Robert south. Nurse Dane acknowledges after hearing Robert's story that "He was no longer slave or contraband, no drop of black blood marred him in my sight, but an infinite compassion yearned to save, to help, to comfort him."[53] She persuades Robert to resist murdering his half-brother, telling Robert that love is immortal and that he can be reunited with Lucy in life or in the afterlife. Moved by this argument, Robert releases the nurse and the captain. She sends Robert to Massachusetts so he can begin "a new life as a freeman" far from the Confederate captain.[54] In parting, Nurse Dane gives Robert her Bible with a Madonna and child on its cover, prompting him to remark he never saw his baby. Later, the nurse asks the captain about Lucy, and the former master confirms that the pregnant Lucy killed herself after he sold Robert, information that Nurse Dane writes to Robert. After the 54th Regiment of Massachusetts stormed Fort Wagner in South Carolina, Nurse Dane sees the dying Robert who took part in the bloody battle; another soldier tells Nurse Dane that Robert attacked and killed a Reb he appeared to know and that the Confederate wounded Robert. The nurse witnesses Robert's death: "and in the drawing of a breath my contraband found wife and home, eternal liberty and God."[55] Told from the perspective of the Northern abolitionist nurse, Alcott's story includes the formerly enslaved man's death as a heroic Union soldier as well as the death of the conniving Confederate soldier-slaveholder. Slavery and the ensuing struggle to end it destroy Lucy and both men, showing war's costs for both sides and the limited capacity of the woman abolitionist to resolve political conflict or to protect the freed man.

Postwar Recriminations

More than a decade after the war's end, Constance Fenimore Woolson published a story about a Civil War conflict between two women, a Northern partisan and a Southern sympathizer living on the front lines.[56] Appearing in the March 1876 issue of *Appleton's Journal*, "Crowder's Cove: A Story of the War" demonstrates the continuing interest of postbellum readers in evaluating political opinions concerning the war and aligning domestic differences with sectional division. In a remote cove in the mountains of Tennessee, farmer John Crowder marries Minerva, a middle-aged New Hampshire teacher who invites her sister Elinor to live with them. Minerva also takes in a boarder, a young Southern girl, Sally Trellington. Sally and Elinor are opposites who embody stereotypical aspects of regional characters. Elinor (the Northerner) is efficient, clean, and orderly, albeit somewhat pale, small, and frail, while Sally (the Southerner) is healthy, always looking for fun instead of work, and somewhat large. Sally is generous but careless; she adopts a flying squirrel and fails to provide the creature with appropriate nourishment. Like Ophelia in *Uncle Tom's Cabin* who creates order out of chaos in her cousin's New Orleans household, Elinor takes care of the neglected pet and cleans up Sally's messy room. The girls become friendly, despite their differences, which include their political views concerning the war.

· Although John and Minerva Crowder are too busy with their work on their Tennessee farm to worry about the war and prefer to characterize their politics as neutral, they suffer after guerrillas from the Federals and the Confederacy make separate raids on the farm, taking almost all livestock and supplies before burning down the outbuildings. Later, strangers leave a wounded Southern boy, who is nursed by Elinor and Sally. An Alabama guerrilla passes a message to Elinor for the boy, telling her that the Southerners will try to intercept the Federal troops at Exton. Hoping to share this information to protect her side, each girl sets out on horseback to give the message to those troops. Although both girls fly down the valley, Sally's more spirited, stronger horse, Black Tom, prevails over the gentle Bess, ridden by Elinor. So "the Federals found themselves surrounded" by their enemy, and a captured Elinor is sent north, while "Sally was the pride, and the belle, and the glory of Morgan's men that night. Exton woke up and found itself in the hands of friends."[57] The girls are not mentioned in the newspaper account, but years later Elinor hears that Sally married well, and she rather bitterly recalls Sally's courageous act that led to a Confederate victory. The conflict caused by the war appears eternal for these two women, who never discuss slavery during or after the war.

Like the information in Davis's, Alcott's, and Woolson's stories, *Battle-Pieces* points out the costs of the war on home ground, noting the trauma of breaking apart the Union and of exposing soldiers and citizens to violence. Melville characterizes partisans as brothers in strife, and his "Supplement" presents a case for reconciliation rather than revenge, while acknowledging "that heroic band—those children of the furnace who, in regions like Texas and Tennessee, maintained their fidelity through terrible trials—we of the North felt for them, and profoundly we honor them."[58] "John Lamar," "The Brothers," and "Crowder's Cove: A Story of the War" reference political disagreements in families that lead to difficulties in trusting relatives and friends. Women and minorities play constrained roles in these fictions, but the texts point out that whether those living on the border of war sympathized with the Union or the Confederacy, or were undecided, people on all sides bore the violent, traumatic consequences of the destructive conflict even if they preferred peace and reconciliation. The stories by Davis, Alcott, and Woolson reveal deeply personal conflicts between partisans as observed by the women focalizers: Lamar is killed by a man he enslaved, the half-brothers in Alcott's story fight to the death, and the young women from North and South in Woolson's story risk their lives to serve as spies. Like *Battle-Pieces*, the three stories only briefly acknowledge slavery as a precipitating factor in the war, instead focusing on the trauma of fratricidal division and evincing hope for a better future after abolition in a reconciled nation.[59] Textual information points to sectional difference, racial inequality, and women's oppression as threats to the nation.

Suffrage in Fiction

Many popular fictions published between 1850 and 1920 recommended that women should be able to vote, while others took positions against women's suffrage, including arguing that it was unnecessary because men already had women's interests at heart.[60] Claire Delahaye points to Laura Curtis Bullard's *Christine, or Woman's Trials and Triumphs* (1856) as the first literary text about suffrage in the US, noting that suffragists would "promote the cause until the passage of the 19th amendment in 1920"; using "literature and politics to express women's power: they provided a space or a framework for participation in political debates thanks to the dialogic form; they were pedagogical tools to educate the reader; they used humor as a political weapon to subvert authority and demonstrate that woman suffrage was necessary."[61] Delahaye cites a claim from a 1914

The New York Tribune article ("Literary Lights Are Lined Up for Votes") that "no best seller [was] complete nowadays without a few suffragettes mixing in the plot—see any publisher's latest list."[62]

Romancing the Vote: Feminist Activism in American Fiction 1870–1920, Leslie Petty's history of US suffrage fictions, notes both communitarian and racist aspects of women's suffrage arguments in tracing how many writers pressed for rights for white women, often acknowledging "collective" values that ignore inequities for women of color. Petty considers activist novels such as Lizzie Boynton Harbert's *Out of Her Sphere* (1871) and Lillie Devereux Blake's *Fettered for Life, or Lord and Master* (1874) as fictions explaining the ways that women can heal the world if they are allowed the authority and opportunity to do so. Petty discerns that these novels "also contributed to a narrow-mindedness about race. . . . Such myopia is a central concern of Frances Ellen Watkins Harper's *Iola Leroy* and Hamlin Garland's *A Spoil of Office*, neither of which is about the women's rights movement per se."[63] Harper's and Garland's works, published respectively in 1892 and 1897, regard the woman's rights movement as "only part of a larger agitation for humanity's freedom," pointing to the importance of forming "oppositional communities that acknowledge the connections between racism, classism, and sexism in America."[64] Although such communities were not common across the US, during Reconstruction mixed-race communities did form in New Orleans and Charleston, encouraging Louisiana and South Carolina to provide constitutional rights to Blacks and to allow women leadership roles.[65]

Harper's *Iola Leroy, or Shadows Uplifted* (1892) illustrates how families suffered abuse, enslavement, violent separation, and death, before and during the war and how some members manage to survive. Iola's white father and her Black mother, who was manumitted by her husband before marrying him, do not tell their children the truth about their mixed race, instead raising their son and two daughters as white. Unfortunately, the father's untimely death places his wife and children in jeopardy, for his heir forces the widowed Mrs. Leroy and her older daughter Iola into slavery. The fiction recognizes Black contributions to the Union victory and sketches problems and prospects during Reconstruction for those formerly enslaved. Harper's novel combines a sentimental plot, political debate, and religious affirmation to share Iola's story of transformation and empowerment. Being privileged before her father's death does not prevent her from later suffering enslavement, but experiencing oppression influences her politics; she endorses progress and works to improve the lives of Blacks. Iola leaves slavery to become an army nurse during the Civil War, while her brother Harry enlists in a Black regiment. After the war, the mother and her two surviving children reunite. Refusing a marriage proposal from the Northern white doctor she worked with during the war, the mixed-race Iola identifies as Black, which subjects her to the discriminatory attitudes of many employers and peers when she works as a clerk. Her brother Harry marries a woman of unadulterated African heritage who is a teacher and a role model for her race. Iola also becomes a teacher of Black children and later marries a man of mixed race who joins her in working for racial uplift of the formerly enslaved.

Iola Leroy points to postwar inequities for those freed from slavery, offering advice, hope, and persuasive rhetoric to inspire women and men to move forward and to engage in social actions designed to create an equitable society for women and men, Blacks and whites. Harper references Christianity and temperance as positive influences in connecting sentiment and politics, detailing personal and political conversations among the family members and their acquaintances and discussions in churches. Information in these conversations reveal postwar outcomes for freed Blacks who struggle to overcome the abuses of bondage and prejudice and who sometimes overindulge in alcohol. Iola and other women commit to working on behalf of equity and social uplift, including through temperance, church, and educational initiatives, and help to develop a community supporting newly enfranchised Blacks. Freedom, enfranchisement, and collective action enable social progress by nurturing mutual respect with women taking leadership roles in their communities. In this way, the narrative informs readers about how women's contributions can lead to equity.

Gendered Opportunities

A book endorsing feminism that is often cited as influencing the development of girls and young women, Louisa May Alcott's novel *Little Women* (1868–1869) explores nineteenth-century domestic ideologies of gender in ways that continue to resonate with audiences. The novel acknowledges separate spheres for women and men, describing how Marmee educates her four daughters (Meg, Jo, Beth, and Amy March) to work within their home and in others' homes while their patriarch serves as a chaplain supporting the Union cause during the Civil War. Sarah Elbert regards the themes of the novel as "domesticity, work, and true love, all of them interdependent and each necessary to the achievement of its heroine's individual identity."[66] Self-sacrifice, compassion, generosity toward others, and the importance of respecting love over money are among the lessons the mother imparts to her girls.

Various cinematic adaptations of *Little Women* reference these lessons along with Jo's chafing at domestic expectations; however, with each passing decade, film adaptations of Alcott's text have leaned increasingly into exploring gender inequities affecting the March girls and their mother.[67] Jo's pursuit of a writing career aligns with dilemmas her three sisters navigate as they seek to develop their talents and interests within a society limiting women to being wives and mothers or spinsters. In her essay "Portraying *Little Women* through the Ages," Anne Hollander surveys three film versions of the novel—those by directors George Cukor (1933), Mervyn LeRoy (1949), and Gillian Armstrong (1995)—to argue that "each one displays the current fashion in what groups of girls in movies should be like."[68] Hollander sums up the films' differences: "The 1933 version had the Sweetheart and the Siren trumped by the Enthusiast, with Mother an aging character part. The 1949 version had the Girl Next Door take precedence over two types of Prom Queen, and Mother was still lovely. And the current version [Armstrong's] offers a range of Self-Realized Women of all ages—today nobody is old."[69] The "19th-century tone" of Cukor's film gives "the comfortable glow of nostalgia" to the March family's poverty, and LeRoy's "celebrates the fresh postwar pleasure of acquiring sleek new possessions," depicting the girls' consumerism during shopping excursions.[70] Armstrong's version quotes Alcott's journal within a voice-over narration with "wholly modern-sounding dialogue" referencing Transcendentalism, temperance, and women's suffrage, issues that also appear in the novel.[71]

Greta Gerwig's 2019 film adapts Alcott's novel to emphasize immigration issues along with highlighting the mother's incessant work, the father's fecklessness, and personal challenges faced by the March girls, who wish to live authentically in a world requiring that women sacrifice themselves for others. Film critic Richard Brody sees Gerwig's *Little Women* as "the tale of the birth of an artist—a female artist at a time that's hostile to women and the telling of stories of women's lives from women's point of view."[72] Highlighting Jo's ambitions to write and her negotiations with a publisher, scenes from Gerwig's film enact the daughters' uncomfortable confrontations with social expectations and constraints inhibiting women's activities, outlooks, and opportunities. While attending a ball Meg realizes that she does not like wearing fashionable, constrictive clothing and boots lent by her peers on this special occasion and later acknowledges to her mother that she would be happy marrying Laurie's tutor instead of a wealthy man. Despite benefiting from art lessons in Europe, Amy understands that her talent is no match for the genius of others and that she could not make a living from her art. She accepts Aunt March's advice that, as a poor girl, Amy would do best to marry a congenial, rich man; however, Amy won't marry for money alone, even if doing so would help her family, and she pushes back against Laurie's initial proposal because she thinks he may still love Jo. The introverted Beth's ambitions are musical, charitable, and familial. She overcomes her shyness to practice piano at Mr. Laurence's, and she insists on following her mother's injunction to take care of the Hummels, a request her sisters have ignored. Bringing provisions to the poor immigrant family, Beth becomes infected with smallpox; after a long illness, she dies claiming that she has lived as she wished in the loving embraces of her parents and sisters. Critic Jessica Bennett notices that Gerwig's 2019 film allows Jo to learn of her mother's anger: "In one of the film's most poignant scenes—which was plucked from the book but has not made it into most previous adaptations—Jo confides her own anger to Marmee."

"You remind me of myself," Marmee tells her.
"But you're never angry," Jo replies.
"I'm angry nearly every day of my life," Marmee says.
"You are?" Jo whispers back.[73]

Marmee's repressed anger flashes near the end of the film when the visiting Professor Bhaer mentions that he intends to go west. Mr. March expresses interest in accompanying his daughter's friend, but Marmee remarks that the trip would be impossible for her husband to undertake and shuts down further discussion of travel for Mr. March.

As depicted in Alcott's novel and Gerwig's film, each March sister is a little woman striving to be true to her own interests and identity, although she recognizes that the social customs of her time foreclose many opportunities. Viewers contributing reviews to the Internet Movie Database praised the well-known actors' performances, admired the cinematography, and noted the honest presentation of marital discord between Meg and her husband about finances and friction between the practical Mrs. March and the peripatetic Mr. March. Comments on the site also acknowledged positive aspects of two of Gerwig's innovations: reordering the time scheme of the mostly linear novel and ending the film with the publication of Jo's book *Little Women*, rather than as the novel does with her marriage to Friedrich Bhaer. Having the narrative jump backward and forward in time enabled the director to present material about each March sister rather than narrowly focusing attention on Jo's development as a writer, while the film's celebratory conclusion allows Jo to have her moment as a writer observing the printing of her novel. Wendy Ide's review explains the director's interest in the material: "It was her love affair with Jo as a character that prompted Gerwig to embark on this, the latest interpretation of a book that has already been adapted for the screen, stage, television, opera and anime about 20 times. But it is the generosity of Gerwig's affections, drawing the other members of the family, and Alcott herself, into the warm embrace of the film, that makes it such a joyous, tumultuous collision of pleasures."[74] Gerwig reconfigures Alcott's text to create a story about the pleasures and costs of marriage and domesticity for all women, indicating family's mixed influence on Jo's public success, as social conventions inhibit and motivate her literary production.

Gerwig's film recognizes the Marches as encouraging Jo, even as they seek to tame her so that she can function in a rigidly gendered society. Going to New York allows her to have new experiences in an urban environment different from Concord, Massachusetts. She has been educated by a family that believes in the power of philosophy to effect social justice. Encouraged by Professor Bhaer, Jo forthrightly expresses her views to win the philosophical debate enjoyed by the young men in his conversational circle. Clearly, if she lived in a society that allowed women's access to university educations, Jo would shine. That she competes so well without a formal education demonstrates hope for a future in which women will go further. At the same time, the film indicates that she succeeds by writing about domestic dilemmas and resolutions, while avoiding a traditional marriage that might prevent her from writing. Like Alcott's novel, Gerwig's film looks to a future in which women are peers and a publisher might more readily accept work by women, thus fostering professional opportunities for them.

Voting Rights for Women

Laura Curtis Bullard's *Christine, or Woman's Trials and Triumphs* (1856) tracks its protagonist from girlhood as she navigates parental disapproval, social discrimination, unjust accusations, illegal confinement, and her fiancé's betrayal before coming into her own as a woman's rights speaker and activist. Christine's beliefs in equality motivate her relatives to confine her in an asylum. After she gains her freedom, they remain estranged from her; however, Christine's faith helps her persist in preaching to women and working on their behalf, and she eventually forgives her relatives. Composed of dramatic, suspenseful episodes testing Christine, the novel allows her to make a decent living as an advocate for women before later in life marrying the fiancé who disappointed her. Nevertheless, the fiction ends short of representing success for her cause.

Christine anticipates the eventual success of the women's rights movement, "for the truth must succeed, sooner or later. All reform movements are slow in their beginnings. They are like the avalanche, which creeps on so gently at first, that its onward course is almost imperceptible, but gathering strength and velocity as it proceeds, it rushes on, bearing before it all that men had deemed most stable and immovable."[75] Her adopted daughter Rosa resists taking up a public role as an advocate for women's rights to become a doctor's wife and to run a household. Rosa's wedding provides a moment for Christine to reflect on her life: "She had regained the love of those, who, for a time, had been estranged from her; she had been enabled to triumph over all the wrong done her—even to turn the evil into good, and as she looked on the happy faces about her, and at Rosa's bright smile, she felt that she had not lived entirely in vain, though she had not attained what she had once hoped to see, the results of her labors, her theory in successful operation."[76] Although her speeches about women's rights attract audiences and produce income, Christine regrets that all women are not as devoted to the cause as she is and that women have not yet earned the vote. Instead, her founding of the Home is her significant legacy enabling women to advance a step toward establishing a future incorporating suffrage and equality.

Sketching political roles for women interested in improving society, Henry James's *The Bostonians* (1885–1886) and George Gissing's *The Odd Women* (1893) illustrate prospects for gender equity in depicting how class divisions and political debates about women's legal rights intersect with personal, romantic interests. The fictions represent women's efforts to intercede in political discourse, to overcome social divisions, and to encourage citizens to contribute to enhancing equity in their communities and the nation. Gissing's *The Odd Women* is often regarded as his best novel, and Leslie Petty describes *The Bostonians* as "the only canonical text from the nineteenth-century whose central heroines are women's rights activists."[77] Like Christine, Olive Chancellor and Verena Tarrant, the women's rights advocates in *The Bostonians*, fail to achieve any social change within the novel. As Petty notes, "the novel warns its readers of the inherent instability and ineffectiveness of a feminist reform community that does not originate from two essential elements, revolutionary love and existential communitarianism."[78] James's novel criticizes the women's rights advocates but suggests there may be prospects for gender equity.

The Bostonians presses readers to consider which path is more appropriate for them: work (or more specifically work for the cause of women's rights) or marriage. The novel considers the issue of women's equality as a passion for many women and as anathema for the lawyer and former Confederate soldier who sets his sights on marrying the youngest, prettiest reformer. Marriage to Basil Ransom seems a career-ender for women's reformer Verena Tarrant after he prevents her speech at the Music Hall when he takes her away from her mentor and his cousin Olive Chancellor, who also seeks Verena's affections. Taking Verena's place on the stage, Olive realizes that despite her reluctance and her lack of confidence in her own rhetorical abilities, she must articulate the women's cause to the restive audience. James's narrator explains what Basil observed as Olive mounted the platform: "She might have suggested to him some feminine firebrand of Paris revolutions, erect on a barricade, or even the sacrificial figure of Hypatia, whirled through the furious mob of Alexandria."[79] The first analogy is to the allegorical figure of Liberty depicted in Eugène Delacroix's painting *Liberty Leading the People* (1830), and the second to the classical philosopher, mathematician, and teacher Hypatia who was murdered by Christian monks, according to Charles Kingsley's 1853 novel *Hypatia*, which regards her as a martyr for women's rights.[80] Whether one knows these intertexts or not, readers recognize the novel's representation of women reformers as sacrificing their lives for their cause.[81] The elderly reformer Miss Birdseye embodies "pathetic nobility," according to Horace Scudder, indicating that sacrifices are necessary to ensure eventual reforms benefiting women. Scudder's 1886 review of the novel in *The Atlantic* argues that James's depiction of Olive is nuanced in showing her transformation: "the admixture of passionate, womanly appropriation of the girl whom she looks upon as the young priestess of the new church of womanhood; and the manner in which the woman is always getting the better of the doctrinaire strikes us as showing more completely than anything else in the book how thoroughly Mr. James has possessed himself of this character."[82] Yet Scudder faults the novel's abrupt ending: "in the final scene of the book, which ought to have been the climax; instead of which, by its noise and confusion, and its almost indecent exposure of Miss Chancellor's mind, this scene allows the story just to tumble down at the end."[83] The conclusion describes Olive as she ascends the platform but does not provide the text of her remarks, so each reader must imagine her message and audience responses.

At least two women writers proposed sequels to James's novel that offer happier endings than martyrdom or confusion. Petty points out that in 1887, Celia B. Whitehead, under the pseudonym "Henrietta James," published a pamphlet titled *The Other Bostonians*, describing how Olive succeeds as a speaker and forgives Verena for her marriage to Basil who becomes bored with Verena.[84] Elaine Showalter offers a similar ending for an imagined sequel: "In this novel, perhaps, Verena would not leave Olive and would not be silenced; she would give her great speech, 'A Woman's Reason,' to cheering crowds at the Boston Music Hall, and Basil would go back to his pathetic dreams of avenging the fallen South."[85] If readers imagine Olive's or Verena's delivering a persuasive speech endorsing women's rights, we are a step closer to envisioning a more equitable future.

That imagined, successful speech in adaptations of the novel in print and film extends the narrative into a progressive political discourse. Roger Ebert's review of the 1984 film adaptation of James's novel favorably compares it to an adaptation of James's *The Europeans* developed by the same collaborative team, emphasizing the disappointed lives of *Bostonian* principals, as Olive, Basil, and Verena fail to achieve what they desire: "This is a much better film, intelligent and subtle and open to the underlying tragedy of a woman who does not know what she wants, a man who does not care what he wants, and a girl who does not need what she wants."[86] Other viewers accept Olive as a heroine who loses the love of her life while coming into her own as a forceful leader fighting for women's rights. David Sterritt argues that the film adaptation has a celebratory ending: "Only at the end does the screenplay make its own perspective clear, allowing the passionately committed Olive to air her views in a speech instead of vaguely dismissing her as James does on the last page."[87] The film puts Olive on a public platform: her project to cultivate the talented Verena as the cause's representative gives way to accepting her own duty to defend women's rights.

Changing cultural views of feminism affect audience interpretations of *The Bostonians*. Rita Felski describes her students' reactions to James's novel as follows:

I remember being struck by the vehemence with which one or two students condemned what they saw as the novel's complicity with patriarchal values. These students sided passionately with the character of Olive, a genteel Bostonian feminist who forges an intimate friendship with the younger Verena and takes her under her wing. Conversely, they saw Basil, the impoverished southerner who adamantly pursues and ultimately wins Verena, as a stalker, a sexual predator, and a thug. They read the novel, in other words, through the lens of a certain brand of feminism that celebrates the nurturing bonds of female friendship and condemns the violent brutality of men. Here was a particularly telling example of reading as resistance.

The problem with this view was not simply that it failed to account for many of the details of *The Bostonians*. It was also that these students seemed unaware that the novel had anticipated their own reading and presented it in a highly ironic light. . . . The power Olive seeks to exercise over her female friend is more covert than that of Basil's confident pursuit of Verena, but it is a form of control nonetheless.[88]

Felski argues that James represents both Olive and Basil as pursuers of Verena; both seek to control her future based on their own desires. Yet even as *The Bostonians* details how lovers (heterosexual and homosexual) manipulate others in pursuing goals, the narrative focuses our attention on women's choices: Verena's concerns whether she should marry rather than continue working for reform, and Olive's on her decision to take her protégée's place on the podium or not. We could regard the novel as a satire of reformers in which an opponent to women's rights defeats women's advocates by courting and stealing Verena, their most appealing representative, a tactic that forces Olive, the least promising orator to take the stage. Or we could be more hopeful as readers who admire women's advocates and believe that Olive's speech about the women's cause would succeed in persuading her audience.

Work for Women

Like *The Bostonians*, *The Odd Women* offers mixed portraits of women's advocates with selfish and altruistic motives, detailing their difficulties with intimate relationships and their heroic attempts to improve conditions for women. Gissing's novel also addresses interrelated social problems, including women's lack of educational and career opportunities, class constraints that inhibit individual economic mobility, and rigid bonds of marriage that make it an uncomfortable arrangement for many women and some men. The novel's information highlights the predicament of the orphaned Madden sisters left with limited financial means and opportunities; their educations have not suited them to work other than as a governess or a lady's companion, and their small inheritance makes them unattractive marriage partners to most men. The plot follows the three surviving sisters—Virginia, Alice, and Monica—as they respectively navigate exhausting employment as companion, governess, and retail clerk. Rhoda Nunn, an acquaintance who trains women for good positions in offices and schools, suggests to the Maddens that their small capital might allow the two eldest sisters to start a school and the youngest to train as a typist, occupations that offer greater autonomy, less physical labor, and better remuneration than their positions. But Virginia and Alice are too cautious to invest capital in a school they would manage, and Monica thinks that working as a typist is harder than marrying a wealthy man.

The women's advocates—Rhoda and her mentor, Mary Barfoot—do their best to prepare women to work and to live independently, but temperaments and circumstances make those pursuits difficult for some of their protégées, including the Madden sisters. Most successful are those women who take part in the women's group meetings, attend lectures, finish their training, and become model employees. Mildred Vesper is exemplary because she is a disciplined worker and a careful manager of her finances, and she avoids drinking alcohol and promiscuity. Mildred counsels her roommate Monica Madden to stick with the women's movement, continue working, and develop an independent life in an office clerkship rather than becoming the wife of someone older and not suited to her, but Monica decides to marry Edmund Widdowson, who, although she does not love him, has pledged his love and fortune to her.

Gissing portrays women's choices between family and work as distinct for most. Mary Barfoot and Rhoda Nunn are model advocates who work tirelessly on behalf of women and resist impulses to marry and have children. In addition to the Widdowsons' tragic relationship, many other unhappy marriages are noted in the novel: the Beauforts', the Poppletones', and the Orchards'; as chapter 8 details, these relationships founder because of selfishness on the part of one partner, grating temperamental differences, and diverging interests. The only happy marriage in the novel is that between Everard Barfoot's friend Micklewaite, a mathematician, and the former Miss Wheatley. They waited seventeen years to marry, and their house is "very small and of very low rental" and furnished with hand-me-down items from the bride's deceased parents.[89] Eventually after years of living apart, the couple are thrilled to marry and congenially live on their small income, which they stretch to care for the bride's blind sister.

Despite their collaboration on the women's movement, Mary and Rhoda have different views of marriage, with the former accepting that some women fall in love and want to be wives and the latter arguing that marriages are too constraining for women. Oddly, they each harbor affection for the same man, Everard Barfoot, Mary's cousin, but both women question his integrity and his behavior with other women. Mary might have become engaged to her cousin, but his cruel treatment of a woman who bore his child discourages her from establishing any intimate relationship. After Everard is suspected of alienating Monica's affections from her husband, Mary warns Rhoda, whose attraction for Everard wanes even after he is proved innocent of this charge.

Both Mary and Rhoda disregard and oppose many social conventions because they are inspired to create changes to improve the lives of women. The middle of the novel reproduces Mary's speech, "Woman as Invader"; in it she argues that women need to invade professions beyond the ones traditionally regarded as womanly (nurse, governess, companion, domestic servant): "If woman is no longer to be womanish, but a human being of powers and responsibilities, she must become militant, defiant. She must push her claims to the extremity."[90] Mary foresees that the world will change: "Most likely we shall have a revolution in the social order greater than any that yet seems possible. Let it come, and let *us* help its coming. . . . I am ready to cry: Let the world perish in tumult rather than things go on in this way!"[91] Her speech ends with an acknowledgment that change will also improve men's lives: "We are working for the advantage of men as well as for our own. Let the responsibility for disorder rest on those who have made us despise our old selves. At any cost—at any cost— we will free ourselves from the heritage of weakness and contempt!"[92] Olive Chancellor might have uttered similar ideas after she ascended the platform to speak at the end of *The Bostonians*.

But Mary's speech does not conclude *The Odd Women*, for the novel's second half details Widdowson's jealousy concerning any interest outside of household management that Monica may have, her efforts to escape her constraining marriage and stalking husband, and the inevitable conflict between them. Monica tentatively attempts to pursue an extra-marital relationship with Bevis, but the young man's fears of losing his job and of being separated by rigid social conventions from his mother and sisters make him unable to elope with or marry Monica. She recognizes that Widdowson's rigid sense of proprieties and his monitoring her every activity means that she and her husband will never have a stable, happy marriage. Too late, she regrets that she did not follow the counsel of women's advocates to pursue independent work instead of marriage. Because Widdowson suspects Monica of adultery (which she did not commit), he claims he is not sure whether he is the parent of her child and opts for separation.

Recognizing that marriage is problematic institution, albeit one she has engaged in more than once, Widdowson's sister-in-law lectures him that he should not have married, but Lady Horrocks also counsels Widdowson that he should forgive his wife and accept the child as his, advice he refuses to follow. In a letter to her husband, Monica confesses her relationship with Bevis, which was romantic but unconsummated, assuring Widdowson that she is having her husband's child. He tells her sister to let Monica know that he forgives her and agrees to see the child; however, Monica dies soon after childbirth. Widdowson resists fatherhood and arranges for the surviving Madden sisters to take care of the baby girl. Virginia and Alice plan to open a school as an appropriate way of earning money while raising their niece.

The novel ends ambiguously. Rhoda notices the infant has her mother's "dark bright eye" and exclaims "Poor little child!"[93] Readers hope Mary Barfoot's anticipation of a revolution enabling gender equity might come to pass, helping Monica's daughter and other women, but that revolution requires more women to choose work and compatible marriage rather than marrying for money. The novel's illustrations of bad marriages and wayward relationships warn women away from Monica's example of marrying an unsuitable man even if he has money. Mary and Rhoda avoid marriage as limiting their autonomy, but their efforts to train clerks and inspire women to independent lives could only be successful if taken up by more women.

Abolitionists and women's rights advocates develop narratives that convey information about oppression and inequities, containing evidence and arguments to persuade readers to work for equality. Freedom narratives and novels such as *Iola Leroy* depict women whose advancement bears benefits for their communities. Realist fictions describe constraints for women and minorities in society and recommend education, work, and equitable marriage as mechanisms to improve gender equity, recognizing that women and men benefit when opportunities are available. *Christine, Little Women, The Bostonians,* and *The Odd Women* illustrate limited educational and professional options for women beyond working as women's advocates, but they imagine future possibilities for women who could have more autonomy and lead more satisfying and interesting lives.

Women's problems are noted in many realist novels, even those texts that do not recommend ways to improve equity but rather decry the limitations of women's domestic pursuits. Ending enslavement and ensuring political rights for all are fundamental democratic principles asserted in the feminist realist narratives discussed in this chapter. While didactic fictions aim to teach moral principles and utopian fictions provide glimpses of innovations in society, realist narratives advance equity, first by pointing to problems associated with social, economic, and legal treatment of gender and racial differences, and then by suggesting the need for reforms such as enfranchisement, equal access in education and employment, and enforcement of laws designed to eliminate disparate treatment and discrimination. As information systems, feminist realist novels offer persuasive illustrations of individuals who pursue social and legal reforms that promote opportunities for education, work, and political rights for women and minorities. These texts outline circumstances that move progressives to initiate changes that ensure social equity.

Chapter 3

Feminist Marriage and the Academic Novel

The University is a Paradise, Rivers of Knowledge are there, Arts and Sciences flow from thence.

—John Donne, *Sermon XIV* (1624)[1]

The academy is not paradise. But learning is a place where paradise can be created. The classroom, with all its limitations, remains a location of possibility. In that field of possibility we have the opportunity to labor for freedom, to demand of ourselves and our comrades, an openness of mind and heart that allows us to face reality even as we collectively imagine ways to move beyond boundaries, to transgress. This is education as the practice of freedom.

—bell hooks, *Teaching to Transgress* (1994)[2]

Despite Donne's celebration of the university as an ideal, universities have not been paradises for all, for they have not always welcomed women, hence the development of women's colleges in Great Britain and the US.[3] Continuing bias and discrimination against women affirms the persistent need to support their pursuing education, an endeavor that encourages freedom of mind, according to bell hooks. As Jacqueline Littman, then president of a women's college, explained in a 2018 alumni publication, "Each chapter of Douglass's history resonates with issues still in play in higher education and in our society. One of the continuing threads is the need for a level playing field for women and for constant institutional change and self-reflection."[4] In the modern era, universities provide fictional settings, characterizations, and plots that connect the development of knowledge and the education of young women and men with issues of personal fulfillment, social mores and advancement, and ethical conduct.

This chapter looks at three British novels considering feminist concerns, including suffrage and women's entrance into university education in the early part of the twentieth century, and concludes with discussion of a novel referencing biases that US women undergraduates confronted in the late twentieth century. These texts illustrate tensions between women's pursuit of scholarly research and advancement and their establishing satisfactory intimate relationships and fulfilling work, while suggesting that the future for educated women seems bright. C. P. Snow's *The Search* (1934), Dorothy Sayers's *Gaudy Night* (1935), and Penelope Fitzgerald's *The Gate of Angels* (1990) detail the attitudes toward women expressed by students and staff at Cambridge, Oxford, and other elite institutions, acknowledging how campus environments and university rituals shaped and are shaped by faculty and student interests, including those influencing ethical conduct. Set between 1912 and 1935, these three novels note hierarchies and protocols at these institutions, describing the costs and benefits of education and of marriage for men and women in the academy. Snow and Sayers build on fictional discussions of the marriage question (whether women should marry) to outline early-twentieth-century perspectives on the scientific and the scholarly as pursuits in tension with common thinking and domestic responsibilities. Fitzgerald's contemporary novel looks through a feminist lens at higher education before women's liberation. Also connecting marriage and women's university education, Jeffrey Eugenides's 2011 novel *The Marriage Plot* focuses on a Brown University coed whose romantic life threatens to forestall her academic accomplishments. Each text considers what constitutes ethical conduct in scholarship, while asserting a woman's right to a higher education, whether she pursues intimate relationships or not.

Ethics and Equity

These twentieth-century narratives considering women's interests in education evaluate academic social values and rituals. The "Oxbridge" plots of the British novels illustrate lapses in standards of moral integrity and professional ethics within discussions recommending the enrollment and employment of women and working-class men in elite universities. Published over six decades, *The Gate of Angels*, *Gaudy Night*, and *The Search* are remarkably similar in providing progressive responses to the questions of whether women should enter universities, whether educated women should be permitted to work as academic researchers, and whether men and women in universities should marry. Snow, Sayers, and Fitzgerald recognize persistent gender inequities and develop portraits of compatible marriages in these novels, acknowledging the ways that academic success affects the capacities of scholars to establish equitable marital relationships, while also pointing out that less equitable marriages produce disappointment. Plots conclude by recognizing that women's devotion to academic success requires calibrating learning and romantic happiness, suggesting that readers can look forward to a future era in which both professional and personal ambitions flourish.[5] An optimism about the future also surfaces in the ending of *The Marriage Plot*, which identifies access and equity in higher learning as enabled by feminist values influencing women's access to opportunities and their confidence in pursuing intellectual endeavors.

Blending romance and mystery, plots of the three British novels depict university scholars confronting the ways that cheating and sexual discrimination threaten integrity and truth across disciplines. *The Search* details hurdles for women pursuing higher-education degrees and culminates in an ethical dilemma resolved by its first-person narrator, a scientist who changes his career because his enthusiasm for scientific truth gives way to his ambivalence about scientific research. *The Gate of Angels* and *Gaudy Night* highlight conflicts between those opposed to higher education for women and heroic characters who support women's scholarship. In the three novels, characters with regressive notions of women's rights are morally flawed individuals who object to women entering academic disciplines; they are villains who commit dangerous crimes for selfish gain. Less dramatically, other sexist characters also lie and take advantage of others, undermining academic integrity in university communities.

Believing that women should work in the home but not outside it, critics of women's education in the fictions argue that marriage is the best vocation for women, while asserting men's right to work in universities to support families. Academic science in Snow's and Fitzgerald's novels appears as sex-segregated, while Sayers describes Oxford University—excepting its women's colleges—as a bulwark of male privilege. In contrast, progressive protagonists advocate modern marriages that enable education and work for women, asserting that a husband and a wife should be considered equals despite these egalitarian ideas seeming radical and suspect to other characters. Thus, *The Search*, *Gaudy Night*, and *The Gate of Angels* share a commitment to feminist principles, albeit to degrees and dimensions aligning with values of the different eras in which they were published. The novels are alike in noting the positive influence of ethical women in universities and in proposing that women and men ought to be able to pursue careers according to their personal interests and abilities and not according to their genders. Commenting on a female undergraduate's challenges in university and her trials and tribulations with romantic partners, *The Marriage Plot* envisions gender equity in higher education as a future prospect yet to be attained.

University Access

Social mobility in late-nineteenth- and early-twentieth-century Britain depended on one's capacity to complete a university education, a challenge depicted in novels such as Thomas Hardy's *Jude the Obscure* (1895), in which the eponymous character has limited economic and professional prospects because he fails to earn a university degree. The first British universities were created to serve the needs of the monarchy and adapted to the education of women over time as social roles changed. The University of Oxford website explains that the university began with teaching as early as 1096 and developed rapidly into a scholarly community from 1167.[6] The University of Cambridge was founded in 1231 and developed its first college (Peterhouse) in 1284. The first colleges at Oxford (University College, Balliol, and Merton) were established between 1249 and 1264. Allowing women to study at Oxford and Cambridge initially required developing additional colleges dedicated to their separate education. The first Cambridge colleges for women were Girton College, founded in 1869; Newnham College, founded in 1872, and Hughes Hall in 1885. The first Oxford colleges for women, Lady Margaret Hall and Somerville, opened in 1879, but women did not become full members of the University of Oxford who were allowed to receive degrees until 1920.[7]

In the early twentieth century, the period in which the three British novels discussed here are set, universities offered some new educational opportunities for women, but one's gender—like one's race/ethnicity and class—presented obstacles for many who wished to join elite institutions.

The Search, Gaudy Night, and *The Gate of Angels* provide individual accounts of this history of exclusion and prejudice. Snow's novel describes sex segregation in employment: educated, yet marginalized women pursue degrees in history and literature with scarce opportunities for professional employment, while men with the same level of education compete as academic scientists in the 1930s. Acknowledging sexism in universities and society, Fitzgerald and Sayers, respectively, detail the criticism against educated women at Cambridge in 1912 and at Oxford in the mid-1930s. Their novels incorporate issues from nineteenth- and early-twentieth-century debates about women's rights, taking as a common subject the proper role for women in society, as characters disagree about whether women should have access to higher education. Although women enroll at Brown University in the 1980s, the setting of Eugenides's novel, his heroine struggles to assert her intellectual views in the undergraduate classroom and to pursue a graduate degree.

Mixing fact and fiction to depict women's intrusion into the highly rarified social world of the British university dates to Virginia Woolf, who wrote the first draft of what became *A Room of One's Own* (1929) as a response to an invitation to provide a university talk about women and fiction. Woolf's formal education was limited to the Ladies' Department of King's College in London between 1897 and 1901, while her brothers Adrian and Julian studied at Cambridge. She based *A Room of One's Own* on two papers she had given in October 1928 to two Cambridge groups: the Arts Society at Newnham College and the Odtaa, a literary society at Girton College. As she describes near the opening of the book,

> All I could do was to offer you an opinion upon one minor point—a woman must have money and a room of her own if she is to write fiction; and that, as you will see, leaves the great problem of the true nature of woman and the true nature of fiction unsolved. I have shirked the duty of coming to a conclusion upon these two questions—women and fiction remain, so far as I am concerned, unsolved problems. But in order to make some amends I am going to do what I can to show you how I arrived at this opinion about the room and the money.[8]

Woolf organizes her book to resemble a fictional narrative, one that takes place at "Oxbridge," a place with social rules recognized by her and her readers. She explains in her first chapter,

> It was thus that I found myself walking with extreme rapidity across a grass plot. Instantly a man's figure rose to intercept me. Nor did I at first understand that the gesticulations of a curious-looking object, in a cut-away coat and evening shirt, were aimed at me. His face expressed horror and indignation. Instinct rather than reason came to my help, he was a Beadle; I was a woman. This was the turf; there was the path. Only the Fellows and Scholars are allowed here; the gravel is the place for me. Such thoughts were the work of a moment.[9]

Woolf acknowledges her visceral response to the university authority's angry look: she is put in her place as a woman, for she is a visitor dependent on its hospitality, which is not generous to those of her sex. She later contrasts the bounty at a men's college dinner with the meager dinner served at the impoverished women's college.

To counter arguments from historians and clerics about the supposed limited talents and capacities of women, Woolf's third chapter of *A Room of One's Own* presents a famous hypothetical case, that of Shakespeare's sister who is imagined as not receiving the education, parental encouragement, or protection of male privilege that her brother enjoys. Woolf speculates that the girl, whom she calls Judith Shakespeare, would have been as talented as her brother and would have run away from a father beating her because she refused to submit to an arranged marriage. According to Woolf's hypothetical, the actor-manager who "took pity on" Judith abandons her when she is pregnant.[10] Both the invented story of the talented Judith, who is not permitted to pursue a vocation in the theater, and Woolf's testimony of Oxbridge hostility exhibited while she is within university walls illustrate persistent inequities that trouble women's lives, acknowledging that public opinion inhibits women from accessing educational opportunities and resources traditionally reserved for men. For centuries, women were limited by attitudes and actions assuming their place should be in the home as a deferential helpmate to a husband. The academic novels evoke Woolf's description of stark gender disparities to illustrate bias and discrimination while suggesting that attitudes should evolve and that the future university will endorse equity and enable women to succeed as students and faculty.

Many working-class men and women were not able to attend British universities until the post–World War II era, when the government began to award stipends for those in need; however, even the limited prospects for nonelite men in universities were generally rosier than those for women. C. P. Snow was the son of a church organist and choirmaster and was educated at Leicester and Cambridge before succeeding as a scientist and university administrator and subsequently a novelist.[11] *The Search*'s first-person narrator also comes from a family without significant means, and he enters King's College, London, despite not understanding the system: "No one at school had any clear idea of open scholarships to Oxford and Cambridge."[12] Like other men from modest circumstances, the narrator, Arthur Miles, graduates and becomes a hard-working, ambitious, and successful scientist. He rises in his profession until he makes a critical error in reporting experimental results; this mistake sets back his career and tarnishes his enthusiasm for science as it keeps him from fulfilling his ambition to direct his own institute.

In contrast with men of modest means who entered university in the early part of the twentieth century, the first generations of women who studied at Oxford and Cambridge were mostly from wealthier families; however, even women completing degrees had limited professional prospects. Considered by some the first feminist mystery writer, Dorothy Sayers finished her program from Somerville College at Oxford in 1915, but she had to wait until 1920 to receive her degree, as women were previously not allowed to earn degrees. Sayers studied modern languages and medieval literature and pursued a career in advertising before becoming a full-time writer of popular mysteries and scholarly works, including translations of Dante's *The Divine Comedy*. Penelope Fitzgerald's mother, Christina Knox, was also one of the first women to study at Somerville; after leaving university, Christina "wrote occasional pieces for the *Manchester Guardian* and contributed [commentaries] through the 1920s and early 1930s to the English Literature Series, editions of annotated, abridged classic texts."[13] According to Hermione Lee, "*The College Record* for autumn 1935 noted Miss Dorothy Sayers had succeeded Mrs. E. V. Knox as chairman of the Association of Senior Members, and that Mrs. Knox's daughter was 'carrying on the tradition of scholarship and of close association with Somerville.'"[14] Penelope Fitzgerald (maiden name Penelope Knox), studied literature and graduated from Somerville College in 1939. Her postgraduate professional employment included working for the BBC, writing as a freelancer for various publications, and tutoring students preparing to enter university. Not until she was in her sixties was Fitzgerald able to earn enough income from her novels, allowing her to pursue writing full time.

Scholarly Values

The Search, *The Gate of Angels*, and *Gaudy Night* detail facilities, events, and conventions associated with early-twentieth-century academic life; the novels describe places and activities off limits to women and reference practices and policies of Oxford and Cambridge that constrained women's participation in the academy and their postgraduate success. While Snow describes London, Manchester, and Cambridge universities as settings for his characters, Sayers and Fitzgerald locate their plots in fictional colleges at Oxford and Cambridge. Applying terms introduced in Jacques Rancière's discussion of space and narrative, I recognize tensions between "the truth of the place" and "the knowledge of the narrative" in these novels.[15] *The Search*, *The Gate of Angels*, and *Gaudy Night* represent "the truth of the place" by sketching imposing physical spaces (quadrangles, buildings, entrance gates) and by describing social and academic rituals of the universities collectively understood as "Oxbridge." Yet the promises that a university enshrines truth and promotes scholarship conflict with "the knowledge of the narrative," which points to how women's accomplishments are not supported in the universities represented in the novels. Claiming that the university privileges truth and rewards merit contradicts the narrative findings ("the knowledge of the narrative") that describe constraints placed on women, including discounting their scholarly contributions. This knowledge recognizes that barriers to women's participation, including discriminations against them, should be eliminated in the future.

Although in these three novels males enjoy social privileges and educational opportunities not available to females, not all men succeed at universities. The narrator of *The Search*, Arthur Miles, admits to his own accidental scholarly error, which cost him a desired position. Yet later in the novel, Arthur refuses to correct a friend's professional lie because he realizes that he would rather help the man and his wife, who is a former girlfriend of Arthur's, than report the man's misconduct. *The Search* allows Arthur to overlook a friend's error instead of reporting it to authorities. "The knowledge of the narrative" in *Gaudy Night* notes inequitable treatment of women students and faculty, even as female scholars working at women's colleges uphold scholarly integrity. Similarly, "the knowledge of the narrative" in *The Gate of Angels* shows that the search for truth is the province of men while reflecting late twentieth-century concerns about women being subjected to sexual harassment and discrimination. Women find advancing in careers difficult: Daisy Saunders, a working-class young woman, and Mrs. Wrayburn, the degreed wife of a college professor, are rebuked as dismantlers of institutional prestige and male privilege.

In the three British novels discussed here, female characters exhibit more integrity, common sense, and human sympathy than their male counterparts, including men holding distinguished university posts, encouraging readers to appreciate women's capacities and to hope for more equitable treatment by educational institutions. Many novels explore the ways in which women's integrity and intelligence may not enable their success, and in many cases may inhibit their prospects. Information in *The Search*, *Gaudy Night*, and *The Gate of Angels* concentrates on depicting sex bias and discrimination as features of academic environment. The novels recommend enhancing women's rights as an ethical solution to resolve gender disparities in education and work and argue that dismantling barriers for women in higher education will make the university a more ethical, humane, and successful endeavor.

Research Ethics

Like Snow, Sayers and Fitzgerald mention ethical dilemmas related to research in their novels. *Gaudy Night* explicitly references Snow's novel, specifically Arthur Miles's decision to keep quiet about his friend's error. *The Gate of Angels* also alludes to difficulties for scientists who pursue personal happiness while seeking to expand scientific knowledge. *The Search*'s first-person narrator, Arthur is an ambitious chemistry student motivated to spend weeks taking photographs and making measurements in the lab. But his hard work causes him to neglect his lover Audrey, who ends up marrying Arthur's philandering friend Charles Sheriff, a less talented scientist. Readers learn that men succeed in their scientific careers by working long hours, collaborating, and sometimes by cheating; however, there are limited opportunities for educated women in Snow's novel to pursue careers. Audrey is a desultory student of history who attaches herself first to Arthur and then to Sheriff, for she realizes that academic and other social conventions demand that she subordinate her interests and needs to those of her breadwinning, philandering husband who can earn a significant income.

One of Arthur's published papers includes a data error because was busy playing politics on the committee developing the institute that he hopes to direct, and he does not carefully review experimental results collected by his laboratory assistant. His scientific misconduct (negligently publishing false results) slows down his career, but Arthur finds love with Ruth, a rich woman. He elects to write general interest books instead of experimenting and submitting scientific papers, a preference that satisfies him more than the prospect of future success in science. Helping his friends, Arthur guides Sheriff to pursue a scientific problem that the latter will most certainly solve, assuring his scholarly reputation and career success. But Sheriff did not want to waste time undertaking the tedious observation and analysis that Arthur's problem required; instead, Sheriff took a shortcut and published a paper with a critical error.

After some reflection, Arthur realizes that if he does not alert the world to the error, Sheriff's paper will likely earn the author a professorship and his wife's respect. Arthur never reports his friend's error, realizing that his own passion for science has been extinguished and that he is relieved to leave that career. Ruth's inheritance means he is not obliged to earn a living, and his writing offers an easier way to earn income rather than continuously angling for professional attention and academic positions as a scientist. *The Search* illustrates Arthur's ambitions as being in tension with his search for personal and romantic happiness until he gives up on science, which he realizes is a profession that can only be undertaken in relentless fashion while one is searching for a discovery. Turning a blind eye to scientific misconduct allows him to feel "free of a cloud" and "to be liberated from all the faiths and superstitions."[16] *The Search* ends with Arthur anticipating a satisfying future: "With a deep content, I walked towards the house, whose lights were streaming through the tranquil twilight."[17] Recognizing that science is corrupted by political maneuverings and selfish ambitions, Arthur turns away from a scientific world dominated by a never-ending sequence of observation, analysis, and publication that may or may not result in advancement and fame.

Pursuing a scientific career is not available to the female characters in *The Search*: Audrey and Ruth are constrained from entering science and other fields. Arthur does not tell the wives about Sheriff's misconduct or his own refusal to report the error. Thus, Arthur's silence keeps the women as nonparticipants in science. That they cannot enter scientific and other university careers seems acceptable to Arthur, who is coping with the aftermath of his own error, his loss of enthusiasm for the tedious work, and his impatience with colleagues. Yet even after Arthur admits his error, he remains involved in many committee deliberations and is offered the post of associate director, while Audrey, Ruth, and other women have limited prospects. They do not sit on committees, nor are they contenders for institute positions. Although gendered dimensions of science are not examined comprehensively in *The Search*, its depiction of academic misconduct becomes an illustrative context for conversations among the female dons in Sayers's novel, which references arguments concerning women's education at Oxford.

Romance and Scholarship

Like *The Search*, *Gaudy Night* considers ethical dilemmas that academics confront while managing romance, marriage, and professional success. Sayers's protagonist Harriet Vane and her admirer Lord Peter Wimsey collaborate to solve a poison pen mystery causing chaos at her alma mater. *Gaudy Night* opens with Harriet deciding to return to her college for its annual celebration so that she can catch up with former classmates. She is a well-known novelist, but as two earlier novels by Sayers illustrate, Harriet has a scandalous past. In *Strong Poison* (1930) Harriet is accused of murdering her former lover, Philip Boyes. After Lord Peter Wimsey figures out that the murderer had to have benefited from Philip's death, Harriet is acquitted. Peter is besotted with Harriet, who is clever, forthright, and professionally successful, and he repeatedly asks for her hand in marriage. In *Have His Carcase* (1932), Harriet stumbles on a corpse of a male Russian ballroom dancer on a beach, and she works with Peter and police to identify the murderers.

Romance and mystery are linked in Sayers's Vane-Wimsey novels, as the detectives Harriet and Peter observe and learn from the ways that love goes wrong in others' relationships. In the first two Vane-Wimsey novels, Harriet distrusts Peter's proposals, which are issued too quickly and frequently to be sincere. Nevertheless, she harbors a great attraction to him and realizes there would be benefits if she were to wed a successful, handsome man with an aristocratic title and money. Profits from her mystery books already provide her with a comfortable living, allowing Harriet to remain single if she wishes, but she appreciates his steady regard for logic and truth and his clever wit.

Harriet resents popular opinion that pigeonholes her as a writer of mysteries, for she also enjoys more serious intellectual pursuits, including scholarly research. Attending her college reunion enables her (and

readers) to notice career paths that other women followed after graduation. On college grounds, while speaking with Miss Lydgate, the English
tutor, Harriet "marveled, not for the first time, at the untiring consci-
entiousness of administrative women."[18] Observing her classmates, she
realizes how boring and annoying some have become. Alumnae include
a rude American eugenicist, a dull farmwife, and an invalid who speaks
only of marriage. Harriet becomes irritated with those who criticize her
mystery novels. One classmate proposes a plot that Harriet finds clichéd,
while others pose trivial questions about the books. In contrast, Harriet
enjoys conversing with her favorite classmate Phoebe, an archaeologist
who collaborates with her husband on fieldwork and publications, and
who manages her family life with children as an extension of her professional life.

In the first part of *Gaudy Night*, Harriet mulls over the possibility of
marriage to Peter as she reflects on the lives of her classmates attending
the gaudy celebration. Her complicated path to an engagement is elaborated in the second half of the novel. She appreciates Peter more after she
observes him in action as a detective in Oxford and realizes how much
others admire him. Women she respects, including the female faculty of
Shrewsbury College, offer compliments about Peter that reinforce Harriet's
affections. Despite the differences between his upper-class background
and her modest upbringing, she realizes they like talking about the same
subjects: books, history, current affairs, politics, psychology, and crime.
Their discussions of marriage in the novel compete with their consideration of the crimes that bedevil Harriet's alma mater.

Sayers archly explains in her "Author's Note" that her depiction of
the fictional Shrewsbury College, with a name embodying criticism of
women, "is entirely imaginary," suggesting that physical aspects of the
invented women's college resemble attributes of Balliol, the alma mater
of Peter Wimsey.[19] Shrewsbury women faculty and students enjoy the
privilege of being in an Oxford college, but they also resent that women's
colleges, as Woolf also noted, have limited resources compared with the
wealthier colleges catering to men. Harriet finds university life appealing
and is drawn back into the world of scholarship, at least temporarily, to
solve the mystery of who sends poison pen letters like the one placed in
her unattended academic robe during the gaudy: "YOU DIRTY MUR-
DERESS. AREN'T YOU ASHAMED TO SHOW YOUR FACE?"[20] Ever
the diplomatic guest, Harriet does not tell anyone about the letter until

the dean calls her back to Shrewsbury to figure out who has played many such pranks on faculty and students there.

Reacting to criticism against women's education, Harriet sends a letter of correction to a London daily paper employing derogatory terms—"Undergraduettes" and "Lady Head"—in reporting "a bonfire of gowns on Shrewsbury Quad" and characterizing the women students as "Lady Undergrads" and "sweet girl-graduates."[21] Harriet complains to Peter "that this kind of vulgarity was typical of the average man's attitude to women's intellectual interests," and he responds that "bad manners always made him sick; but was it any worse than headlining foreign monarchs by their Christian names, untitled?"[22] Peter's prim response reveals that he is concerned with maintaining standards of taste and protocols, but he shares Harriet's progressive attitudes toward women's education. Other characters harbor more conservative opinions about social propriety, class, and gender.

The novel's dominant question concerns whether marriage and family are more appropriate activities for women than establishing careers, but *Gaudy Night* also reflects class and ethnic biases. Set in 1935 as England watches Adolf Hitler, the novel includes characters' comments about the German leader's politics and remarks about Jews that make readers wonder whether Sayers was an anti-Semite. The porter Padgett seems to forgive young ladies who act up at college like young gentlemen do. Yet after the "decorators' foreman" asserts that young women should behave appropriately, Padgett replies "Wot this country wants . . . is a 'Itler."[23] The porter's and the foreman's admiring remarks about the German dictator reveal questionable, fascist, and traitorous political ideas.

While sleuthing at Shrewsbury, Harriet tries to identify the community member who holds "a grudge against the S.C.R." (Senior Common Room).[24] She keeps watch and analyzes evidence: the poison pen letters, a damaged copy of *The Search*, the destruction of Miss Lydgate's manuscript proof, an effigy of a woman scholar left in the chapel, and the vandalized New Library and Science lecture-room. Faculty in the SCR mull over clues and possible suspects, agreeing with Harriet that public statements would only alert the wrongdoer, who is likely to become more circumspect. The all-female Shrewsbury faculty and administrators exchange disparate opinions about scouts, maids, and other working-class characters. Some scholars suspect working-class staff members of wrongdoing, but others can't believe that their scouts and maids vandalized property or sent offensive letters. Since all staff members, except two senior maids, are locked in their rooms during the night, suspecting staff seems a dead end.

Faculty argue about whether married women and mothers can be dedicated staff members, complaining about the frequent absences of the dean's secretary, Mrs. Goodwin, who does not work if her school-age son falls ill. Some faculty members divide women into two groups—scholars and mothers—with no one belonging to both groups. Other administrators and faculty have a soft spot for mothers, particularly Annie, a widowed scout who boards her children with the Jukes family. Mr. Jukes was dismissed from Shrewsbury for stealing while he was a porter, but the Warden and the Dean augmented the family's income by encouraging Annie to place her two young girls with the Jukes family while the maid resides in college. This arrangement lasts until Jukes blackmails an Oxford undergraduate, and Annie must find a more suitable home for her daughters. She teaches her girls to become wives and mothers instead of entering professions, and she reports to Harriet when they accidentally meet outside of college: "It seems to me a dreadful thing to see all these unmarried ladies living together [in college]. It isn't natural, is it?"[25] Annie doesn't hesitate to share her negative views of women scholars.

Harriet's midnight rambles to keep watch around the college grounds introduce her to Pomfret, an Oxford undergraduate who one night helps the drunken Miss Cattermole back to her Shrewsbury residence. Harriet advises the latter to study more, helps save the depressed student, Miss Newland, from committing suicide, and becomes an authoritative adviser to Peter's collegian nephew, Saint-George. After the nephew learns she is searching for someone intent on wrecking Shrewsbury, he tells her that he spotted an odd figure on the grounds: someone with beastly eyes who threatened him when she found him sneaking into the women's college: "We murder beautiful boys like you and eat their hearts out."[26] Helping his uncle Peter and "aunt" Harriet with the case, Saint-George observes Shrewsbury routines one day to see if he can identify the suspect.

Visiting Oxford to see his nephew, Peter also analyzes clues and interviews witnesses with Harriet. She likes that he appreciates her references to literature, history, and politics and can engage in witty dialogue with her. He quotes; she quotes. They share an interest in promoting ethical and equitable actions as they act as informal educators in university. Harriet cannot resist lecturing Saint-George and other undergraduates she encounters to be more responsible to themselves and others. As philosopher Susan Haack argues, "The plot of Sayers's story turns precisely on a character's concern for truth and the disastrous series of reactions it prompts, and an important preoccupation is the relation of epistemological to other values: why is honesty valuable in scientific and other inquiry? Is suppressing a fact as bad as telling a lie? What is the relation between epistemological and ethical values? Do the obligations of one's job always, or ever, override considerations of personal loyalty?"[27] In *Gaudy Night*, questions of truth and ethical responsibility are tied to references to Snow's novel, after a mutilated copy of *The Search*, likely left by the poison pen writer threatening the women's college, turns up. Lord Peter Wimsey cites Snow's novel in solving the mystery, commenting on the scientist's decision in *The Search*: "If we do not penalise false statements made in error, we open the way for false statements by intention. And a false statement of fact, made deliberately, is the most serious crime a scientist can commit."[28] Senior Common Room faculty considering the topic of "Deliberate falsification" agree with the character Arthur Miles's decision to leave science after making an error because they understand that scholarship must have integrity and that falsehood in science is "indefensible."[29] The newest scholar to join Shrewsbury, Miss de Vine, raises another example of misconduct: she uncovered one scholar's attempt to hide archival evidence contradicting his research. Her former university punished the scholar by firing him, causing a hardship for his family. The privileged female dons debate whether the man's wife, someone from the working class, would be at all concerned about his honor or would resent the termination as an unnecessary cruelty.

Speaking privately with Miss de Vine, Peter hears the complete account of Arthur Robinson's attempt to earn an academic post by stealing and hiding a historical document that countermanded his thesis. Peter tries to figure out who at Shrewsbury might be connected to Robinson, digging up the first names of the man's wife and daughter to determine that Annie must be guilty. The Warden insists that Annie be brought to the Senior Common Room to defend herself from charges, but instead of offering a defense, the scout inveighs against the system that punished her husband, pushing him into insecure jobs and alcoholism before he "blew his brains out."[30] Annie's bitterness and bile upsets everyone. Susan Haack comments on the scene:

> When Harriet, with the help of Lord Peter Wimsey, exposes her as the criminal, Annie—the desperately angry Total Woman—is defiant: "Couldn't you leave my man alone? He told a lie about

someone who was dead and dust hundreds of years ago. . . . You broke him and killed him—all for nothing. Do you think that's a woman's job?" Annie thinks women should be wives and mothers; these women dons, and the women students for that matter, are unnatural creatures, taking away men's jobs.[31]

Despite being horrified by Annie's rant, faculty members affirm their commitment to the college's mission to advance women's educational and professional prospects. The dons advocate for women's pursuits of research and teaching, and they agree that their colleague Miss de Vine was correct in helping to terminate Annie's husband.

As a strong-minded woman, Harriet believes that women should be educated and should be able to enter whatever professions they choose. She is grateful to Peter for his help in determining the threat against Shrewsbury, but she does not want gratitude to be the reason she marries him. Instead, it is their compatibility, mutual interests, shared political views, and their joy in being together that links them. After they attend a concert in Oxford, he asks her in Latin to marry him as they walk through the beautiful university, and she accepts, also in Latin. The novel approves women enrolling in higher education and highlights integrity in scholarly work along with equity and compatibility in marriage as critical factors in enabling women's advancement.

Accidental Romance and Science

Published much later than the novels by Snow and Sayers and reflecting feminist perspectives in looking back at women's lives in the early-twentieth century, Penelope Fitzgerald's novel examines ethical concerns regarding how academics pursue career success and conduct courtships leading to marriage. The novel acknowledges the need to expand opportunities for women in higher education and the workplace. *The Gate of Angels* is set in London and Cambridge during a period rife with change: early twentieth-century physicists proposed conflicting theories of atomic structure while political activists agitated for women's rights. Erwin Hiebert writes,

Physicists around 1900 were caught up in a spirit of scientific speculation that would have been considered quite reckless ten years earlier. At least it is apparent to me that the majority of physicists around 1900 were far more willing to challenge the fixity of the traditional categories of physics than they had been a decade earlier, when mechanics, heat, light, electricity, and magnetism were lumped together theoretically under dynamics, thermodynamics, and electrodynamics.[32]

Political ferment occurred concomitantly with scientific discoveries in Britain: "Between 1870 and 1884 debates on women's suffrage took place almost every year in Parliament."[33] By 1912 suffragists employed violent tactics "such as chaining themselves to railings, setting fire to mailbox contents, smashing windows and occasionally detonating bombs."[34] Feminist issues pop up in *The Gate of Angels* as frequently as scientific theories; the novel references suffragists sent to prison, public campaigns for women's suffrage, women's limited opportunities in higher education and professions, and everyday sexual harassment, assault, and abuse against women.

The Gate of Angels begins with a description of "disorder," a storm bedeviling bicyclists, including Fred Fairly, a university lecturer recovering from an earlier accident that resulted in an unexpected sentimental conclusion. This unmarried postdoctoral fellow in physics determined after the earlier accident that the woman who was also knocked unconscious at the same time as him was the love of his life. The chance encounter of the Cambridge physicist and Daisy Saunders, a young, working-class woman, initiates a romance and a mystery. The novel culminates in an inquest resolving two questions: Who drove the vehicle that hit Fred and Daisy while they were bicycling on the same road? And who was the witness who left the injured bicyclists at the scene of the accident?

The first chapter of *The Gate of Angels* describes Fred Fairly's disorder, confusion, and economically precarious life as a junior fellow: he misses dinner, muses about Daisy, and has an odd conversation with the master. The narrator explains to readers that Cambridge protocols are frequently breached at his college and that fellows like Fred are not certain of what to do, although after he found himself in bed with Daisy, he decided that he wished to marry her despite St. Angelicus College prohibitions. Fred's sudden infatuation with Daisy provides counterpoint to scientific debates mentioned in the novel. Scholars at Angels have stakes in physics debates about atomic structure, but Fred does not have much time for research, and he cannot manage to find time to write a letter explaining his feelings to Daisy. His colleagues and supervisors subject him to interruptions, including notes that explain what one thinks might have happened on an occasion, what the writer meant to say instead of what it might appear was said, and/or what the recipient should do. Writers do not always want responses; many notes are written to gratify the sender rather than the recipient, and they often contain observations that may not be accurate. The community is insular, peculiar, and steadfast in keeping to its inconvenient traditions, as the narrator dryly remarks; however, during this period of rapid scientific and social change, readers understand that cumbersome, inefficient conventions might be transformed in the future.

The early history of the college's origins notices that a person always has enemies, for it was founded by a dethroned pope who staved off a poisoning attempt before dying in old age. Other notable features of the college include that it is "the smallest college in Cambridge" and it "resembled a fortress, a toy fortress" lacking many of the facilities one would expect of a Cambridge college: "There were no cloisters, no infirmary, no hospice, no welcome (to be honest), to those strangers or not, arriving from outside, no house apart for the Master."[35] Students have no quarters on the college campus, and there is not "room in their court for their bicycles which had to remain stacked outside the Great Gate. Over the gate the heraldic arms, weathered almost flat with the wall, showed two angels asleep."[36] The college motto, "*Estoy in mis trece* . . . is translated as 'I have not changed my mind,' but 'nothing doing' might be nearer."[37] Angelicus appears a small, marginal college without amenities, tough on students, considered heretical, and identified with persistent, stubborn, inefficient conservatism.

College procedures are haphazard. Fred's appointment as Junior Fellow was arranged informally after he met a professor at a reception for those with a First Class in science. The professor assigns Fred "to instruct his students in physics and take them off his hands," and to a number of other assorted duties: "to lend a hand with the library, the catering and the accounts, act as assistant organist and keep the collection of fifteenth-century musical instruments in repair and, as far as possible, tuned."[38] As the age of the instruments and the mixed responsibilities of stewardship indicate, the college clings to traditions it cannot afford. Understanding that Fred's father is a somewhat poor minister, Flowerdew pays Fred out of his own pocket and arranges an Angels fellowship for the young man.

Fred also becomes associated with the Cavendish Laboratory. The chaos caused by the rainstorm in the book's first chapter signals instability, not only concerning Fred's romantic state, his casual position, and the college's finances, but also to the uncertainty related to scientific claims. *The Gate of Angels* looks at how scientists in this corner of Cambridge react to new discoveries in atomic physics emerging from the north of England. A physics graduate of Cambridge and later director of the Cavendish Laboratory (1919–1937), Ernest Rutherford was working at the University of Manchester when he discovered the atomic nucleus in 1911.[39] His discoveries inspire Fred and his peer group of young scientists, while annoying conservative Cavendish scientists such as Flowerdew. More interested in believing in what he observes than in speculating about theoretical possibilities, Professor Flowerdew embodies the stubbornness identified with Angels and objects to what many see as a plausible scientific discovery, telling Fred that he does not believe in Rutherford's atomic structure because it is not observable reality. Historian of science Stanley Jaki describes Rutherford's more nuanced sense of reality:

> Rutherford not only believed his eyes when seeing the evidence on a scintillating screen, but he also believed that there ought to be another reality beneath that which he had seen. The reality was that of the atom with a very small hard core and with a very large, almost empty periphery, the realm of orbital electrons. It was a reality which he could see only with the eyes of the mind, but he held it to be as real as what he could see and touch.[40]

In contrast with Rutherford who "sees" reality beneath what he observes, Flowerdew follows Ernst Mach who insists on believing only what he can observe to be real.[41] Flowerdew explains his caution to Fred:

> An atom is not a reality, it is just a provisional idea, so how can we say that it is situated in space? We ought to feel suspicious of it when we find that it has been given characteristics which absolutely contradict those which have been observed in any other body. There is a continuity of scientific thought, you know. The continuity is now being thrown out the window. Let us hope we shall remember where it is when, at long last, we find that we can't do without it.[42]

Flowerdew refuses to entertain what Neil Cameron describes as "a compromise between established conventions and the meritocratic and philistine imperatives of nineteenth-century sciences," for the professor prefers

"The preservation of tradition and the benevolent feudalism of the Laboratory."[43] Fred appreciates that while Flowerdew finds the new ideas in atomic physics "unsound," the professor is not dogmatic or authoritarian; he does not demand that Fred agree with him about atomic theory to retain the Angels fellowship, which allows a small but secure income. The college environment is hard on fellows, for they cannot marry and must take on extra labor to increase their income. Nevertheless, Fred appears reasonably content and on friendly terms with his most eccentric colleagues.

Fitzgerald's historical novel considers various forms of communication, including those that do not convey information. What someone really means is often thrown into question in this novel. Fred and his friends are members of the Disobligers' Society, and they posture by speaking against true beliefs during meetings encouraging ironic versions of intellectual debates. No Disobliger who speaks at the meetings believes what he is saying, which cheapens academic discourse in general, even though the Disobligers see their meetings as a critical, extracurricular practice of venting about their difficult conditions. The unbelieving son of a minister, Fred is assigned to speak for the soul in the meeting that his friend Skippey presses him to attend. Fred later walks with the provost who comically assumes that as a Disobliger Fred *always* says the opposite of what he means. The blind master writes Fred a note indicating, contrary to what he said to Fred when they met in the quadrangle, that the master "recognized" him by his footsteps in the courtyard. It is unclear whether the master's statement means he understood Fred believed in the soul, as his Disobligers speech indicates, or whether the master knew Fred was saying he does not believe in the soul, as the conventions of the Disobligers Society require.

This confusion regarding what to believe about the master is another textual example of the novel's ambiguities concerning the reliability of information; these include questioning if the new atomic theory is correct, inconclusiveness regarding whether Fred and Daisy marry, and other scenes about uncertain speculations. Cambridge academics include the provost of St. James College, Dr. Matthews, who researches archaeological sites and makes up ghost stories, including a rumor of corpses under a road that influences the local court reviewing Fred's and Daisy's accident on that same road. Fred's love at first sight for Daisy, why the unknown driver caused their accident, Flowerdew's suspicions of atomic theory, the Disobligers' reversing positions, and Dr. Matthews's insistence on finding supernatural explanations cause characters (and readers) to question which information and beliefs can be trusted.

A random event, the bicycle accident bringing Fred and Daisy to the Wrayburns' house prompts his romantic interest in Daisy after they mysteriously wake up without their clothes and in bed together. This mystery is explained: after the vehicle struck Fred and Daisy from their bicycles, a farmer's son brought them to the Wrayburns' house, which is near the site of the accident. Mrs. Wrayburn assumed the injured Fred and Daisy were married because Daisy was wearing a wedding ring and the young people appeared to be traveling together. But her assumption that Fred and Daisy constitute a couple was inaccurate. There remains an air of uncertainty about the accident, as characters and readers wonder who drove the vehicle that hit Fred and Daisy? And who was the third bicyclist, the man who rode away?

Fitzgerald inserts Daisy's history within a flashback telling how she came to be riding a bicycle on the outskirts of Cambridge and wearing a wedding ring. The explanation boils down to issues of class and gender: Daisy Saunders has experienced poor economic prospects and a history of sexual harassment by her male employers.[44] She grew up in London dealing with depressing circumstances of working-class life, which are illustrated in Fitzgerald's description of a neighborhood full of "the smells of vinegar, gin, coal smoke, paraffin, sulphur, horse-dung from backyard stables, chloride of lime from the backstreet factories, and baking bread every morning."[45] Poor and fatherless, she minded babies to supplement her mother's meager earnings from a bottle-capping factory. Daisy attended school until she was fifteen, when she found full-time employment as a clerk. Taking public transit to her work, Daisy put up her hair, placed her aunt's wedding ring on her finger, and kept a pin in her pocket to fend off the wandering hands of male passengers. The narrator explains,

> Those who did the approaching, in the stifling proximity of the tram, were inclined not to believe in the wedding-ring, and knew what else Daisy was wearing as well as she did. It was a battle with no accepted rules and when the tram began to roll with its plunging, strong-smelling human freight, men put their hands over their ticket and money pockets while schoolboys protected their genitals and women every point of contact, fore and aft.[46]

Men at Daisy's clerical jobs also subjected her to sexual harassment. The aunt's wedding ring was not enough to protect Daisy from grabby men on the tram, and her self-possession was not enough to keep her bosses from pressing her to engage in sexual relations.

After her mother died, seventeen-year-old Daisy was left penniless. She was remarkably lucky to be hired as a probationer in a hospital, a job that also provided her with a home, and she hoped to work her way up to being a nurse. Her performance in the hospital was excellent until her generous impulse to assist a patient was held against her. She was terminated because she tried to cheer a man rescued from suicide by drowning; Daisy convinced a local newspaper to print an item about the gentleman so that he would feel better. After the article "Mystery of 'Ministering Angel'" is published, she was recognized as the person who reported the patient to the newspaper, and she was fired from the hospital because, as matron reminds her, she acted independently and outside doctor's orders.[47] Daisy's revealing information is treated as a misstep, one endangering her economic prospects.

Homeless, unemployed, and without support from family or friends in London or elsewhere, Daisy decides to ask for work at the Cambridge asylum run by a kind doctor. Kelly, the unscrupulous editor who wrote the article that ended Daisy's nursing career, stalks her and bullies her. At King's Cross Station he maneuvers the poor girl into going to Cambridge with him so that he can teach her how to have sex for money. Daisy feels "pity for them both," but she agrees to go with Kelly because she has nowhere else to go and no one to help her.[48] "What a pair we make, she thought. He doesn't deserve any better, no more do I."[49] Having spent her life fending off men's attentions, Daisy realizes that her desperate straits push her to a new low. Fitzgerald presents the conversation without narrative mediation to emphasize Kelly's relentless, exploitive pursuit of Daisy, whose miserable situation makes her sympathetic to readers. Kelly harmed the young woman: by publishing the newspaper article he caused her to become friendless, homeless, unemployed, and hopeless. He knew the article would cause her to be fired from her hospital job, but he doesn't even warn her before printing the information. Then he took advantage of her to point out that her only remaining option was to have sex with him. His promise to "look after" Daisy came with an oath: "I'll give you my dickybird."[50] He might have meant he gives her his word to be her protector, but the word "dickybird" connotes "penis," and the conversation makes them appear to be pimp and prostitute. Daisy's precarious economic state makes her accept his relentless propositioning that they travel together to Cambridge.

Kelly's manipulation of Daisy ends part 2 of the novel, while part 3 returns to Fred's present-day anxieties about writing to her: "After seeing Daisy at close quarters for let us say half an hour . . . he knew he must marry her. There was from that point of view, nothing more to say."[51] Daisy for a time goes back to London, but she returns to Cambridge to work as a part-time domestic for the Wrayburns in exchange for living in their attic. She also has a full-time job ironing linens at Dr. Sage's mental hospital when she and Fred next see each other. Daisy's difficulties in finding a respectable position at a decent living wage and Mrs. Wrayburn's limited professional prospects despite her being an educated woman, albeit without official degree, illustrate how hard it was for women to earn enough income to be self-supporting.

After Daisy returns to Cambridge, Fred invites her to spend the day with him taking a walk in the country, and at a public house he asks her to marry him. Daisy does not refuse or accept: "I don't say I won't Fred."[52] Mr. Wrayburn later mentions the example of La Traviata—the story of a father intervening to keep his son from marrying a courtesan—to Daisy, for he hopes this indirect reference would discourage her from being involved with Fred if she knew their marriage would put an end to his job at Angels. Daisy does not know the opera, but she understands Mr. Wrayburn's point that Fred would be terminated from his position if he married. Not caring about losing his job, Fred invites Daisy to meet his family when they come to Cambridge. His mother and sisters work for the suffrage cause and allude in indirect ways to Daisy's politics. Although Mrs. Fairly is doubtful that Daisy is the right companion for Fred, his sister Hester remarks, "I can imagine her selling Votes for Women," and his sister Julia tells their mother that she is behaving "like the father in that opera."[53] The Fairly sisters' opinion of Daisy is high, as is Professor Flowerdew's of Fred, offering sympathetic perspectives on the young people's romance that counter Mr. Wrayburn's opinion.

Part 4 of The Gate of Angels presents Dr. Matthews's speculations about the man who caused Fred and Daisy's accident and the missing witness; these men were not seen immediately after the event but are later identified. Matthews links a supernatural experience to the road accident involving Fred and Daisy, so locals spread the rumor that "the Provost of St. James believed there was someone—perhaps two people—buried quite recently underneath the Guestingly Road, just a few miles before you come to Dr. Sage's lunatic asylum."[54] The provost's reputation as someone who "carried weight" beyond their community pressures the police to serve a summons "on George Turner, farmer, for having provided a carter or driver, with whom he had a master and servant relationship, with an unsafe vehicle not showing front lights or rear lights . . . holding him responsible as an employer for the wrongs committed by his employee who, on March 2nd 1911, drove the above-mentioned cart without reasonable care and foresight," crashing into Fred and Daisy on their bikes.[55] Although the men causing the accident are identified, uncertainty remains because the question of who can be trusted to provide accurate testimony affects the legal proceedings. At Turner's trial, Fred's "reliability" as to what he saw that night is questioned because he is a scientist, and the judge determines that Mrs. Wrayburn cannot be recognized as a scholar. She points out under oath that if the university presented degrees to women, then she would be a graduate; however, the inspector insists she is a housewife. Daisy knows who the witness was, but she refuses to reveal the name of the third bicyclist. Readers realize the man was Kelly, but she does not want to admit publicly that she knew him. The accident prevented Daisy from reaching the hotel and falling victim to Kelly's predatory intentions. Called as a witness at Turner's trial, Kelly reports that he was afraid to come forward earlier because "I did not wish to cock it all up for Miss Saunders"; however, later he admits, "I've changed my mind . . . Jesus' eyes, now I do want to cock it all up for her."[56] Kelly's bitterness about Daisy's escape from his clutches overcomes any desire he might have to protect himself from criminal charges.

After hearing Kelly's testimony, Fred waits for hours in the café across the street from the court until the odious editor exits. Fred grabs and punches him without saying a word to this man who intimidated Daisy and nearly raped her. Fred's friend Skippey comes along and helps Fred carry the unconscious Kelly to the Botanical Garden, where they dump him. Along the way, Fred learns that Skippey is looking for someone to work as an assistant testing the Michelson-Morley experiments. Fred goes off to present a lecture to his freshman physics students, but he is still thinking of Daisy when he finishes the class by telling them to remember "that scientists are not dispassionate."[57] Acting on his passion, Fred asks Daisy about Kelly, only to hear her say she doesn't love Kelly. The narrator describes the lovers as "in despair," for "there seemed to be another law or regulation by which they were obliged to say to each other what they did not mean to attack what they wished to defend."[58]

After they fight, Daisy tells Fred not to look for her again because she will leave Cambridge.

But Daisy misses the bus back to London and gets lost before she passes by the college where she hears a man suffering. Running into the Angels quadrangle, she revives the blind master by applying her nursing training and diagnosing syncope to the men who come running, "crying out in dismay" to see why there is a woman on college grounds: "She must have spent five minutes in there, not much more. The slight delay, however, meant that she met Fred Fairly walking slowly back to St. Angelicus."[59] The novel's conclusion does not specify if Daisy will accept Fred's marriage proposal; however, readers know that she cares about him even though she hesitated to agree to his earlier proposal. Daisy and Fred are drawn to each other, so one can only assume that they wed.

There is a nice symmetry to the plot in that Daisy and Fred meet by accident and reconcile by accident, although readers might be uncertain about whether they are right for each other. Fred is not sure what the correct atomic structure is, but he is willing to stake his career on further investigations in physics. He is more certain of his feelings for Daisy than he is of anything else. Daisy is a tough, but kind girl; her family situation and economic circumstances have made her so. Based on Daisy's and Fred's comfortable interactions with each other and their kindness to others as well as her practicality and Fred's admitted love for her, we can speculate that they will happily marry. Angels will terminate Fred if he marries, but he has the possibility of working for Skippey, or he can go off to Manchester to work with Rutherford. As a minister's son already managing with little money, Fred is not worried about his finances. Daisy's future circumstances will be improved by marriage, and there is no doubt that she will work hard after she marries Fred. Fitzgerald herself regarded the novel as the only one she wrote with a happy ending.[60]

According to information in these novels, science and romance develop knowledge based on integrity and trust, incorporating these as necessary elements in university settings and in intimate relations. In *The Search*, the male protagonist retreats from science because he prefers being loyal to his friend to confirming the man's cheating. Snow's novel acknowledges that many men use women for sex and put their own careers ahead of their romantic relationships, while the protagonist gives up science for a happy marriage. Set in the 1930s, *Gaudy Night* depicts ideal marriage as a commitment of equals developing out of romantic love. Similarly, in *The Gate of Angels*, Fred loves and respects Daisy. Mutual attraction and respect bring couples together after a period of uncertainty, entering relationships based on enjoyment of one another's company and their somewhat progressive views of sex roles. The three novels point to sex discrimination in employment, noting difficulties for women whose education and work are limited, although there's a sense that conditions may improve in the future. Higher education is compatible with marriage, depending on the interests of the partners, and female characters adapt to situations. Mrs. Wrayburn's domestic life overwhelms her much as Harriet is overwhelmed by the mail she receives from fans. The solution is the same: a woman who can afford help does so to manage domestic and professional work. Mrs. Wrayburn hires Daisy, and Harriet hires a secretary.

Another message in these books is that men should espouse and live by feminist principles. Although some male characters act in egalitarian ways and respect women's rights to the vote, education, and work, men are not always respected or rewarded for having these ideas. Arthur Miles gives up science because doing so improves his domestic happiness and his friend Sheriff's. Lord Peter Wimsey does not suffer for his feminism, but he loses the respect of traditionally minded men and women. Fred Fairly seems a too amiable man until his love for Daisy gives him enough backbone to knock out the dangerously misogynistic Kelly, enabling him to marry and accept new employment.

Links among the three novels encourage readers to understand how the plot of *The Search* influences *Gaudy Night* and to appreciate Fitzgerald's similar representation of the slow march of progress for women's rights. Readers recognize the need for university education and votes for women, while appreciating the value of a happy marriage. *The Gate of Angels* offers a retrospective look at women's roles in and out of academe in the early twentieth century, an account that elegantly weaves together concerns about women's education and work noted in the earlier novels while developing conjoined, postmodern stories—one of how Daisy and Fred court and another of how physicists of the period worked through differences to understand atomic structure. According to this analogy, principles of the universe and features of a romantic relationship may yield ambiguous information yet still develop new understanding.

Independence and the Marriage Plot

Jeffrey Eugenides's *The Marriage Plot* (2011) also presents a positive view of women in higher education. Tracking three US undergraduates in

Brown University's class of 1982, the novel explores romantic and intellectual entanglements. Madeleine and Leonard become attracted to one other when they are enrolled in the same semiotics class and begin to function as a couple, a situation perplexing their classmate Mitchell, who is in love with Madeleine. After graduation, Mitchell travels and studies religions, while Madeleine's study of nineteenth-century novels encourages her to commit to a partner rather than make her own choices. Her four years of college were dominated by her intense pursuit of romance, as her graduation day illustrates; instead of attending the commencement, Madeleine skips the ceremony to help Leonard check out of the mental hospital where he has admitted himself. His severe manic depression makes their relationship difficult, but she decides to live with him after graduation. She believes in Leonard, and she resists acting independently or accepting others' advice. After graduating from Brown, Madeleine becomes a companion to Leonard, who as a promising scientist has been rewarded with a fellowship at a fictional version of Woods Hole Laboratories.

During the summer, Madeline meets a woman resembling the famous scientist Barbara McClintock on the beach and realizes that some successful women avoid marriage.[61] In September, Madeline attends a conference on Victorian literature stoking her interest in pursuing graduate study, but she puts aside plans to do so because of Leonard's mental illness. Instead, she feels compelled to marry him, so that she can help him get better. Their relationship shatters during their European honeymoon after Leonard's odd purchase of an opera cape in Paris begins an odyssey of unstable acts: excessive drinking in Marseille, forcing Madeleine to have rough sex in Nice, and maniacal gambling in Monte Carlo. Madeleine tracks him down to the casino, but Leonard escapes and doesn't surface for two days, during which time she enlists her father's help and that of the American ambassador. Her mother flies to Monaco to meet Madeleine, who is "frantic with worry that Leonard might hurt himself, or be arrested."[62] Eventually, authorities alert Madeleine that an injured Leonard has been found in a hospital, where he is treated with a French drug that brings him back to lucidity.

Madeleine and Leonard return to the United States to live with her parents in New Jersey, but Leonard's continuing depression makes married life difficult. With great effort, she manages to bring him to Manhattan so she can look for an apartment near Columbia, where she will attend graduate school in English. Leonard's unwillingness to shackle Madeline makes him abandon the marriage. At first Madeleine is despondent, but she also feels relieved and turns to Mitchell, who for a moment takes

Leonard's place as her partner. Mitchell loves her and enjoys having sex with her, but he understands that she is escaping her bad marriage. Familiar with her first scholarly publication on the marriage plot in the novel, Mitchell asks her a critical question:

> From the books you read for your thesis, and for your article—the Austen and the James and everything—was there any novel where the heroine gets married to the wrong guy and then realizes it, and then the other suitor shows up, some guy who's always been in love with her, and then *they* get together, but finally the second suitor realizes that the last thing the woman needs is to get married again, that she's got more important things to do with her life? And so finally the guy doesn't propose at all, even though he still loves her? Is there any book that ends like that?[63]

Madeleine responds that there isn't a novel like that, although she happily agrees it would be a good ending. The novel's conclusion allows that Madeleine will part from Leonard, that she will live independently while pursuing a graduate degree in English, and that she feels fine about not jumping into another romantic relationship. At least for now.

Providing information about marriage's negative dimensions for women, many realist novels about romantic relationships and marriage end in tragedy, relationships with poor prospects, or women living alone (*Hard Times, The House of Mirth, The Ambassadors, The Awakening, Quicksand, The Odd Women, The Women's Room*, to name a few). Even in narratives allowing some women to find love in marriage (*Mansfield Park, Middlemarch, Little Women, Normal People*), others are disappointed by marital constraints. The novels discussed in this chapter examine complications of love, education, and work for women, but these elements are not always part of the equation. *The Marriage Plot* offers an unusual ending, reconfiguring the conventions we associate with a realist novel focusing on gender relations and marriage, for it suggests that graduate school is more important than settling down with a mate. Mitchell's hesitation to woo and wed Madeleine reveals his sincere affection and respect for her and understanding of what is important to her. His unwillingness to press a vulnerable Madeleine into a relationship acknowledges what she needs, for his caution enables her to express her own desire to pursue graduate education rather than entering a committed relationship. Whether this is a pause or a shift from his earlier desire, it is also what Mitchell needs to move forward, to explore what matters to him. Such a conclusion informs readers that romance can be successful without marriage if partners pursue vocations that interest them. The single marine biologist who loves her work provided Madeleine with a model of a single woman who succeeded professionally. Self-fulfillment comes before marriage and may replace it for many in the contemporary world, as stories about women who choose scientific careers over husbands illustrate.

Chapter 4

Feminism Meets Science in Recent Narratives

When woman penetrates at last—always through a side door—into
this mysterious masculine world from which she was for so long
excluded (this center of so many marvelous adventures recounted in
song and story, surrounded by the aura of a long-forbidden culture),
she is struck by the fact that abstraction dominates in two ways:
system and hierarchy.

—Claudine Hermann, "The Virile System" (1976)[1]

The female feminist question then becomes how to affirm sexual
difference not as "the other," the other pole of a binary opposition
conveniently arranged so as to uphold a power-system, but rather as
the active process of empowering the difference that women make
to culture and to society. Woman is no longer different from but
different so as to bring about new values.

—Rosi Braidotti, "The Subject in Feminism" (1991)[2]

Depictions of women scientists in contemporary narratives about science
stage troubling issues about scientific environments and practices that
feminist philosophers and social scientists raise in scholarship: identifying
discriminations and barriers to accessing education and jobs and linking
epistemological claims about scientific objectivity and method with masculinity.[3] Since the 1970s, national governments have sought to diversify
the science, technology, engineering, and mathematics (STEM) workforce.

The US National Science Foundation and national science councils in Europe developed initiatives addressing the advancement of women researchers. In the US, the 1971 Comprehensive Health Manpower Act prohibited discrimination in university admissions, contributing to an increased number of female STEM graduates.[4] Although women obtain bachelor's degrees in some scientific fields at almost the same rates as men, fewer women than men attend graduate school in STEM or pursue careers as scientists, and women remain underrepresented at all levels of employment in engineering, computer sciences, and physics.[5]

Women exiting STEM career pathways report workplace discrimination, sexual harassment, and unequal opportunities for scientific collaboration in addition to citing family, medical, and other personal reasons to leave their positions.[6] Histories of women in scientific and technical fields have focused on exceptional figures such as Maria Mitchell, Rosalind Franklin, Lise Meitner, and Barbara McClintock, who persisted and succeeded in making important contributions to their fields despite being challenged by cultural sexism and discriminatory professional practices. This chapter considers information about STEM environments and personnel in novels describing female scientists and their working conditions, connecting fictional observations to feminist critiques of science.

Gendered Stereotypes

Media stereotypes affect perceptions of women in science, influencing viewers' ideas about who should work in science and what constitutes science.[7] For centuries, media stereotypes have represented scientists as evil, greedy, mad, dangerous, and male.[8] Like the protagonists in Goethe's *Faust* and Mary Shelley's *Frankenstein*, many scientific characters act on ambitions to control nature.[9] Women scientists in popular fiction and film adhere to other media stereotypes, appearing glamorous and feminine, or quirky and androgynous. Sexual stereotypes present challenges for women scientists. In a toast at the 2015 World Conference of Science Journalists, Nobel laureate Sir Timothy Hunt commented that the problem with "girls in the lab" was that "you fall in love with them, they fall in love with you, and when you criticize them they cry."[10] His remarks went viral on social media, eliciting a barrage of photos of women scientists posing in their labs with goggles, lab coats, or technical equipment and captioned #Dis-

a Chinese father and a German mother. The chapter concludes with discussion of a nonfiction book and its film adaptation about Black women mathematicians who contributed to US space projects.[14]

Representing women scientists navigating barriers and biases, *The Signature of All Things* (2013) by Elizabeth Gilbert; *A Whistling Woman* (2002) by A. S. Byatt; *Brazzaville Beach* (1990) by William Boyd; *Carbon Dreams* (2001) by Susan Gaines; *Intuition* (2006) by Allegra Goodman; *State of Wonder* (2011) by Ann Patchett, and *The Tenth Muse* (2019) by Catherine Chung point out challenges for women in science and offer recommendations to improve their professional outcomes. Gender issues in these novels align with elements of Margot Lee Shetterly's history, *Hidden Figures: The American Dream and the Untold Story of the Black Women Who Helped Win the Space Race* (2016), and the film adapted from it, *Hidden Figures* (Dir. Theodore Melfi, 2016); both book and film detail strategies to reduce bias and discrimination. These texts cover a range of historical periods and scientific fields, referencing feminist critiques of science in describing "gender in the cultures of sciences" and "gender in the substance of science" and depicting women scientists who confront sexism and racism.[15]

Discovering Evolution

Gilbert's historical novel *The Signature of All Things* depicts Alma Whittaker, an unusual nineteenth-century American woman who was educated in math and science—first by her botanist mother, and then by tutors hired by her father. Her inherited wealth, unhappy romantic life, and excellent education encourage her devotion to scientific collection, observation, and analysis.[16] Like other accomplished women scientists who benefited from family connections, including Margaret Cavendish (taught by her brothers), Caroline Herschel (worked with her brother), and Maria Mitchell (educated by her father), Alma was fortunate to have a mother who nurtured her scientific endeavors. Like many "gentleman scientists" of the time, she did not worry about money or equipment. That scientists were usually gentlemen and not ladies in the nineteenth century owes to the professionalization of the sciences in the period. As Margaret Rossiter describes, women easily pursued scientific work until professional societies established standards of educational and scholarly credentials presenting barriers eliminating women "amateurs" from their ranks.[17] In the late nineteenth century, US women's colleges hired women like Maria Mitchell as faculty who could serve as role models and mentors for their students, but other professional positions for women in science were rare.

Despite enjoying privileges enabled by family wealth, Alma realizes that social conventions and family responsibilities owing to her gender limit her work. "The task of a naturalist, as Alma understood it, was to discover," but as a woman, she cannot travel on expeditions to make observations and discoveries like male naturalists of her time.[18] Instead, she turns to the study of mosses, which no one has paid much attention to, for she appreciates that the rocks around the family's estate contain "ancient, unexplored galaxies."[19] Twenty years of watching moss colonies grow and reading works by Charles Lyell and John Phillips enable Alma to develop a taxonomy of time—Human Time, Moss Time, Geological Time, and Divine Time. After her father dies, she finally breaks free of his estate and travels to Tahiti, where, inspired by the exotic landscape and her island experiences, she develops the "theory of competitive alteration," hypothesizing that "the struggle for existence—when played out over vast periods of time—did not merely *define* life on earth; it had *created* life on earth. It had certainly created the staggering variety of life on earth. Struggle was the mechanism."[20] *The Signature of All Things* rewrites the history of evolutionary biology, revealing how a talented woman scientist, despite being constrained by gender stereotypes and social conventions, managed to develop a theory, albeit unpublished, on par with Charles Darwin's theory of evolution by natural selection, published in *On the Origin of Species* (1859), and with Alfred Russel Wallace's similar theory.

Scholars documenting the accomplishments of exceptional women of science in the nineteenth and twentieth centuries describe their struggles to establish secure professional positions and relationships. They developed knowledge in relative isolation, based on careful observations and analyses, an approach also followed by Alma. Marie Curie enjoyed a successful collaboration and happy marriage with Pierre Curie, followed by his early death, her rejection by the French Academy, and her scandalous love affair with a married scientist.[21] Without Rosalind Franklin's knowledge, her colleague Maurice Wilkins shared her data and photographs with James Watson and Francis Crick, who identified the molecular structure of genes; but "fortune did her no favors," as Franklin's contributions to the discovery of DNA were not well known until after she died in 1958 at age thirty-seven of ovarian cancer.[22] Geneticist Barbara McClintock could not secure professorships as easily as her mid-twentieth-century male peers and spent the majority of her scientific career in a Cold Springs Harbor research lab doing limited collaborative work and much more solitary research on the mobility of genes. Temperamental characteristics encouraged McClintock's isolated work: she acknowledged her "capacity to be alone began in the cradle," and, similar to Alma, she "discovered, if one looked hard enough and carefully enough, a single organism would reveal its secrets."[23]

Alma travels late in life to visit her mother's family in Amsterdam, becoming curator of mosses at the city's botanical garden and furthering her ideas about evolution. She shares her writing with Alfred Russel Wallace during his visit to Amsterdam, and she is pleased that his response groups her with him and Charles Darwin—"This means there were three of us!" Yet she never publishes her manuscript because she believes it is not "scientifically incontrovertible"; she is "a perfectionist" who is "not going to be caught publishing a theory with a hole in it, even a small hole."[24] She feels her scientific "study of the world" made her "the most fortunate woman who ever lived" and does not regret lacking recognition.[25] Disadvantaged by nineteenth-century social conventions that discouraged women from participating in scientific circles and encouraged deference to male authorities, Alma possessed autonomy and time, circumstances that allowed her to monitor the undisturbed mosses on her large estate and to observe their evolution over years. Social constraints and lack of educational opportunities influence prospects for women in science, but Alma's unusual, albeit fictional, life offers an inspirational model for contemporary readers.

Obstacles could have prevented Alma from pursuing a scientific career, but she persisted by going around them to make a great discovery. Not able to make long voyages as Darwin and Wallace did, she investigated organisms and environments that were available to her. The novel's information explains how women held back by social conventions, legal restrictions, and sex discrimination can still propose new theories. Alma's discovery of evolution by natural selection owes to her individual and social circumstances: her talent and capacity for hard work, her luck in escaping a constrictive marriage and in gaining family wealth after surviving her parents, and her adventurous spirit. Imagining a nineteenth-century female scientist's success in navigating gender-based constraints, Gilbert's novel offers hope for the future in illustrating a spectacular example of a woman who was Darwin's peer. The novel considers that many talented women excel in science to make discoveries, that environments should transform to nurture their work, and that their work should be recognized.

Women's Liberation

A. S. Byatt's *A Whistling Woman* brings together more than fifty characters in entangled plots touching on university reforms, a religious cult, and television production to examine social and intellectual preoccupations of 1960s England, including feminism, psychology, and sociobiology.[26] One of several characters grappling with changing opportunities for women, Jacqueline Winwar is a biology student enthralled with studying Darwinian selection in snails: "She was beginning to recognize the inexorable force of her own curiosity, her desire to know the next thing, and then the next, and then the next."[27] Determined to continue research after graduation, she asks Professor Bowman to hire her to pursue postdoctoral study of snail neurons and the physiology of memory. Bowman asks while interviewing her for a job if she has a boyfriend; responding no, Jacqueline thought she "tried to see her sex—with some success—as a problem and an obstacle, to be solved and surmounted."[28] Bowman's negative attitude about women in science does not prevent him from hiring her in autumn 1968, and later propositioning her at a conference, which she expected. She has sex with him despite his backhanded "compliments": he tells her that she does not dress well, looks "*comfortable*," and doesn't say much. Jacqueline finds him "at once repellent and irresistible," after he calls her "a good girl," words that haunt her: "at twenty-nine she is hardly any longer a girl, was indeed a woman who was heading beyond the natural age for easy child-bearing."[29] She does not want to repeat going to bed with Bowman, but "he created in her a kind of angry hunger for sex," a desire propelling her into a misguided engagement with her colleague Luk.[30] After her miscarriage, Jacqueline ends the romance and tells Luk, "You must let me know what I want—and I do know. . . . There doesn't have to be a reason. As long as I know. And I know."[31]

At a university conference, Jacqueline realizes that Bowman has absorbed her research data in his presentation: she "sat there and heard her results described, and so to speak, claimed, without acknowledgement. It was her work—her months of trial and error, failure and triumph, smoothly taken over as part of the Lab's generally excellent performance."[32] Despite Bowman's taking credit, Jacqueline wants to remain in science.

Later Daniel, a local pastor and friend, informs her that their late mutual friend Ruth has "bequeathed" her baby to Jacqueline. Jacqueline responds she wants "to do what's right," but Daniel, who knows she is committed to science, reminds her that she doesn't want a child. She realizes that she wants to "go to Paris and work with French neuroscientists on the electricity and chemistry of memory" and that "she had also got to get away from Lyon Bowman. Who treated his lab like—like a harem."[33] Jacqueline will leave his lab to go to France and will not adopt the baby. Even if she pursues a relationship with Daniel, she will continue to work in science.

Scientific Ambition

The two topics—romance for scientists and recognition for scientific discoveries—are also addressed in *Brazzaville Beach*, in which author William Boyd tracks scientist Hope Dunbar Clearwater's graduate education, her problematic marriage in England, and her love affair in Africa.[34] Hope comes of age in 1960s Britain and does graduate work in botany before shifting to ethology. As a graduate student, Hope married mathematician John Clearwater, whose income allows her to enjoy a brief, happy "hiatus," during which she "read and shopped, visited friends and went to films in the afternoon" and "repainted their bedroom and looked vaguely for a larger flat."[35] Hope delayed applying for jobs even after receiving her doctorate: "She had published one article [in *Nature*] and done some reading, but little more."[36] Her faculty mentor incorporated her data in his symposium talk and presses her to accept a scientific position. Irritated with her marriage, she takes a job dating hedgerows in Dorset, but her husband remains in London, and their relationship becomes rockier. He struggles with mental illness, fails to achieve mathematical discoveries, engages in an affair, and commits suicide. Hope joins a team doing fieldwork on primates in Africa. Boyd's novel threads together Hope's reflections on her present-day life in a Congolese beach house with her recollections of her marriage to John and his decline into madness, her research on British hedgerows, and her study of chimpanzee behavior in war-torn West Africa.

In Africa, Hope works in the Grosso Arvore wildlife preserve, a research station run by famous primatologist Eugene Mallabar. A project latecomer and the only single woman on the team, she is treated as a third-class citizen, lodged in the least private tent, propositioned by male members of the research team, and treated coldly by their wives, who despite their educations and expertise are limited to secondary roles as assistants. She enters a casual love affair with Usman, an Egyptian pilot working as a mercenary. Her professional problems begin when her observations of chimpanzee behavior challenge Mallabar's ideas developed over twenty years of his research at Grosso Arvore.

Jeanne Altmann explained that women primatologists developed "New methods that encouraged the inclusion of formerly ignored research subjects—both females and low-status males."[37] Primatologists Thelma Rowell, Jane Goodall, and Altmann have been credited with "canceling out" the bias of their male counterparts by focusing on female primates: "But arguably their more profound contribution was to prompt a significant reorientation in both methods and understanding. Whereas previously the emphasis was primarily on theory, and observation was done mostly at a distance (from a jeep), the women entrants went to extraordinary lengths, virtually living amongst the apes or monkeys, to get to know and observe the individual animals at close quarters."[38] Sidelined by professional colleagues and daring to use unconventional means, women primatologists reduced the distance between animal subject and scientific investigator and were able to develop new understanding of species behavior.

Brazzaville Beach explores the gendered aspects of observation methods, describing how a woman scientist's marginal status on a scientific team enables new discoveries. Hope's in-the-wild observations resemble those of Rowell, Goodall, and Altman, while Mallabar's research depends on his observations of chimps in a man-made enclosure. He concentrates on securing funding, content to incorporate his team's field observations of chimp behavior in his books. In contrast, Hope does not let the discomforts of working in the bush interfere as she tracks the breakaway southern chimpanzees assigned to her; however, after northern chimps attack her group, she also begins to follow the movements of the northern patrol. She watches chimpanzees committing cruel, violent acts, including killing and cannibalism, and she realizes the two groups of chimps are fighting over a female chimp. Hope's careful observations of the chimps' personalities and their social dynamics inspire new information as she develops her theory of chimp infanticide and cannibalism.

Because Hope's theory of chimp violence could overturn decades of research from Grosso Arvore, Mallabar, who is completing another book about the chimpanzees' peaceful, cooperative behavior, initially refuses to believe her observations. He and his team are too invested in their ideas about chimp sociability; they fear losing funding and prestige and go so far as to manufacture evidence to convince Hope that predators have killed the chimps. Her tent, where her research notes are stored, mysteriously catches fire, but Hope's assistants have preserved copies of her notes. Realizing that her theory could make her famous, Hope secretly mails a paper with her data and analysis to a journal to ensure recognition: "*Hope was aware, from very early days, that there was every chance that it would be her name forever associated with this new knowledge and understanding.*"[39] She is concerned about the northern chimps' attacks on the southern group and wonders if researchers should intervene to end the violence between the two groups. She eventually convinces Mallabar to accompany her to observe the chimps' behavior for himself, but he is shocked by the violence he sees, becomes irrational, accuses her of damaging the chimps, and strikes her. To escape, Hope jumps into a vehicle driven by a colleague leaving on a supply run.

Hope and the other researcher are kidnapped by rebel fighters and held captive for some days before escaping during an attack on the rebels. Rescued after nine days, Hope learns that her lover Usman disappeared on a mission, and she inherits his gun. While she was absent from the project site, Mallabar suffered a nervous breakdown, and his colleagues revised his book manuscript to incorporate Hope's insights, although only mentioning her work in a footnote. She is banned from the research station and prevented from publishing her findings, including the article she sent for review, because she signed an employment contract giving publication rights to the Grosso Arvore project. She returns to the reserve to track down her southern chimps, arriving to observe their massacre by invading northerners and to see the southern alpha male Conrad dying a slow, painful death. She uses Usman's gun to kill Conrad and the marauding northern males, ending violence between the two groups.

Boyd comments in the paratext "About the Book," included as an appendix to a recent edition, that "Everything Hope does at the end of the novel is . . . the morally right thing to do. She is both human and humane. She carries out, with a clear conscience, a small act of redemption for our species."[40] Feminist philosopher Hilary Rose describes how science as a system depends on its relationship with "other forms of power: cultural, economic, and military."[41] Her manifesto for love applies to Hope's empathy for the chimps: "We see feminism bringing love to knowledge and power. It is love, as caring respect for both people and nature, that offers an ethic to reshape knowledge, and with it society."[42] The conclusion of *Brazzaville Beach* reflects on Hope's new life at the margins of science: she works as a driver ferrying supplies and researchers for the Grosso Arvore project while living in Usman's beach bungalow. Abandoning romantic love and professional recognition, she wonders if her lover survived the plane crash and meditates on what she calls "my indecision, my moral limbo."[43] Others take credit for her scientific research, and personal losses have left her isolated, but she remains philosophical. Readers understand that Hope acted with integrity and compassion and that she made an important discovery in primatology, even if Mallabar forbids her proper credit, illustrating that sexual discrimination and unrecognized achievements negatively affect the careers of fictional women scientists and impede science.

Dreaming Discoveries

Set in the early 1980s, Susan M. Gaines's *Carbon Dreams* describes a young geochemist studying climates of the distant geologic past, who is thrust into the growing controversy over contemporary global warming, while managing intimacies and developing a scientific reputation.[44] Tina Arenas is a postdoctoral researcher at the Brayton Institute of Oceanography (BIO) in northern California, where she occupies the lab of a senior researcher on sabbatical. *Carbon Dreams* exposes a creative, intuitive dimension of scientific process, revealing how Tina's dreams, speculations, and casual conversations merge with hard data and analysis to form her experimental designs and theories. She works long hours and has little social life. Her father is a widowed Mexican immigrant with high expectations; he is proud of her educational achievements, but he wants her to marry and have children. Her helpful, friendly mentor and role model is a famous, older male professor, her graduate adviser's adviser who works at a neighboring university and who collaborates with her. He offers steady scientific advice; however, he does not recognize social dimensions constraining women scientists.

Young women entered science in large numbers in the 1980s, but there are few women with PhDs on the BIO research staff, as Tina's friend Katharine, a doctoral student, mentions: "I wonder what [these old guys] think happens to all those students. . . . Are we supposed to fade away into domestic bliss with our PhDs? Spend six years of our lives as indentured servants subject to miscellaneous forms of psychological torture so that we'll make better wives and technicians?"[45] Tina's and Katharine's friendship exemplifies female camaraderie that helps women scientists navigate minority status, making up for a lack of role models. Katharine, who works for the only female full professor at BIO, the successful, famous Sylvia Orloff, recognizes her boss as a deeply flawed mentor who discourages young women: "She just believes that the way to prepare a young woman for a life in science is to work her to death, encourage cutthroat competition and tell anyone who isn't ten times better than the best of the men that she will never amount to a heap of beans. . . . Sylvia actually believes it herself, that there's no such thing as a good woman scientist, only a brilliant one. Just because that's how *she* made it."[46] Katharine's insightful explanations identify persistent academic barriers for women, including biases that diminish women's achievements.

Tina becomes involved with an environmentally conscious organic farmer who learns her research is misrepresented in a *New York Times* article about climate change. Chip convinces her she has responsibilities to get the science right and to clarify climate issues for the public. He supports her decision to terminate a pregnancy, but he hopes their future includes children. Tina finds the abortion physically and emotionally difficult; however, the next day she goes back to work with the only famous female scientist she knows. The childless Sylvia Orloff is furious after Katharine decides to marry and follow her husband to San Diego, where she has accepted a job in a government research lab. "Sylvia," Katharine explains, "sees herself as the creator of superwoman scientists—meaning tenure-track academic scientists publishing in *Nature* and *Science*. . . . It adds to her power, having us scattered throughout the country's finest research labs. . . . But now we're betraying her right and left."[47] Tina lands a coveted tenure-track position, which is more than many male peers do, because of her excellent analysis, hard work, and willingness to make personal sacrifices. Although Chip will not give up his farm to start over in an unfamiliar place, Tina accepts the East Coast job and ends their relationship. Ironically, her new position allows her to pursue the socially responsible climate change research that Chip encouraged. A male scientist could choose work in addition to romance. His female partner might not have a job, or she might have a more portable career than scientist, for "Being a scientist and a wife and mother is a burden in a society that expects women more often than men to put family ahead of career."[48] Only a feminist, flexible partner could change the formula; Tina could partner with a feminist who could build a life around her demanding scientific work.

Feminism and Scientific Ethics

Allegra Goodman's *Intuition* describes such a feminist man: Jacob Mendelssohn, a former child prodigy who is a postdoc when he encounters college freshman Marion, whom he recognizes will be a successful scientist: "When they were twenty he asked her to marry him. She was only a girl, but he believed she would make radical discoveries. This was why Jacob dedicated himself to Marion."[49] As the novel opens in the mid-1980s, Marion Mendelssohn directs a lab in a Massachusetts cancer research institute. She supervises technicians and postdocs, including Robin and Cliff who are romantically entangled, but Marion and the institute codirector, medical doctor Sandy Glass, fail to closely monitor their employees' work or provide necessary mentoring. After Cliff's R-7 tumor-reducing project shows promise and becomes the focus of the lab's work, Robin, the senior postdoc who has struggled for years on an impossible assigned project, expresses her resentment about having to work on "his" research, which she cannot replicate, and breaks up with Cliff. She investigates Cliff's data because they seem manufactured, informed by Jacob's remark that "The results seem almost too good to be true."[50] Two women scientists, Marion and Robin, begin as mentor and mentee, find themselves on opposite sides of the ethics complaint about Cliff's work, and appear in the novel's conclusion as two collegial scientists in dialogue about science.

Echoing experiences of historical and fictional women scientists, *Intuition* points to two ways sexism affects scientific practice: employment inequities and men's appropriation of women's results. Robin's adviser Uppington made her and other women students wait to graduate: "like younger daughters waiting to marry . . . because the whole lab was concentrating on pushing another [male] student out the door."[51] Robin's resentment of Cliff builds on the disparities between the Mendelssohn lab's treatment of him and of her: "He had come in as heir apparent to the lab. . . . He'd usurped Robin's position, beating her out for money, space, time, attention. From the first day he'd had special treatment, and it infuriated her that he would not acknowledge that."[52] Marion also suffered career disadvantages and lacks appropriate recognition (circumstances like those described by Margaret Rossiter in her account of the Matilda effect), including having her research discoveries scooped by a peer.[53] Harvard Professor Art "Ginsburg had stolen Marion's ideas in the past. Years ago, hearing of her metabolic work with mice, he'd pursued a similar line himself and then presented his results first at major conference, effectively stealing her thunder."[54] Marion's temperamental caution ensures the high quality of her science, but it delays her publications. Her overconfident partner, Glass, presses Marion to publish Cliff's data quickly, a mistake she comes to regret.

Intuition illustrates an intermingling of scientific, political, and social issues surrounding Robin's careful, persistent investigation of her ex-boyfriend Cliff's results and her complaint about his concealing certain R-7 data. Meeting with external scientists, Robin produces a graph of Cliff's published results, which "cluster beautifully," and one of his unpublished results, which "scatter."[55] Marion and Sandy disagree with Robin's conclusion about several torn-out pages she found stashed in the animal facility, putting her and her supervisors on opposite sides of a mediation and a subsequent congressional hearing examining practices at the Mendelssohn-Glass lab. Although Cliff and the lab are not sanctioned, Marion insists on withdrawing Cliff's paper from publication. The novel suggests that Cliff may have thrown out data that didn't fit his hypothesis: "He had sifted out what was significant, and the rest had floated off like chaff."[56] Others cannot replicate his results with R-7; tumors recur in mice treated with it. In addition, his sloppy record keeping and his eagerness to promote the effectiveness of the R-7 drug, which he twice administered to mice after Sandy and Marion told him to stop, throw doubt on his results. Although Robin is embarrassed that her discovery is of Cliff's cheating, she continues to dedicate herself to science and accepts what her new boss, Art Ginsburg, tells her: sometimes being right must be enough.

The novel ends with Marion's presentation at the annual cancer meeting in San Francisco. She notices Art Ginsburg and Robin sitting next to each other in the audience: "Ginsburg had deeper pockets than Marion, the more formidable reputation, the more aggressive approach. Still, he was not above competing with her."[57] Her talk is marred by "trouble with her transparencies," and her speaking too quietly and too fast. To Robin, Marion looks "fussy and nervous," but she has "new results on metastasis" that interest the audience: "She was not charismatic, but her ideas were. And when she launched her propositions, she was the archer, shooting arrows into the audience; each of her statements incisive, brilliant, and characteristically self-critical."[58] Pleased attendees want to ask questions or comment, Marion realizes she can remedy her previous neglect of Robin whose hand is up along with nine others: "What did she need? In that calm, clear, nearly joyous moment after her talk, the answer began to come to Marion. Ah, yes, of course, she thought with some surprise. And she called on Robin."[59] This conclusion redeems both Robin and Marion, illustrating that they navigate bias and discrimination to persist in science.

Robin overcomes disadvantages she faced because of her gender, and she continues her career after coping with neglectful mentors and a competitive, unsupportive boyfriend. At the conference she takes her place as a scientist in a public forum to discuss Marion's paper. Nanette, the female lab technician, had told Robin, "Don't you know women are always meanest to other women? Especially women scientists," but the narrative allows that Marion becomes a mentor.[60] Marion understands that she should help Robin, her former postdoc, advance. Exploring a case of academic misconduct, the novel argues that practices routinely available to men (having role models, supportive mentoring, and respect from peers) must also be available to women, as these are critical, necessary resources enabling scientists' satisfaction and career prospects. Identifying the importance of nurturing good science, whether performed by women or men, becomes the core lesson of Goodman's novel.

Overcoming Error

Thematically similar to Joseph Conrad's *Heart of Darkness* and focusing on a woman scientist thrust into a foreign adventure, Ann Patchett's *State of Wonder* follows Indian-American pharmacologist and medical doctor Marina Singh, whose boss and lover Mr. Fox, a CEO of a pharmaceutical company, sends her to the Amazon to investigate the Vogel company's project studying a plant-derived fertility drug.[61] Mr. Fox tells Marina that her colleague Anders Eckman died of an unknown illness during a journey he took to report on the uncommunicative Dr. Annick Swenson's project. Although Marina "succeeded in life because she so rarely declined any request that was made of her," she resists her boss's request that she undertake the same trip.[62] Her resistance stems from her experiencing in childhood hallucinatory effects from taking medication while traveling between her mother in Minnesota and her father in India. She is also reluctant to see Dr. Swenson, who supervised Marina's medical residency until she quit after a surgical error. Only after Anders's wife Karen pleads with Marina does she agree to look for her missing colleague.

Despite reacting poorly to an antimalarial drug, losing her luggage and cell phone, and being delayed and distracted in Manaus by the Bovenders, the couple living in the city apartment that Vogel rents for Dr. Swenson, Marina eventually makes her way from Minnesota to Dr. Swenson's research station in the Lakashi tribe's remote village. Swenson initially appears not to remember Marina, who is befriended by both Lakashi locals and the project scientists. Under Swenson's guidance, Marina amazes herself by delivering a baby by caesarean section in a tree house. Many Lakashi women are pregnant, including women over sixty, and the seventy-three-year-old Dr. Swenson reveals her own seven-month pregnancy. Lakashi women chew the bark of the local Martin trees to remain fertile. The scientists explain that this practice also protects against malaria: it is "the greatest discovery to be made in relation to the Lakashi tribe," one that Dr. Swenson insists on crediting to her deceased mentor Dr. Martin Rapp, who she claims "saw no limitations for women," for she regards her success as owing to his guidance.[63] Yet Rapp's combining summer research expeditions with his male college students with his love affair with Annick Swenson raises ethical questions for women on Swenson's research team. Nancy Saturn, "a young botanist with a degree in public health," who works on Swenson's project disapproves of Dr. Rapp's extramarital romance with his subordinate and thinks he "wasn't a good man" because of his philandering.[64]

Ethical dilemmas in the novel include the marginalization of women and nonwhite subjects and researchers. Marina doubts herself, particularly questioning her behavior during her long-ago residency: she operated then without Dr. Swenson's required approval, and the baby Marina delivered by caesarean section was blinded in one eye. Dr. Swenson requested that Marina operate on the Lakashi mother giving birth in the tree house even though "interference in the medical needs of an indigenous people suddenly struck Marina as the worst possible idea."[65] Dr. Swenson misrepresented the discoverers of the Martin trees and the Rapps in naming them for her mentor and lover Martin Rapp, and she kept a young boy from another tribe after he was sent to her for treatment. Other ethical issues concern Marina's keeping secret from her Vogel colleagues her intimate relationship with Mr. Fox and not revealing to him that Dr. Swenson's project aims to develop a vaccine against malaria rather than the fertility drug that Vogel funds. Although Marina has qualms about hiding information, she agrees to not to tell her employer because, as Dr. Swenson explains, it is the same drug: though women in the West will pay enormous sums for a fertility drug, a malaria vaccine is only useful in places where people cannot afford it.

The malaria vaccine research is conducted in an ethically questionable manner and does not allow the native population any voice in its operations. The scientists nurture mosquitoes that infect Lakashi men with malaria, supplying cola beverages as an incentive to the subjects and failing to warn the men of the disease's dangers. Dr. Alan Saturn, one of Dr. Rapp's "awestruck" male students, resents Marina's implied criticism of the vaccine study, telling her "Don't make this out to be the Tuskegee Institute," because it is likely the subjects already had malaria and the potential outcome of developing a vaccination to prevent the disease makes shortcuts worthwhile.[66] Claiming "it's good to get out of the American medical system from time to time. . . . It frees a person up, makes them think about what's possible," Alan tries to convince Marina to let the infected mosquitoes bite her to test the vaccine's efficacy; however, she refuses, expressing disapproval of his experiment.[67]

Directed by Barbara Bovender, Mr. Fox suddenly arrives at the Lakashi field site looking for Marina and wanting answers about the fertility drug. Dr. Swenson points to her own pregnancy as proof that the drug works; however, she conceals that the fetus is stillborn and avoids mentioning the drug also prevents malaria. Swenson convinces Marina to deliver the stillbirth and asks her to remain among the Lakashi as project director. Marina is honored but after she refuses the position, Mr. Fox orders her to stay because the fertility drug is effective. Hearing Barbara Bovender's vision of her long dead father during the trip from Manaus to the field site, Marina realizes that Barbara saw Anders, who was captured by a nearby bellicose tribe. Marina gathers bribes and takes off with Swenson's "adopted son" Easter to negotiate the release of her colleague. The tribe insists on taking Easter in trade for Anders, so Marina gives the boy back to his parents to save her colleague.[68] Anders returns with her to the Lakashi site and eventually to Minnesota.

Before Marina returns to Minnesota, she accomplishes many things, including performing obstetrical surgery. Dr. Swenson finally speaks of the error Marina made as a medical resident, relieving her guilt about blinding the baby: "You made a very common mistake that night at the General. You rushed, nothing more than that. . . . In retrospect the real loss was your quitting the program."[69] Recognizing that Dr. Swenson regretted not having children, Marina also experiences maternal instincts stimulated by her own relationship with Easter. If chewing the bark of Martin trees made her fertile, she might become pregnant. Marina understands Mr. Fox manipulated her to go to Brazil to protect the company, and after performing surgery, earning the respect of scientists and natives, and rescuing Anders, she is less submissive toward authority and more confident in her own abilities and judgment.

Hostile Environments

Catherine Chung's novel *The Tenth Muse* about a celebrated woman mathematician combines generic features of bildungsromans, historical novels, and narrative puzzles. The book addresses adoption and cultural difference, issues also highlighted in Lisa Ko's *The Leavers* (2017), a novel about a Chinese American boy whose mother was an undocumented immigrant unexpectedly deported from New York when her American-born son was eleven years old.[70] In Ko's book, Deming's mother disappears to serve time in prison before being sent back to China. Her son is adopted by a kind, but culturally insensitive, liberal, white couple; they never understand the difficulties Deming faces in figuring out who he is and what he should do. He always misses his mother and the family she created with a fellow undocumented immigrant, who also unexpectedly abandons him, and becomes unmoored and unsure of his identity. Ko's and Chung's novels identify how adoptees living among persons of different ethnicities in another country manage uncertainties to sort out their histories and identities.

In *The Tenth Muse*, Chung embeds layered testimonies about the Holocaust and information about mathematicians within a first-person coming-of-age account offered by Katherine, who acknowledges that she tells "a story like a woman: looping into myself, interrupting."[71] She describes her education, professional advancement, and growing understanding of her identity as an adoptee, detailing her attempts to find out who her biological parents were and setting biographical information within a context that recognizes disadvantages women face in the sciences. The many disappointments Katherine faces would make *The Tenth Muse* grim, except that she acknowledges in a flash-forward about a quarter of the way into her account that she succeeded in becoming a famous mathematician, noting that she "was asked to give a talk at MIT in 2005 after Lawrence Summers, then president of Harvard University, gave his infamous speech on the natural abilities (or lack thereof) of women in the sciences."[72] She shares that her talk described her "career and the history of women in math as well as the challenges facing women today," topics also dominating Chung's novel.[73]

Katherine's story begins with a description of her childhood relationship with her parents: a Chinese woman and an American man in an emotionally distant marriage. In 1957, the summer before Katherine enters tenth grade, her mother left the family, but her father resists explaining anything about the family's past until much later when he reveals that both he and her mother adopted her. Readers and Katherine learn about her birth with the unwrapping of each narrative layer. Her father provides a mysterious clue to her identity when he gives her a small brown notebook with the initials S.M. and with graphs, drawings, and writing in German; he describes the notebook as a souvenir from the war, and it is the first thing that Katherine owns. Both adoptive parents encouraged her interests in science and math. Her mother introduced exercises to improve Katherine's observation and concentration, while her father built a ham radio with her and taught her to communicate over her own network, but they worry that limited opportunities for women in science would constrain her educational and career choices. Nevertheless, Katherine persisted in studying math because she is gifted and hard-working, although these attributes seem not enough at times. While in college, Katherine experiences discrimination because of being a woman and being a minority. A close friend copies her work, but when the professor confronts both students, the young white man, who is the son of a famous mathematician, convinces their professor that Katherine copied *his* work. She is devastated that the professor accuses her of plagiarism and that he is unwilling to hear her explanation; however, she persists to graduate as a math major. That professor does not press a plagiarism charge, but he never apologizes even after Katherine succeeds in his class. Katherine ends her friendship with the cheater, her other professors realize her talents, and in her senior year of college she wins the Emmy Noether Award for publishing a paper.

The novel's embedded layers reach into the past: Katherine's account incorporates her father's history of how he came to adopt her and what she later finds out about the woman he brought home from the war. After Katherine enters graduate school with a prestigious scholarship for women, her stepmother reveals to her that the woman who raised Katherine was not her birth mother, prompting her reflection "Katherine ≠ Katherine."[74] Her ill father explains how he began caring for her and her adoptive Chinese mother in the aftermath of World War II. While hospitalized, Katherine's father describes how he came to adopt her as a baby at the end of the war when he was recovering in a military hospital. He shares the first-person account of Liliane, a nun caring for orphans, who explains that she accepted a baby given by a young couple, a Jewish woman and a Chinese man, to the nun's sister. The man who becomes Katherine's father visited the orphanage and accepts the baby as his responsibility. The general "gives" him a Chinese woman, Meiying, who is willing to emigrate, and the three become a family. Her adoptive father's account makes Katherine determined to find out more information about her birth parents.

As an adoptee and a minority woman in a traditionally white, masculine field, Katherine struggles, for she has more questions than answers about her identity, her heritage, and her future as a mathematician. Describing herself as "the only skirt in a sea of pants" in graduate school, she decides that she must excel.[75] Her role models are famous mathematicians, particularly women, including Hypatia, Emmy Noether, and Maria Mayer. Katherine develops close working relationships with peers and professors who help her advance her mathematics research, as she collaborates with physics students and with Peter Hall, a famous math professor who becomes her graduate supervisor and for a time her lover. She could choose love over work and partner in life and work with Peter, but then she would not be recognized in her own right. Maria Mayer herself explains to Katherine that there are some advantages to working in science without a professorial appointment, but Katherine considers that situation demeaning and gives up her romantic relationship to establish an independent career during a time when it is difficult for women to find employment in STEM. Katherine travels to Bonn, Germany, to pursue mathematical research and to solve the mystery of who her birth parents were by following clues in the brown notebook, helped by her first Asian American friend Henrietta, nicknamed Henry.

The two women travel to Gottingen, which was until World War II a famous center for mathematical research, where Katherine learns that her birth mother Sophie Meisenbach informally attended university math courses despite being prevented from enrolling because of her Jewish ethnicity, her gender, and her father's objections. Katherine meets Sophie's cousin Karl Meisenbach, who survived the war because he was not Jewish and chose not to protest the elimination of Jewish professors from the university. Karl benefited from the terminations and was appointed to a professorship. He offers details about Sophie—some true and some false—and photos of her family to Katherine, who lends him her notebook, but Karl is not trustworthy. He keeps the notebook and lies to Katherine about Sophie. Distressed after the notebook was stolen and confused about her heritage, Katherine returns to Gottingen to find an address connected to Sophie's lover Cao Xi Ling. A woman answering at the address explains that she gave her passport to the pregnant Sophie, so that she and Cao could run away in 1943; unfortunately, the young lovers' escape was not successful. Katherine understands that the brown notebook contains Sophie's mathematical discoveries, which match early published work of Karl Meisenbach. Karl rationalizes his submitting Sophie's work with Cao Xi Ling for publication under Karl's name as the only way it would be published. Katherine does not reveal Karl's academic misconduct because of her friendship with Henry, who marries Karl. After Karl's death decades later, Henry sends Katherine a box containing the brown notebook with Sophie's last letter to Karl, which describes Sophie's maternal love for the unborn Katherine. Her origin is no longer a mystery but part of the tragedy of the Holocaust.

Chung's novel describes a woman navigating difficulties in science, noting barriers blocking her advancement and that of her female relatives. Meiying, Katherine's adoptive mother, suffers discrimination and abuse during war. Katherine's Jewish birth mother, Sophie, was unable to work in mathematics in Nazi Germany. Katherine endured sexist jokes and comments and the mistaken assumption of colleagues that her male partner was solely responsible for their jointly published work. Katherine persists, explaining, "I am recognized now as one of the pioneers of dynamical systems and was one of the first to use it to solve problems in other fields like game theory and topology," and "These days I'm casually referred to quite often as 'a genius.' "[76] Sexism, stereotypes, and assault threaten women's achievements, but Katherine's talent, perseverance, and independence enable her professional success.

Feminist Science

Feminist studies of science include historical scholarship describing the lives of women scientists, sociological and anthropological analyses of scientific workplaces, and philosophical accounts of gendered dimensions of knowledge creation. Feminist scholars point to interrelated issues affecting women's progress in science: limited access to educational and professional opportunities; discriminatory practices in scientific settings; scientists' masculinist constructions of science, nature, and gender; and a discourse that identifies objectivity, rationality, power, and privilege as implicitly or explicitly masculine. Philosopher of science Sandra Harding notes that "Modern science has again been reconstructed by a set of interests and values—distinctively Western, bourgeois, and patriarchal."[77] Feminist critiques, including those in fictional form, recognize bias and barriers affecting woman's place in science and consider how gender matters to the outcomes of science. The seven novels discussed in this chapter describe attitudes and social conditions constraining women's careers, while speculating about masculinist bias in science. With conclusions noting women's career outcomes, these narratives, like that of *Hidden Figures*, offer hope by imagining a better future for women in science.

Fictional plots about women scientists navigating barriers and facilitators along professional pathways are set in different historical eras and reference concepts elucidated in feminist studies of science, describing cultural conventions and workplace conditions that present challenges. In *The Signature of All Things*, Alma's recognition is hampered during the nineteenth century, a period in which women did not generally engage in professional activity. *A Whistling Woman* describes Jacqueline's struggles to persist in science during the late 1960s, a time when more women began to enter male-dominated professions. Hope in *Brazzaville Beach* tries to follow the examples of male scientists striving to make celebrated discoveries, but she loses in competing with her employer. *Carbon Dreams* depicts Tina's day-to-day challenges impeding a career pathway while resisting attractions of marriage and family. Scientific fraud and women's disadvantages in science are intertwined themes in *Intuition*, which looks at how Marion's deference to her male senior collaborator and her temperamental caution constrain her research and limit her effectiveness as a mentor to her lab postdocs. *State of Wonder* notes physical and ethical challenges affecting science in an age of globalization, comparing the personal and career choices of women scientists (Annick, Marina, and Nancy) from different generations. Presenting Katherine as a talented mathematician navigating bias and barriers and discovering her heritage, *The Tenth Muse* regards the history of women in science as inspirational.

The cultural belief that women should limit themselves to marriage and children rather than look for professional success fluctuates and affects treatment of women who opt for scientific careers. In the 1960s, ideas about gender roles changed, and women in science could assert themselves. Social scientists Diane Bilimoria and Abigail Stewart use the term "relative isolation" to describe conditions for LGBT minorities in STEM academic departments, allowing that the term also fits women and persons of color: "This isolation has been commonly found for racial-ethnic minorities, and even for heterosexual white women, in science and engineering . . . suggesting that these environments are experienced as powerfully monolithic by people who are not straight white men."[78] Fictions detail environmental conditions in science, with some referencing women's ways of pursuing knowledge. Taken as a group, the seven novels illustrate women scientists' motivations and abilities to advance in science. Limited, bad, or selfish advice and mentoring affect protagonists as each would have benefited from more supportive counsel during her career. Some women suffer because of the gender stereotype that men's careers matter more than women's: Jacqueline and Hope have their work stolen by male employers, and Robin's career is delayed by her adviser and her postdoc supervisors. Dr. Swenson and the Lakashi favor Marina, who reveals her capacities to act ethically and heroically in dangerous circumstances, while the narrator of *The Tenth Muse* overcomes obstacles to embrace a career allowing her to develop important mathematical research.

Exploring women's scientific approaches, the novels reflect and refract cultural assumptions about their emotions and judgment affecting their progress in scientific research and point to career barriers that should be eliminated. Evelyn Keller, who earned her Harvard PhD in physics in the early sixties, called attention to the "deeply rooted popular mythology that casts objectivity, reason, and mind as male, and subjectivity, feeling, and nature as female. In this division of emotional and intellectual labor, women have been the guarantors and protectors of the personal, the emotional, the particular, whereas science—the province par excellence of the impersonal, the rational, and the general—has been the preserve of men."[79] This mythology argues that men's rationality predisposes them to be scientists, actively unveiling nature's truths, whereas women's emotionality and closeness to nature colors their observations and judgment. Tracing these ideas from the roots of modern Western science through contemporary developments in biology, Keller asks two questions: "How is it that the scientific mind can be *seen* at one and the same time as both male and disembodied? How is it that thinking 'objectively,' that is, thinking that is defined as self-detached, impersonal, and transcendent, is also understood as 'thinking like a man'?"[80] If scientific knowledge is objective, and we associate objectivity with masculinity, the only women who could be scientists would be those resisting feminine stereotypes. Feminine characteristics seem to disqualify women from being taken seriously as scientists: Bowman comments on Jacqueline's quiet manner, Mallabar paints Hope as hysterical when she reports chimp infanticide and violence, and Mr. Fox makes decisions for Marina because he thinks she overreacts.

The epistemological questions Keller and other feminist critics raise and respond to consider how scientific knowledge itself might be characterized as gendered. As W. Faulkner and E. A. Kerr ask, "If there were more women in science, would this in any way alter either the way science is practiced or the knowledge produced?"[81] That science practiced by women might turn out differently from that developed by men prompts some to consider the related notion that scientific analyses created by feminists might constitute "feminist science." Two novels considered here represent fictional women scientists who delve intuitively into their scientific practices and methods, suggesting that these female characters develop different approaches to studying nature. *Brazzaville Beach* and *Carbon Dreams* particularly exemplify Donna Haraway's argument that science is situated knowledge, developed by embodied individuals with cultural predispositions who act in particular ways according to contingent circumstances: "Feminism is about a critical vision consequent upon a critical positioning in unhomogenous gendered social space. . . . That is because feminist embodiment resists fixation and is insatiably curious about the webs of differential positioning. There is no single feminist standpoint because our maps require too many dimensions for that metaphor to ground our visions."[82] Tina's dreams blend with her careful data collection and rigorous analysis to produce ingenious results. Hope's chimp interactions and observations inspire her new theory about the species. Such "alternative methods are not directly related to sex or presumed womanly traits," although taking a different perspective informed by marginalization can reveal new information.[83]

In an ethnography comparing physicists in the US and Japan, Sharon Traweek concludes that the "heroic" challenges of working in the discipline of high-energy physics mean that in each culture "the virtues of success, whatever their content, are associated with men."[84] Novels reveal cultural ideals of masculinity pervading science, noting that fictional female scientists work in male-dominated environments. Scientific practice and discovery appear to be intellectual activities controlled by men with resources who compete to advance their own discoveries and to subsume women's work. Women work with and for men, who could nurture their subordinates or who could manipulate or harass them.

These fictions highlight gender-related advantages and disadvantages in material resources and point to how influences of colleagues, family, and friends affect outcomes for women scientists. Plots suggest that by eliminating sexist attitudes, discriminatory behavior, and disadvantageous conditions, women will be more successful in science. The narratives explore circumstances also analyzed in feminist critiques of science to explain how patriarchy, sexism, and bias pervade scientific practice. As information systems, the fictions reveal that male senior scientists take credit for women's research and that many women navigate professional requirements while being subjected to sexism (harassment, discrimination, bias, intimidation), disadvantages not affecting male scientists. Women's scientific practice, their scientific method, and their insights appear in these novels as associated with gender, although to describe the female scientist as exhibiting a "feminine" way of doing science would be mistaken. Women scientists engage in science in various ways: some acquire knowledge for its own sake and are less focused than their male peers on achieving extrinsic rewards, and some seek professional recognition of their achievements. Because women scientists have fewer resources and allies than their male counterparts, they resort to doing science differently: looking at a problem from a different angle, constructing scientific work to accommodate social conventions associated with gender, or pursuing individual interests along with creating new scientific knowledge.

Inspirational Scientists

Hewing closely to the archetype of a woman scientist whose gender sets her apart, fictional female scientists are members of an isolated, yet plucky breed. Delineating the circumstances of scientific work and the ideological biases that affect women's working conditions, the narratives represent women scientists who find the practice of science intellectually interesting, intrinsically rewarding, and socially relevant. They rebut stereotypical views of women as less able than men to perform scientific research, and, by offering a counternarrative of success, they contribute to debates about the underrepresentation of women in science. Personal testimonies of women who persist in science or who develop other career pathways provide positive images that complement and reinforce feminist studies of women in science and of their scientific theories and practices.

Uplifting narratives about women in science inspire young women and all who struggle to advance along scientific pathways; these texts also encourage others to support gender-equitable educational and work environments. *Hidden Figures* (2016) by Margot Lee Shetterly details the history of black women mathematicians working for the 1950s and 1960s US space agency, noting the social and workplace hurdles these women confronted in contributing their expertise to American success in the space race. Shetterly's prologue acknowledges, "The idea that black women had been recruited to work as mathematicians at the NASA installation in the South during the days of segregation defies our expectations and challenges much of what we know about American history."[85] A 2016 film directed by Theodore Melfi based on Shetterly's history represents the somewhat fictionalized experiences of three women at the NASA facility in the Langley Research Center in Hampton, Virginia: Katherine Goble Johnson, Dorothy Vaughan, and Mary Jackson.

In the film, each woman overcomes the double bind of sexism and racism to advance her career. Katherine's superb mathematical abilities enable her to calculate the trajectory of John Glenn's spacecraft. Despite the initial hostilities and doubts of her immediate supervisor and peers, she works around discriminations that force her to drink from a separate coffeepot, to use the distantly located restroom reserved for black women, and to remain focused on her work while enduring abusive, discriminatory comments. Katherine solves a problem bedeviling her white male colleagues by applying an old mathematical formula to determine the needed Project Mercury trajectory. The film depicts how the white male agency head eliminates the segregated restroom and coffeepot and illustrates how Katherine's research contributions are eventually recognized in publication by her previously dismissive white supervisor. Although told by a white woman supervisor to accept increased work responsibilities without benefit of a raise in salary or a promotion, Dorothy subversively teaches herself computer coding to manage the new IBM computer acquired by the space agency, becoming the first black female supervisor of the division. Mary's white, German immigrant supervisor encourages her to pursue further education to become an engineer although no engineering degree programs were open to black women. She overcomes her husband's anxieties about her ambitions and wins a court case to enroll in a degree program by casting a persuasive appeal to the judge. Graduating from the sex- and race-segregated educational program, Mary becomes a NASA engineer. The film documents the mutual mentoring and eventual success of the three women protagonists at the space center.

Hidden Figures was a popular cinematic success, although some critics were troubled by revisions of history, particularly the film's highlighting the white supervisor as eliminating discrimination and its introduction of entertaining elements. The cast, including Taraji P. Henson, Octavia Spencer, Janelle Monáe, Kevin Costner, and Jim Parsons, were awarded the Screen Actors Guild Award for Outstanding Performance by a Cast in a Motion Picture, and a number of individual actors received awards and nominations, including Spencer who was nominated for an Academy Award. Although the film diverged from historical facts, including fictionalized character and plot elements that digressed from the actual experiences of the women pioneers, the movie's appealing features include its happy ending, bouncy music, attractive period costuming and set design, and convincing performances. A. O. Scott's New York Times review acknowledged, "Like many movies about the overcoming of racism, it offers belated acknowledgment of bravery and talent and an overdue reckoning with the sins of the past."[86] In an Australian newspaper, Paul Byrnes more critically remarked, "The truth, as so often in movies 'based on a true story,' is richer and more subtle than the movie allows. . . . Almost every one of the fudges makes the film more entertaining and less truthful. Don't these women deserve better?"[87] The two-and-a-half-hour popular film argues convincingly for increasing the representation of women in STEM and developing a warmer climate to ensure their success, while Shetterly's book provides a more nuanced, detailed historical account of how women at the Langley Space Center overcame challenges, a narrative that credits their actions for bringing social progress in their professional fields during the civil rights era. Connected texts, the Hidden Figures book and the film DVD use the same image of the three film protagonists. The film's production company and individual actors hosted free screenings to promote it across communities. Variety reported: " 'As we celebrate Black History Month and look ahead to Women's History Month in March, this story of empowerment and perseverance is more relevant than ever,' said Liba Rubenstein, 21st Century Fox's senior vice president of Social Impact, 'We at 21CF were inspired by the grassroots movement to bring this film to audiences that wouldn't otherwise be able to see it—audiences that might include future innovators and barrier-breakers—and we wanted to support and extend that movement.'"[88] The free screenings to generate word of mouth increased the number of tickets sold, a form of politically aimed philanthropy informing audiences about racism, sexism, and the need for feminist collective action, messages from Shetterly's book.

Entertaining, inspirational fictions constitute information systems representing females whose discoveries benefit science and society. Women, and men, benefit from broad adoption of feminist principles promoting equal access to education and work and the elimination of sexist and racist stereotypes. Narrative representations of feminist scientists are optimistic about their achievements, pointing to an equitable future that respects scientific evidence and theories while eschewing stereotypes and bias in favor of policies that ensure inclusive excellence in science.

Chapter 5

Reproductive Independence and Collectivity

What we often call the curse in Genesis 3:16, "Your desire shall be for your husband, and he shall rule over you," is part of a broader description of the results of their rebellion on the man and woman's pre-Fall functions. For example, God had commanded them to "be fruitful and multiply." Now, after sin, Eve's part in that function would be by pain and labor (Genesis 3:16).

—"Ordination of Women and the Old Testament" (2010)[1]

We think it a cultural tragedy that women see motherhood as the primary source of status and self-esteem: the maternal imperative seems to us at work in the rise of self-defined infertility patients and in the increasing numbers of teenage mothers who, according to many accounts, feel they must have children to count in the world.

—Helena Michie and Naomi R. Cahn, *Confinements* (1997)[2]

For centuries, menstruation and pregnancy have been regarded as conditions diminishing women's participation in public life. The first epigraph presents an example of conservative biblical commentary regarding women's subordination that touches on a concept known as "Eve's curse" in describing her punishment after she and Adam sinned. Bearing children and caring for them are responsibilities traditionally associated with women, although feminist theories and practices have long sought to revise assumptions of domestic labor and to reconfigure arrangements concerning reproduction, caregiving, household tasks, and paid work, as the second epigraph acknowledges. Dolores Hayden's *The Grand Domestic Revolution* (1982) details a range of nineteenth- and twentieth-century American feminist proposals to improve household design, care of children, and other domestic responsibilities, but few structural reforms around housework and caregiving have been adopted or sustained. John D. Gibson points out "The ability of feminists to push successfully for reforms in employer childbearing and childrearing policies is a linchpin of feminism's vitality as a political movement."[3] Yet while progressive maternity and paternity policies prevail in some European countries, the US and the UK provide limited state support for parents and children.[4] Fictional works set in these countries and media accounts testifying to women's challenges during pregnancy and postpartum point to the need for progressive policies around reproduction to benefit women, their children and partners, and society.

Conveying information about pregnancy, childbirth, and child-rearing, the narratives discussed here elaborate ways that society should respect women's maternal rights and responsibilities. Modern fictional representations of pregnancy illustrate feminist values in privileging women's choices and their concern for children. Two novels—Margaret Drabble's *The Millstone* (1965) and Heather Swain's *Luscious Lemon* (2004)—depict first-person narrators' sexual experiences, pregnancies, and decisions about intimate relationships, while John Irving's *The Cider House Rules* (1985) argues for abortion rights. *Call the Midwife* (2012–2022), a television series based on a British midwife's memoirs, surveys responses to pregnancy and motherhood by considering diverse social, medical, and public health concerns. These fictions affirm pregnancy and motherhood as feminist activities, arguing that women should be able to make independent choices regarding reproduction and that women should be assured access to social and medical resources before, during, and after pregnancy. Aligning with Brit Bennett's 2016 novel *The Mothers*, news reports and scientific studies acknowledge racial disparities related to gynecological care and reproductive technologies. Increased rates of infant and maternal mortality for minorities in the UK and US, and the retrenchment of women's reproductive rights after the 2022 US Supreme Court decision *Dobbs v. Jackson Women's Health Organization*, which overturned *Roe v. Wade* and directed states to establish their own laws concerning abortion, present challenges.

Reproduction and Social Attitudes

The 2020 pandemic and subsequent COVID variants have increased stress on patients, providers, and health systems in an era witnessing rising costs for health care for countries with aging populations. During this period, women's reproductive health concerns have not been prioritized by medical caregivers. Pregnancy and childbirth still incur medical and psychological dangers for women, despite technological improvements in contraception and childbirth and the development of at-home pregnancy tests enabling women to confirm pregnancies. Andrea Tone's history of contraception tracks the manufacture and use of these technologies in America, documenting individual and social concerns regarding controlling reproduction.[5] In a 1995 study of the ways thirty-one New England women managed their pregnancies, Robin Gregg acknowledged that "Pregnancy has increasingly become redefined as a process requiring medical and technological intervention, even before a woman becomes pregnant."[6] Yet accessible contraception and technologies tracking fetal health may not enable an anxiety-free pregnancy and delivery. In earlier centuries, poor hygiene during childbirth meant that women risked developing infections, including puerperal fever, which "affected women within the first three days after childbirth and progressed rapidly, causing acute symptoms of severe abdominal pain, fever and debility."[7] Today, many women, even those in countries with advanced medical systems, suffer postpartum complications, including bleeding, infections, abscess or peritonitis, or psychological disorders.[8]

Attitudes about reproduction fluctuate over time and are entangled with ideologies of sex/gender roles. A number of 1960s films focus on consequences for men and women who engage in extramarital sex, describing how open sexual attitudes and freewheeling experiences diminish their individual socioeconomic prospects. Based on Shelagh Delaney's 1958 play, the film A Taste of Honey (1961) presents working-class, school dropout Jo, who is abandoned first by her alcoholic mother and then by a sailor (Jimmy) with whom she has her first romantic, sexual relationship.[9] Geoffrey, a young gay man, befriends the pregnant Jo, and they set up housekeeping together, settling in a slum flat in congenial, asexual fashion, two marginalized people supporting each other until Jo's mother barges back into her life and evicts Geoffrey. A Taste of Honey concludes on a melancholy note as Jo's close friendship with Geoffrey ends, leaving her with a difficult mother, a new baby, and a rather dismal future. In 1960s

England, men had more professional opportunities and greater latitude in social relations than women, but they also experienced negative consequences of sexual pursuits. Male swinger Alfie engages in extramarital affairs without thought of consequences for him or his partners or their families in the 1966 film bearing his name.[10] He resists marrying Gilda after she becomes pregnant; she decides to marry another man who becomes the father of her son. Alfie's callousness leaves his sexual partners emotionally hurt and mentally anxious, and the end of the film shows him as isolated, without a supportive intimate partner, family, or close friend.

Embracing Motherhood

Two novels depict feminist narrators who feel empowered by their pregnancies, while managing medical and social complications. In Margaret Drabble's *The Millstone* (1965), Rosamund Stacey relies on generous, liberal parents to aid her after she has one sexual encounter resulting in pregnancy. The novel depicts her as she advances from pregnant dissertating graduate student to single mother with a healthy baby, a doctorate, publications, and a university faculty position. The opening of Heather Swain's *Luscious Lemon* (2004) finds the protagonist Ellie (Lemon) Manelli, a young chef and restaurant owner, madly in love with food and her boyfriend. An orphan who was raised by a practical grandmother and intrusive aunts, Ellie faces challenges as pregnancy tests her mental and physical states, her intimate relationships, and her professional career as a chef. Twenty-something Rosamund and Ellie transition from uncertainty and insecurity to adulthood, managing medical circumstances and social attitudes. These women attain stability and maturity in adjusting to unpredictable aspects of pregnancy and child-raising, learning to understand and express their needs as they accept reproductive responsibilities.

Taking advantage of a novel's capacity to reveal consciousness in an immersive form, *The Millstone* focuses on first-person narrator Rosamund Stacey, the Cambridge-educated daughter of parents who are liberal socialists and generous in allowing their daughter to live rent-free in their London apartment while they are abroad. Rosamund spends her days preparing her doctoral dissertation on sixteenth-century poetry and engaging in a limited social life, consisting of her drinking with literary acquaintances and casually dating unsuitable young men. A male companion introduces her to George, a handsome BBC radio announcer. They tumble into bed, and for the first (and perhaps the only) time in her life Rosamund has sex. After she realizes she is pregnant, she fails to induce an abortion by drinking gin and taking a hot bath; however, she decides to remain pregnant, keep the baby, and not reveal the father's name even to him.

The novel explores Rosamund's thoughts about childbirth and motherhood along with describing her prenatal care, interactions with doctors and other caregivers in the National Health Service, and plans for childcare. She does not like to confront people or take advantage of them, which means that in any negotiation she gives more than she gets, but she becomes assertive in her role as a mother. After she discovers that her roommate and part-time sitter Lydia's unpublished novel describes an unmarried pregnant woman resembling her, Rosamund is "both annoyed and upset . . . by the thought that Lydia had been living in my house for nothing and writing all this about me without saying a word."[11] But she never complains to Lydia about being the subject of her novel, perhaps because its mediocre reception appears just recompense for its author's deception.

Rosamund's circumstances—generous parents, steady academic advancement, and cautious, private personality—undergird her choices about childbirth and parenting. A feminist socialist like her mother, Rosamund is independent, cognizant of her privilege in being well educated, so she avoids acting in ways that could be perceived as aggressive. Her "career has always been marked by a strange mixture of confidence and cowardice," but motherhood encourages her to stand up to authority.[12] Pregnancy and childbirth proceed smoothly, and Rosamund is happy after the birth, perhaps the happiest she has ever been: "my stay in the hospital was one of the more cheerful and sociable patches of my life," and she learns that as a mother she must mature to prioritize her daughter's needs.[13] Nancy Hardin remarks, "As a result of Rosamund's commitment to her pregnancy and subsequently to Octavia, she achieves a true synthesis both within herself and with the outside world."[14] Although the novel's title hints that Octavia might be a burden for Rosamund, she is anxious only when the baby is ill and requires medical attention.

Rosamund worries after Octavia's heart surgery that her infant is alone in the hospital. Despite disliking confrontation, she screams so loudly after being barred from Octavia's room that she is one of the rare parents allowed to be with her sick baby: "It was no longer a question of what I wanted, this time there was someone else involved."[15] Visiting her daughter in hospital, Rosamund converses with the mother of another young patient; the women exchange information about gaining hospital visiting privileges, and Rosamund feels comfortable enough to ask this stranger how she bears her daughter's illness. The woman explains that she doesn't bear it and that she used "to pretend not to mind . . . and laugh it off with my friends" until she "got tired of pretending it was nothing just to save other people's feelings," remarking "Now I don't care who sees I care."[16] Rosamund asks if the other mother is concerned about all sick children, but she responds that she has stopped worrying about others' children because her limited energy and attention mean that she can only concentrate on taking care of her own children. Rosamund similarly commits to Octavia instead of assuaging her liberal guilt and prioritizing others' needs as more important or by politely accommodating herself to official protocols that interfere with her relationship with her child.

Before becoming a mother, Rosamund resisted asking others for help. She allows Lydia to share her apartment because this arrangement offers the benefit of an occasional babysitter. But emergency assistance is also needed; one night while Lydia is out, Rosamund must pick up a prescription for her sleeping baby, so she calls on neighbors to look out for Octavia. In a flash-forward we learn that they were happy to help in this way. Although she recognizes that it would be nice to have a partner help with her tax return, Rosamund so thoroughly falls in love with her baby that she does not miss romantic intimacy. Meeting George accidentally, she invites him into her apartment and lets him see Octavia sleeping: "compared with the perplexed fitful illuminations of George, Octavia shone there with a faint, constant and pearly brightness quite strong enough to eclipse any more garish future blaze. A bad investment, I knew, this affection and one that would leave me in the dark and the cold in years to come; but then what warmer passion ever lasted longer than six months?"[17] Rosamund's love for Octavia protects them from others' demands. George and Rosamund may stay in touch, but the novel resists a conclusion that brings the couple together or even one indicating she will tell him that Octavia is his child.

Rosamund need not marry or acknowledge her child's father. She finished her PhD, published her thesis, and earned a faculty appointment, circumstances that shield her and her baby from discrimination due to illegitimacy. Her parents hear from the surgeon about Octavia's birth and surgery, and they write her to explain they will extend their time abroad, allowing their daughter and granddaughter to continue living in their apartment. An independent, confident scholar, Rosamund appreciates her parents' generosity. She found it difficult to "ask for love or friendship" before experiencing childbirth; however, becoming a mother enables this feminist to negotiate with others and "to ask for help, and from strangers too."[18] Drabble shows motherhood as benefiting Rosamund, who accepts its responsibilities as enhancing her emotional life while recognizing that there is support if she asks for it.

Feminism, Technology, and Reproduction

In *Feminism Confronts Technology* Judy Wajcman claims that "Nowhere is the relationship between gender and technology more vigorously contested than in the sphere of human biological reproduction," noticing that while technology is frequently identified as masculine, "Women are the bearers, and in most societies the primary nurturers of children."[19] Wajcman understands social views shape and are shaped by reproductive technologies such as contraception, in vitro fertilization, ultrasound, and fetal heart monitoring, but she resists technological determinism: "Although women are the prime targets of medical experimentation, reproductive technology cannot be analyzed in terms of a patriarchal conspiracy. Instead a complex web of interests has been woven here—those of professional and capitalist interests overlaid with gender."[20] Recognizing this "complex web of interests" enables us to better understand, as Rosalind Petchesky argues, "the pregnant woman, not as an abstraction, but within her total framework of relationships, economic and health needs, and desires."[21] Bettyann Kevles describes the history of ultrasound technologies and their reception by physicians and patients to explain how the women's liberation movement encouraged each pregnant woman "to take back control over pregnancy" by undergoing ultrasounds revealing the status of her fetus.[22] More critically, Kevles points out that technology encourages physicians to concentrate on the fetus instead of the mother. Technologies such as fetal heart monitoring shape experiences of pregnancy and childbirth by focusing attention on the fetus or images of it, contributing to constructions of fetal personhood.[23]

Acknowledging feminist concerns regarding the medicalization of childbirth, Heather Swain's novel *Luscious Lemon* captures empowering and constraining aspects of reproduction and technologies. Swain's novel focuses on Ellie Manelli aka Lemon, who experiences an unplanned pregnancy that after twelve weeks ends in an unexpected miscarriage. *Luscious Lemon* explores her and her boyfriend's reactions to parenthood and notices their engagement with reproductive technologies, including contraception, pregnancy tests, ultrasound imaging, and fetal heart monitoring. Technological management of mother and fetus and the unpredictable outcomes of pregnancy constitute two thematic threads in the novel, as the protagonist (Lemon) and her boyfriend (Eddie) learn that technologies supply limited information about reproduction. Lemon forgets to take her birth control pills because she is stressed from the hectic pace of work at her restaurant, and she later tracks her pregnancy via successive ultrasounds. The issues of who is in control of the pregnancy and what information technologies supply loom large in Lemon's first-person narrative describing her evolving relationship with her family.

Swain's fiction incorporates details from the author's miscarriage, first revealed in a 2003 *Salon* essay, which began as a response to her husband's suggestion that writing about loss would allow Swain to cope with it. Yet she initially resists managing her grief in the following way:

> How could I ever do that, I wondered? How could I write about my miscarriage when I wanted the story of my daughter to remain interred? Wrapped in the gauzy fabric of my sadness. Enclosed in the intricate carvings of my womb. But my husband was right. The emotional devastation and physical pain of miscarriage stays hidden too often. No one ever talks about it, least of all the pregnancy books women consult.
>
> So I grappled with my grief. Gestated it until I could smooth it black and white across the page, a story with a beginning, middle and end. I exposed myself in graphic detail in order to create this eulogy for my daughter. To give her the final and proper burial that she never received.[24]

Swain's essay becomes a starting point for her novel about a pregnancy ending as hers did. Both essay and novel are mechanisms devised to cope with the author's grief while also offering solace to others. One in four pregnancies end in miscarriage, and many women experience at least one, but until the 1990s miscarriage was rarely discussed in print or conversation.

Linking two perspectives, *Luscious Lemon* experiments with narrative elements to describe the protagonist's pregnancy as a form of "transformative motherhood," to borrow Linda Layne's phrase.[25] Lemon's narrative focuses on present-day action and mentions related past events. The other narrative addresses the fetus and comes from an unnamed, omniscient narrator who shares information about conception and tracks the physiological development of the fetus. Lemon's first-person account and the chronologically organized fetal narrative combine to explain what anticipating a child signifies for her. Orphaned at age six after her parents die in a train accident, Lemon was raised by her maternal grandmother and supervised by aunts. The maternal matrix connects Lemon and her fetus to the rest of the Calabria clan, whose vast experience with pregnancy and childbirth supplement information revealed by an over-the-counter pregnancy test, ultrasound tests, and a pragmatic obstetrician-gynecologist. The novel tracks the course of Lemon's pregnancy, her miscarriage, and her emotional recuperation from it, allowing her to share intimate details about her parents' deaths and her vulnerabilities. The conjoined narratives of Luscious Lemon chart the protagonist's development over time, combining present-day scenes with flashbacks to Lemon's past experiences, and the short history of her fetus's development and demise.

Lemon's first-person account moves from sexual encounter to mature acceptance, along the way describing her childhood, work, love of food, family genealogy, and love life, while the second-person account by an omniscient narrator speaking to the embryo describes the transformation from zygote into a fetus. Lemon's narrative is frank but unreliable, for her discussion of her sexual past and of her resistance to family authority and involvement proceeds by indirection. Punctuating her testimony are the titled (rather than numbered) poetic, scientifically informed passages describing the pregnancy's progression from conception through miscarriage. In these titled sections the omniscient narrator addresses the embryo in Lemon's uterus as "you," asking questions and revealing information about its kin and history. Passages about the fetus provide information about its biological development and genealogical information about its forebears, increasing our understanding of Lemon.

Pregnancy presents a new stage of maturation for Lemon, an orphan who has long struggled to understand why her musician parents worked on the road and left Lemon behind with her maternal grandmother. The slowly revealed circumstances of her parents' deaths, her vulnerabilities, and her fears about the future increase reader sympathy for Lemon, who in the first chapter appears to be assured—a cynical, hip, Italian American New Yorker who resists settling down to marry and have a family and who keeps her extended, intrusive family at a distance. Lemon's narrative initially prefers to focus on her new, popular restaurant and her satisfaction with her coworkers, who are like a second family to her. Direct statements made by the narrator to the fetus reference its mother (Lemon) and grandmother (Lemon's deceased mother) and point to Lemon's mixed emotions about this pregnancy, heightening her description of her mother's difficult choices concerning motherhood and work. Her capacity to decide what is good for herself, the baby she expects, and Eddie improves through the narrative as she manages crises and disappointments.

Luscious Lemon's first pages celebrate how she and Eddie mark the first anniversary of her restaurant by making love on the rooftop, an act she describes in referencing cooking, her past, and her family: "Tonight is my night, and I could devour the world. Catch it by the heels . . . Skin it, fillet it, sauté it. Serve it on a platter with bitter wild leeks and potentially poisonous mushrooms shaped like flying saucers. Surround it with delicacies of the rivers and the sea. (Gifts from my long-dead mother). Exotics from my larder . . . An eclectic stew of me."[26] But the last line of the first chapter foretells difficulties: "Watch out, I warn, as I roar with delight. Nothing can stop me now."[27] Lemon's exultation about being on top of the world forecasts a prospective fall from success and the beginning of a phase with new challenges and tribulations. "Egg and Sperm," the separate titled passage following the first numbered chapter, provides an inside look at what is happening in Lemon's body while she and Eddie have sex: "Both [egg and sperm] hurl through space and time until one of those brave swimmers unites its chromosomes with that spaceship egg."[28] The egg is fertilized, an event noted by the omniscient narrator's statement to it: "And suddenly, there you are."[29] Thus, conception is established for readers before Lemon and Eddie know about the pregnancy, a biological process that is out of their control despite their efforts to manage and understand it.

Although imaging technologies focus on the fetus, feminist framing of pregnancy and childbirth resists recognizing the fetus as a floating, detached object privileged above the mother. Instead, feminist scholars consider convergent interests of mother and fetus. In an essay about fetal personhood and popular culture, Lauren Berlant argues, "The pregnant woman and the fetus thus register changes in the social meanings of gender and maternity."[30] She planned her essay to "be about the reinvention of American personhood from the point of fetal inner space," mentioning narratives representing fetal voices speaking to viewers.[31] *Luscious*

Lemon similarly connects a narrative of "fetal inner space" provided by the uncharacterized narrator who speaks about Lemon's pregnancy in the titled passages while Lemon's first-person account of family and friends who constitute "the web of interests" surrounding the pregnancy appears in the numbered chapters.[32]

Swain follows the description of fetal conception with intimate revelations about Lemon, who details her history gradually in her present-day commentary, revealing and refining details about her experiences and emotions. The narrator tells us that at eight weeks the fetus is about "an inch. Your mother's thumb tip," addressing "her" to explain that this pregnancy will allow Lemon to recuperate from her mother's death: "she likes the idea of a daughter. Someone to replace the missing link of her life of long-ago abandonment. But what she does not yet understand is, although you are inside her, although she is giving you life, although without her you are literally nothing, already you are your own person, and her life will be endless variations of letting you go."[33] Connecting pregnancy and death links Lemon's feelings about her fetus and her mother; in this way, *Luscious Lemon* captures the physical and emotional complexities many pregnant women experience in bonding with their future offspring.

Feminist sociologist Barbara Katz Rothman decries tendencies of parents to consider the fetus as a commodity, while Robin Gregg points out that under the medical model pregnancy has two patients: mother and fetus.[34] Gregg's informants understand their pregnancies as "embedded in a number of contexts: their other pregnancies, other aspects and circumstances of their lives, and the larger social, cultural, and political environment."[35] They recognize benefits of technologies such as chorionic villi sampling and amniocentesis to determine abnormalities, responding in ways that align with information supplied by the genetic counselors interviewed by Rothman.

Even as medical treatment received by mothers and newborns has in many ways improved with the incorporation of amniocentesis, ultrasound, in vitro fertilization, and drug therapy for premature infants, technologies intrude on pregnancy and childbirth. Swain's novel speaks to the ambivalence of patients and doctors regarding technical mechanisms. During Lemon's first prenatal visit, Dr. Shin asks the couple about whether they would prefer natural childbirth, hearing that Eddie does prefer it while Lemon doesn't. The doctor advises Lemon and Eddie to stay away from the hospital until Lemon is ready to deliver: " 'I'll tell you the best thing. You go into labor, you open a bottle of wine and start drinking,' " says Dr.

Shin. . . . " 'Save up your energy. Childbirth's hard work. So stay home. Have a nice time together. Wait until you're eight centimeters dilated. Then you call me, and we meet.' "[36] Lemon is unimpressed by the image of the fetus on the ultrasound screen ("It seems so small and ordinary") until Dr. Shin points out the heartbeat.[37] Seeing "a tiny pulsating light . . . at the center of the blob," Lemon and Eddie gasp with delight and recognize "an itty-bitty foot . . . beneath the curved body.[38] Rosalind Petchesky notices that "women . . . see in fetal images what they are told they ought to see" and that "the meanings of fetal images . . . differ depending on whether a woman wishes to be pregnant or not."[39] Swain constructs the ultrasound scene as a demonstration of how Dr. Shin's expertise and the ultrasound image frame what Lemon and Eddie see.

But what does one see at the end of a pregnancy that does not result in childbirth? In the novel's section titled "Ten Weeks" the narrator signals the fragility of the fetus by informing readers that it looks "vaguely human now. . . . You move, jerky involuntary motions with your limbs. Or, are you really waving to your mother? . . . You are a girl, as your mother has suspected . . . Your mother is bookended by the two of you. Mother, daughter. She is forever both now." This final sentence of "Ten Weeks" connects Lemon's deceased mother to the fetus, hinting that it will not survive. Midway through the novel, Lemon begins to bleed. Because an ultrasound does not reveal any anomalies, Dr. Shin sends Lemon home, telling her patient to rest and not worry. Lemon falls asleep, wakes up in the night with a cramp, dreams that the "egg begins to rumble, shimmy, shake, vibrate beneath me," feels no second heartbeat, and remembers the day she learned her parents died in a train wreck in New Jersey.[40] In a delirium Lemon sees her dead mother and calls out for her grandmother. She manages to get to the bathroom, where she feels the fetus "slip inside" of her and "fall" in "some kind of clot."[41] She calls Eddie, who is on a business trip in Italy, but she can only leave a voice mail message. Next Lemon calls Dr. Shin, who tells the hysterical Lemon, "If you are going to lose it, it's because it's no good. It means something is wrong with the fetus."[42] Eddie alerts Lemon's aunts who rush over to clean up her apartment and guide her to her grandmother's house, where she recuperates.

The aunts try to console Lemon, but their words offend her. Lemon prepared herself for a healthy pregnancy and feels cheated by the miscarriage. Dr. Shin and the aunts understand that many pregnancies do not result in healthy births. Because miscarriage remains unacknowledged in our culture except as a failed pregnancy, Lemon is unprepared for any outcome other than a healthy baby. As an orphan, she bets that she has already seen her share of trouble, but Dr. Shin knows that the miscarriage cannot be prevented, however one might wish that. Barbara Katz Rothman contrasts the medical management that terminates a troubled pregnancy with care practiced by Dutch midwives who "asked a question that simply makes no sense in the medical understanding of pregnancy. If the baby is going to die anyway, the midwives asked, 'Why spoil the pregnancy?'"[43] This outlook understands "that pregnancy itself has a meaning and a value in a woman's life, and that for women who want to become mothers, a good pregnancy and a good birth are good things to have."[44] Missing out on a good birth, Lemon learns to accept and share her pregnancy loss with others.

At first she feels guilty and angry that Eddie seems to blame her for the miscarriage, but improved communication between them becomes critical to Lemon's grieving process. Just as significant are Lemon's conversations with her grandmother, Eddie's mother, and Makiko, the pastry chef from her restaurant, who soothe her feelings in different ways. Her grandmother patiently lets Lemon visit every day and not talk about this painful experience. Eddie's mother calls and allows Lemon to talk without having to express any guilt. Makiko brings back a water baby (*mizuko jizo*) from Japan for Lemon, explaining: "We think that when a baby dies, it's too young to have a soul and so it gets stranded on the banks of the river that separates life and death. So we have these statues to remember the babies and to try to make them feel better."[45] In Japan, Makiko visited her mother and her water baby that she had placed for the fetus she lost to an abortion when she was in her teens. Learning to accept that others also suffer, Lemon matures by acknowledging that her miscarriage is like Makiko's abortion because both experiences confirm that "sorrow is a part of life."[46] Swain's novel describes overlapping connections of food and family that enable Lemon to process her grief about the miscarriage. Formative cooking experiences enabled Lemon to grieve for her dead parents while bonding with her grandmother and her great-aunt Poppy. While recuperating from her miscarriage at her grandmother's, Lemon realizes that the menu at her Manhattan restaurant was unnecessarily fussy and complicated, and she begins to envision how she might start a new Brooklyn restaurant based on her great-aunt Poppy's simple recipes. Grieving the loss of her fetus allows Lemon time to cope with her loss and to undertake new projects when she is ready.

At the end of *Luscious Lemon*, Lemon and Eddie bring the *mizuko jizo* to rest in her grandmother's backyard, where she retreated the day of her parents' funeral. The two narratives become one as Lemon memorializes the miscarriage in a ritual of placing the *mizuko jizo* to connect family and friends with the unborn. *Luscious Lemon* acknowledges that women should carefully utilize reproductive technologies, illustrating that while tests, scans, and other technologies provide data, this information should be supplemented with a woman's knowledge of her own body, appropriate cultural rituals, and the support of her partner, family, and friends. Linda Layne analyzes how miscarriage often enables "transformative motherhood," a way of redeeming pregnancy loss by recognizing the unborn child as a "gift" to parents who achieve greater understanding and appreciation for life in memorializing their loss.[47] Swain's novel connects miscarriage to abortion, allowing Lemon and Makiko to mourn without guilt. Demonstrating that pregnancy requires community support, *Luscious Lemon* relies on Lemon's first-person narration and the omniscient narrator's fetal discourse to explore miscarriage as a convergence of birth, maternity, and death.

The Lord's Work and the Devil's Work

The Millstone and *Luscious Lemon* acknowledge how medical institutions and technologies manage women's health, while asserting that women require medical care that thoughtfully engages with technologies. John Irving's novel *The Cider House Rules* describes the career of Dr. Wilbur Larch, an obstetrician battling his gonorrhea and addiction to ether while he helps women. In the early twentieth century, when he trained in the South End of Boston, Dr. Larch observed where pregnant women receive abortions and was appalled by an abortionist's lack of knowledge and the unsanitary, deadly conditions of the surgery. He realizes that women and girls needing abortions come from all classes: some are prostitutes impregnated by clients, while others are raped by relatives or abandoned by lovers; however, any woman may need and seek an abortion to survive. Dr. Larch sympathizes with them, and he aims to protect their rights to elect abortions after reading Mrs. W. H. Maxwell's *A Female Physician to the Ladies of the United States* (1860): "The authoress . . . believes that in view of the uncharitableness of general society towards the erring, it is fit that the unfortunate should have some sanctuary to which to flee, in whose shade they may have undisturbed opportunity to reflect, and hiding forever their present unhappiness, nerve themselves to be wiser in the future. The true physician's soul cannot be too broad and gentle."[48]

Young Dr. Larch is invited to a rich family's home, where instead of being treated as a guest he is asked to undertake an abortion on a young pregnant girl. After completing the surgery, the doctor finds a bulky envelope filled with cash, which he takes great pains to disperse to the servants in the household because he resents that the family hosted him to perform the termination. Dr. Larch realizes that changing attitudes toward the procedure have increased difficulties for women seeking to end pregnancies.

> [He] reflected on the last century of medical history—when abortion was legal, when many more complex procedures than simple abortion were routinely taught to medical students: such things as utero decapitation and fetal pulverization (these in lieu of the more dangerous Caesarean section). He mumbled those words to himself: utero decapitation, fetal pulverization. By the time he got back to Portland, he had worked the matter out. He was an obstetrician: he delivered babies to the world. His colleagues called this "the Lord's work." And he was an abortionist: he delivered mothers too. His colleagues called this "the Devil's work," but it was *all* the Lord's work to Wilbur Larch. As Mrs. Maxwell had observed: "The true physician's soul cannot be too broad and gentle."[49]

To do this work, Dr. Larch becomes head of the remote St. Cloud orphanage, where over a long career he welcomes pregnant women in need of an abortion or a place to give birth. The nurses who work with him are equally devoted to helping women and to raising the orphans, including Homer Wells.

Although other orphans are adopted before they reach adolescence, Homer never finds suitable foster parents; instead, he remains at St. Cloud's and becomes a surrogate son to Dr. Larch, who trains his protégé to work as an obstetrician. At age thirteen Homer finds a fetus and asks the doctor why many mothers and pregnant women come to the orphanage. Dr. Larch explains that sometimes a woman realizes she cannot keep a baby and brings it to the orphanage and sometimes "the woman knows very early in her pregnancy that this child is unwanted."[50] Allowing each woman authority, Dr. Larch clarifies his own role to Homer: "I'm just the doctor. I help them have what they want. An orphan or an abortion."[51] By the time he is twenty, Homer demonstrates that he is an accomplished obstetrician, albeit one without a formal education. When Dr. Larch is away one day, Homer saves a premature baby and the baby's mother, a woman with eclampsia who suffered puerperal convulsions. The nurses and Dr. Larch are proud and impressed with the young man's surgical skills, and Homer is pleased because the doctor gives him fatherly kisses in approval. But unlike Dr. Larch, who affirms the rights of women to choose whether or not to bear children, Homer does not want to have anything to do with abortions; however, he has no objections to delivering babies. Caring for a woman who stabbed herself in attempting to abort her pregnancy, Homer realizes that his beliefs differ from Dr. Larch's.

> That quick and not-quick stuff: it didn't work for Homer Wells. You can *call* it a fetus or an embryo or the products of conception, thought Homer Wells, but whatever you call it, it's alive. And whatever you do to it, Homer thought—and whatever you call what you do—you're killing it. He looked at the severed pulmonary artery, which was perfectly displayed in the open chest of the baby from Three Mile Falls. Let Larch call it whatever he wants, thought Homer Wells. It's his choice—if it's a fetus, to him, that's fine. It's a baby to me, thought Homer Wells. If Larch has a choice, I have a choice too.[52]

Kristen Luker notes in her history of abortion in the US that one's preference for using the term *fetus* or that of *baby* reflects one's ideology concerning abortion, whether it is the right of women to elect the procedure or whether you think the procedure is tantamount to murder.[53] Employing the word *choice*, Irving contrasts the different outlooks of Dr. Larch and Homer, recognizing medical caregivers exert significant authority over a woman's pregnancy.

Homer wants "to be of use" at the orphanage, but he doesn't want to be a doctor or perform abortions.[54] Dr. Larch accepts Homer's decision to avoid performing abortions on the same day that a young golden couple—Candy Kendall and Wally Worthington—visit St. Cloud. After Candy introduces herself to Homer and apologizes to him for "interrupting," he thinks, "You are interrupting two abortions, one birth, one death, two autopsies and an argument," and he might have added "a possible interview for an adoption," as one of the orphans is desperate to be whisked away in the couple's white Cadillac.[55] Homer falls in love with Candy, who meets with Dr. Larch for an abortion, while Wally distracts himself by advising Homer that the orphanage should plant apples and that the young man should to leave St. Cloud to work with Wally at the Worthington orchard on the coast.

Ambiguities and untruths constitute the backbone of this novel. Dr. Larch agrees that Homer should leave the orphanage and encourages him to get to know Wally's parents so that he might stay at the orchard, but the doctor also hopes that Homer will one day return to St. Cloud to take over as the head doctor. Homer's leaving disappoints nurses and orphans, especially Melony, the oldest female orphan who had extracted a promise from him that he wouldn't move from the orphanage without her; she nurses a grudge against him for leaving her, and through decades she looks in every Maine apple orchard to find him. While Homer works at the orchard during the war, Wally enlists, is sent to the Pacific theater, goes missing, is injured, and suffers partial paralysis. After Wally is reported missing in action, Homer and Candy begin a long affair that produces a son, Angel, who grows up thinking that Homer is his adoptive father, a fiction that persists after Wally returns and remains married to Candy.

About fifteen years after Homer left St. Cloud, the aging Dr. Larch writes a pleading letter asking him to let go of his anti-abortion stance and to return to the orphanage as Dr. Fuzzy Stone, a fictional persona invented by Dr. Larch.

> If abortions were legal, you could refuse—in fact, given your beliefs you *should* refuse. But as long as they're against the law, how can you refuse? How can you allow yourself a choice in the matter when there are so many women who haven't the freedom to make the choice themselves? The women have no choice. I know you know that's not right, but how can you— you of all people, knowing what you know—HOW CAN YOU FEEL FREE TO CHOOSE NOT TO HELP PEOPLE WHO ARE NOT FREE TO GET OTHER HELP? You have to help them because you know how. Think about who's going to help them if you refuse.[56]

Nurse Caroline also writes Homer to tell him that he shouldn't be "a hypocrite" and that he is the only one who can take Dr. Larch's place.[57] Homer replies he is not a doctor, he believes the fetus has a soul, and he's sorry for not returning to the orphanage. Dr. Larch's next letter disagrees, and he dies after mailing it.

Meanwhile at the orchard, Homer faces a dilemma related to abortion. His teenage son Angel falls in love with Rose Rose, one of the migrant pickers and mother of a toddler. Rose Rose becomes pregnant a second time, this time by her father who is the crew chief. Angel and Candy are desperate to protect the young woman, and Rose Rose asks Angel to help her get an abortion. Homer contacts the orphanage to ask Dr. Larch to perform the abortion, but the old man has already died, and Nurse Caroline tells Homer that he will have to do it himself. Homer realizes that he would even perform an abortion on Melony, his nemesis, if she needed one, and he makes up his mind to "be a hero."[58] While performing the procedure on Rose Rose, Homer realizes that he could not "refuse to help a stranger": "I'll just give them what they want . . . An orphan or an abortion."[59] Piling on more dramatic scenes, Irving has Rose Rose run off with her child after stabbing her father, while Mr. Rose arranges his injury to look like he stabbed himself, bleeding out until he dies.

Homer's decision to perform abortions leads to his return to St. Cloud, where he adopts the dead orphan Fuzzy Stone's biography, a legacy Larch has left to him. Over time the doctor secretly created two fictional biographies in his medical files: one describing Homer as ill with a weak heart who will die in middle age, and another under the name of Fuzzy, an orphan who is a model of success with stellar achievements, including earning a medical degree and undertaking missionary work. Dr. Larch prepared the nurses to alert the board of trustees to hire as his replacement the accomplished, young Dr. Fuzzy Stone. After a slight delay to complete the apple harvest, a period Homer uses to grow a beard and develop a tan under a sunlamp, he becomes Dr. Stone, returns to the orphanage, and takes up Dr. Larch's work caring for women through their pregnancies and abortions.

Irving's novel acknowledges incompatible views on abortion while privileging a woman's right to choose, a position often regarded as foundational to feminism. Dr. Larch and the nurses at the orphanage support a woman's right to elect termination before quickening, but other characters, notably Homer for a time, want to protect what they regard as viable life. Helena Wahlström explains "the novel rejects a 'pro-life' stance in favor of a woman's rights perspective, and clearly illustrates that abortion does not preclude or negate motherhood."[60] Homer understands from Rose Rose (after she has been raped by her father) that sometimes an abortion is a necessity for a woman and that Homer must intervene to help her, even if it means that his assistance requires him to take on a new identity.

Janet Engstrom and Ramona Hunter employed Irving's novel as part of a project to teach reproductive options within the context of women's and children's health and family nursing. This project teaches future health care professionals about

> many issues in this book that are relevant to reproductive and overall health. The obvious issues relate to contraception and its availability and the absence of safe and legal abortion services. But, like any good novel, the book includes many stories, many of which relate to sexuality and unintended pregnancy such as adultery, incest, sexual orientation, sexually transmitted infections, substance abuse, domestic violence, racism, parenting, dishonesty in describing reproductive options, lack of access to reproductive services, and poverty.[61]

Social and medical circumstances frame women's pregnancies and childbirths in Irving's novel. Characters' perspectives encourage readers to appreciate that a woman should have the right to elect an abortion and that supportive medical caregivers should respect her choices and ensure her positive health outcomes.

Empowering Women Caregivers

Many medical dramas depict people collaboratively working and combining technical and social skills, illustrating the ways they partner in investigations and treatments while navigating bias and discrimination. Set in post–World War II London and first broadcast in 2012, the British television show *Call the Midwife* depicts women's expertise as medical caregivers, notably as midwives and nurses, and describes how they work collectively to care for pregnant women, their families, and others needing medical attention. The series explores late 1950s and 1960s cultural changes in British society related to gender, immigration, and improvements in medicine, including the development of the National Health Service. Plots outline medical challenges for caregivers and patients and note improvements in technologies, education, and work for women.

Call the Midwife represents how collective action helps women escape abuse, confront sexism, and improve their health. Female characters are path breakers in supporting ethnic diversity and gender equity, extending scientific and technical knowledge, sharing information, and applying it to improve individuals, families, and society. The BBC One series features heroic female nurses and midwives who meet the medical needs of a struggling urban population, particularly women and children, featuring early episodes based on Jennifer Worth's four memoirs about her experience as a midwife in 1950s Poplar, a poor section of East End London: *Call the Midwife* (2002), *Shadows of the Workhouse* (2005), *Farewell to the East End* (2009), and *In the Midst of Life* (2010).[62] Producer Heidi Thomas and others invent episodes consonant with Worth's memoirs in *Call the Midwife*'s later seasons.[63]

Call the Midwife depicts the gradual acceptance of feminism and medical innovations, illustrating how midwives and nurses rely on supportive peers and advisers to cope with professional and personal difficulties and to provide medical treatment to patients. The series criticizes the rigidity of 1950s and 1960s gender roles and expectations of normativity while recommending cultural and institutional reforms to eliminate the harassment, abuse, exploitation, and discrimination that plague women and the poor and to extoll the benefits of female friendship. Episodes recognize the necessity of women's participation in medical care, noting how their contributions benefit individuals, families, and communities. Midwives and nurses, both nuns and secular women, are role models inspiring contemporary girls and women to pursue education and work and teaching patients to accept innovations in diagnosis and treatment.[64]

The secular and religious midwives help London's East Enders cope with pregnancies and births, assist new mothers by promoting healthy antenatal and natal practices, and offer preventive and therapeutic care to many other patients. Helped by a doctor and medical personnel operating emergency vans or working in hospitals, the nurse-midwives promote good hygiene and foster health in straitened economic circumstances. The focal protagonist of the drama's first episodes is Jenny Lee, a nurse and newly qualified midwife who trained in more privileged places, including the home counties surrounding London and Paris, before arriving at Nonnatus House in the poor Poplar district of East London. Vanessa Redgrave provides the voice-over for the mature Jenny's remarks that open and close each show, while Jessica Raine plays the part of the twenty-two-year-old Jenny, who is shocked by the terrible living and health conditions in the Poplar community in 1957. Surprised to find that her new home is a convent, she learns to appreciate the company of the resilient, caring nuns who survived the Blitz and the young, secular nurse-midwives who work hard to help Poplar's challenged residents. Trixie is a fun-loving character invented by the producers, and Cynthia is based on Jennifer Worth's lifelong friend and steady confidante of the same name. The popular actress Miranda Hart plays the role of Camilla "Chummy" Fortescue-Cholmondely-Browne, a gawky society debutante whose missionary zeal inspires her to pursue midwifery in London and then in Africa. As Worth explains in her memoirs, the nuns were amazing women. Sister Monica Joan left a life of privilege, and Sister Evangelina grew up poor, but these differences matter little as they struggle to help others. Sister Julienne serves as a gentle leader and guide for the nuns and the secular nurse-midwives. Later seasons of the series introduce additional nuns and midwives of different ages and ethnicities who confront various personal, medical, and social challenges.

Each episode of *Call the Midwife* links the lives of the nurse-midwives with those of their patients. In the first season, Jenny's romantic problems include that she had been in love with a married man. When she meets Molly Brignall, a pregnant mother in an abusive marriage, Jenny realizes that some forms of love are unhealthy: Molly's husband threatens harm to her and their children unless she prostitutes herself to earn money. Eventually, Molly and her husband are sent to jail for neglecting their children, forcing Molly's mother to raise her grandchildren and providing a lesson to Jenny who must control her affections to avoid a relationship with a man who might mistreat her. Other romances have mixed outcomes: Trixie confronts sexual harassment, Chummy and the medical orderly Jane find romantic partners, and Sister Bernadette and the doctor realize they are in love and decide to marry.

The nuns and secular midwives discuss their cases and political views, and they work collaboratively to support their patients, mothers, and babies who suffer various ailments, including preeclampsia, premature birth, breach birth, rickets, and many other pregnancy and childbirth complications. The women—caregivers and patients—are bound together because they believe that Poplar residents deserve better social conditions. Reviewers understand the series' appeal as a feminist call to arms: "Alison Graham in the *Radio Times* dubbed *Call the Midwife* 'a magnificently subversive drama' and 'the torchbearer of feminism on television,'" and "Caitlin Moran claimed the series encapsulated 'how unbelievably terrifying, dreary and vile it was to be a working-class woman 60 years ago.' "[65] Midwives work to keep mothers and babies healthy, while addressing social problems such as race and sex discrimination, domestic abuse, prostitution, poverty, and the frustrations of women worn out by reproduction in the years before the birth control pill was available. The antenatal clinic and maternity home showcase their medical work, allowing them to monitor the health conditions of pregnant women, new mothers, and new babies and to encourage improved diet, hygiene, and exercise practices to raise the living standards of families and community.

Conchita Warren, the Spanish mother of twenty-four bilingual children, becomes the first Poplar case that Jenny handles by herself after Mrs. Warren (who speaks only Spanish) falls and goes into premature labor. With Conchita's English husband helping during the birth, Jenny delivers a tiny infant who is hand-fed by the mother. This family takes positive actions, for the mother insists the premature infant remain at home under her care instead of languishing in hospital. Married to an unemployed laborer, a poor woman facing her ninth pregnancy is unable to feed her children; Nora Harding tries to induce abortion but only succeeds in injuring herself. Fortunately, Jenny and the midwives get her to hospital so she can recover, and the episode ends endorsing access to contraception as a basic right of women.

Technological medical innovations, particularly contraception, vaccinations, and antibiotics, usually, but not always, improve health outcomes for women and children. The midwives insist on home inspections before delivery and mandate institutional care in the maternity home or in hospital for mothers whose homes and family situations cannot meet certain standards. In addition to the National Health Service package of materials (paper to protect the mattress, hygiene supplies) needed for home births, midwives and doctor bring medical technologies, including "gas and air" (anesthesia) to alleviate pain during labor, and they develop community educational programs focusing on disease prevention. The nurses and nun midwives also address medical issues affecting poor, elderly residents who have not had much medical care. The program documents post–World War II development of the National Health Service that allows Jenny to care for Joe, an elderly, lonely veteran whose legs have chilblains, and for Mrs. Jenkins, an older woman whose children died in the workhouse, where she also labored and which she barely survived. Later seasons describe medical cases involving African, Asian, and Caribbean immigrants who seek jobs and better lives in London.

Viewers observe that while the female caregivers come from diverse class and ethnic backgrounds and have varied spiritual interests and family experiences, the nuns and the secular midwives nevertheless share a common interest to keep patients healthy and to help them pursue happiness according to their own ways, respecting individual values and priorities. One nun leaves the sisterhood to marry the doctor working with the Nonnatus caregivers, and one midwife becomes a nun. Faith and cultural practices are sympathetically compared. Each episode links three or more subplots: one tracks personal and/or professional circumstances related to the nurse and nun midwives and their small community, a second incorporates problems and prospects of pregnancies and other medical cases in Poplar, and a third looks at social challenges affecting women and families: gender and ethnic discrimination, domestic abuse, incest, violent attacks on vulnerable women, lack of safe housing, poor working conditions, and mental illness.

Over the course of eleven seasons (as of 2022 with a twelfth promised in 2023), the long arc narrative notes changes in 1950s and 1960s Poplar, tracking the growth of women's independence from traditional, subservient roles.[66] Opportunities for women in education, work, and intimate relationships illustrate a gradual acceptance of feminist ideas, including that women should be able to access contraception and abortion. Secular midwives, particularly Trixie and Valerie Dyer, who was raised in Poplar and served as a nurse in wartime, encourage women to be true to themselves and to accept modern ideas about women's sexuality, fashion, and values that sometimes trouble the nuns. Nurse Phyllis Crane, older than the other midwives, recommends that her colleagues embrace opportunities to learn and to experience life. Homosexuality is still a suppressed subject, so midwife Patsy Mount and nurse Delia Busby conduct their affair as quietly as possible. After Phyllis witnesses them kissing in the convent, she offers friendly counsel and keeps their secret.

The growing acceptance of feminism in the series aligns with features of globalization, including mobility, migration, and inequality. *Call the Midwife* includes episodes documenting discrimination against the poor, who are accused of being lazy, as well as biases against Irish travelers, Romanis, blacks, and immigrants from other countries. In an episode in the ninth series, nurse midwife Lucille Anderson, who is Black and from Jamaica, is subjected to hostile remarks from bigots, including a woman patient she helps deliver while they are stuck in an elevator. Different cultural values inform episodes as residents from various Commonwealth countries move into Poplar, and the midwives in different seasons travel around England and to Scotland and South Africa to treat patients while learning about regional cultures and medical practices.

Midwives and nurses assist with childbirths in homes, in the maternity home sponsored by Nonnatus House, and in hospitals, providing patients with customized care and informative communication, sometimes in extreme conditions. In different episodes, viewers observe the Nonnatus caregivers successfully deliver babies in harsh physical locations (on a ship, a barge, a remote island during a storm) and tense situations for families in crises. Together with Dr. Turner and occasionally with other providers, the midwives and nurses confront a range of physical and mental illnesses, disabilities, and injuries affecting their patients and sometimes their medical colleagues. They conduct clinics and work to prevent and treat illnesses and diseases, including cancer, Huntington's chorea, polio, smallpox, typhoid, tuberculosis, postpartum depression, and anxiety, using whatever methods and therapies are at hand. These heroic caregivers promote the incorporation of the best available information, technologies, technical processes, and treatments to benefit Poplar residents. The Nonnatus women also help women avoid prostitution and resist abusive violence, sometimes intervening with violent husbands and other hostile relatives. The caregivers dispel fears about vaccinations, rare diseases, and cancer treatments, and some provide contraception even though its use conflicts with church teachings.

Incorporating lively period music and attractive costumes and filming in locations and on sets that reproduce the sounds and looks of the 1950s and 1960s, *Call the Midwife* illustrates how the Nonnatus caregivers employed scientific and technical methods for social good in the decades following the war. Not all innovations are positive; seasons 5 and 6 describe how intensive analysis of medical records confirms that thalidomide, which Dr. Turner prescribed for morning sickness, had devastating effects on the offspring of several mothers. Plotlines converge around medical cases, personal empowerment, and female bonding while noting shifting social attitudes toward disabilities. Episodes point to stereotypes constraining prospects for women and minorities, defining the midwives' medical care as a feminist reform project planting seeds for subsequent efforts to improve health. The Nonnatus women consult with hospital personnel, public health officials, social workers, and police, providing informative examples of how individuals in communities work together to overcome poverty, sexual discrimination, abuse, and exploitation. The nurse-midwives assisting with pregnancies and births devote their time and take risks to save lives. Addressing public health and safety, they solve medical problems and improve the lives of women and men who grimly cope with postwar difficulties. *Call the Midwife* highlights role models, pointing to improved health and economic prospects for women.

Fictions about reproduction discussed in this chapter constitute information systems representing pregnancy, childbirth, and parenting as important concerns for women that affect their maturation, economic well-being, social advancement, and mental health; pregnancy and its treatment may enhance or derail women's lives. Reproduction can bring a community together, or it can make individual lives and family and social relationships intolerable if women are not provided sufficient support. Narratives provide insight into changing attitudes surrounding pregnancy and motherhood by acknowledging how fictional women in *The Millstone*, *Luscious Lemon*, *The Cider House Rules*, and *Call the Midwife* manage childbirth, which is an unpredictable process in that each pregnancy follows its own course. A 2022 British government report notices that realities for pregnant women are not as rosy as optimistic fictions, while promising to reduce inequalities such as "the difference in the stillbirth and neonatal mortality rate per 1,000 births between that for women from an ethnic minority group and the national average."[67] Fictional feminist narratives about pregnancy, childbirth, and parenting argue that women's medical and social interests ought to be supported with appropriate resources to ensure a healthy, equitable future.[68]

Agreeing that successful births require resources and family support, Brit Bennett's 2016 novel *The Mothers* describes how young Black women and men cope with fluctuating emotions as they make decisions about pregnancy, abortion, and infertility.[69] Bennett's book considers how the teenagers' choices influence their future romances, educations, and work and lead to regret later in life. This nuanced novel is about much more than women's reproductive lives as its editor notes: "It's such a compelling and accessible book, and yet it's much more ambitious than you initially realize. . . . It's a story about living up to expectations in contemporary black America."[70] In noting Black reproductive regrets, Bennett's novel aligns with media accounts considering how technologies and social circumstances affect Black women's reproductive choices and their health outcomes. Researchers report traumatic stress for Black women and often inadequate medical care resulting in health complications such as misdiagnoses, dangerous childbirths, and higher infant and maternal mortality rates. Dorothy Roberts points out that while Black women are more likely to experience infertility, they are less likely to have access to in vitro reproductive technologies, an outcome of what she references as "the devaluation of Black reproduction" and "the proliferation of rhetoric and policies that degrade Black women's procreative decisions."[71] Instead of supporting IVF procedures that are high-risk, expensive, and available to relatively few women, Roberts recommends that the US federal government enhance support for "Research designed to reduce infertility, programs that facilitate adoption, and the general provision of human needs," particularly those addressing "the endemic spread of chlamydia, an STD that affects millions of people and contributes to especially high infertility rates among young Black women."[72]

Miscarriages, infant deaths, and postpartum complications for mothers are more likely for Black women, regardless of their economic or educational status. Linda Villarosa points out racial disparities: "Education and income offer little protection. In fact, a black woman with an advanced degree is more likely to lose her baby than a white woman with less than an eighth-grade education."[73] Testimonies concern poor medical diagnoses of infertility and the tone-deaf responses of doctors to postpregnancy complications of Black women, as actress Gabrielle Union and tennis player Serena Williams assert in describing how they did not receive appropriate medical treatment for their reproductive needs. Union explained in an interview with Oprah and a *Time* article that she had several miscarriages, a diagnosis of adenomyosis, and IVF treatments before she was eventually counseled to use a gestational surrogate.[74] Her resistance to surrogacy stemmed in part from her own wish to experience pregnancy and her disquiet about racial dimensions of surrogacy: "I got the sense a lot of white families-to-be were more comfortable with brown people as surrogates—Latina and South Asian—who were often classified as 'breeders.' "[75] Serena Williams shared in interviews that her difficulties postpregnancy were due to her doctors not believing what she said about her symptoms.[76] Anne Pollock describes Williams's postpartum treatment as typical yet paradoxical given the tennis star's wealth and fame, "Even with all the resources, expertise, and assertiveness that she was able to muster, Williams faced challenges in receiving the attention and intervention she desperately needed."[77]

Medical studies document that "Black women have higher morbidity and mortality in pregnancy and postpartum, compared with women of other races/ethnicities, including white and Hispanic women. Pregnancy-associated deaths are rising in the USA and are higher than in other developed nations. Pregnancy-associated mortality rates are disproportionately higher among non-Hispanic black women."[78] "Weathering," lifelong stress, and implicit bias are significant factors contributing to Black women's higher risk in pregnancy. Kira Johnson's husband described her dying in 2016 after experiencing a "sloppy C-section" performed in a Los Angeles hospital.[79] Since her death, he has advocated for legislation to prevent maternal death.[80] Shalon Irving's story of her poor health after delivery has been cited as typical for Black women in that her physical condition worsened despite numerous visits with physicians who did not treat her serious symptoms of hypertension.[81]

These cases document racial disparities in reproductive care, while fictional narratives explain collectivity around reproduction as a means of empowering women and speculative dystopic fictions foresee dismal prospects.[82] After the US Supreme Court overturned *Roe v. Wade* in June 2022, women's reproductive futures in many states appear uncertain and require concerted efforts to address health outcomes and legal rights. News media report diminished access to contraception, reproductive technologies, and prenatal care, resulting in poor reproductive outcomes, particularly for nonwhite women, and barriers to reproductive choice for all.[83] Noticing problems is a small step toward improvement.

Chapter 6

Overcoming Violence against Women

The absolute necessity to raise these questions in the world: where, when, and under what conditions have women acted and been acted-on, as women? Wherever people are struggling against subjection, the specific subjection of women, through our location in a female body, from now on has to be addressed. The necessity to go on speaking of it, refusing to let the discussion go on as before, speaking where silence has been advised and enforced, not just about our subjection but about our active presence and practice as women.

—Adrienne Rich, "Notes toward a Politics of Location" (1985)[1]

when you walk alone at night
carry your keys in your fist
points sticking out
past the knuckles
just in case

—Janine DeBaise, *from* "What We Learn" (2019)[2]

Television crime franchises such as *Law and Order*, *NCIS*, and *CSI* feature ensemble casts of men and women detectives responding to abuses heaped on female victims, their children, and other vulnerable individuals. Feminist women detectives and forensic pathologists navigate obstacles, including gendered stereotypes confronted at work and at home, to solve crimes or endure them as survivors.[3] Fictional narratives describe sexism and other inequalities influencing the criminal justice system, arguing that preventing violent crimes against women is a necessary component of gender equity. As Amnesty International reports, "Worldwide, one in three women experiences physical, sexual or emotional violence in her lifetime; one in five experiences rape or attempted rape."[4] "Patterns of violence" against Black women, immigrants and undocumented women, women in the military, women in detention, and Native American women are "shocking" as domestic abuse and rape statistics indicate.[5]

Including more women in positions of authority in prosecutorial offices, reconfiguring civic security arrangements, and eliminating negative social stereotypes about gender and sexual orientation are three ways to reduce violence against women that are represented in narratives. This chapter examines fictions centering on violent attacks on women, discussing two novels about rape and murder—Toni Morrison's *Paradise* (1997) and Louise Erdrich's *The Round House* (2012)—and *The Closer* (2005–2012), a television series focusing on a female chief of detectives pursuing a serial rapist-murderer. Plots about women's safety suggest that legal mechanisms are insufficient to prevent or respond to acts of physical violence, which reinforce existing gender inequities. Violent acts threaten, intimidate, and silence women. The fictions share a common master plot: women transgressing against social norms are subjected to attacks that could incite revenge. Audiences read these narratives allegorically, recognizing that female characters "are less individuals than figures for a social group," to adopt a phrase from Michael Denning.[6] Readers recognize that sexual and physical violence are problems that many, if not all, women face because of unequal power relations.[7] Narratives acknowledge few remedies to overcome violence, suggesting that finding ways to eliminate and to respond to attacks remain significant concerns for feminists.

Patriarchal Trauma

Fictions describing violent crimes that subordinate women suggest legal and extralegal mechanisms that could enable justice and enhance gender equity if appropriately developed. The last novel in a trilogy that includes *Beloved* (1987) and *Jazz* (1992), Toni Morrison's *Paradise* (1998), considers historical events that provide a context for pervasive sexual abuse and violent crimes against women. The novel presents a large cast of characters, including founders of an African American community and their progeny who maintain its patriarchal legacy, opening with a shocking attack on a group of women who live in a mansion, formerly a convent, on the outskirts of town. Men from three different churches in Ruby, Oklahoma, unite to kill these women. The bloody violence makes it difficult for readers to accept, as some citizens do, that these men were justified in committing the mass murder of independent women who transgressed social norms. The convent women who live off the land shelter the abused and dispossessed and support each other, an arrangement that allows this women's collective for a time to escape from discrimination and physical dangers.

Oppositions in the novel reference race/ethnicity, age, sexual interest and experience, and education. The males murdering the Convent women react to past grievances, as a long simmering gendered conflict in Ruby erupts. Reviewers disagreed over whether the structure and story in the best-selling *Paradise* emphasize gender and other differences in simplistic ways.[8] Yet scholars find value in the gendered structure, as Marni Gauthier explains:

> Although the narrative centers on the Ruby township, ruled by men, the novel relates its true story primarily through women whose individual names entitle each chapter: these include each of the Convent women, and Patricia and Lone (Ruby's resident midwife). Men's voices do enter the narratives . . . where they convey the town's heritage and guiding principles, but the women's stories consistently reveal the men's perspectives to be skewed.[9]

Gauthier understands that Morrison's patterning of oppositions conveys meaning, arguing that "the gender dichotomy is only one part of a larger series of oppositions that the novel stages and then explodes for its central project of interrogating the processes by which popular national histories are made and sustained."[10] The community was founded as a refuge for former slaves, but individual differences influence social divisions in the town. Promoting equitable treatment for Blacks, the principle on which the town was founded, gives way in Ruby to inequities harming women, but the narrative also recognizes that societies evolve and suggests that people, even those harmed by violence, could be guided toward tolerance rather than nursing grievances leading to more violence.

Historical references in Morrison's novel appear as a long series of past injustices against Blacks, according to Channette Romero: "*Paradise* seems written in response to the failures of the Civil Rights Movement and the Black Nationalist Movement to bring about full equality and social justice for all Americans, what Martin Luther King, Jr., envisioned as the 'beloved community.' "[11] Romero explains that Morrison "shows contemporary readers a richer, less-reactionary African American past . . . and suggests that recovering this history and tolerance for difference will help bring about cultural transformation."[12] Simone Drake indicates that differences between the townspeople of Ruby and the marginalized women include how they practice love: "Out of all this discourse on love emerges a truth: Ruby loved itself too much, and the Convent women did not love themselves enough."[13] The novel suggests that developing a diverse, loving community to protect and nurture residents requires accepting difference and compromise, which many women characters endorse and men resist.

Many men in Ruby did not value women's ways of cooperating and sharing; instead, the men feel compelled to destroy what they do not understand. The murderers demonize the Convent women who transgress conservative patriarchal norms of behavior and who resist being controlled by men and narrow social conventions. As Romero explains,

> These women willingly accept into their house individuals who have been marginalized by the rigid code of behavior in Ruby: adulterers, unmarried pregnant women, alcoholics, and women fighting with their husbands or other authority figures in the community. These women also work collectively to heal the violent traumas of their own lives under the instruction of a former Catholic nun, Consolata, a woman who speaks to multiple deities, reads minds, and raises the dead. The town leaders are outraged by the idea that these women live without men or the Christian God in their lives.[14]

Gauthier places the deadly, gendered conflict within a larger historical framework describing injustices meted out to Blacks: "Armed with invented disparaging myths about the Convent women, they effectively execute a lynching in which the perpetrators, not the victims, are all black men."[15] Thus, *Paradise* becomes "a fantasy of black nationhood, arising from a mythology and history that correspond to the evolution of the United States, [that] devolves into a dystopia," according to Gauthier.[16] Warning that the suppressed, unleashed rage of an oppressed minority destroys those even more marginalized, the novel argues that violent actors intend to ensure power while criticizing those who believe that past crimes justify the commission of violence.

The men in Ruby have suffered, but they choose to exert violence against women rather than working to reduce inequities and enable social justice. Reverend Richard Misner's complaint against the murderers' selfishness reflects this social devolution:

> They think they have outfoxed the whiteman when in fact they imitate him. They think they are protecting their wives and children, when in fact they are maiming them. And when the maimed children ask for help, they look elsewhere for the cause. Born out of an old hatred, one that began when one kind of black man scorned another kind and that kind took the hatred to another level, their selfishness had trashed two hundred years of suffering and triumph in a moment of such pomposity and error and callousness it froze the mind.[17]

One townswoman who has not lived in the Convent investigates the town's history. But Pat does not share with Misner the information that she collected for her genealogy of its residents: "that nine 8-rocks murdered five harmless women: (a) because the women were impure (not 8-rock); (b) because the women were unholy (fornicators at the least, abortionists at most); (c) because they could."[18] She burns her history, believing that written accounts are skewed and should be cast aside; however, Morrison's novel takes the place of that genealogy in serving as an account of Ruby's intolerance and murder.

Memorializing the Convent women's murders could provide reconciliation across divisions that would prevent another crime like it. Descriptions of selfish, violent men contrast with scenes of the women helping and consoling each another. Sometimes the Convent women are in conflict, as scenes that occur after new arrivals move into the Convent illustrate; however, the place maintains a general atmosphere of comfort for those in need until that home is violated. After fighting with her mother (Pat) and leaving her family home, Billie Delia benefits from the kindness of the Convent women. Reflecting on the conflict between the men and the women, she regards Ruby as: "a backward noplace ruled by men whose power to control was out of control and who had the nerve to say who could live and who not and where; who had seen in lively, free, unarmed females the mutiny of the mares and so got rid of them. She hoped with all her heart that the women were out there, darkly burnished, biding their time, brass-metaling their incisors—but out there. Which is to say she hoped for a miracle."[19] The stories that the Convent women share with each other, their personal testimonials of abuse and suffering, provide a way they overcome their traumas to heal, "using narration as the means of reconnecting to others and the natural world," as Romero notes.[20] At the same time, the ability of the Convent women to come to terms with their pasts exposes the failure of Ruby's citizens to confront and manage their own traumatic histories. Trauma cannot be erased, but future iterations could be prevented if we recognize inequity and abuse as warning signs of incipient violence and if we enact feminist principles to eliminate inequalities leading to resentments.

Justice and Revenge

Similar to the way *Paradise* sets a history of racial inequities affecting African Americans against its account of men's violence against women, Louise Erdrich's *The Round House* (2012) links historical racial injustice with contemporary gendered violence. This novel points to US law as insufficient in prosecuting and punishing crimes committed against women attacked on reservations, while recognizing that tribal histories are critical to a rape investigation. Many of Erdrich's fictions represent the history of Native Americans and their social marginality within connected family stories set on a fictional reservation and towns in North Dakota. *The Round House* incorporates oral accounts as a predominating dimension of the interconnected narratives in Erdrich's oeuvre, supplementing the history of the Pillager family elaborated in *Love Medicine* (1984), *The Beet Queen* (1986), *Tracks* (1988), and *The Bingo Palace* (1994). *The Round House* (2012) relies on Joe Coutts, a first-person homodiegetic narrator who describes what happened after his mother Geraldine was raped when he was thirteen, combining family history with a political argument about sexism, legal inequity, social injustice, and flawed public policy, especially the lack of legal protection and remedies for people living in Indian country who are victimized by non-Indians. The main plot focuses on the question of legal jurisdiction and the evidence against the non-Indian man who attacked Geraldine, while the interpolated tales shared with Joe by various characters highlight the problems of finding justice for victimized women. The overarching plot and interpolated tales acknowledge violence against women on the reservation as the legacy of historical crimes against Indian tribes deprived of their land and self-governance.

Set in 1988, *The Round House* illustrates how members of the Ojibwe tribe endure despite the failure of the law to compensate them for historical cases of federal land grabbing accompanied by violence, racial oppression, and gender discrimination. The novel references Gabriel Dumont and Louis Riel, men who fought in the region for Indian rights only to see tribes lose their land and their capacity for legal authority, developments that lead to the impoverishment and social marginality of Native Americans. Joe's father, who is a tribal judge, explains to his son the limited jurisdictional authority allowed his court and afforded people who live on reservations. The 1978 US Supreme Court decision, *Oliphant v. Suquamish Indian Tribe* (435 US 191 [1978]), muddled jurisdictional authority on reservations for Native Americans victimized by non-Indians: "The decision stated that Indian tribal courts do not have inherent criminal jurisdiction to try and to punish non-Indians, and hence may not assume such jurisdiction unless specifically authorized to do so by Congress."[21] The lack of jurisdictional authority incurs costs borne by reservation residents.

In March 2011, the Assistant Secretary of the Bureau of Indian Affairs acknowledged: "American Indian women experience among the highest domestic violence victimization rates in the country and more than half of all married Indian women have non-Indian husbands," noting that legislation to recognize tribal jurisdiction over non-Indian offenders "provides tools to tribal governments to address the problem of domestic violence much more completely on Indian reservations."[22] Soon after *The Round House* was published, Erdrich argued in an opinion piece appearing in the February 26, 2013, issue of the *New York Times* that the US House should renew the Violence against Women Act that had been approved by the Senate. Her article "Rape on the Reservation" cites appalling statistics.

> The Justice Department reports that one in three Native women is raped over her lifetime, while other sources report that many Native women are too demoralized to report rape. Perhaps this is because federal prosecutors decline to prosecute 67 percent of sexual abuse cases, according to the Government Accountability Office. Further tearing at the social fabric of communities, a Native woman battered by her non-Native

husband has no recourse for justice in tribal courts, even if both live on reservation ground. More than 80 percent of sex crimes on reservations are committed by non-Indian men who are immune from prosecution by tribal courts.[23]

Erdrich's article recommended a solution: "To protect Native women, tribal authorities must be able to apprehend, charge, and try rapists—regardless of race. Tribal courts had such jurisdiction until 1978. . . . The Senate bill would restore limited jurisdiction over non-Indians suspected of perpetrating sex crimes."[24] On Friday, March 1, 2013, President Obama praised the 113th Congress for authorizing S.47, the Violence against Women Act to close the loophole. According to *Indianz*, a website devoted to news about Native Americans, the bill included a landmark section recognizing tribal jurisdiction over non-Indians who commit domestic violence offenses on reservations, a provision that first surfaced in a July 2011 Department of Justice proposal.[25] Since publication of *The Round House*, laws have changed to prevent the legal dilemma outlined in Erdrich's novel. In May 2020, a coalition of states attorneys general pressed Congress to reauthorize the act, although the US Department of Justice indicated its protections remained in force regardless of legislative action.[26] In March 2022, President Biden signed into law the Violence against Women Act of 2022; it allows "special criminal jurisdiction of Tribal courts to cover non-Native perpetrators of sexual assault, child abuse, stalking, sex trafficking, and assaults on tribal law enforcement officers on tribal lands."[27]

The round house of the novel's title is a sacred place, one dedicated to purging and healing rituals. An Indian-hating rapist deliberately chose this location, which in 1988 was out of tribal jurisdiction, as the place to bring Geraldine and his other victims. Joe barely understands what rape is when his mother arrives at the "white" hospital to be tested and treated for it, but he quickly learns about its traumatic effects after his mother becomes too fearful and depressed to function. Joe and his father want to know why Geraldine was attacked. One clue is that just before the attack she retrieved a legal file from her office that was related to her work as the tribe's genealogy expert. After being treated at the hospital, she takes to her bed, refusing to identify the rapist, to explain the information in the file, or to acknowledge details of the crime. The young Indian mother, Mayla, and her infant daughter were kidnapped and went missing after Geraldine managed to escape, while the attacker remains at large. Joe and his father recognize that the location of the rape in being outside tribal jurisdiction affects which authorities can prosecute the crime. They review his father's court cases, learning relevant details about likely motives and legal strategies while documenting how difficult it is for the reservation community to redress inequities and for their legal authorities to prosecute criminals.

The choice of an adolescent male to narrate a novel about a complex legal tangle surrounding a sex crime was a careful one. In an interview, Erdrich explained that she "had to find a way to go straight in, and Joe gave me the way in with the innocence and the heart. Well, he's not all that innocent. He's a 13-year-old kid, but he's so protective of his mother and so ambivalent as a 13-year-old about both his mother and his father. So he's growing up in a tremendously short time over the course of a summer."[28] Joe deals with his own maturing sexuality in the aftermath of his mother's rape, narrating events with few flashbacks or flash-forwards. Intelligent, curious, and likable, he is quick-tempered and has few positive adult role models. Although a judge, Joe's father appears tentative about investigating the crime against Geraldine, but Joe sees his father's attitude as realistic in recognizing the limitations of what a tribal court can review. Other adult men on the reservation are at best sober and at worst violent, while many women and children suffer neglect and abuse. Joe's friend Angus and his mother are frequently beaten by her boyfriend, while Joe's friend Cappy lives in a household of men who avoid domestic routines.

Joe is a typical teenager in many ways; he enjoys riding his bike and role-playing *Star Trek: The Next Generation* games with his friends, who share his taste in scatological and sexual humor. The boys drink illegally obtained alcohol and smoke cigarettes and marijuana, hiding these actions from their parents and guardians. After Joe's friend finds beer at the crime scene, the boys drink it, not understanding that they have consumed evidence that might identify Geraldine's attacker.[29] Joe commits to learning who hurt his mother, so he persists in investigating the crime, although both parents warn him to stop because they are worried about what might happen to him. He spends his summer looking for the rapist, examining evidence at the crime scene, chasing leads, interrogating witnesses, and speculating about the offender's motivation and a way to punish him. He realizes his father's cases point to people and legal principles associated with the attack against his mother.[30] Goading his mother to testify, even though she refuses to leave her bed much less her home, Joe tells her, "I'm going to find him and I'm going to burn him. I'm going to kill him for you . . . I'll do it. There is nothing to stop me. I know who he is and I'm going after him. You can't stop me because you're here in bed. You can't get out. You're trapped in here."[31] Joe's conclusions—about the attacker's movements on the day of the crime and the methods the man used to capture and abuse his victims—prove correct, and Joe follows through on his promise to his mother to destroy her attacker.

Relatives and friends help him solve the case by feeding and shelter-ing him and sharing tribal history. Joe visits several homes and hears sto-ries that teach him about other women—Linda Wishkob, Akiikwe, Mayla, and Sonja—who suffer from domestic abuse. A white woman adopted into an Indian family, Linda Wishkob was born a twin and was abandoned at birth by her white birth parents, the Larks. Believing Linda was deformed, possibly brain damaged, because her head, arm, and leg were misshapen, the parents instructed the obstetrician to allow Linda to die, although they brought home her twin brother Linden. Betty Wishkob, an Indian janitor on duty at the time of Linda's birth, saves and heals the girl. Betty and her husband adopt her, fighting social services to raise her with the three Wishkob children. After the Wishkob parents die and their other children move away from the area, Linda remains in their family home located on the reservation. When Linda is middle-aged, Grace Lark sues to take control of her daughter and the Wishkob tribal properties, including the home Linda occupies after her Indian parents die. Joe's father objected to this legal maneuver and wrote a decision preventing the release of the Wishkob land from tribal control. Later, Linda's Indian family is surprised when she agreed to donate her kidney to her Indian-hating twin brother Linden. Linda regrets too late that her organ donation helped this evil man live.

Over time Joe's mother reveals details of her assault, and Joe pieces this information together with the physical evidence he observes to fig-ure out what happened. After Geraldine learned that the governor would adopt an Indian child and that the child's mother was missing, she told her husband and son what she remembered of the attack. That day she drove to the round house to meet Mayla, who had begun to enroll her daughter into tribal membership, which required naming the child's father. Geral-dine explains that on her way to the round house she was attacked by a man who wanted the file with information about Mayla and her daughter. He rapes Geraldine because she won't give him the documents. Unfor-tunately, she was hooded and does not know precisely where she was attacked in the area where "Tribal trust, state, and fee" land meet.[32] The rapist understood that the complexities of justice affecting federal, state, and tribal systems would make it difficult for authorities to prosecute any crime committed by a non-Indian on the reservation. The man's frustrated desire for Mayla set in motion his plan to punish her for engaging in sexual relations with the former governor and bearing that man's child. Geraldine fights against her kidnapper and destroys the attacker's matches by urinating on them; after the rapist leaves to find more matches to burn the women and the child, Geraldine escapes. She tells her husband and her son about the attack before going back into the hospital.

Helped by his *dooedam* (guiding spirit), Joe traces clues concerning Mayla and her child. He finds a doll containing $40,000 that was submerged in the lake near the Round House, and he takes the money, which is later confirmed to be hush money the governor paid Mayla. Joe asks his uncle Whitey's girlfriend Sonja for help, and, acting as Joe's guardian, Sonja sets up bank accounts around the area. She tells Joe that the money will help him go to a good college; however, she can't resist spending some on clothes and jewelry, causing Whitey to wonder jealously who gave her these items. Joe tries to protect Sonja and unconvincingly lies that he gave her the jewelry as they flee from Whitey, but Joe also asks Sonja, who was formerly a professional stripper, to put on a show for Joe's grandfather Mooshum as a birthday present. After Joe blackmails her to see her strip and shows signs of trying to dominate her, Sonja tells him she has been abused by men. She admits she felt inferior and never pressed Whitey to marry her, telling Joe that he is "another piece of shit guy. Another gimme-gimme asshole."[33] Then she leaves town with most of the money he found in the lake.

Erdrich organizes episodes concerning Joe's investigation, his interactions with Sonja, and scenes describing Mooshum's dream about his ancestor Akiikwe, Earth Mother. Over one hundred years old and quite poor in 1988, Mooshum understands that his family might have prospered if the Métis rebellion in 1885 against the Canadian government had been successful: "If Louis Riel had let Dumont ambush the [US] militia back then, 'I'd be a retired prime minister.' "[34] A dreaming Mooshum also tells Joe a legend about Akiikwe, the wife and mother who survived her husband and others in the tribe trying to murder her. She found (with her son Nanapush's help) the buffalo her tribe requires for sustenance, and the men who tried to kill Akiikwe were ashamed after she returned to the tribe. After Joe learns that his mother's rapist, Linden Lark, Linda's twin brother, is released from jail, he complains to his father about the tribe's inability to punish his mother's attacker. Joe's father points to the corrupt history of federal law preventing Indians from fully enforcing their system of justice, explaining to his son that he and "many other tribal judges try to make . . . solid decisions . . . to build a solid base . . . for our sovereignty. . . . We want the right to prosecute criminals of all races within our original boundaries."[35] Connecting Indian myths, personal accounts, and laws, Erdrich's novel links present-day gender inequities on the reservation with historical land grabs and persistent sexism and abuse.

Helped by friends, Joe punishes Linden Lark, who raped Geraldine, killed Mayla, and kidnapped Mayla's daughter. Joe determines Linden's routine by asking Linda about her twin brother's habits, and he obtains a gun and learns to shoot so that he can attack Linden at the golf course. Joe hits his target, but it is his friend Cappy's bullet that kills Linden. Although Joe is an accomplice to a murder, he is protected because Cappy was killed in an auto accident during a desperate trip to leave the reservation and never revealed any information about who shot Linden Lark. Joe put the gun under Linda's front porch, and she hides its pieces to protect Joe. She absolves Joe by telling him that he should not let the killing destroy him and that she should have shot Linden herself. Joe indicates that some years after the period he describes in the narrative he becomes a lawyer and marries an Indian girl he met that very summer.

The novel connects the mystery about the crimes committed by Geraldine's attacker with related stories identifying how Native Americans, particularly women, have been shortchanged by the US justice system. Indians have been cheated, discriminated against, subjected to violence, and constrained from seeking legal remedies. Erdrich details the historical oppression of tribes, greedy schemes of bigoted politicians to control them, and a troubled economy for Native Americans to illustrate how these factors diminish individuals and families in Indian country. The central plot follows the boy's developing sense of masculinity, as he learns to protect rather than to dominate women, while the embedded stories describe violent abuses of women and point to the need for individuals to fix what the law does not. Joe's account of his investigation offers insight into the ways in which individuals seek justice after the law and policy fail them, while the interpolated stories provide mythic, ethical, and legal justifications for his murder of his mother's rapist. Erdrich's novel establishes sympathy for Joe as well his family, friends, and tribe by weaving together historical and current-day examples of discrimination and crimes against Indians and women. Because legal, officially sanctioned mechanisms of punishment against his mother's rapist appear impossible, it is difficult for readers to object to the killing of Linden Lark, who is a rapist, kidnapper, and murderer. In this way, the narrative structure of *The Round House* with its tales and related personal and legal testimonies maintains reader sympathy for Geraldine and other victims of violence as well as their loved ones. Each reader must connect information in the intertwined narratives about abused characters to recognize the historical injustices dealt to Native Americans, applying the lesson learned from oral histories—that women should not be abused—to what Joe shares about his family and friends.

Analyzing the narrative structure and strategies of the novel's interpolated historical tales and legal and personal accounts along with its main plot about Geraldine's rape and Joe's solving of the crime fuels reader sympathy for the actions of past figures and present-day characters who redress crimes. Embedded stories about Akiiwe and Linda Wishkob acknowledge violent, abusive acts that damage women, while the account of Joe figuring out Geraldine's rapist and punishing the malefactor reveals the limits of the law. Readers are led to conclude that there are cases in which individuals feel forced to take matters into their own hands to achieve retribution. This lesson applies to Sonja's theft of the hush money that Joe retrieved, rationalizing her stealing because, like Mayla, its intended recipient, she has suffered abuse because of male dominance. Joe should not have made Sonja strip for his grandfather, but the result of his action is that she teaches him that all women should be respected and not exploited for others' gain.

The Round House illustrates continuing discriminations against Native Americans and women, recommending that the US correct jurisdictional issues. Fictions by Morrison and Erdrich, respectively, argue for protecting women's independence and establishing legal grounds to try criminals on Indian reservations. Information in the novels about insufficient legal protections encourages us to help women by contributing needed resources—healthy environment, education, jobs, and equitable laws—so that individuals can live safely and productively. Economic resources and legal protections developed with community interests in mind are fundamental components of enabling justice and developing a safer, feminist society.

Hunting Criminals

In *The Closer* (TNT 2005–2012), a television detective series linking professional and personal plots centering on a female protagonist, the audience simultaneously recognizes women's independence and vulnerability, while considering that any woman can be a victim of men's anger and a lagging legal system.[36] Recent television series demonstrate narrative complexity in establishing their fictional worlds and by developing round and flat characters that engage over time within intersecting narrative arcs. As Jason Mittell explains, "Narrative complexity is a redefinition of episodic forms under the influence of serial narration—not necessarily a complete merger' of episodic and serial forms but a shifting balance. Rejecting the need for plot closure within every episode that typifies conventional episodic form, narrative complexity foregrounds ongoing stories across a range of genres."[37] Adhering to the narrative conventions of the police procedural, *The Closer* references the work of real-world detectives, incorporates information about forensic techniques, and includes personal details about major fictional characters to amplify feminist messages concerning social inequities and legal limitations. Interdependent elements of character and action in the drama's weekly subplots develop the portrait of a female police chief of detectives who is vulnerable to male violence. The series sketches how her professional authority and feminist principles affect her interactions with family, friends, colleagues, witnesses, and criminals, revealing the nuances of pursuing justice in a world dominated by male hierarchies of power.

Although most episodes of the show introduce and resolve homicides or other major crimes, the major narrative arc of *The Closer* weaves a multiyear story line around this white female detective's long pursuit of a particular criminal, a lawyer who uses his knowledge of his women clients to stalk, rape, and kill them. *The Closer* reconfigures genre conventions and gender stereotypes associated with police procedurals, focusing on Chief Johnson's position as a woman in authority within a male-dominated work environment and encouraging viewers to consider how her feminism and femininity influence her work.[38] Brenda's method of solving murder cases draws on her abilities to put together evidence and to extract confessions, "tough" abilities that contrast with her "soft" appearance and speech. The series highlights her unusual style and questions her relentless pursuit of justice for victims, describing her rise and fall as chief of a major police division and encouraging ethical criticism of her lapses as a chief determined to convict criminals by whatever means necessary.

Peter Rabinowitz explains that a name in the title of a fiction marks the character as "Showing up in a position privileged by a rule of notice," which is "one way of attracting attention."[39] *The Closer* is a moniker rather than a proper name; however, using the phrase in the show's title draws attention to the protagonist and her special abilities concerning interrogating suspects and analyzing forensic evidence. The series highlights character and action as equally important. As Shlomith Rimmon-Kenan argues, "It is legitimate to subordinate character to action when we study action, but equally legitimate to subordinate action to character when the latter is the focus of our study."[40] The interdependence of character and action in *The Closer* highlights gender issues and questions the law-and-order ideology of police procedurals. The series resets gender codes in acknowledging the female protagonist's weaknesses and strengths in relation to her effectiveness as an investigator and as a manager who blends stereotypes in combining a feminine appearance and masculine work methods.

Kyra Sedgwick plays Brenda Leigh Johnson, a confident, attractive woman who left the Atlanta Police Department to take charge of a Los Angeles police squad of homicide experts drawn from various divisions. Chief Johnson and her squad usually resolve one case within a one-hour episode, while details from earlier episodes crop up in later ones as Brenda's character transforms. Brenda initially appears as a feminine, Southern interloper entering the hard-boiled masculine world of homicide investigators who work by competing, upstaging, and yelling. She quickly learns that many of her new colleagues resent her; some members of her squad threaten to quit rather than work with her. Over time Brenda wins the respect of her new employees and peers because she is an excellent detective and leader of her elite unit; it helps that she is extremely polite and that her deliberative approach to work convinces them that each case must be dissected to discern which elements in testimonies are out of place and which story is not credible. Her distinctive abilities as "the closer," whose deft handling of interrogations results in convictions, make her admired until her dogged determination to solve crimes triggers her ethical lapse and incurs financial liability and embarrassment for the city.

Brenda's girlish, feminine appearance and her commanding authority attract attention. Most episodes begin at a crime scene with detectives looking for clues as Chief Johnson arrives. The typical first camera shot of Brenda, an eyeline match that fits Laura Mulvey's formulation of "the male gaze," begins at the character's feet and travels up her body before keeping her in a medium shot at the scene or in the Los Angeles Police Department (LAPD) offices.[41] Robert Dale Parker notes that "Mulvey describes classical Hollywood cinema as organized around a binary opposition between a masculine spectator, the subject, and what we might call a feminine spectated, the object."[42] Viewers observe Brenda shod in high heels, wearing pastel or brightly colored sweaters or highly stylized jackets with flowing, often flowery skirts, with her hair long and loose or tied up as if for prom, and carrying a large black shoulder bag that holds a combination of work files, material evidence, and personal stuff, including a cache of sweets. As the camera pans out from her figure, Brenda compels viewers' attention as her outfit—skirt and sweater, dress, or trench coat in beige, pink, coral, red, or white—stands out among the ensemble of dark-gray and black suits worn by her colleagues.

As the highest-ranking female in the Los Angeles Police Department, Brenda has a reputation for closing difficult cases by encouraging murderers and witnesses to talk, largely by employing "soft" communication skills she honed while working for the Central Intelligence Agency, where she learned about forensic techniques that make her a sharp interrogator.

The series rewrites gender stereotypes in its characterizations of the chief and her team: crusty and aggressive male detectives reveal sentimental streaks, while their chief appears to be a glamour girl with a heart of steel. Chief Johnson combines traits typed as masculine (assertiveness, aggression, risk-taking, and authoritative decision-making) and as feminine (attractive appearance, polite speech, emotionality, and flirtatiousness). Brenda's strong Southern accent, overly polite manners, and entrenched candy habit supplement her expertise. While interrogating witnesses and criminals, she sometimes adopts a persona that appears sympathetic to the interviewees, particularly when she leads them to believe she does not work for the police so that they will be more open in speaking with her. By the end of each episode, Brenda appears more authoritative and more admirable as a detective and as a woman because she adroitly combines masculine and feminine strengths in achieving successful outcomes for investigations.

As a cultural figure, the television female detective embodies stereotypes of femininity blended with methods of ratiocination, a quality shared with other fictional detectives, including Auguste Dupin, Sherlock Holmes, Miss Marple, and Jessica Fletcher. The female detective's appearance in print, television, and film narratives about crimes acknowledges her moral commitment to determine truth and her professional duty to punish the guilty, although her methods are frequently unorthodox and run counter to those employed by her male counterparts. Priscilla Walton and Manina Jones argue that the cinematic representation of an attractive female police officer focuses on "the conflation of sexuality and power" that appears "as both a contradiction and a threat."[43] Other recent television series set the female detective's sensuality, competence, and compassion within legal institutions, largely police stations and courts, contexts that highlight gender, ethnic, and class differences and problems of gender equity in institutions.

Police dramas reinforce social norms and ideologies of law and order, as series starring women illustrate their subversive tendencies to skirt official procedures, to resort to informal channels of communication, or to use other extra-procedural ways of collecting and analyzing evidence. Gender inequities in detective stories are dramatized and visually represented by a character's different physical stance, wardrobe, and emotions. Institutional settings highlight tensions when there are many more men than women, when men's authority dominates or represses women, or when a woman's professional style, attitude, or workspace is depicted as stereotypically feminine. The female detective can seem uncomfortable in domestic settings, sometimes cast as a fish out of water because of her inadequate domestic skills. Brenda has limited cooking abilities and tends to be sloppy at home. During the series, her emotional vulnerabilities emerge after she learns she is in early menopause. Few television procedurals link criminal investigations as closely to one detective's personal life as *The Closer* does in delving into Johnson's health and reproductive status, her sexual history, her relationships with her husband and parents, and her home and pet ownership. Each episode links particular aspects of her life to details in the cases investigated by her and her squad, connecting details to elaborate a portrait of a woman using any means necessary to protect herself and others in a chaotic urban environment.

Most people have no idea what they are up against when they speak with Chief Johnson, who looks like a model but who always remains focused on solving crime. Brenda's sensitivity, including her skill in interpreting facial expressions and body language, enables her to monitor the emotions of suspects during investigations and to judge the veracity of their statements during interrogations. She suggests that she will help witnesses and suspects if they tell the truth, but these offers are attempts to bait interlocutors into confessions of guilt. For example, in the penultimate episode of the series, after Brenda suggests to a female teenage suspect that mitigating circumstances may set the girl free, the teenager admits that she lied by identifying an innocent man as her rapist because she hoped to protect her boyfriend from her domineering father's rage.

Brenda arrests both the girl and her father for the second-degree murder of a war hero falsely accused of rape by the teenager and killed by the father.

The narrative arc of the series moves from highlighting Brenda's success at work, which makes her home life problematic, to examining her moral integrity by questioning her specific aggressive decisions and actions as deputy chief. Her traditionally feminine, radically feminist, and distinctly quirky traits constrain and enable her ability to solve cases and to work with peers and supervisors who question her behavior and actions. Difficulties in Brenda's personal life, notably vicissitudes in romantic and family relationships, health concerns (including learning that she is no longer fertile), and anxieties about driving and finding a suitable home in a strange city, compete with the challenges of managing her team of headstrong detectives as they investigate and solve cases. At first, Brenda appears to be a stickler for the rules, but over time she bends protocol and procedures to protect her squad and to close cases, which highlight conflicts between men and women leading to murder, for, as Lt. Provenza claims, it is usually an intimate partner who is guilty of homicide. During the series, Brenda matures emotionally as she learns to communicate productively with her family and coworkers.

Her obsession with arresting and convicting criminals is represented as a kind of competitiveness: she does not want criminals to beat the system, and she will use any means possible to incarcerate the guilty. Her core integrity is questioned in later episodes by colleagues, the press, and attorneys who complain that she follows her own rules to force confessions and to trample on the rights of criminal suspects. Narrative critic James Phelan points out that ethics and aesthetics are always interconnected.[44] The ethics and aesthetics of *The Closer* illustrate the problems associated with the protagonist's admirable efficiency in closing cases, as Brenda's relentless pursuit of the guilty puts her in a morally precarious position when she overreaches to punish a confessed criminal who received immunity from prosecution.

Brenda's supervisor, the chief of police, indicates that she has a hard time understanding that there are other people in the world, and her squad for a time regards her compulsion to analyze evidence and to determine guilt as problems. Even after earning the respect of her subordinates, Brenda remains marginalized as her methods are scrutinized in the department and beyond by those who worry about the legal and ethical rights of criminals. Creators of *The Closer* were inspired by Helen Mirren's performance as Detective Chief Inspector Jane Tennison in the British television series *Prime Suspect*, which debuted in 1991. Tennison is an idiosyncratic, effective, and culturally sensitive investigator who becomes sexually involved with colleagues and who manages hostility from the dominating men she works with by being as tough as they are until she gets home. While Tennison's determination at work makes her appear as rugged as the boys, Brenda takes a different way to demonstrate her authority. Media critic Maddy Dychtwald points out that Brenda "retains (and revels in) her femininity, keeps her composure, can handle the two 'sexist pigs' who bait her due to their jealousy and insecurities, and not lose her head."[45] Unlike male colleagues who are louder and more obnoxious to assert their authority, Brenda works in a low but effective register with her steely glance, cool words, and extreme courtesy.

The chief's gender and her feminine ways become advantages in many cases. During her second case in Los Angeles (*About Face*, season 1, episode 2), Brenda enters the world of Heather Kingsley (Helen Tucker), a former model, who died at home from nicotine poisoning. Although many on Brenda's squad assume the husband, a Hollywood movie star, is the logical murder suspect, she insists on interviewing all who had contact with Heather before the murder; this trail leads Chief Johnson and Sgt. David Gabriel (Corey Reynolds) from a hairdresser's salon to a dress shop and then to a makeup artist's studio before arriving at a restaurant. Interviewing a series of witnesses, Brenda gets a makeover along the way. She adopts a becoming hairstyle; buys a red, fitted, V-neck dress with white trim around the empire waist and neckline; and has her makeup done by a professional. Her investigative method of putting herself in the victim's footsteps coincides with her transformation into a glamorous Californian. By following the victim's trail, Brenda realizes that the husband's extramarital affairs embarrassed the victim into looking her best for a confrontation with a rival. After the coroner's autopsy shows that nicotine entered through the victim's hair, Brenda concludes that the husband's affair with the pregnant hairdresser motivated the latter to kill her lover's wife.

Brenda's past includes some missteps, information that surfaces after she moves to Los Angeles. Her career in Atlanta was harmed by a morals charge instigated by her ex-husband, although it was later dismissed. Before being hired by Will Pope (J. K. Simmons) to work in Los Angeles's Police Department, Brenda worked for him in the Washington, DC, police department. They had an affair while she was single and he was married to his first wife, information not initially known by her squad. Her past reputation positions Brenda as a less than perfect human being like others in the Los Angeles Police Department. The real-world backstory for the series highlights the police force's diminished reputation, which was tarnished by various high-profile cases, including the Rampart scandal in which seventy police officers were implicated in crimes that took place from March 1997 to December 2001.[46] Brenda's squad lived through those difficult times, although they did not participate in crimes and were not accused of corruption. The Closer aligns the department's troubled history with Brenda's ethical lapses.

Brenda's subordinates exhibited distinct hostility toward her after she joins the LAPD, and many comments reveal the department's toxic environment for women. Senior detective Lt. Provenza has four ex-wives about whom he frequently offers criticism. Lt. Flynn, who is also a divorced white male senior officer, is known for his cynicism and his smart quips at murder scenes; his disparagement of the decision to appoint a woman as division chief motivates him to ask that Brenda be terminated. Detective Julio Sanchez (Raymond Cruz) knows about Los Angeles gangs and seems on the make whenever speaking with a pretty woman. Detective Irene Daniels (Gina Ravera) is a highly qualified investigator of financial malfeasance, while Detective David Gabriel is the first squad member to support Brenda as chief. Daniels and Gabriel have a short romance that results in her leaving the squad. Over time, squad members, who moved from different divisions, bond with each other and with Brenda by acting in a coordinated fashion to analyze physical evidence, witness statements, and interrogations associated with each case to formulate a credible narrative of how and why the crime was committed. Each episode concentrates on an investigation of a crime with a gendered dimension, depicting detectives who speculate about methods, motives, and opportunities to solve cases.

Focusing on a woman with a high-profile job, talented subordinates, and a handsome, accomplished husband, The Closer depicts Brenda's trials and tribulations as typical of female professionals while also appealing to anyone struggling to manage work and a personal life. Brenda relies on her superior interrogation techniques, sensitivity to cues revealing when someone is lying, and efficient management of talented squad members to close each case. She applies information or principles learned outside her job and a deft understanding of diverse human needs and interests to press criminals to confess. Relentlessly working to resolve each case and rarely leaving work at the office, she frequently consults with Fritz at home to get his perspective and access to FBI information and technology. Brenda is so obsessed with murder that when playing tourist in Hollywood with her mother and husband, she asks about the cause of death at each star's home that they visit. Although Brenda's main job is solving homicides, she also investigates sex crimes. Brenda remains haunted by the women victims stalked and deceived by serial rapist and murderer Philip Stroh, so she investigates his activities on her own time, retaining in her home many files relevant to cases involving this lawyer who used his position to commit rapes and murders.

Brenda elicits testimony from suspects, witnesses, and officers that supply necessary, yet otherwise overlooked details to construct a narrative accounting for each crime and sometimes its cover-up. She notices contradictions in testimony, asking questions and making assertions that prompt people to reveal key information they are trying to hide. Often her interlocutors don't realize they are speaking to a police officer when Brenda conducts interviews because she will lie and say she is an administrative assistant, a social worker, or even a lawyer.

Brenda uses deception and coercion to solve cases, doing so by establishing an "illusion of intimacy," as Richard Leo argues.[47] As Mark Godsey notes, "Police have developed fraud-based interrogation techniques because they assume that every suspect under interrogation is guilty and needs some coercion and trickery to come clean, and because the police 'view themselves as agents of the prosecution and thus the suspect's adversary.'"[48] Adversarial communication between suspect and police must be carefully controlled to produce a reliable outcome. The model interrogation method promoted in US police departments is the Reid technique, which relies on three primary phases of a process to solve a crime: collecting and analyzing evidence to determine the investigation's direction and to establish insight into the suspect, conducting a nonaccusatory interview of the suspect to ask behavior-provoking questions to interpret a subject's responses, and managing an accusatory interrogation to elicit further evidence.

The Closer depicts police work following phases of the Reid technique, although Brenda often independently discovers (or sometimes manufactures) evidence that she mentions to the suspect in the accusatory interrogation.[49] Chief Johnson argues that lying to suspects is a logical, if unethical, procedure because she believes the suspects are also lying. She and her squad deceive assumed criminals by encouraging them to confess to crimes whether the police have physical evidence in the cases or not. A forced confession is a critical tool in the police arsenal, so the series illustrates how a skilled interviewer can persuade or trick a suspect into confessing, which will conclude the investigation and allow the case to go to trial. The value of a coerced confession may be questionable, but "in fact confessions have more impact on case outcomes than other persuasive forms of evidence."[50] Brenda and her squad are rarely called into courtrooms on the show. Therefore, viewers don't often get to see whether confessions produce convictions.

Brenda is like the femme fatale in film noir, who, according to Walton and Jones, "represents female power in the social and economic realm as inappropriate, deviant, and unlawful," and who can be regarded as "configuring an ambivalent relationship to the institution of the law."[51] In seasons 3 and 4, Brenda must deal with a journalist shadowing her and questioning her actions, and, in season 5, Internal Affairs Captain Sharon Raydor tracks Brenda's every step as ethical and legal aspects of Brenda's methods are questioned. Early seasons of *The Closer* point to Brenda's work as an antidote to the corrupt practices that long pervaded the LAPD, but later episodes punish her overzealousness to root out crime and to punish criminals.

Concomitantly, while solving high profile murder cases in subversive ways, Brenda matures during the series. In later episodes, she is married rather than being a single woman in a scandalous extramarital affair, she and Fritz find a better home than her first one (a house vacated because the occupant was murdered), she becomes a parental substitute on a sometime basis to her niece, and she learns Los Angeles geography and manners. The last two seasons of *The Closer* depict complications stemming from Brenda's unorthodox strategies to prompt criminal confessions. Her decisions lead to civil actions harming the police department's reputation and affecting the city's finances. Culminating in episodes in which Brenda is subject to continuing oversight, season 7 focuses on the question of whether her actions are legal and ethical. Over others' objections, Brenda ordered her squad to leave the man receiving immunity to be released to his home in a dangerous neighborhood, where gang members sought revenge and quickly killed him. The man's family subsequently filed a civil lawsuit against Brenda because she left him without any police protection in known gang territory. The 2011–2012 season includes Captain Raydor's Internal Affairs audit, a leak from someone with knowledge of Brenda's division, and the suit filed by the family's zealous attorney. Although a judge stops the lawsuit, its documentation reveals that in many cases Brenda's suspects die in police custody, evidence that serves as the basis of a federal lawsuit against Brenda for violating the civil rights of the accused by using deceptive practices.

The portrait of a feminist woman in authority who uses violence and deception to end violence against women contributes to dramatic suspense, although violence begetting violence offers little satisfaction to viewers in search of optimistic solutions. Brenda is replaced in the subsequent series with a feminist woman leader solving crimes without deception and violence. The final episodes in the final season of *The Closer* transition to the new series, *Major Crimes*, starring Mary McDonnell as Captain Sharon Raydor, who is committed to protecting victims according to procedure. The culmination of *The Closer* introduces Rusty Beck (Graham Patrick Martin) as a witness to rapist and serial killer Philip Stroh's burial of a corpse. Stroh chases and attacks Rusty, but the teenager manages to escape. After a security camera in a department store connects Stroh to the dead woman, Brenda uses Rusty, who has previously prostituted himself, as bait to lure Stroh on to the street where he is arrested for cruising.

Even with Rusty as a witness, the police cannot arrest Stroh because they do not have physical evidence to connect him to the murders of several women buried in Griffith Park. Frustrated and clever, Brenda attacks Stroh in the elevator of the police building. Deputy District Attorney Hobbs accompanies Rusty and Brenda to the coroner's office, where the pathologist with the DA's permission takes Stroh's DNA, collected by Brenda, and inserts it in the wool cap that Rusty pulled off Stroh's head during the attack in the park. Brenda brings Rusty home to encourage him to share evidence. Stroh surreptitiously enters Brenda's house and takes Rusty hostage, holds a knife at the boy's throat, and threatens to kill him, prompting Brenda to tell Stroh that she manufactured evidence against him and to let the boy go. Cool in a crisis, Brenda remembers that Rusty told her how he protected himself from dangerous men, and she tells Rusty to "go slack," that he should flip Stroh over. After Rusty knocks down Stroh and there is a safe distance between them, Brenda finds her gun and shoots Stroh through her handbag.

Brenda does not kill Stroh, and she refuses to hear him talk about his crimes. As Matt Webb Mitovich points out, "*Brenda lives on*. She was not killed off in some hero's death. She did not leave in disgrace. She theoretically could resurface. . . . And she moves on to her new career with needed closure, knowing that Phillip Stroh will prey no more."[52] The conclusion highlights Brenda's effectiveness in capturing a wily criminal who raped and killed women. Although Brenda manufactured evidence to bait Stroh, she stopped his campaign of violence against women without killing him. Brenda raised herself in the estimation of viewers, who may be critical of her deceptions, by not killing Stroh. Other narratives discussed in this chapter illustrate that extraordinary means is used to stop violence against women. *Paradise* acknowledges that men in Ruby kill the Convent women, but the men are not punished and may kill again. *The Round House* illustrates how vigilante violence kills a rapist-murderer who might otherwise go free. Brenda entraps Stroh to stop his campaign of violence and to protect herself.

Yet Brenda is no longer "the closer" because there is no scene of Stroh being interrogated or confessing. In the last two episodes of *The Closer*, Brenda realizes that she is tired of listening to bad people, that she is weary after her mother's unexpected death, and that she needs to spend more time with the living. She accepts a job as chief of the district attorney's bureau of investigation and negotiates to bring David Gabriel with her. *The Closer* was a popular and critical success in the US, and Sedgwick won numerous awards for her performance over seven seasons. From 2006 to 2010, she "made history as being the only female actor in the history of television to be nominated for an Emmy, Golden Globe, and Screen Actors Guild award every year that the show aired in the eligibility period."[53] The syndicated series was successfully exported to many European countries, Korea, and South Africa. The show's focus on a competent, attractive professional woman managing a squad of detectives and facing down criminals reconfigures stereotypes of femininity, illustrating Brenda's transformation from an enthusiastic, effective chief of detectives to a weary, mourning leader.

Brenda's last scene with her squad shows her accepting their parting gift: a handbag like the one destroyed by her shooting of Stroh. In replacing their chief's signature item, an object combining associations with femininity and technical expertise, the team seeks to heal her wounds; they filled the new handbag with small chocolate cakes with cream. Her final words to the team are "It looks like love," spoken in her gentle voice as she is tearing up. Leaving the squad, Brenda enters the elevator to depart her old job while unwrapping and eating a small cake. The character of Brenda regains integrity in the narrative by refusing to kill

Stroh and by leaving a job that encourages her to make bad people talk. Stroh is incarcerated, and Brenda is free to establish a healthier life in a less demanding position.

Writing about the interdependence of character and action, Porter Abbott notes that "Characters, to put this in narratological terms, have *agency*; they cause things to happen. Conversely, as these people drive the action, they necessarily reveal who they are in terms of their motives, their strength, weakness, trustworthiness, capacity to love, hate, cherish, adore, deplore, and so on. By their actions do we know them."[54] Providing a character study of a feminist woman detective, *The Closer* illustrates its protagonist's competence in closing cases as intertwined with her personal traits. To be "a closer," means that she is quick to judge, slow to forgive, and eager to punish criminals, even those not convicted by the legal system. Her actions drive the narrative. She forces confessions in some cases in ways that provoke ethical criticism regarding her means and their outcomes. Over the course of the series, Brenda becomes less concerned about following procedure and protecting criminals' rights, but her faults stem from her desire to close cases regardless of the costs; these are forgiven as she leaves her job as chief. The series flirts with feminism in its characterization of Brenda, whose rigorous technical skills and toughness make her an example for women in technical and other nontraditional careers. By leaving her job as chief to take a position allowing her to have more personal time, she models a healthier and more domestic lifestyle.

Texts about violent crimes directed against women acknowledge that gender discrimination, bias, and social stereotypes of masculine and feminine roles provide social contexts for understanding what might seem to be anomalous individual transgressions. *Paradise*, *The Round House*, and *The Closer* indicate that systemic, structural circumstances contribute to criminal transgressions and foster injustices against women. Information in these narratives contributes to the argument that society should eliminate antiwomen rhetoric, practices, and actions. Necessary reforms include changing laws, encouraging women's leadership, being more sensitive to victims and survivors, and protecting historically vulnerable social groups from violence and abuse. The narratives indicate that if legal and ethical means fail, people will act in transgressive and dangerous ways, while noting feminist examples of heroism and collective support from like-minded individuals to recommend mechanisms protecting women and enhancing gender equity.

Chapter 7

Feminist Politics in Fiction

Perhaps the queer point would be to suggest that we don't have to choose between pessimism and optimism. We can explore the strange and perverse mixtures of hope and despair, of optimism and pessimism, within forms of politics that take as a starting point a critique of the world as it is and a belief that the world can be different.

—Sara Ahmed, "Happy Futures, Perhaps" (2011)[1]

The world urgently needs your leadership. Recognize that you are the unique person you are, with your own special power to shape the future—for yourself and for our country.

—Nancy Pelosi, Smith College Commencement Address (2020)[2]

Focusing on cultural shifts prompted by eighteenth- and nineteenth-century literature, Nancy Armstrong's *Desire and Domestic Fiction* explicates the ways in which "novels were supposed to rewrite political history as personal histories that elaborated on the courtship procedures ensuring a happy domestic life."[3] Many novels steered clear of national and world politics or submerged political issues, but they interrogated social categories: "fiction was particularly good at picking up fragments of an agrarian and artisan culture when it recast them as gender differences and contained them within a domestic framework."[4] Armstrong references Elaine Showalter's explanation: "The belief that essential differences distinguished men from women and gave each powers that the other did not possess provided the basis . . . on which a feminine subculture sought to extend women's power."[5] Class conflicts in fictional narratives existed alongside struggles between men and women, with novels positing political and moral ideas related to improving individuals and society.

Today women occupy some leadership positions in business and education, but they are still not proportionally represented in governments and therefore have less influence in determining how public funds should be spent.[6] Similarly, there are relatively few transgender and non-cis-gendered individuals who serve at local and state levels of government in the US and in the UK.[7] According to statistics cited by UN Women, "Only 25 per cent of all national parliamentarians were women" as of October 2020 and "As of 1 September 2021, 26 women are serving as Heads of State and/or Government in 24 countries."[8] UN Women's call to action regarding parliamentarians indicates that there has been progress toward greater gender equality around the world since the 1995 Beijing Declaration and Proclamation for Action, but as of 2019 "not a single country can claim to have achieved gender equality and multiple obstacles remain unchanged in law and in culture."[9] "Key acceleration points" in the call to action are "ending discriminatory laws; increasing the number of women in parliaments, cabinets and leadership; implementing progressive law reforms; challenging norms and traditional gender stereotyping; and supporting other women in politics."[10] These initiatives influence attitudes, practices, and laws to create a just society, part of a feminist vision incorporating women's leadership, minority rights, and gender equity.

Media representations of progressive politics educate the public about feminism's prospects and the benefits of electing women and minorities to legislative office while acknowledging the complexities of politics as a profession.[11] Popular US and British film and televisual fictional narratives about politicians include realistic characterizations of nonwhite and nonmale politicians and government officials.[12] Various genres, including comedies, satires, romances, dramas, thrillers, and fictionalized documentaries, show government activities, achievements, and scandals.[13] This chapter considers fictional representations of women political leaders as information illustrating feminist motives and initiatives and inspiring hopes for reform.

Countering Expectations

Offering a comic story about a woman president, the film *Kisses for My President* (1964) with Polly Bergen and Fred McMurray focuses on a married couple adopting political roles after the wife is elected and the husband becomes "first lady": "Even though he had his own business, he forgoes that to stay at home and becomes bored with the duties that are usually given to ladies in that position: planning the banquets, what's for supper, guiding the tours, etc."[14] In the 1960s, US social views regarding employment and leadership for women and minorities were shifting, but not fast enough. Until the passage of Title VII of the Civil Rights Act in 1964, which prohibits employment discrimination based on race, color, religion, sex and national origin, women were more likely to be home-makers than employees or public leaders. Modeling a domestic role in the White House, First Lady Jacqueline Bouvier Kennedy worked to restore and preserve the building and gardens; her contributions were shared in television and other press coverage, and it may have influenced the film-makers' decision to emphasize domestic tasks for McMurray's character.[15] Polly Bergen also played the mother of a female president in the short-lived television drama *Commander in Chief* (2005–06), starring Geena Davis as Mackenzie Allen, a former university chancellor serving as the first female vice president who unexpectedly becomes president after her predecessor has a stroke in his second year of office. Allen's husband was a state attorney general, but he works as her chief of staff until becoming "First Person" while the president's mother serves as hostess. Episodes of *Commander in Chief* combine stories about the Allen family with national and international political challenges requiring that the president apply her gender lens to governing.

Like *Kisses for My President* and *Commander in Chief*, *Veep* (2012–2019) foregrounds gender inversions and family complications worked out in a political environment.[16] Taking a different tone from the dramas *Scandal* (2012–2018) and *House of Cards* (2013–2018), which encompass politically driven plot lines playing with stereotypes of feminism and fem-ininity, the comic satire *Veep* points out foibles and failings of a woman who serves as an ignored vice president until the president resigns. Unlike *The West Wing* (1999–2006), which offered an idealistic administration pursuing progressive policies, *Veep* depicts the ugly side of politics, using caricatured characters and provocative dialogue to show "the idiocy and narcissism and vitriol fueling the US government" along with the "mal-ice and incompetence" of politicians and their staffs.[17] *Veep*'s protagonist Selina Meyer (Julia Louis-Dreyfus) appears to be an "antiheroine" in that she is foul-mouthed, unethical, prone to illegal actions, and lacking in all loyalty, ultimately allowing her faithful, admiring body man, Gary, to be blamed and imprisoned for overseeing financial improprieties of her

Meyer fund; evading responsibility for the crime, Selina can finally take office in her own right as president. In *Veep*'s last season, Selina's presidential campaign has its ups and down, largely because she offers no substantive policy ideas during a lackluster campaign marred by incompetence. She receives a big boost in public support only after telling her opponent Senator Kemi Talbot, who is multiracial, attractive, hopeful, and leading in the polls, that Kemi, and by extension all women, should stop complaining about bias and barriers and should "man up." This improvised argument dismissing women's concerns as petty gripes captured public attention, earned the party's nomination, and won the presidency for her. Selina's feminism focuses on her advancement; she feels constrained by her gender and objects to gender inequities and discrimination, but her dominant ideological principles combine egotism, defensiveness, and revenge. Her willingness to do anything to be elected stems from neurotic desperation, and her policy positions aim to make her popular rather than solving social problems. A narcissist, Selena is not regarded by anyone else as a feminist.

Feminist Ethics in Politics

More serious in tone than *Veep* and more insightful about women who manage government and family, the television series *The Amazing Mrs. Pritchard* (2006), *Borgen* (2010–2013) and *Borgen: Power and Glory* (2022), and *Madam Secretary* (2014–2019) represent the political leadership of feminist women who strive to infuse integrity and ethics into governance. These series outline limits and prospects of feminism in domestic and international politics, suggesting a near future more concerned with social investments than armed conflicts. Respectively produced in three countries—Britain, Denmark, and the United States—and detailing different national political processes, *The Amazing Mrs. Pritchard*, *Borgen*, and *Madam Secretary* identify professional and personal challenges faced by Prime Minister Rosamund Pritchard, Minister Birgitte Nyborg, and Secretary of State Elizabeth McCord. These feminist women politicians strive to develop a more equitable, ethical world despite barriers raised by colleagues, institutions, and social conventions. Pritchard, Nyborg, and McCord inject feminist principles into politics but compromise when circumstances demand. The promise of a feminist future created by women activists concludes Meg Wolitzer's novel *The Female Persuasion* (2018), which describes feminist women from successive generations who work in nonprofit and media organizations as they press for needed progressive policy and social reforms. These narratives outline challenges for women in politics while offering sympathetic, hopeful feminists as role models and detailing realistic plots that encourage viewers and readers to develop equitable social practices and legislative policies.

Feminist leaders who rise swiftly and unexpectedly to powerful political positions, Pritchard, Nyborg, and McCord struggle with domestic problems while intervening in national and international crises. They sacrifice time with spouses and children and have few personal interests because they spend their waking lives working on behalf of their governments to protect citizens and national interests. Plots elaborate how feminist principles of equity are difficult to enact in policy and legislation and how women suffer slights and discrimination in pursuing political agendas and policy change. Conflicts emerge: these women, who were elected or appointed based on their honesty, integrity, and flexibility and their commitments to social equity and gender equality, realize they are asked to bend their principles to reach their goals, to help allies, or to stay in power. In this way, the narratives acknowledge limitations in establishing political equality, while sketching the utopian attractiveness of feminist ideas that promise a better future. The series depict woman politicians who tap into community concerns to meet social challenges. Although tracking different forms of government—Britain and Denmark are homes to parliamentary forms of representative democracies, while in the US representative democracy in the legislative branch complements executive and judicial power—The Amazing Mrs. Pritchard, Borgen, and Madam Secretary offer comparable characterizations of female politicians whose values of equity, agency, and consultation guide their careers.

Feminist politicians in these shows advocate for women's and children's rights and support equality initiatives as well as those related to environment, health, education, and social welfare. These leaders encourage democratic debate and collaborative decision-making, trends that emulate those in the real world of national politics.[18] Toril Moi pointed out in 1988 "that since the 1960s, socialist feminism in its various forms has been the dominant trend in British and Scandinavian feminism, both inside and outside academic institutions."[19] Henrietta Moore identifies dimensions of feminism that resonate with strengths of political leadership: "In a minimalist definition, feminism could be taken to refer to the awareness of women's oppression and exploitation at work, in the home and in society as well as to the conscious political action taken by women to change this situation."[20]Aligning with these descriptions, the three television series in the main represent women politicians whose feminist beliefs infuse their policies and practices. Prime Ministers Rosamund Pritchard and Birgitte Nyborg and Secretary of State Elizabeth McCord often express their ethical concerns to protect and care for citizens of their own and other nations rather than selfishly seeking to enlarge their political power and privilege. Even *Borgen: Power and Glory*, which focuses on foreign minister Birgitte Nyborg's struggle for power with the female prime minister, has its long arc narrative culminate with women realizing that good governance and management matter more than individual success. Feminist politicians in these narratives serve their countries because they are committed to equity, justice, and democracy.

Family Problems

Like others who combine work and family, fictional women with high-powered jobs as Prime Minister and Secretary of State have domestic responsibilities related to cooking, cleaning, and parenting. *The Amazing Mrs. Pritchard* (2006), a six-part BBC One series, details the rise and fall of Rosalind Pritchard (Jane Horrocks) as she learns the political ropes and eventually becomes tied up by them. *Mrs. Pritchard* kicks off with an episode in which Ros, a successful supermarket manager and efficient homemaker who at the end of her long workday simultaneously cleans the kitchen, prepares dinner, and debriefs her family without missing a beat, becomes well-known and respected by the British public after she is interviewed on television. When opposing politicians running for parliamentary election tussle in front of her store, an irritated Ros separates the men. She tells them and the television news journalists who ask about her involvement that even though she doesn't know much about politics she could do a better job than these male candidates. Encouraged by female coworkers, her daughters, an angel investor, and a political strategist, Ros runs for election and forms a new party, the Purple Democratic Alliance. Ordinary and high-powered women decide to run as part of Ros's new party, combining efforts to win a record number of seats and earning Ros the post of prime minister. In her opening speech in front of 10 Downing Street, Ros promises that she will never lie and that she will always be transparent. She exemplifies integrity and truth while campaigning, but once elected she has difficulties in running the government along these lines because daily crises challenge Ros's plans to open the business of government to "the great British people."

Inspired by an idea shared by her daughter's teacher, Ros proposes to transfer the seat of government from London to Bradford and to sell Westminster; however, the prospect of moving Parliament horrifies ministers who resist Ros's attempts to push forward with reformist plans to save money and to connect the government to previously neglected regions. Ros becomes less flexible, less willing to compromise tactics and strategy, in the subsequent year of her administration. While attending an international climate summit, she impulsively commits Great Britain to a green initiative: car-free Wednesdays. Cabinet ministers advise against phasing in this plan, but she decides to implement it quickly. Her struggles at home with her husband and oldest daughter run along similar lines as Ros's rapid decisions override her family's wishes. She forces her husband to find a new job and move to London so the family can stay together while she is in office. Yet on both fronts, family and government, Ros can only push so far against those who disagree, or she risks being dictatorial or outmaneuvered.

The most damaging crises for Ros's administration concern money; one involves her accountant husband Ian's past illegal behavior laundering criminal money, while another ethical problem concerns her angel investor who loaned money to women politicians so they would defect to the Purple Alliance. Ros's investor Kitty and her political strategist Miranda conceal for a time that Ian was forced by his employer to approve illegal business transfers fifteen years earlier. A drunken Ian later reveals his crime to his and Ros's daughter Emily, who reacts badly and tells her mother despite Kitty and Miranda pressing Emily not to tell Ros about Ian's misdeed to preserve the prime minister's deniability.

Another ethical dilemma arises as Ros's cabinet ministers worry about her awarding a lucrative information technology contract to Kitty's neophyte firm. Hillary reaches out to her former political rival Catherine who tells the prime minister that the contract is not appropriate. Ros realizes that Catherine is correct and that there are only two options: Ros could divorce Ian and stay in power, or she could give up being prime minister to remain quiet about her husband's crime. The two women make different choices affecting their personal lives and political careers. Ros wants to stay married and does not want to endanger her legacy as an upright prime minister, so she resigns the post. Catherine and her young lover break up after she refuses to tarnish her public profile by kissing him in public, and she becomes prime minister. Circumstances beyond Ros's control—her investor's bribing candidates and her husband's laundering money—weaken her political position. The series does not allow women to be successful in two domains, although it suggests that feminist politics could offer a promising future if women avoid the missteps of family and supporters or if the electorate disregards personal problems and relationships. Women who wish to enact a feminist agenda affirming equity must also manage the quid pro quo negotiation in governing that often takes the place of bipartisan compromise. Nevertheless, *The Amazing Mrs. Pritchard* makes plausible the prospect that governments could transform to promote gender equity if leaders (and their supporters) maintain integrity.[21]

Ethics and Democracy

In thirty episodes broadcast over three seasons, *Borgen* (2010–2013) highlights the intermingling of political and media interests in Denmark by developing a story line around the country's first female prime minister, while the 2022 season encompasses eight episodes centering on an older, more politically savvy Birgitte Nyborg (Sidse Babett Knudsen).[22] The Danish series connects politicians with media personalities Kasper Juul, Katrine Fonsmark, and Torben Friis. Most characters in the first three seasons exhibit flaws and make mistakes, although the four central characters—Birgitte, Kasper, Katrine, and Torben—are idealistic and sympathetic because they strive to act ethically in managing political circumstances and personal challenges. Kasper and Katrine serve at different times as "spin doctors" for Birgitte and for a time are romantically involved with each other. Katrine shifts from being an investigative reporter and political correspondent to working for a politician, while Kasper moves in the opposite direction, going from spin doctor to becoming a political pundit co-anchoring a television show with Torben, a respected journalist and political commentator. The 2022 season depicts Birgitte as a cabinet minister, while Katrine and Torben work, respectively, as the manager of a television news division and a television political commentator.

Early episodes of *Borgen* follow Birgitte Nyborg's transformation as she evolves from serving as a committed minority party leader of Moderates to negotiating a new government as Royal Investigator. The Moderates are a minority party compared with the Liberals and Labor, but "as always in Danish politics . . . the fight is over the center" (season 1: episode 1). Birgitte's success depends on her vision, political strategies, and collaborative skills. She is a genuine Moderate aiming for consensus while staying true to her goals to make Denmark more equitable and economically sustainable than it was under the rule of Liberal and Conservative governments. As a feminist, she promotes equality and laws respecting women's different choices. To push through her Moderate reform agenda concentrating on enhancing welfare, the environment, and the health system, Birgitte persuades others that these are commonsense goals benefiting all citizens, but she must compromise features of her plans to satisfy her coalition partners.[23] Birgitte is an effective leader of a small party that partners with larger parties because she is a masterful negotiator and consensus builder, skills she refined as a union leader.

In the first stage of her political career, Birgitte works for a Moderate agenda: investing in health care, enhancing environmental protection, and ensuring social equity. She exhibits integrity and refuses to win control of the government by the devious means employed by her rival Michael Laugeson. After Birgitte's spin doctor Kasper obtains proof that Hesselboe, the prime minister, paid for his wife's purchases with a government credit card before reimbursing the government, Birgitte refuses to leak this information to the press, but Laugeson reveals the document incriminating Hesselboe during the last televised election debate. This mean-spirited political ploy—airing Hesselboe's dirty laundry—causes the Liberal party to suffer dramatic losses, while Birgitte's Moderates gain seats after her excellent debate performance. The second episode of the first season details how Birgitte as royal investigator negotiates with parties angling for power and hoping to have one of their own party members selected as prime minister. The negotiation benefits Birgitte, who after caucusing with different parties, establishes a coalition and support to become prime minister. Instead of a major party (Liberals or Labor) gaining the position, she leverages political alliances, and as prime minister brings together various progressive parties: Labor, Solidarity, Greens, and her Moderates.

In contrast to Birgitte, other politicians act unethically in pursuing their ambitions. Politicians Troels Hoxenhaven, Jakob Kruse, and Hans Christian Thorsen, and television executive Alex Hjort follow selfish, corrupt agendas as they aim to increase their power, often by deceit or intimidation. Instead Birgitte works strategically to enhance democratic processes in Denmark and eliminate social inequities. She attacks problems by listening to concerns and negotiating priorities of different constituencies rather than by acting to shore up her political power. She respects and reinforces democratic processes because in her mind they are equitable and good for Denmark. By the end of the first season, Birgitte no longer expects party leaders to do the right thing without her influence; instead, she persuades others to support democratic initiatives.

Compelling concerns related to feminism motivate story lines in the long arc of *Borgen*. The series represents challenges that women face in taking up professional roles and the conflicts that any politician must resolve to maintain a trusted public image while managing messy personal and family complications. Certain politicians resign their government posts after contradictions between image and reality become apparent. Birgitte supports minister of business Henriette Klitgaard's plan to force companies to include 47 percent women on executive boards; however, after learning that the young minister's résumé includes fraudulent educational credentials, Birgitte demands Henriette's resignation (season 1: episode 5). Birgitte acts with integrity and makes ethical decisions, although in certain episodes, viewers see that she commits critical errors. After her marriage breaks up, she has a spontaneous one-night sexual fling with her chauffeur, an affair that leaves her vulnerable to his claims of discrimination after he is terminated from his position as her driver. And she underestimates the capacities of her coalition partners to betray each other. Yet these errors of judgment do not become public knowledge, so her reputation for honesty and integrity does not suffer. She sacrifices her self-interest and her family's needs when she deems national interest more important than her ambitions. In season 1: episode 9, after the media attack the foreign minister H. C. Thorsen for accepting gifts while negotiating a government contract, Birgitte tries to regain public trust by forcing her then husband to resign from his new job with a company supplying parts for a government project. Critic John Powers explains,

> I'm not sure I've ever seen a show that's better at capturing the personal cost of political life. For Birgitte, power doesn't so much corrupt as isolate. The more successful she becomes as PM, the more her private world dwindles. Her circle of friends shrinks, her children feel neglected, and her marriage to the funny, liberal-minded Philip—a onetime CEO who's put his career on hold—starts to founder. Losing her knack

for intimacy, she begins talking to him like a prime minister making points in a cabinet meeting.[24]

Birgitte's husband eventually tells her he no longer wants to sacrifice for the sake of national interests and commits to a new partner rather than subordinating his life to her political career. The male politicians in the series do not sacrifice their interests to personal relationships, and they are not represented as isolated in advancing professionally like Birgitte. The men are also less inclined to notice issues of social inequity, preferring to work toward amassing power for themselves and their parties.

Borgen excels in showing how Birgitte's wins in government short-change her personal relationships. Her great success in managing a peace negotiation between two warring African nations (season 2: episode 8) is followed by a family crisis: her teenage daughter Laura suffers from severe anxiety attacks and must be admitted to a private mental health facility (season 2: episode 19). Philip, Laura's father and Birgitte's ex-husband, has private health insurance that could pay 85 percent of the costs to treat Laura's illness, but Birgitte and her adviser Kasper agree that the family should not access these private benefits while Birgitte works to reduce government subsidies of private health care (she would rather develop more extensive publicly funded accessible care). Meanwhile, her nemesis Laugeson, now editor of the newspaper *Express*, argues that it is the media's responsibility to publicize government officials' actions. He assigns photographers to stalk the mental health facility where Laura receives treatment, causing chaos there and forcing Birgitte to take a month's leave from being prime minister until her daughter's health improves and press interest diminishes. Both Hesselboe, who angles to return to the post of prime minister, and Laugeson, who resents Birgitte's becoming prime minister, characterize her monthlong family leave as a gender problem. Their public criticism advances the view that women politicians cannot balance home and work and that any woman with a conscience would quit politics to stay home and take care of her family. Women broadcasters at TV1 are troubled by this argument as they understand that Birgitte's family-friendly politics and her caretaking of her family enact her core values, which are close to those of many women. For a time, Birgitte takes a leave from her duties to care for Laura, but she resists defending her choices and her administration in the public forum. Later, Laura's doctor, also a working mother, and Birgitte's party adviser and long-standing friend

Bent separately tell her that Laura's improved condition means Birgitte should return to work, which she does.

Kasper tells journalists and Bent shares with Birgitte that she is the best prime minister that Denmark has ever had. During her three years of serving as prime minister of a coalition government, Birgitte achieves her reform agenda's three goals related to welfare, environment, and health. These successes motivate Birgitte to address parliament, reminding them that women have had official roles in the body since 1918. Her statement serves as a rejoinder to her rivals' criticism that women should manage their families rather than their nation. Birgitte takes advantage of public attention to claim that women belong in Parliament and surprises members, especially Hesselboe, who has been laying the groundwork to return as prime minister, by calling immediately for an election (season 2: episode 20).

Questions of whether a woman holding the job of prime minister can also enjoy a satisfying intimate relationship or a private family life remain unresolved until the third season when Birgitte becomes involved with a British businessman who values her extraordinary abilities to strategize; his career is enhanced by Birgitte's status, and he welcomes the role of being her plus one. Viewers do not see male politicians struggle to combine a satisfying family life with political success, a topic dominating the first two seasons of *Borgen*. The third season depicts the talented Birgitte as building a party and another coalition to further enhance life in Denmark; she is an outsider returning to politics after a two-year absence to manage a difficult campaign with a new party. In the last episodes of season three, she negotiates for a coalition government, but this time with her as foreign minister and Hesselboe remaining as prime minister. That at this point in her life Birgitte chooses to have a secondary role in the governing of the country demonstrates that she is a public servant inspired by feminist, progressive principles rather than being motivated by ambition or greed.

Birgitte is true to herself and her politics in engineering a solution that is best for her country. Some reviewers complained Birgitte is "implausibly ethical" and "Who wouldn't have grabbed the premiership?" but as Serena Davis argues, "This is why *Borgen* is better than the rather more abstract ethics of altruistic politicking in that great American series about power in a democracy, *The West Wing*. This is also why the most moving moment in the final episode of season three of *Borgen* wasn't the news that Birgitte didn't have cancer anymore but the moment when she looked up at the Danish parliament and called it her 'second home.' "[25] Birgitte cares less about being prime minister than working for a better Denmark, one that keeps its citizens safe, educated, healthy, and on equal footing. She recognizes that not all are as privileged as she is, and she works to ensure that equity remains the foundation of government policy.

Borgen represents a successful women politician who brings her personal skills to the national stage, allowing her work life and her home life to merge, if not seamlessly, at least enough to permit professional achievement and personal satisfaction and to promise a better future enabled by feminist principles privileging health, environment, and education. In the fourth season of the series, televised in 2022, the world is different, and the female politician has changed with it. In this season, Birgitte no longer has dependent children, and she occupies a different position: as the foreign minister she often engages in tense debates with the female prime minister. Lisa Abend describes the older Birgitte as more ambitious and tougher: "Highly principled and idealistic in the past—a Danish version of *The West Wing*'s Jed Bartlett—she now abandons some values in favor of political expediency, betrays allies and even family members, and undermines anyone she perceives as threatening her power—which, in this case, happens to be a lot of other women."[26] As head of the news division, Katrine is professionally successful but less admirable than her younger self as she struggles to meet demands of her bosses and to constrain reporters. As media studies scholar Susanne Eichner notes, "There is also something progressive in that the show allows women to feel the whole spectrum, to be good and evil, broken and ambivalent."[27] The last episode indicates that Birgitte and Katrine resolve their conflicts between work and family as they see fit.

Madam President

The CBS series *Madam Secretary* (2014–2019) stars Téa Leoni as a former Central Intelligence Agency (CIA) officer whose former agency boss becomes president and appoints her to the cabinet post of secretary of State. Professor Elizabeth McCord moves from the university to Washington, DC, with her husband Henry (Tim Daly), another professor and former CIA officer, and their three teenage children. Many episodes of *Madam Secretary* explore international crises alongside domestic issues requiring the secretary's effort. Like Ros Pritchard and Birgitte Nyborg who after stressful days at the office clean up their kitchens and catch up with family, Elizabeth manages a second shift of domestic tasks. In early episodes, Henry is a professor at a military college, but he later works in national security and in the 2018 season reports to the president as ethics adviser. Elizabeth and Henry keep their spy lives mostly hidden from their children; however, the three McCord children cannot ignore that their parents serve as representatives of President Dalton's moderate administration.

Two episodes in *Madam Secretary*'s second season provide useful comparisons with *The Amazing Mrs. Pritchard* and *Borgen*. "The Show Must Go On" (series episode 23/season 2: episode 1) and "Invasive Species" (series episode 35/season 2: episode 12) illustrate primary dimensions of Elizabeth McCord's character. In "The Show Must Go On," Elizabeth, a strong cabinet secretary who must negotiate inevitable turf battles and overlaps of authority, takes a one-day turn as president after the president's plane goes missing, the vice president undergoes surgery, and others ahead of Elizabeth in the line of succession are unable to assume these duties. As she takes up her acting president duties in the Oval Office, the president's chief of staff Russell Jackson offers two cautions, telling Elizabeth not to do anything and to be ready to give an order to shoot down Air Force One if everyone onboard is dead, a prospect that terrifies her. Anxious that she will upset the president's agenda and his chances for reelection, Russell admits the president has without consulting her appointed Elizabeth's nemesis Craig Sterling as National Security adviser, because the president "can do whatever he wants." Elizabeth concludes from this conversation that as acting president she has authority to do what she wants, so she takes her opportunity as a one-day president to pardon her children's heroine, a journalist who leaked government secrets. "The Show Must Go On" ends with the president's plane safely returned. After the president asks about the pardon, Elizabeth reminds him that he appointed Sterling without consulting her. The episode ends with her being satisfied with accomplishing one good deed on a frightening day.

In "Invasive Species" Elizabeth helps her husband Henry and his siblings deal with the sudden death of their father. Tensions simmer during a family visit because Henry's sister Maureen resents that she assumed the largest role in caring for their ailing parents, now deceased. Maureen's snide comments about arrogance and privilege reveal she is jealous of Henry's career success and Elizabeth's position as secretary of state. Elizabeth ignores many slights and assists Maureen in picking out a casket; at the funeral home, they find that the father's burial policy lapsed, so Elizabeth pays for the casket and service. Courtesy of Elizabeth's request to the State Department to investigate, the McCord family learns that Henry's father committed suicide. He was conned out of his savings by a person he met on an internet dating site, someone he thought was a girlfriend but who turned out to be a male acquaintance seeking a way out of his own financial troubles. Mourning their father doesn't prevent the McCord siblings from bickering and blaming each other. Peeved about the three sport utility vehicles with Secret Service agents following Elizabeth's car, Maureen calls her sister-in-law "Queen Elizabeth" and incurs Henry's ire for trashing his wife. Elizabeth and Henry's oldest daughter Stevie is mystified by Maureen's attacks and her strong mother's passivity in the face of such insults. After Stevie asks, "Why don't you fight back?" Elizabeth explains that she treasures the raucous McCords because after Elizabeth's own parents passed away, she had only her brother to call family until she fell in love with Henry. Although the episode focusing on Henry's father's funeral takes place far from the White House, Elizabeth resolves family tensions in the same way that she solves international crises: by being attentive, respecting others' views, refusing to insult provocative interlocutors, and staying on high moral ground.

Many episodes of *Madam Secretary* illustrate foreign crises the State Department deals with, including assassinations, coups, dictators, human rights abuses, defectors, civil and international conflicts, terrorist attacks, revolutions, and the threat of nuclear war. Elizabeth works for peace and stability, while safeguarding US interests around the world. She prefers diplomacy to force in effectively negotiating to protect US interests in accordance with laws and ethics. As the lead administrator in charge of embassy staff, she also protects Americans working abroad. Many have personal connections: her husband Henry works for a time in the National Security Agency (NSA), and her brother, who is a physician, works with a nonprofit medical organization in war-torn Syria.

Like other political shows highlighting women, *Madam Secretary* depicts Elizabeth switching gears between work and home, as Téa Leoni, the actor playing her points out: "I like the idea that I could be unleashed to be as steely and strong as I needed to be professionally because I could come home and make mistakes, burn eggs, give the wrong advice to my child and be human. . . . I think that's a fun ride, and it's interesting to watch. I get offended by this idea that if you're a strong woman then you've lost your femininity."[28] At work Elizabeth's feminist-infused politics combine care for individuals and country. She watches out for stresses and illnesses that could sideline her staff, and she expresses concern for everyone she interacts with, including US political opponents and foreign diplomatic liaisons. A role model for citizens in public service, Elizabeth demonstrates consistent integrity and humanity along with flexibility and courtesy, including when she learns her daughter is dating a political opponent's son.

Elizabeth plays a leading role in constraining the president after his bellicose comments make his judgment questionable. "Sound and Fury" (Episode 80/season 4: episode 12) also known as the Twenty-fifth Amendment episode, was broadcast January 14, 2018. The title is derived from Shakespeare's *Macbeth*, with the "sound" referring to what is believed to be a sonic attack on an American embassy and the "fury" describing the response from President Dalton, played by Keith Carradine.[29] The episode depicts an unusual event: a cabinet discussion about temporarily removing the president from office so he can receive medical care.[30] Advised by Elizabeth, First Lady Lydia Dalton (Christine Ebersole), and others, Dalton agrees to be hospitalized for "a benign brain tumor that had been pushing on his frontal lobe," an injury affecting executive function.[31] After his operation and recovery, the president returns to the Oval Office, expressing gratitude to those who prevented him from forcing a war.

Women collaborate on producing *Madam Secretary*, and many women have played secondary characters in the series, including the director of the FBI, US legislators, journalists, and staff members in the State Department, the White House, and Congress, as well as a Russian president, a French foreign minister, and a representative of the Algerian government. One powerful woman, Vice President Teresa Hurst, a former senior senator from Pennsylvania, was the driving force behind President Dalton's win as an independent candidate; however, after she threatens to contravene State Department policy, Hurst must be reminded by Elizabeth that a vice president should not act independently of administrative policies.[32] Hurst, who harbors presidential ambitions, regards Elizabeth as a rival until they agree that their political fortunes matter less than ensuring the US remains the preeminent democracy on the world stage.

The series combines realism with doses of fantasy. Although the US has not elected a woman president and women candidates could not get past the stage of speaking in debates during the 2020 presidential election, *Madam Secretary* has Elizabeth, encouraged by President Dalton and his chief strategist, elected as president in the show's final season, which was titled *Madam President*.[33] She injects ethics into diplomacy and governance even though her administration is hampered by an impeachment investigation and a congressional hearing. The series finale depicts her daughter's White House wedding, a celebration with McCords and staff negotiating a congressional deal with reception guests. The last scene ends on a hopeful note, with Elizabeth undertaking a whistle-stop train tour to persuade more states to approve the Equal Rights Amendment.[34]

Femininity and Feminism

Nancy Rothbard, a professor at the Wharton School, remarks on the positive outcomes for businesswomen who embrace femininity: "For women to be successful in the workplace, research shows, we need to exhibit both competence and warmth, and feminine qualities are warm."[35] Femininity also appears in a semiotic register in television shows about governing as each woman politician undergoes a fashion makeover. In *Madam Secretary* Elizabeth enters the White House and is ordered to accept fashion advice from a stylist. In *Borgen* once Birgitte becomes prime minister, she appears in suits and rides in a chauffeured limo rather than wearing jeans and riding a bike to Parliament. After briefly going undercover in a workman's jacket to speak with her former supermarket subordinate, Ros in *The Amazing Mrs. Pritchard* also begins wearing business suits. The woman politician should be elegantly dressed, carefully coiffed, and in heels.

Prioritizing equity, women political leaders demonstrate integrity, technical expertise, and a disciplined work ethic, while being sensitive to others and demonstrating what should be done to minimize damage and to maximize success. Their intelligence, adaptability, flexibility, and patience serve them well at home and in government. As women who collaborate rather than competing with an endless stream of rivals, the three television protagonists listen and learn, acting decisively. Women politicians in the optimistic television series considered in this chapter spend more time resolving problems instead of shoring up their power or ensuring their popularity. These feminists resolve national and international conflicts, acting collaboratively and consensually, accepting information and opinions from superiors, peers, and subordinates while pursuing logical arguments and strategies. The series acknowledge the exceptional careers and anomalous positions of the three women politicians who unexpectedly reach powerful roles. Ros accidentally enters politics, Birgitte becomes prime minister after negotiations as investigator, and Elizabeth accepts the cabinet appointment offered by her former boss. These shows recognize constraints affecting women's political careers; after all, until the 1970s, many women entered politics by following their husbands or fathers and that is still a path for some.[36]

Other television shows and films depict women whose optimism concerning politics influences men in power. The 1937 film *First Lady* (Dir. Stanley Logan) stars Kay Francis as granddaughter of a US president and as a presidential aspirant's wife whose patriotism motivates her to derail a less worthy man's candidacy and clear the way for her husband's campaign.[37] Two 2022 cable television series—*The First Lady* (Showtime; Dir. Susanne Bier) and *Gaslit* (Starz; Dir. Matt Ross)—present fictionalized accounts of historical women who influenced the actions and reputations of their spouses.[38] Weaving together biographies of Eleanor Roosevelt, Betty Ford, and Michelle Obama, *The First Lady* depicts events "through the lens of the First Ladies" and "delves deep into the Ladies' personal and political lives. Exploring everything from their journeys to Washington, family life, and world-changing political contributions."[39] Its episodes illustrate sacrifices, moral integrity, and savvy political advice as women's positive, critical contributions to presidential legacies. Eleanor Roosevelt counsels Franklin Roosevelt on administrative appointments, expands the role of First Lady, and offers political commentary to guide women to vote in their own interests. After Gerald Ford supplies Richard Nixon with a controversial pardon, Betty Ford shares her battle with breast cancer with the public to demonstrate White House transparency and works on behalf of the Equal Rights Amendment. Michelle Obama urges Barak Obama to declare the 1996 Defense of Marriage Act as unconstitutional and to work for health-care reform.[40] *Gaslit*'s eight episodes depict the Watergate conspirators working in the White House, their attempts to cover up their crimes, and how women assist law enforcement and the press in uncovering them. Martha Mitchell tells all to journalists to protect her husband from being blamed as the architect of the conspiracy, and Maureen Dean and Gail Magruder act in similarly protective fashion in pressing their partners to cooperate with federal prosecutors.

Other dramas represent less idealistic women as politicians. In season 7 of *24* (2001–2014) Cherry Jones began playing President Allison Taylor, who the actor "described as nothing like Hillary Clinton"; Taylor instead resembles "a combination of Lyndon Johnson, Eleanor Roosevelt,

Golda Meir, and John Wayne" with "similar opinions to Barack Obama" who must sacrifice her integrity at a critical juncture.[41] As Elizabeth Marvel, the actor who played President Elizabeth Keane in *Homeland* (2011–2020) remarked about that character, a woman who imprisons former allies if she thinks they threaten her leadership, "I also really appreciated that they did not just paint her as this noble virtuous hero. She was a survivor. She was a very complicated individual that they created."[42] Offering the woman president as a secondary character mixing virtues and vices provides texture and complexity in drama; however, there is at least one television narrative that characterizes a totally evil woman who serves as president.

Political wife and politician, Claire Underwood in the sixth and last season (2018) of the US television series *House of Cards* uses feminism as a weapon while imitating the ruthless, selfish, and vengeful methods demonstrated by many male politicians, including her husband and predecessor. As one reviewer explains, "Season 5 of *House of Cards* ended with Robin Wright's character Claire Underwood wresting control from her husband to become president of the United States, herself. 'My turn,' she says directly to the camera, in one of the most successful finale twists the show has pulled off. The flip became a moment of unexpected foreshadowing, both for the direction of the show and for the nationwide conversation on the continued struggle for gender equality."[43] Compared with Lady Macbeth in her jockeying for power and her tendencies to lie and deceive, Claire resents being told what to do and resists doing it, character traits illustrated in flashbacks to her fury as a child punished by her parents and later as a teenager who quit her role as Lysistrata in a play because acting seemed pointless (season 6, episode 5). Her initial decisions as president combine her desire to be perceived as ethical while applying political force and devious tactics to defeat her enemies. Her actions are always aligned with her narrow interests. For example, in the second episode of the last season Claire presses the governor of a state affected by a chemical leak to declare a state of emergency. She threatens him until he agrees; although the declaration benefits the public, it also damages the Shepherds, brother and sister power brokers who seek to control Claire and are therefore her enemies.

As part of Claire's complicated scheme to fire her cabinet secretaries and to eviscerate the political future of her vice president, she performs as mentally disturbed to encourage her enemies to paint her as a hysterical, incompetent woman and to pursue the Twenty-fifth Amendment to try to dislodge her from the White House. Subsequently, she announces (to viewers) that she will "weaponize feminism" and appoints an all-female cabinet to replace those who were disloyal. After the Shepherds release information about Claire's abortions, she spins a heart-wrenching account of her supposed medical condition: she claims the Underwoods struggled with infertility and that a four-month pregnancy was not viable. Then she uses her deceased husband Frank Underwood's sperm to become pregnant and appear maternal. This strategy pays off: she can neutralize the Shepherds' influence and increase her popularity and power. Her character in *House of Cards* is a Machiavellian schemer pretending to be a feminist to avoid losing or deferring to anyone.

Claire is always fighting, always acting in a military mode. Emphasizing this dimension of her character, costumers for the show put her in outfits bearing the features of military uniforms: various pantsuits and dresses are severely tailored in dark colors (navy, dark green, and black) and accentuated with brass buttons. Dressing this way enables Claire to appear as a leader of troops when she stands next to dark-suited politicians or soldiers in uniform. In similar fashion, Claire's "feminist" tactics veil selfish motives while making her seem caring. The series ends with Claire destroying all those who might disagree with that profile.

Optimistic Feminism

Meg Wolitzer's novel *The Female Persuasion* (2018) focuses on a celebrated US feminist social reformer who began her advocacy for gender equity in the 1960s and subsequently exerted great influence on younger generations. The novel addresses critical questions about power and equity: "What does it mean to be powerful? How do people measure their impact upon the world and upon one another? Does all of this look different for men than it does for women?"[44] Spanning different decades, the novel connects college students Greer Kadetsky, Corey Pinto, and Zee Eisenstadt with the older, respected feminist Faith Frank, who is modeled in some ways on Gloria Steinem. Greer embraces feminism after being assaulted by a male student at a 2006 frat party, and the novel follows her through college and her twenties, ending with a description of a 2018 party celebrating her best-selling book *Outside Voices*, encouraging women to speak out against inequities and to promote reforms. The narrative of Greer's life alternates with flashbacks to a similar call to consciousness and feminist success of Faith Frank, who was raised in the 1950s and emerged at the forefront of the women's movement in the late 1970s to write her 1984 feminist manifesto *The Female Persuasion*.

Faith's commitment to feminist politics informs the magazine she edits and later Loci, the feminist foundation she directs. Speaking on the Ryland College campus, Faith meets Greer, then a freshman. Faith's speech explains feminism by describing a conversation with "young women" who claim not to identify with its principles. They

> "say, 'I'm not a feminist, but . . .' By which they mean, 'I don't call myself a feminist, but I want equal pay, and I want to have equal relationships with men, and of course I want to have an equal right to sexual pleasure. I want to have a fair and good life. I don't want to be held back because I'm a woman' . . . And I always want to reply . . . 'What do you think feminism is, other than that? How do you think you're going to get those things if you deny the political movement that is all about obtaining that life that you want?' "[45]

Following the speech, Greer asks Faith a question referencing the Ryland administration's unwillingness to expel the male student who attacked her and other women. Greer bluntly asks Faith: "What are we supposed to do?"[46] Faith responds with concern about "how alarmingly improvised the legal process is on campus," indicating that although she is unfamiliar with the circumstances she recommends that "you and your friends should definitely keep the conversation going," advice that Greer follows in pursuing feminist initiatives.[47]

After Greer graduates, she goes to work for Faith, whose feminist foundation organizes leadership summits for women. Faith explains her commitment to feminism by acknowledging that hers is a particular type:

> "I do what I can . . . I do it for women. Not everyone agrees with the way I do it. Women in powerful positions are never safe from criticism. The kind of feminism I've practiced is one way to go about it. There are plenty of others, and that's great. There are impassioned and radical young woman out there, telling multiple stories. I applaud them. We need them. We need as many women fighting as possible. I learned early on from the wonderful Gloria Steinem that the world is big

enough for different kinds of feminism to coexist, people who want to emphasize different aspects of the fight for equality. God knows the injustices are endless, and I am going to use whatever resources are at my disposal to fight in the way I know how."[48]

Faith's arguments inspire those who read her books and hear her speeches, while her informal conversations influence young people to follow their own personal and professional interests in enhancing equity, even if these do not align with traditional gender roles or with existing examples of feminism. Advising individuals and developing a public role based on her integrity and sincere commitment to women, Faith nurtures progressive social change; however, as times change, circumstances and forms of feminism evolve.

Greer is thrilled with her job working in Faith's foundation until generational differences affect their responses to a problem: the variance between the foundation's public image and its questionable, secretive practices concerning financial support of a new initiative. Greer and Faith vehemently disagree about whether the Loci foundation, which is funded largely by ShraderCapital, should admit to a lack of integrity. Greer learns that a prominent Loci project to save women in Guatemala from sex traffickers and to provide them with mentors did not complete its second phase because ShraderCapital executives hired a local contact to manage the project instead of the carefully vetted, experienced woman selected by Faith and Loci leaders. After Greer gives a highly publicized speech about the success of the mentoring program, she hears from Kim, a former ShraderCapital executive, who tells her that the Guatemalan women were saved from traffickers but were not matched with women mentors as Loci and Greer publicly claim. Kim tells Greer that the venture capital firm did not want to admit their failure: "They decided that would be terrible PR. So they just allowed it to keep going, which is, as you can imagine, illegal. And of course Loci's name is all over the brochure."[49] Greer realizes that because she highlighted the project as a success, she is also accountable.

Faith and Greer react differently to ShraderCapital's "incompetence" in managing the Guatemala project. Male executives at ShraderCapital were not worried that donations for it were still being collected or about the discrepancy between publicity and reality; one asserted that donations would be saved for another Loci project, an idea that seemed fine to Emmett Shrader, the firm's distracted head. After Greer tells Faith about

Kim's admission that the survivors lacked mentors, Greer expects that Faith will break off the relationship between Loci and ShraderCapital. But Faith has no intentions of losing Shrader's funding and appreciates that at least the Guatemalan women were saved from trafficking. Greer quits Loci because Faith will not stop publicizing the nonexistent mentoring program.

The differences between the two women appear according to a values divide signaled by their names. Faith Frank is honest and faithful to cause and person, although pragmatic in protecting the interests of feminism, while Greer, whose name evokes feminist Germaine Greer, seems a radically doctrinaire feminist through much of the novel. Faith is a public figure who has worked for decades in personal, private, patient ways to effect changes improving women's lives, while Greer is a twenty-something who for some years ignored the needs of her parents, best friend, and boyfriend as she identifies with the abstract feminist cause of helping women. Greer commits to the ideal of improving women's access and opportunities, but she criticizes her parents' life choices, sacrifices her friend Zee's interests, and breaks up with her boyfriend Corey while he deals with a family tragedy. In contrast, Faith has been loyal to her old friend Annie instead of advancing the cause of feminist politics by revealing Anne McCauley's secret: "Whenever Faith saw Senator McCauley on television, she thought of how easy it would be to tell the truth publicly about her, to simply release a statement to the press saying eleven years before Senator McCauley became such a strong and vocal opponent of legal abortion, she had in fact undergone an illegal one in Las Vegas."[50] Greer resigns from Loci and rebukes Faith for refusing to confess publicly about the lack of mentors in Guatemala, but Faith reminds Greer that she lied to keep her college buddy Zee from working at Loci, information that serves as leverage to ensure that after Greer leaves the foundation she will not publicize the lack of mentoring.

Wolitzer weaves details about the lives of feminist characters to track their consciousness-raising, noting the increased opportunities that feminism makes possible. Disturbed by her adolescent experience of being a gay woman betrayed by her therapist, Zee transforms from activist college student to unhappy paralegal, becoming a depressed inner-city schoolteacher and later finding satisfying work as a trauma specialist. The narrative follows the shift from Faith's brief 1960s affair with Emmett Shrader to their mature professional friendship ensuring funding for Loci. Emmett could have divorced his heiress wife to stay romantically involved with Faith; instead, he is persuaded by his wife to accept money to start his venture capital firm. In 2010 after his wife divorces him, Emmett persuades Faith to accept ShraderCapital funds to start the Loci foundation.

Greer's feminism colors her relationship with her parents, whom she has generally disdained for their counterculture lifestyle and for limiting her educational ambitions after their failure to file financial aid forms makes it impossible for her to enroll at Yale. Her ideas about feminism also affect her fluctuating relationship with Corey Pinto, who is influenced by Greer and his mother to become a feminist. Corey's mother accidentally kills her younger son. Princeton graduate Corey leaves his financially rewarding consulting job to return home after this tragedy so that he can take care of his mother who is devastated, overcome by posttraumatic stress, and abandoned by his father. Greer respects Corey's caring for his mother but criticizes his choice to quit his well-compensated consulting job. Instead, Corey lives with his mentally unstable mother and cleans houses to earn income. For a time, Greer and Corey break up and pursue other relationships; however, after Greer resigns from her job at the foundation, she returns to her childhood home. She and Corey are again neighbors, and she starts to think differently about his decision to quit his consulting job. Greer's father asks her over dinner one night what Corey is doing, and Greer answers that he works at a computer store, is inventing a computer game, and is cleaning houses, noting, "So I guess that's what he's up to. Not that much."[51] Reacting to the "Not that much," Greer's mother Laurel Kadetsky, who works as a library clown, a job demeaned by Greer, chides her daughter:

> "It seems to me, said her mother, "and this is really outside
> my sphere of knowledge, since I'm not the one who's been
> working at a feminist foundation. But here's this person who
> gave up his plans when his family fell apart. He moves back
> in with his mother and takes care of her. Oh, and he cleans
> his own house, and the ones she used to clean. I don't know.
> But I feel like Cory is kind of a big feminist, right?"[52]

Laurel's question remains unanswered as the chapter ends, but readers are likely to agree with the assessment that caring for others reflects feminist values.

Sweethearts in high school and through college, Corey and Greer reunite as maturing adults to construct lives based on personal values, including a commitment to feminism. Greer worked as a barista while writing her nonfiction feminist manifesto *Outside Voices*. The best-selling book makes her rich, and she attains new status as a public figure helping women improve their lives. She and Corey marry, parent their daughter Emilia, and live in Brooklyn, where he continues to create respected sleeper video games while taking care of home and child. The financial success of Greer's book and related merchandising allows them to provide for their parents and to live comfortably but not lavishly. We learn in the last chapter that by 2018,

> The world . . . changed so stunningly. Even now, years in, no one could get used to it; and conversation at parties still centered around the ways no one had seen it coming. They could not believe what had happened to the country. "The big terribleness," said a tall, spindly, and intense woman . . . "The thing that really gets me," she said, "is that the *worst* kind of man, the kind that you would *never* allow yourself to be alone with, because you would know he was a danger to you, was left alone with all of us."[53]

The novel's ending circles back after twelve years to its opening concerns about misogyny and sexual predation.

The conclusion of *The Female Persuasion* indicates that Greer's feminism will, like Faith's version, soon have competition from ideas issued by a younger generation. Emilia's sitter Kay is a high school student who does not hesitate to tell Greer that despite being impressed with her employer, Kay prefers a more powerful version of feminism: "I look at everything that women did and said in recent history, and somehow we still got to a caveman moment. And our responses to it just aren't enough, because the structures are still in place, right?"[54] Greer encourages her, recognizing that all feminist voices and efforts are needed to continue agitating for long desired change, including upending what Kay explains is the assumption that "the white, cisgender, binary view of everything was the correct one, the only one, when it fact it wasn't. We're done with that for good."[55] The narrative outlines a trajectory in which feminism enables social changes and suggests future enhancements. Theory and practice sketch feminist visions for an equitable world. Optimism enables change and fuels further progress as readers imagine a just society on the horizon.

The Power of Feminist Narratives

Feminism's Progress considers the ways in which fictional print and media narratives influence audiences to believe in the power of feminism to empower individuals and enhance society. Evolutionary biologist Richard Prum, near the conclusion of his book about Charles Darwin's theory of mate choice, writes that "feminism is not an ideology of power or control over others; rather it is an ideology of freedom of choice."[56] Prum asserts that "Female sexual autonomy and same-sex behavior have both evolved to be disruptive to male hierarchical power and culture," explaining that human desire and attraction "are not just tools of subjugation but individual and collective instruments of social empowerment."[57] Arguing *Lysistrata*'s "lessons are clear," he considers "Individuals can transform human society through their affirmative sexual choices."[58]

Fictional narratives elaborate the ways feminist principles of equity and collaboration enable women to endure, even though at times characters suffer bias and discrimination in pursuing their personal and political agendas. Admirable women serve the public interest, doing so because of their honesty, integrity, and their commitments to work collaboratively and collectively for social equity and gender equality. They navigate obstacles, informed by ethical principles to reach their goals, help allies, and stay in power as they contribute to the creation of the beloved community. They follow the advice of Elizabeth Grosz about what to remember and what to forget: "This may provide a possible path, with careful reworking, for any politics of the oppressed: to remember what one needs to move on to the future with more resources than the present can provide, while at the same time forgetting what one must, what has hurt, damaged, injured or rendered one passive. A paradoxical impulse: to know what one must forget, to know in order to forget it."[59] Narratives featuring women in government and public policy reveal utopian hopes based on moving forward by embedding feminist principles into political practices and working for equitable outcomes to improve citizens' lives.

Feminist realist fictions entertain and educate, presenting plausible scenarios promising social change to inspire viewers and readers to establish reforms. Print and media narratives note social conditions inhibiting equity and identify needed structural changes to improve human lives. Narratives discussed in this book were authored or produced by those willing to present positive aspects of feminist principles and practices and to illustrate possible ways to work toward equality; however, such texts do not always receive significant attention. As Nicole Rudick reminds us,

> The history of literature is a history of publication—who gets published, in what form, by whom, and when, a host of factors that conspire to determine whether an author gains renown or disappears from the literary landscape. If we examine the history of literary achievement (a critical mass of awards, magazine profiles, reviews, inclusion in anthologies and course offerings), it is largely white, male, and middle class—a homogeneity enabled by a similar constituency in the editorial departments of periodicals and books.[60]

The fictions discussed in this book offer the promise of gender equity and describe feminism's power to create it, while noting barriers women navigate and suggesting progressive strategies.

Authors submit texts and publishers manage the means of production, and readers respond to ideologies in fictions. Desire for change and hope for better prospects follow our reading of fictions recounting discrimination and violence against women, as Toni Morrison's novels inspire reader identification with her protagonists' visions rather than their antagonists such as the Ruby men who kill the Convent women for transgressing social norms. Fiction offers information promoting social change by encouraging readers' and viewers' emotional responses to characters and social dynamics in created worlds that resemble our own experiences or that we can translate into our experience.[61] Narratives are powerful in pointing out that while we might still see evidence of a patriarchal sex/gender system, we understand that feminism evolves to eliminate inequities and to create a future promoting equity.

Epilogue

Feminism has within it the seeds of a genuine world view. Like every real system of thought it is able to refer itself to everything in our lives, thereby rescuing the old, forgotten knowledge that is locked deep inside each of us. But if, in the end, in our ideological lunge toward retribution, we use it as a means of abdicating our responsibility *to be true to every part of our experience*—we are lost.

—Vivian Gornick, "On the Progress of Feminism" (1970)[1]

If we are to come out of this crisis less selfish than when we went in, we have to let ourselves be touched by others' pain.

—Pope Francis, "A Crisis Reveals What Is in Our Hearts" (2020)[2]

And what keeps me going is that hope is a discipline.

—Mariame Kaba, "Hope is a discipline." (2021)[3]

I don't talk about hope, I believe in being determined. Hope feels good, but I'm not optimistic or pessimistic. I am determined.

—"Stacey Abrams in Conversation with Charlayne Hunter-Gault" (2021)[4]

This book traces the theme of hope in a feminist future as it appears in fictional narratives representing women's resistance to patriarchal values and their determination to overcome them. Calling out discrimination against

231

women, the poor, and minorities, realist feminist texts share optimism in envisioning changes that eliminate socioeconomic and racial disparities and that promote equity-based reforms. As Raffaella Baritono and Valeria Gennero acknowledge, there is an inherent link between political advocacy and theory in women's studies: "Since their inception, feminist movements have confronted the necessity to articulate the connections between political action and theoretical reflections, as they tried to build a usable past out of the omissions which framed traditional history."[5] Each feminist makes decisions that are personal and political, drawing strength from inspirational role models and historical gains that have improved equity. As a white, cis-gendered woman living in a city proud of its diversity and tolerance, I acknowledge my privilege as a college professor as well as my motivation to work toward eliminating inequities, including sexism, racism, and homophobia.[6] My professional life encompasses researching, teaching, and writing about narratives and about women's advancement in higher education, while administering educational programs that increase satisfaction and advancement of women and minorities. I draw inspiration for my university work from post-Romantic fictions that explore social inequities and recommend change, including those discussed within this book.

I am grateful to generations of feminist writers for their efforts to explore women's potentials and to convey their concerns to general audiences, as journalist Susan Faludi does in *Backlash: The Undeclared War against Women* (1993), her account of how women's rights, including those related to education, work, and reproduction, were denigrated in the 1980s by traditionalist, conservative, and misogynist individuals and institutions. Faludi's book describes the work of activists, politicians, corporate leaders, journalists, Hollywood filmmakers, and others who objected to women's independence; her subjects felt threatened by their loss of power and created false media narratives of harms caused by the women's movement to erode public perception of gender equity. Although women had gained educational, employment, financial, and reproductive rights, Faludi noticed these rights were being undermined and in danger of being eliminated. Yet her epilogue points to a remedy: "In the past women have proven they can react in a meaningful way, when they have a clear agenda that is unsanitized and unapologetic, a mobilized mass that is forceful and public, and a conviction that is uncompromising and relentless."[7] In the middle of 2022, we are again at a moment in which women's rights are in contention and requiring us to act collectively.

I completed a draft of this book in January 2021, after a polarizing US presidential election and during a period in which the United Kingdom and the European Union were figuring out how Brexit would affect their political agreements and trade relationships. Revising the manuscript in summer 2022, I notice more troubling major news: worldwide COVID-19 deaths surpassed six million lives lost, the Russian invasion of Ukraine caused thousands of deaths and displacements of eight million citizens, and, in the first half of the year, there have been hundreds of mass shootings in the US, including many racially motivated attacks against Blacks, Asians, Asian Americans, and Pacific Islanders.[8] As referenced in chapter 5, a US Supreme Court June 2022 ruling overturned *Roe v. Wade* and eliminated a federal right to abortion, making women's reproductive futures uncertain in many US states.[9] News accounts report lack of access to abortions, contraception, reproductive technologies, and prenatal care, resulting in disparate outcomes in pregnancy and childbirth, particularly for nonwhite and poor women.[10] Subsequent to the Supreme Court ruling on *Dobbs v. Jackson Women's Health Organization*, a number of states have also limited access to abortions.[11] The loss of reproductive rights, social inequalities, sex- and sexuality-based biases, and systemic racism remain concerns for feminists and for the majority of citizens.

In July 2022, Michelle Goldberg acknowledged Faludi's pioneering feminist work in a *New York Times* discussion with Ezra Klein, indicating that what's needed to overcome the backlash against feminism and to push forward on equity issues is collective action.[12] Mobilizing individuals and groups to vote and demonstrate on behalf of women's reproductive rights and other equity issues could garner attention on the order of the Women's March in 2017, a demonstration that anticipated the retrenchment of women's rights in protesting the election of Donald J. Trump as president. After taking office in January 2017, Trump, the forty-fifth US president, took aim at the Affordable Care Act (ACA); ended multinational and national commitments concerning health, climate control, and environmental protections; and separated immigrant families at the southern US border. Low morale, feelings of fragility, loss of productivity, and concerns about financial stability still affect individuals and communities as they confront racial divisions, economic uncertainty, a viral pandemic, climate change, and outbursts of violence.

Pandemic Problems

2020 saw rising rates of an unexpected viral infection spreading worldwide, with extraordinarily high numbers of individuals dying from the

COVID-19 virus, while scientists at US agencies, including the Centers for Disease Control and the National Institutes of Health, struggled with politicians who were more concerned with the president's reelection than with following medical evidence that identified mask-wearing, social distancing, testing, tracing, and isolation as medically necessary ways to contain the outbreak until vaccinations were possible.[13] Increasing numbers of infections and deaths in 2020 led to lockdowns and general panic about how to survive a pandemic. Resulting unemployment, decreased wages, and numbers of evictions motivated Congress to supplement unemployment checks and to offer some individuals, businesses, and nonprofits stimulus money, but that minimal funding did not meet the significant economic and medical needs of many citizens who in desperation lined up at food banks and at the limited number of COVID testing centers arranged by states. Schools and colleges were forced to shift abruptly in March 2020 to remote operations, and nearly 100,000 US businesses ended up closing by October 2020.[14]

Women were more likely than men to have lost or been forced to quit jobs in the health, education, and service sectors in 2020.[15] During the early days of the pandemic, many working mothers lost jobs or had to manage caring for and teaching their children while working remotely. Helen Lewis anticipated in the March 2020 issue of *The Atlantic* that "the choices of many couples over the next few months will make perfect economic sense. What do pandemic patients need? Looking after. What do self-isolating older people need? Looking after. What do children kept home from school need? Looking after. All this looking after—this unpaid caring labor—will fall more heavily on women, because of the existing structure of the workforce."[16] "Structure of the workforce" includes the income disparity between men and women, as Lewis identifies: "According to the British government's figures, 40 percent of employed women work part-time, compared with only 13 percent of men. In heterosexual relationships, women are more likely to be the lower earners, meaning their jobs are considered a lower priority when disruptions come along."[17] Similar conditions prevailed in the US.

During an era in which schooling functioned remotely, and the risk of infection made it complicated to hire individuals outside the family, parents, usually mothers, assumed responsibility for care.[18] Angela Garbes, a US writer and a mother who spoke with Terry Gross, recounted her own pandemic experience of abandoning a book project in the first months of the pandemic because her children needed care and her husband's better-paying job with health benefits made it critical to prioritize his work over hers. Garbes explained in June 2022 that once Child Tax Credit benefits expired after a year, the government did not offer additional help to families: "We live in [a culture] that doesn't value care work and that doesn't value mothers and that doesn't value women," she says. "America doesn't have a social safety net; America has mothers."[19] Sam Smethers noted the disparity between benefits awarded in Britain to mothers and those to fathers: "The reason for this inequality lies partly in the way parental leave is structured, with just two weeks of paid paternity leave for fathers compared with nine months' paid maternity leave (plus three months unpaid) for mothers—most of which she can then choose to transfer to her partner. The presumption is that the mother is the primary carer."[20] Paid parental leave is less common in the US, which should incorporate Smethers's recommendations: increase pay for caregivers, equalize salaries, and provide government support for childcare businesses. Caregiving is as essential as transportation for anyone with a family and a job.

Racial Disparities and Protests

The Economic Policy Institute issued a report in June 2020 testifying to dire conditions for persons of color in the US.

> Evidence to date suggests that black and Hispanic workers face much more economic and health insecurity from COVID-19 than white workers. Although the current strain of the coronavirus is one that humans have never experienced before, the disparate racial impact of the virus is deeply rooted in historic and ongoing social and economic injustices. Persistent racial disparities in health status, access to health care, wealth, employment, wages, housing, income, and poverty all contribute to greater susceptibility to the virus—both economically and physically.[21]

Influencing health and lifespan, labor disparities and pay inequities have immediate and long-lasting effects, including on retirement income, for women, particularly women of color.[22]

Pandemic and economic disruptions and horrific episodes of racial violence continue to dominate US news reports. Since 2019, iconic civil rights leaders and pioneers, including Elijah Cummings, Katherine Johnson, Joseph Lowery, C. T. Vivian, John Lewis, Bruce Boynton, and David Dinkins, have died of various causes.[23] Their heroic achievements as recounted in obituaries appear alongside tragic news of young Black Americans murdered by police.[24] After May 25, 2020, many citizens around the US and around the world protested against police violence and deadly force, including racist treatment and murders of Blacks.[25] Video taken that day by bystander Darnella Frazier documented Minneapolis police officers arresting George Floyd; her Pulitzer Prize–winning footage supplements "the transcripts of bodycam footage from officers" that "show Mr. Floyd said more than 20 times he could not breathe as he was restrained. He was also pleading for his mother and begging 'please, please, please.'"[26] Before being suffocated by the officer leaning on his neck, Mr. Floyd also managed to say, "Can't believe this, man. Mom, love you. Love you. Tell my kids I love them. I'm dead."[27] In reaction to his murder and to the killings of Breonna Taylor, Ahmaud Arbery, Eric Garner, Michael Brown, and many others, in 2020 Black Lives Matter and Black Trans Lives Matter activists staged marches across the US and around the world to protest white supremacist attacks, racist violence, and discrimination.[28]

In summer 2020, athletes on US professional teams conducted anti-racism protests at their events. All twenty-two US women soccer players wore Black Lives Matter T-shirts and kneeled during a moment of silence before the Challenge Cup.[29] Some athletes also endorsed progressive candidates in addition to protesting racism. On August 4, 2020, women on the WNBA Dream wore T-shirts supporting Democrat Rev. Raphael Warnock, who was running for election as a US senator from Georgia. Consulting with former Georgia state minority leader and voting rights advocate Stacey Abrams, the players agreed to support Warnock, a decision that put them in conflict with an owner of their team, Senator Kelly Loeffler, the incumbent Republican running for the same seat who had objected to the WNBA dedicating its season to social justice.[30]

Black Lives Matter and Black Trans Lives Matter protests in summer 2020 attracted people of all ages, ethnicities, and socioeconomic backgrounds in many cities in the US and abroad. Protesters reacted to incidents of police violence against Blacks, surges in COVID-19 infections, and economic declines that disproportionately affected racial minorities, women, and children, with many citizens calling for defunding the police. In July 2020 Dan Balz reported that "white Democrats have become more like black Democrats in their perceptions of racism, discrimination and policing. . . . A *Washington Post/Ipsos* survey showed that 95 percent of black Democrats and those who lean Democratic, along with 89 percent of white Democrats and leaners, said the country needs to continue to make changes to give black people equal rights with white people."[31] Attempting to catalyze change and reduce systemic racism, many educational institutions, organizations, and community groups in 2020 developed virtual workshops, events, book discussions, and other activities to eliminate racist policies and practices and to develop antiracist environments. For example, TIME'S UP, an organization founded in 2018 by Hollywood celebrities to raise funds for legal cases related to sexual discrimination and harassment, extended its social justice goals, developing the online guide "Building an Anti-Racist Workplace."[32]

Popular artists also responded to the tense atmosphere in the country. Objecting to racist killings and Donald Trump's frequent calls for law, order, and violence to quell demonstrators, musicians produced protest songs, including "I Can't Breathe," H.E.R.'s composition referencing "the last words of both George Floyd and Eric Garner as they died as a result of police brutality."[33] In June 2020 H.E.R. (Gabriella Wilson) released online lyrics reminding listeners of the dead and the families and friends mourning them.[34] Pop star Demi Lovato issued "Commander in Chief," a song accusing President Trump of selfishness and greed. The singer explained in a CNN interview that she wrote the song to speak directly to Donald Trump, "calling out his response to racial injustice, the Covid-19 crisis and more."[35] On October 14, 2020, during the Billboard Music Awards show and in front of a large VOTE sign, Lovato sang the composition, playing piano and accompanied by appropriately distanced, female back-up singers.[36] Her lyrics, as posted online, detail the deadly consequences of Trump's actions and inactions, his greed, and hypocrisy.[37] Fans were divided about whether Lovato's political views matter, but one critic found "Commander in Chief" "the most damning protest song of the Trump era."[38] The video released with the song depicts persons of different genders, ages, and ethnicities lip-syncing and signing lyrics evoking Trump-era corruption scandals, the separation of families at the southern border, and insufficient government responses to COVID-19 and concurrent economic problems.[39] In 2020 COVID-19 infections surged while hospital personnel and resources became strained, fewer beds were available in many US and UK locations, and medical workers were under great stress.

Backlash and Resistance

Faludi's *Backlash* cataloged how women's rights, including those related to education, work, and reproduction, had been opposed and diminished by traditionalist, conservative, and misogynist individuals and institutions. In the first decades of the twentieth-century anti-abortion rights activists continued to relentlessly promote their cause, while many women's advocates voiced concerns that *Roe v. Wade* (1973) appeared threatened by opportunistic abortion bans related to COVID-19 in several states.[40] After US Supreme Court Associate Justice Ruth Bader Ginsburg died in September 2020, her seat was quickly filled by Amy Coney Barrett, a conservative woman judge whose writings oppose the Affordable Care Act (ACA) and whose expressed Catholic beliefs conflict with LGBTQ protections and abortion rights.[41] In the weeks before the November 3, 2020, US presidential election, voters worried about the prospect of women losing reproductive rights, increasing unemployment, persistent racial violence, and the Trump administration's incompetent response to the pandemic, which disproportionately affected persons of color. Progressive rage in 2020 and the fact that many states sought to reduce the spread of COVID-19 by issuing absentee ballots motivated the largest voter turnout in history for a presidential election.

A few days before the November 2020 US election, Michelle Goldberg pointed out in the *New York Times*, "It's hard to catalog all the things we lost under the presidency of Donald Trump."[42] Anxiety about the election, which was anticipated to have a close margin and to be succeeded by a period during which results might be called into question, motivated Goldberg to consult Meg Wolitzer, "who still feels the manic churn of current events fraying her concentration"; the novelist's remarks revealed her worry about uncertainty: "Right now it's all about, 'How will this end?' Wolitzer said. 'And that is so different from how we read fiction, because it's about the desire to stay in this world, to be suspended in this world.' "[43] Her comment suggests that in a world dominated by shocking political events fiction could offer a respite and a way forward. Immersing ourselves in narratives modeling community engagement, ethics, and equity can inspire real-world plans, including feminist reforms that may appear as emerging rather than accomplished.

Citizens made a difference when they voted in 2020. Georgia turned blue in the fall after massive voter registration and get-out-the-vote efforts. Many National Basketball Association players (all genders) adopted shirts emblazoned with "Vote," and player representatives convinced management to open sports stadiums and arenas as locations for early voting in Georgia and other states.[44] Their collective efforts complemented work by voting rights advocates, including Stacey Abrams, the former Georgia state legislator who lost a bid in 2018 to become the state's governor by 55,000 votes in an election overseen by her rival Brian Kemp, who was serving as secretary of State.[45] In 2013 Abrams founded the New Georgia Project, an organization to register voters and to expand the electorate, and after "witnessing the gross mismanagement of the 2018 election by the Secretary of State's office, Abrams launched *Fair Fight* to ensure every American has a voice in our election system."[46] In the months before the 2020 presidential election, Abrams was a ubiquitous presence on television and radio imploring citizens to register and to vote. On November 9, 2020, her achievement in increasing the number of eligible Georgia voters was invoked during most major local and national news shows as a factor in the Democratic victory. In Atlanta on that November Saturday after the election had been called for Biden-Harris just before noon, the weather was balmy, and thousands of people of all ages stepped out of their homes and into public outdoor spaces in many neighborhoods to congratulate each other and to exult in the possibility of change.

The announcement that Biden's ticket won the presidential election led to spontaneous celebrations for some, while many Trump supporters expressed disbelief and denial, rejecting election tallies and without evidence speculating about voter fraud. Frustrations with the federal government's poor response to the pandemic, a weak economy, and rising white nationalism motivated women and minorities to vote for the Democratic presidential candidate Joe Biden in the 2020 election, even in states that had formerly voted for Trump. According to Erin Delmore, "While Biden made gains among college-educated, white women voters who supported him in greater numbers than they did Hillary Clinton four years ago, Black women voters carried him over the finish line."[47] Delmore points to several factors that influenced women to vote for the Biden-Harris ticket, which promised "to build better." Although the Trump campaign pitched "a law and order" message to white, suburban women, according to Delmore, "an early exit poll found that more than half of white suburban women said they have a favorable view of the Black Lives Matter movement and nearly half said they believed that the justice system is unfair to Black people."[48]

On November 6, 2020, *Washington Post* reporters parsing "mixed election results" noted that "women still face a sexist political culture" to explain why women were motivated in part to cast their ballots for the

Democratic ticket, which included Senator Kamala Harris, the first woman of color to run as a major party candidate.[49] Women voters responded to the Democratic commitment to address gender disparities.

> Joe Biden is going to build our country back better after this economic crisis and that includes ensuring we get closer to full inclusion of and equality for women. Women—particularly women of color—have *never* had a fair shot to get ahead in this country. Today, too many women are struggling to make ends meet and support their families and are worried about the economic future for their children. This was true before the COVID-19 crisis, but the current global health crisis has exacerbated these realities for women.[50]

Biden's platform indicated his willingness to work with progressives to develop comprehensive reforms addressing care of children and elders, public health, climate, and infrastructural needs. Although the Trump project Operation Warp Speed rapidly produced the first COVID-19 vaccines, with the first injections occurring in December 2020 in the US, the Trump administration neglected to produce robust plans for vaccine dissemination, forcing Biden to push states to develop systems implementing distribution across the country beginning in January 2021.[51]

Historic US senatorial elections in Georgia on January 5, 2021, resulted in victories for two Democrats: Raphael Warnock was elected the first Black senator from Georgia, and Jon Ossoff was elected the first Jewish senator from Georgia. Neither had ever won an election before, and their vote margins over their opponents were small, but their wins ensured narrow Democratic control of the US Senate to complement a Democratic president and a Democratic majority in the House of Representatives. Only hours after the twin Democratic senatorial victories in Georgia were confirmed, white nationalist, Q-Anon, Proud Boys, and other Trump supporters on January 6, 2021, attacked police and invaded the US Capitol Building. The insurrectionists toted weapons and wore combat gear; they were incited to sedition by President Trump, who claimed election fraud. He had filed more than sixty unsuccessful lawsuits before holding a rally that day near the Ellipse during which he encouraged his followers to march on the Capitol "to stop the steal." In a last desperate maneuver, Trump urged his followers to interfere with Congress's count of Electoral College ballots for the November 2020 US presidential election as a way to prevent Joe Biden from being confirmed as the next president.[52] The mob invasion on January 6, 2021, of the US Capitol caused chaos for hours until security forces could clear the rioters who invaded the building, injuring police and protesters and yelling death threats against lawmakers, including Speaker of the House Nancy Pelosi and Vice President Mike Pence. Hundreds of mostly white male insurrectionists stole, damaged, and destroyed property that day, and investigations into the deaths of US Capitol officers and of insurrectionists continue as of this writing after hundreds of arrests and some convictions.[53]

Although during the January 6, 2021, Capitol invasion legislators were moved to secure areas until the building was deemed safe, they returned to the legislative chambers and remained through the night to complete the confirmation process declaring Biden president. In the weeks following the failed insurrection, social media platforms banned Trump, cabinet secretaries and other members of his administration resigned, former donors and allies refused to contribute to the senators who objected "to the certification of election results in Arizona and Pennsylvania," and many politicians and other citizens asked for resignations from those legislators supporting the failed coup.[54] In response to the insurrectionists' murderous anger fueling their claims of being dispossessed of "their" country, some political leaders called for breaching the political divide and ending the presidency of hate and division, while others pressed for investigations, arrests of insurrectionists, and hearings to determine the roots of the January 6 attack on the Capitol. On January 13, 2021, the House of Representatives voted on impeachment: "to formally charge President Trump with inciting violence against the government of the United States, 10 Republicans cast their votes in favor."[55] The historic second impeachment trial of the out-of-office Donald Trump resulted in acquittal on February 13, 2021, although even Republicans had discussed censuring the former president for his actions and inactions.[56] Commentators looking ahead to a 2022 midterm election noted that Trump's speeches and informal remarks fueled violent rhetoric and violence and appear to be accepted by many Republican leaders, candidates, and voters.[57] In summer 2022, the US House of Representatives Select Committee to Investigate the January 6th Attack on the US Capitol held numerous hearings to share evidence collected about the insurrection and planned fall hearings to examine the lack of response to the insurrection on the part of the Trump administration.[58]

Immediately following the violence around and in the Capitol, feminist political commentators looked forward to the possibility of Democrats gaining traction to pass progressive legislation. Roxane Gay in

January 2021 called on the Democrats "to use their power . . . and legislate without worrying about how Republican voters will respond. Cancel student loan debt. Pass another voting rights act that enfranchises as many Americans as possible. Create a true path to citizenship for undocumented Americans. Institute a $15 minimum wage. Enact 'Medicare for all.' Realistically, only so much is possible with a slender majority in the Senate, but the opportunity to make the most of the next two years is there."[59] Gay's list contains proposals aligning with feminist values of increasing equality and empowerment and dismantling hierarchies of privilege.[60] Biden announced before taking office that he would address several issues, including the pandemic, economic problems, racial injustice, climate change, student loan debt, and immigration.[61] Conservative fears of socialism, communism, and feminism, stemming from anxieties that some may benefit at the expense of others, and thin margins of Democrats in Congress complicated the Biden administration's capacity to effect Gay's proposals, as well as other proposals articulated by progressive legislators aiming to meet the needs of Americans burdened by sexism, racial oppression, and pandemic conditions.

Inclusion and Aspiration

January 20, 2021, inaugural ceremonies for President Biden and Vice-President Kamala Harris followed a memorial service the evening prior that honored 400,000 US deaths due to COVID-19. Many speakers and performers at the memorial, the inauguration, and the evening televised celebration after the inauguration focused on hopes for the future; their texts reflected on the need to work together to negotiate differences and unify the US according to core principles of democracy. Both singers at the memorial service were Black females. Kamala Harris is the first female vice president as well as being the first Black person and first of Asian descent to be elected to that office. The inauguration ceremony highlighted the participation of women and persons of color, including Justice Sonia Sotomayor, who swore in Harris as vice president; firefighter Andrea Hall, who led the Pledge of Allegiance; and singer Jennifer Lopez, who translated part of the pledge into Spanish and included it in her medley. Amanda Gorman, the youngest poet ever to speak at an inaugural ceremony, described herself in her poem as "a skinny black girl descended from slaves" who was "raised by a single mother," pointing out that "we have our eyes on the future" and ending on these hopeful lines:

The new dawn blooms as we free it.
For there is always light if only we're brave enough to see it,
If only we're brave enough to be it.[62]

Gorman delivered the inaugural poem at the invitation of incoming First Lady Dr. Jill Biden, who was also responsible for selecting *Landscape with Rainbow* by nineteenth-century Black artist Robert S. Duncanson as the inaugural painting. In tune with these optimistic references, Joe Biden's inaugural speech recognized a range of challenges for his administration, appealed to all to work together to eliminate divisions, and included his pledge to be "President for all Americans."[63] Diverse participation in the inaugural events helped the Biden-Harris team to lift the spirits of those in the audience worried about whether there would be a repeat of the January 6 insurrection against the Capitol.

Speeches and performances at the inauguration of the forty-sixth president focused on aspirations and the future, on moving forward and correcting actions of the previous administration, and on being as inclusive and transparent as possible in decisions and actions. Biden's cabinet picks were highly competent, experienced, and reflect the country they serve. This group had more women, more persons of color, and likely greater expertise than any US cabinet in history, although some observers expressed a concern that the president appointed mostly white men to key positions. On his first day in the Oval Office Biden signed seventeen executive actions that followed up on his inaugural address about unity, truth, and understanding; many of these executive actions aimed to eliminate racist and sexist practices and many responded to continuing problems of COVID-19.[64] The vice president's first actions in the Senate included presiding over the swearing in of three new senators, all Democrats who tipped the balance in the chamber to Democratic control.

What Next?

Susan Faludi's last sentences in *Backlash* respond to a feminist's pessimism about whether the 1990s would really be a decade seeing the empowerment of women; her words remind readers that they can counter efforts to diminish women's rights and lives:

> One might hope, or dream, that [Ruth] Mandel's gloomy pre-
> diction is proved wrong. But more productively, women can
> act. Because there really is no good reason why the '90s can't
> be their decade. Because the demographics and the opinion
> polls are on women's side. Because women's hour on the stage
> is long, long overdue. Because, whatever new obstacles are
> mounted against the future march toward equality, whatever
> new myths invented, penalties levied, opportunities rescinded,
> or degradations imposed, no one can ever take from the
> American woman the justness of her cause.[65]

Refusing to be daunted by opposition and moving forward collectively to accomplish the just cause of gender equity remain the watch-
words of the day. As Katharine M. Marino and Susan Ware assert in
"Rethinking 'First Wave' Feminisms: An Introduction," "feminism is an
ongoing struggle that has never been quiescent and a fight that is far from
over."[66] The US and the UK face political crises fueled by male leaders
whose selfishness and lack of care for citizens impeded national responses
to climate change, inflation, and a pandemic: Boris Johnson resigned in
2022 as prime minister of Great Britain and former president Donald
Trump may face criminal charges.

During the summer of 2022, the US House of Representatives January 6th committee revealed in several televised hearings the results of
their investigation into the 2021 insurrection at the Capitol, and then
President Trump's actions contributing to the riot and his resistance to
calling in law enforcement to end it. The committee's eight carefully produced hearings presented an evidence-based argument supported with
video clips and witness testimony and framed by comments from its chair,
Rep. Bennie Thompson, and its vice-chair, Rep. Liz Cheney.[67] Concluding
the eighth hearing, Cheney thanked the women who testified, including a
Capitol police officer, election workers, and Trump appointees, and praised
them as "an inspiration to American women and American girls."[68] NPR
reported that Cheney wore "a symbolic white blazer" and "acknowledged
the history of the room the hearing was held in—the site of the Committee on Women's Suffrage, a powerful force in helping women gain the

right to vote," quoting her remarks: " 'in 1918, the Committee on Women's Suffrage convened to discuss and debate whether women should be granted the right to vote. . . . This room is full of history, and we on this committee know we have a solemn obligation not to idly squander what so many Americans fought and died for.' "[69] In this way, feminist past and present actions and hopes for the future inspire change and continue to move toward greater equity.

In the third year of the pandemic, hope may sometimes appear elusive, but it should never be absent, as Beverly Daniel Tatum argued in her 2022 Smith College commencement speech encouraging graduates "to cast out fear and replace it with hope."[70] Tatum pointed to the recent "pushback" against progress as a reason to continue to press for change: "There is no question that we are living through such a period of 'counterrevolution' today—a retrenchment of women's rights, voting rights, human rights! Yet when we feel the pushback, we must remember it comes in response to change. If there had been no change—no advancement in women's rights—there would be no pushback against that advancement."[71] She reminded graduates of Dr. King's statement, "The moral arc of the universe bends toward justice," asserting "our collective responsibility [is] to help it bend faster," and explained that her courage is also informed by the examples of Italian women who fought fascism, the French who resisted Nazi occupation, and Ida B. Wells, who campaigned for US anti-lynching laws.[72] Dr. Tatum reminds us that appreciating those who demonstrated resilience in the face of oppression and who are represented in historical narratives helps us understand that persistence and cooperation among allies results in progress toward equity.

Equity advocates are also inspired by fictional narratives that track similar examples of resistance and courage in the face of oppression. In that spirit, I conclude this book about fictional representations of feminist optimism by quoting from a contemporary novel set in 1950 Mexico to note how its plot references misogynist threats drawing on myths and pseudoscience to elaborate how supernatural forces collude with colonialist eugenicists to terrorize and enslave young women. Two women and their allies survive by demonstrating courage and resilience, allowing the women to escape their captivity as breeders. Silvia Moreno-Garcia's *Mexican Gothic* (2020) details many episodes in which females confront patriarchal powers that they cannot understand and for a long time must endure; however, the novel ends with the protagonist's speculation about what comes next: "The future, she thought, could not be predicted, and the shape of things could not be divined. To think otherwise was absurd. But they were young that morning, and they could cling to hope. Hope that the world could be remade, kinder and sweeter."[73] Feminist principles in fiction, myth, and history make change possible.

Notes

Prologue

1. Kimberlé Williams Crenshaw, "Mapping the Margins: Intersectionality, Identity Politics, and Violence against Women of Color," 13. https://www.racial equitytools.org/resourcefiles/mapping-margins.pdf.

2. Robin Truth Goodman, "Introduction," in *The Bloomsbury Handbook of 21st-Century Feminist Theory*, ed. Robin Truth Goodman (London: Bloomsbury, 2019), 1–18: 13.

3. Susan Hekman, "Subject," in *The Bloomsbury Handbook of 21st-Century Feminist Theory*, ed. Robin Truth Goodman (London: Bloomsbury, 2019), 21–31: 22.

4. Lauren Berlant, *Cruel Optimism* (Durham: Duke University Press, 2011), 121–22.

5. Berlant, *Cruel Optimism*, 123.

6. Emilie Walezak reassesses realist fiction by British women writers considering feminism and posthumanism. See Emilie Walezak, *Rethinking Contemporary British Women's Writing: Realism, Feminism, Materialism* (London: Bloomsbury, 2021).

7. Martin Eve, *Literature against Criticism: University English and Contemporary Fiction in Conflict* (Cambridge, UK: Open Book Publishers, 2016), 88.

8. William G. Thomas III, "Television News and the Civil Rights Struggle: The Views in Virginia and Mississippi," *Southern Spaces* (November 3, 2004). https://southernspaces.org/2004/television-news-and-civil-rights-struggle-v iews-virginia-and-mississippi/.

9. From "Mission Statement," *Trans Book Review*, https://transbookreviews. wordpress.com/.

10. Diana Fuss, *Essentially Speaking: Feminism, Nature and Difference* (London: Routledge, 1989), 102, 24.

11. Ellen Rooney, "The Literary Politics of Feminist Theory," in *The Cambridge Companion to Feminist Literary Theory*, ed. Ellen Rooney (Cambridge:

Cambridge University Press, 2006), 85–86, https://www.cambridge.org/core/books/cambridge-companion-to-feminist-literary-theory/literary-politics-of-feminist-theory/4FB72144874474CE592D1EC2AC59B0C4.

12. Parveen Adams, "A Note on the Distinction between Sexual Division and Sexual Differences," in *The Woman in Question*, ed. Parveen Adams and Elizabeth Cowie (Cambridge: MIT Press, 1990), 103, cited in Rooney, "The Literary Politics of Feminist Theory," 88.

13. Sylvia Walby, "Beyond the Politics of Location," *Feminist Theory* 1, no. 2 (2000): 189–206; Dale Bauer and Priscilla Wald, "Complaining, Conversing, Coalescing," *Signs* 25, no. 4 (2000): 1299–1303, cited in Judith Lorber, *Gender Inequality: Feminist Theories and Politics* (Los Angeles: Roxbury, 2005), 318, 319.

14. "The Combahee River Collective Statement," 1978, November 6, 2020. https://combaheerivercollective.weebly.com/the-combahee-river-collective-statement.html.

15. Judith Fetterley, *The Resisting Reader: A Feminist Approach to American Fiction*, (Bloomington: Indiana University Press, 1978), xxii.

16. Ellen Messer Davidow, "The Philosophical Bases of Feminist Literary Criticisms," *New Literary History* 19 (Autumn 1987): 65–103, 91–92.

17. R.W. Connell, *Masculinities* (Berkeley: University of California Press, 2005), 243.

18. See Catharine Stimpson, "Reading for Love: Canons, Paracanons, and Whistling Jo March," in *Little Women and the Feminist Imagination: Criticism, Controversy, Personal Essay*, ed. Janice M. Alberghene and Beverly Lyon Clark (New York: Garland Publishing, 1999), 63–81.

19. Elizabeth Freeman, *Time Binds: Queer Temporalities, Queer Histories* (Durham: Duke University Press, 2010), xvii.

20. For example, see the collection *Little Women and the Feminist Imagination: Criticism, Controversy, Personal Essays*.

Introduction

1. Mary Ellmann, *Thinking about Women* (New York: Harcourt Brace Jovanovich, 1968), 205.

2. Audre Lorde, "The Transformation of Silence, into Language and Action," in *Sister Outsider* (1984), cited in *Feminist Literary Theory and Criticism*, ed. Sandra M. Gilbert and Susan Gubar (New York: W. W. Norton, 2007), 226.

3. Gloria Anzaldúa, *Borderlands/La Frontera* (San Francisco: Aunt Lute Books, 1989), 100.

4. Moira Ferguson, "Preface," in *First Feminists: British Women Writers, 1578–1799*, ed. Moira Ferguson (Bloomington: Indiana University Press, 1985), xi.

5. Kristen Grogan, "An Interview with Rachel Blau DuPlessis," *The Oxonian* 29, no. 4 (December 5, 2015), http://www.oxonianreview.org/wp/an-interview-with-rachel-blau-duplessis/.

6. bell hooks, *Feminism Is for Everybody: Passionate Politics* (Routledge, 2014), xii.

7. Catherine Belsey, "Constructing the Subject," in *Feminisms: An Anthology of Literary Theory and Criticism*, 2nd ed., ed. Robyn Warhol and Diane Price Herndl (New Brunswick: Rutgers University Press, 1997), 661.

8. On intersectionality, see Kimberlé Williams Crenshaw, "Mapping the Margins: Intersectionality, Identity Politics, and Violence against Women of Color," https://www.racialequitytools.org/resourcefiles/mapping-margins.pdf, and Elizabeth Evans, "What Makes a (Third) Wave?" *International Feminist Journal of Politics* 18, no. 3 (2016): 409–28.

9. Laura R. Fisher, *Reading for Reform: The Social Work of Literature in the Progressive Era* (Minneapolis: University of Minnesota Press, 2019), 4–5.

10. Fisher, *Reading for Reform*, 68.

11. Fisher, *Reading for Reform*, 227.

12. Simone de Beauvoir, *The Second Sex* (New York: Random House/Vintage, 1974), 301.

13. Rosi Braidotti, "The Subject in Feminism," *Hypatia* 6, no. 2 (Summer 1991), 155–72, 158.

14. Annette Kolodny, "Dancing through the Minefield," *Feminist Studies* 6, no. 1 (Spring 1980): 1–25, 2.

15. Barbara Christian, "The Race for Theory," *Feminist Studies* 14, no. 1 (Spring 1988), 67–79, 75.

16. Finke cites Donna Haraway's essay, "A Manifesto for Cyborgs," *Socialist Review* 80 (1985): 65–107, 100. See Laurie Finke, "A Powerful Infidel Heteroglossia: Toward a Feminist Theory of Complexity," in *Feminist Theory, Women's Writing* (Ithaca: Cornell University Press, 2018), 5.

17. Judith Butler, "Imitation and Gender Insubordination," in *Feminist Theory and Criticism*, ed. Sandra M. Gilbert and Susan Gubar (New York: Norton, 2007), 708–22, 722.

18. See Dan Levin, "The Human Experience Is Infinite," *New York Times*, June 28, 2019, https://www.nytimes.com/interactive/2019/06/28/us/pride-identity.html.

19. US Department of Labor, "DOL Policies on Gender Identity: Rights and Responsibilities": "Gender identity discrimination can affect anyone. Policies barring gender identity discrimination not only protect those who openly identify as transgender or express their gender in a non-conforming way. They also protect other people against sex stereotyping—for instance, women who some people think are 'too masculine' or men who some people think are 'too feminine.'" Accessed August 2, 2022, https://www.dol.gov/agencies/oasam/centers-offices/civil-rightscenter/internal/policies/gender-identity.

20. For a discussion of how intersex discourses in medicine "informed the invention of gender," see Julian Gill-Peterson, *Histories of the Transgender Child* (Minneapolis: University of Minnesota Press, 2018), 16–17.

21. Carol Colatrella, "Introduction" and "On Technology and Humanity," in *Technology and Humanity*, Salem Press/EBSCO, 2012: vii–xv, 1–23.

22. Judith Butler, "A Dissenting View from the Humanities on the AAUP's Statement on Knowledge: In Defense of Critical Inquiry," *Academe* 106, no. 2 (Spring 2020), https://www.aaup.org/article/dissenting-view-human-ities-aaup%E2%80%99s-statement-knowledge#.X_Dj6elKhZ0.

23. Ann Ardis, *New Women, New Novels: Feminism and Early Modernism* (New Brunswick: Rutgers University Press, 1990), 117. Critical analyses of media recognizing audience desire include Susan Douglas, *Where the Girls Are: Growing Up Female with Mass Media* (New York: Random House, 1995), and Bonnie Dow, *Prime Time Feminism: Television, Media Culture, and the Women's Movement Since 1970* (Philadelphia: University of Pennsylvania Press, 1996).

24. NPR Staff, Interview with Laurie Frankel, *NPR* " 'This Is How It Always Is' " Was Inspired by Its Author's Transgender Child," January 30, 2017, https://www.npr.org/2017/01/30/512030431/this-is-how-it-always-is-was-inspired-by-its-authors-transgender-child.

25. Laurie Frankel, *This Is How It Always Is* (New York: Flatiron Books, 2017), 237.

26. *Kathoey* is a term applied in Thailand to a male-to-female transgender person or person of a third gender or an effeminate homosexual male. *Kathoey*, *Wikipedia*. Accessed August 2, 2022, https://en.wikipedia.org/wiki/Kathoey.

27. Josiah Royce coined the term, but it was popularized in the civil rights era by the Reverend Dr. Martin Luther King Jr. See "The Beloved Community," on the website of the King Center, https://thekingcenter.org/about-tkc/the-king-phi-losophy/. Accessed August 15, 2022.

28. Alexandra Alter, "How Feminist Dystopian Fiction Is Channeling Women's Anger and Anxiety," *New York Times*, October 10, 2018, https://www.nytimes.com/2018/10/08/books/feminist-dystopian-fiction-margaret-atwood-wom-en-metoo.html.

29. See two Margaret Atwood interviews on *YouTube*: "*The Handmaid's Tale* is being read differently" (2018?), https://www.youtube.com/watch?v=7a8LnKCzsBw; Margaret Atwood, "Handmaid's Relevance after Election" (2017?), https://www.youtube.com/watch?v=BvIpWyWVTdE.

30. Mervyn Rothstein, "No Balm in Gilead for Margaret Atwood," *New York Times*, February 17, 1986, https://archive.nytimes.com/www.nytimes.com/books/00/09/03/specials/atwood-gilead.html.

31. Sophie Gilbert, "The Remarkable Rise of the Feminist Dystopia," *Atlantic,* October 4, 2018, https://www.theatlantic.com/entertainment/archive/2018/10/feminist-speculative-fiction-2018/571822/.

32. Virginia Allen, Douglas K. Blair, "What We Saw at Protest Outside Justice Amy Coney Barrett's House," *Daily Signal*, May 11, 2022, https://www.dailysignal.com/2022/05/11/what-we-saw-at-protest-outside-justice-amy-coney-barretts-house/.

33. Margaret Atwood, "Introduction," *The Handmaid's Tale* (New York: Doubleday, 2017), xviii.

34. Michelle Goldberg, "Margaret Atwood's Dystopia, and Ours," *New York Times*, September 14, 2019, https://www.nytimes.com/2019/09/14/opinion/sunday/margaret-atwood-the-testaments-handmaids-tale.html.

35. Jennifer Weiner, "How Do I Explain Kavanaugh to My Daughters?" *New York Times,* October 9, 2018, https://www.nytimes.com/2018/10/09/opinion/kavanaugh-justice-princeton-women.html.

36. Peter Rabinowitz, *Before Reading: Narrative Conventions and the Politics of Interpretation* (Columbus: Ohio State University Press, 1998), 225, citing Alice Jardine "Gynesis," *Diacritics* 12 (Summer 1982): 54–65, 56.

37. Rita Felski, *Literature after Feminism* (Chicago: University of Chicago Press, 2003), 3.

38. Rosalind Gill acknowledges that media and views of feminism are diverse and changing, and she notes that television talk shows can offer "anti-normative messages." See Rosalind Gill, *Gender and the Media* (Cambridge, UK: Polity, 2007), 2, 5.

39. Christine Stansell, *The Feminist Promise: 1792 to the Present* (New York: Modern Library, 2011), xiii.

40. Rebecca Coleman and Debra Ferreday, "Introduction: Hope and Feminist Theory," in *Hope and Feminist Theory*, eds. Rebecca Coleman and Debra Ferreday (New York: Routledge, 2018), 3, citing Angela McRobbie, *Feminist Media Studies* 4, no. 3 (2004): 255–64.

41. Janet Todd, *Feminist Literary History: A Defence* (Cambridge: Polity Press, 2007), 137.

42. Stanford professor of history Claybourne Carson explained the reference to Melissa Block during the segment "Theodore Parker And The 'Moral Universe,'" *NPR*, September 2, 2010, http://www.npr.org/templates/story/story.php?storyId=129609461.

43. According to "The Arc of the Moral Universe Is Long, but It Bends toward Justice," Quote Investigator, "A similar statement appears in *Morals and Dogma of the Ancient and Accepted Scottish Rite of Freemasonry*," copyright date of 1871, and publication date of 1905: "We cannot understand the moral Universe. The arc is a long one, and our eyes reach but a little way." https://quoteinvestigator.com/2012/11/15/arc-of-universe/.

44. Weiyi Cai and Scott Clement, "What Americans Think about Feminism Today," *Washington Post*, January 27, 2016, https://www.washingtonpost.com/graphics/national/feminism-project/poll/; Rachael Henry, "Attitudes to Gender in 2016

Britain: 8,000 Sample Study for Fawcett Society," Survation, http://survation.com/uk-attitudes-to-gender-in-2016-survation-for-fawcett-society/; the Equal Protection Clause, the Fourteenth Amendment of the US Constitution offers "equal protection under the laws." "Amendment XIV," *Legal Information Institute*, https://www.law.cornell.edu/constitution/amendmentxiv. The Sex Discrimination Act of 1975 in Great Britain (https://www.legislation.gov.uk/ukpga/1975/65) was superseded by the nation's Equality Act 2010, noting "protected characteristics—age; disability; gender reassignment; marriage and civil partnership; pregnancy and maternity; race; religion or belief; sex; sexual orientation." See Equality Act 2010, legislation.gov.uk, https://www.legislation.gov.uk/ukpga/2010/15/contents.

45. Roxane Gay, *Bad Feminist: Essays* (New York: Harper, 2014), xii.

46. Stansell, *The Feminist Promise*, 104, 124–25.

47. Anna Julia Cooper, *A Voice from the South* (New York: Oxford University Press, 1988).

48. Amanda Taub, "On Social Media's Fringes, Growing Extremism Targets Women," *New York Times*, May 9, 2018, https://www.nytimes.com/2018/05/09/world/americas/incels-toronto-attack.html.

49. Aristotle, *Politics* 1.1253a. https://www.perseus.tufts.edu/hopper/text?doc=Perseus:abo:tlg,0086,035:1:1253a.

50. In the United States, conservative media such as Fox News and Breitbart News stoked the flourishing of right-wing and nationalist groups, while progressive social groups—Occupy Wall Street, Black Lives Matter, Women's Marches, the Dreamers, #MeToo, #TimesUp, and March for Life—command attention in mainstream and progressive media.

51. As of August 15, 2022, Google reported 5,220,000 results referencing "limitations of electoral college."

52. Emma Watson's speech delivered to the UN on September 20, 2014, is on YouTube at https://www.youtube.com/watch?v=p-iFl4qhBsE. The transcript is at U.N. Women, "Emma Watson: Gender Equality Is Your Issue Too," http://www.unwomen.org/en/news/stories/2014/9/emma-watson-gender-equality-is-your-issue-too. Chimamanda Ngozi Adichie's Ted talk "We Should All Be Feminists," delivered December 2012, is available at https://www.ted.com/talks/chimamanda_ngozi_adichie_we_should_all_be_feminists. Sheryl Sandberg's Ted talk "Why We Have Too Few Women Leaders," delivered in December 2010, is available at https://www.ted.com/talks/sheryl_sandberg_why_we_have_too_few_women_leaders.

53. Evan Sawdey, [review] "Beyonce's Lemonade," *Pop Matters*, April 27, 2016, https://www.popmatters.com/beyonce-lemonade-2495435666.html.

54. Meghan Markle's Speech at UN Women 2015, delivered in July 2015, https://www.youtube.com/watch?v=EDvV-xfrqIM.

55. Gay, *Bad Feminist*, 171.

56. In March 2018, accounts of protests against gun violence in schools, largely initiated by student survivors of the February 14, 2018, Parkland

school shooting, referenced #MeToo, noting that senior Emma González from Marjory Stoneman Douglas High School was subject to misogynistic and homophobic criticisms. See Travis Cohen, "This Is What Righteousness Sounds Like: The Importance of Emma González," *Miami New Times*, February 19, 2018, https://www.miaminewtimes.com/arts/emma-gonzalez-stoneman-douglas-survivor-makes-righteous-speech-10100848.

57. The protest continued November 1917 with thirty-three women arrested on what were later deemed to be unconstitutional grounds. See Terence McArdle, "How Women Got the Vote," *Washington Post*, November 10, 2017, https://www.washingtonpost.com/news/retropolis/wp/2017/11/10/night-of-terror-the-suffragists-who-were-beaten-and-tortured-for-seeking-the-vote/?utm_term=.0a7d6fc1331b.

58. Some estimated worldwide attendance at the January 2017 Women's Marches at more than 2.6 million individuals.

59. Beginning in fall 2017, many instances of sexual abuse and discrimination commanded public attention as the #MeToo and #TimesUp movements accused men in business, politics, media, and entertainment of discrimination, harassment, and rape; many accused relinquished their positions.

60. Eleanor Flexner, *Century of Struggle* (Cambridge: Harvard University Press, [1959] 1975), 271–72. For discussion of suffragist ideologies, see Aileen S. Kraditor, *The Ideas of the Women's Suffrage Movement, 1890–1920* (New York: Norton, [1965] 1981).

61. Photographs held by the Library of Congress document the violence against the protesters. For example, see the photo captioned "Sailors attacking pickets, 1917, while policemen look casually on—(Two policemen leaning against fence at left of street lamp pole on right)," Library of Congress, https://www.loc.gov/item/mnwp000210/.

62. The subheading of one article is "When no one is arrested, it's often because no one wants to arrest them"; see Jess Zimmerman, "The Myth of the Well-Behaved Women's March," *New Republic*, January 24, 2017, https://newrepublic.com/article/140065/myth-well-behaved-womens-march.

63. The quotation is from *Recollections*, https://recollections.biz/blog/colors-womens-suffrage/. Also, see *Women's History Bites* blog post "The Colours of the Suffragettes," November 25, 2014, https://irishwomenshistory.blogspot.com/2014/11/the-colours-of-suffragettes.html: "In 1908, the Women's Social and Political Union or WSPU, adopted the colour scheme of purple, white and green, that would not only distinguish them in their political movement, but would also prove to be a huge marketing success."

64. Christine Captidis, "Hillary Wears White Pants Suit to Debate, Internet Goes Crazy," *CBS News* October 20, 2016, http://www.cbsnews.com/news/hillary-wears-white-pants-suit-to-debate-internet-goes-crazy/.

65. Nancy Pelosi on *PBS NewsHour* on election night 2016 commented on her white outfit's connections to suffragists. "Nancy Pelosi offers election night

predictions," *PBS NewsHour*, November 8, 2016, https://www.pbs.org/video/nancy-pelosi-offers-election-night-predictions-1485909178/.

66. Vanessa Friedman, "Kamala Harris in a White Suit, Dressing for History," *New York Times*, November 8, 2020, https://www.nytimes.com/2020/11/08/fashion/kamala-harris-speech-suffrage.html.

67. The Pussyhat Project, "Design Interventions for Social Changes." https://www.pussyhatproject.com/our-story/. Accessed August 17, 2022.

68. Trump's comments were recorded in 2005 as part of a television show and were aired in October 2016. See "Transcript: Donald Trump's Taped Comments about Women," *New York Times*, October 8, 2016, https://www.nytimes.com/2016/10/08/us/donald-trump-tape-transcript.html, and Daniel Victor, "'Access Hollywood' Reminds Trump: 'The Tape Is Very Real,'" *New York Times*, November 28, 2017, https://www.nytimes.com/2017/11/28/us/politics/donald-trump-tape.html.

69. Diana Pearl, "'Pussyhats' Galore: Inside the Pink Toppers Thousands Will Wear to the Women's March on Washington," *People.com*, January 21, 2017, http://people.com/politics/pussyhats-galore-inside-the-pink-toppers-thousands-will-wear-to-the-womens-march-on-washington/. Also see Leanna Garfield, "Thousands of Women Will Wear Pink 'Pussy Hats' the Day after Trump's Inauguration," *Business Insider*, January 18, 2017, http://www.businessinsider.com/pussy-hats-womens-march-washington-trump-inauguration-2017-1.

70. Some photos and related essays appear at "Feminist Resources for #TheResistance," *Signs (Virtual Issue)*, http://signsjournal.org/features/virtual-issues/feminist-resources-for-theresistance/#models. Accessed August 17, 2022.

71. One collection appears online in Alan Taylor, "Photos of the Women's Marches around the World," *Atlantic*, January 21, 2017, https://www.theatlantic.com/photo/2017/01/photos-of-the-womens-marches-around-the-world/514049/.

72. Françoise Mouly, "Cover Story: Abigail Gray Swartz's 'The March,'" *New Yorker*, January 27, 2017, https://www.newyorker.com/culture/culture-desk/cover-story-2017-02-06.

73. "New Yorker Celebrates Intersectional Feminism with New 'Rosie the Riveter' Cover," *The Griot*, January 28, 2017, https://thegrio.com/2017/01/28/new-yorker-celebrates-intersectional-feminism-with-new-rosie-the-riveter-cover/.

74. Maurice Agulhon, *Marianne into Battle: Republican Imagery and Symbolism in France, 1789–1880*, trans. Janet Lloyd (Cambridge: Cambridge University Press, 1981), 3.

75. "The colors associated with women's suffrage represented the many sides of the cause. The British women's suffrage colors were purple, white, and green. Purple, white, and gold were the colors of the American suffrage movement." "The Colors of Women's Suffrage," *Recollections*, June 17, 2019. https://recollections.biz/blog/colors-womens-suffrage.

76. Agulhon, *Marianne into Battle*, 1. A red Phrygian cap is also mentioned in literary works as a signal of a woman's progressive politics and as a way of allegorizing her participation in political events. Émile Zola's first and penultimate Rougon-Macquart novels, *The Fortune of the Rougons* (1871) and *The Debacle* (1892), depict the revolutionary zeal of women wearing such caps.

77. Taylor, "Photos of the Women's Marches around the World," *Atlantic*.

78. See essays in *Nasty Women: Feminism, Resistance, and Revolution in Trump's America*, ed. Samhita Mukhopadhyay and Kate Harding (New York: Picador, 2017).

79. Taylor, "Photos of the Women's Marches around the World," *Atlantic*.

80. Christopher F. Karpowitz and Tali Mendelberg, *The Silent Sex: Gender, Deliberation, and Institutions* (Princeton: Princeton University Press, 2014), 139.

81. This text is adapted from Carol Colatrella's review of Christopher F. Karpowitz and Tali Mendelberg, *The Silent Sex: Gender, Deliberation, and Institutions* in *International Journal of Gender, Science, and Technology* 8, no. 2 (2016): 313–16, http://genderandset.open.ac.uk/index.php/genderandset/article/view/453.

82. John Wagner, "Bernie Sanders Wins Backing of African American Group in Nevada's Largest County," *Washington Post*, February 19, 2016, https://www.washingtonpost.com/news/post-politics/wp/2016/02/19/bernie-sanders-wins-backing-of-african-american-group-in-nevadas-largest-county/.

83. This and the previous paragraph are from Colatrella's review of *Silent Sex* in *International Journal of Gender, Science, and Technology*. Also see Rebecca Traister, *Good and Mad: The Revolutionary Power of Women's Anger* (New York: Simon and Schuster, 2018), 66.

84. Mary Beard, *Women and Power: A Manifesto* (NY: Liveright, 2017), xi.

85. Beard, *Women and Power* 4.

86. Beard, *Women and Power*, 3.

87. Oswyn Murray, "Life and Society in Classical Greece," *The Oxford History of the Classical World*, ed. John Boardman, Jasper Griffin, and Oswyn Murray (Oxford: Oxford University Press, 1986), 212.

88. Sue-Ellen Case, *Feminism and Theatre* (New York: Methuen, 1988), 7.

89. Nancy Sorkin Rabinowitz, *Anxiety Veiled: Euripides and the Traffic in Women* (Ithaca: Cornell University Press, 1993), 7.

90. "Sit in a Drizzle to See Greek Play: Courageous Suffragists in Outdoor Theatre Hear Aristophanes Plead Their Cause," *New York Times*, September 20, 1912, 11, https://www.nytimes.com/1912/09/20/archives/sit-in-a-drizzle-to-see-greek-play-courageous-suffragists-in.html.

91. Scott Rappaport, "Literature professor links Santa Cruz to international theater event for peace," *UC Currents Online*, February 17, 2003, http://www1.ucsc.edu/currents/02-03/02-17/play.html.

92. Nancy Rabinowitz's *Anxiety Veiled: Euripides and the Traffic in Women*, looks at "the relationship between gender, power, and sexuality in tragedy" to "understand its ideological force," recognizing that "left unanalyzed, the dynamic at work in the plays may continue to seem to be universal and thus continue to reinscribe itself in the modern audience" (x).

93. References to various adaptations of *Lysistrata* appear at https://en.wikipedia.org/wiki/Lysistrata.

94. For an extensive analysis, see Nancy Armstrong, *Desire and Domestic Fiction: A Political History of the Novel* (Oxford: Oxford University Press, 1987).

95. Jane Austen, *Pride and Prejudice* (New York: Penguin, 2003), 5.

96. Flexner, *Century of Struggle*, 7.

97. Jill Rappoport, *Giving Women: Alliance and Exchange in Victorian Culture* (Oxford: Oxford University Press, 2012), 5, discusses Charlotte Bronte's *Jane Eyre* (1847) and Elizabeth Gaskell's *Cranford* (1853), among other works.

98. Christine Stansell, "Elizabeth Stuart Phelps: A Study in Female Rebellion," *Massachusetts Review* 13, no. 1/2, Woman: An Issue (Winter–Spring, 1972): 239–56: 250.

99. Feminist Press website for *The Silent Partner*, https://www.feministpress.org/books-n-z/the-silent-partner. Also see Carol Colatrella, *Toys and Tools in Pink* (Columbus: Ohio State University Press, 2011), 86–97.

100. See Charlotte Perkins Gilman, *Suffrage Songs and Verses* (NY: Charlton Company, 2011), in *A Celebration of Women Writers*, http://digital.library.upenn.edu/women/gilman/suffrage/suffrage.html.

101. Robert Shulman, "Introduction," *The Yellow Wallpaper and Other Stories* (Oxford University Press, 1995); Carol Colatrella, "Work for Women: Recuperating Charlotte Perkins Gilman's Reform Fiction," *Research in Science and Technology Studies* (*Knowledge and Society*, vol. 12), ed. Shirley Gorenstein (Stamford: JAI Press, 2000): 53–76.

102. See Ann Heilman, "Introduction" (1–14) and Lisa Ganobcsik-Williams, "Charlotte Perkins Gilman and *The Forerunner*: A New Woman's Changing Perspective on American Immigration" (44–56) in *Feminist Forerunners: New Womanism and Feminism in the Early Twentieth Century*, ed. Ann Heilman (London: Pandora, 2003).

103. Sally Ledger, *The New Woman: Fiction and Feminism at the Fin de Siècle* (Manchester: Manchester University Press, 1997), 5.

104. Alison Harvey, *Feminist Media Studies* (Cambridge: Polity, 2019), 4–5.

105. Harvey, *Feminist Media Studies*, 60.

106. Harvey, *Feminist Media Studies*, 71.

107. Harvey, *Feminist Media Studies*, 143, 142.

108. The blurb appears on the back cover of Lynn Povich, *The Good Girls Revolt: How the Women of Newsweek Sued Their Bosses and Changed the Workplace* (New York: Public Affairs, 2012).

109. The phrase "coming to consciousness" is Povich's and appears in Alexis Sottile, " 'Good Girls Revolt': Inside Landmark Lawsuit behind New Feminist Series: Fact-checking the Fictionalized Account of the 1970 Female Uprising at 'Newsweek,' " *Rolling Stone*, November 3, 2016, https://www.rollingstone.com/culture/news/good-girls-revolt-inside-lawsuit-that-inspired-amazon-show-w447701.

110. Traister, *Good and Mad*, 175.

111. These phrases are chapter titles in Londa Schiebinger, *Has Feminism Changed Science?* (Cambridge: Harvard University Press, 2001).

112. For a definition of the police procedural, see Noah Stewart, "Toward a Definition of the Police Procedural," *Noah's Archives: Curating Genre Fiction since 1972*, March 30, 2014, http://noah-stewart.com/2014/03/30/toward-a-definition-of-the-police-procedural.

Chapter 1

1. Horace, "The Art of Poetry," *Criticism: The Major Texts*, ed. and trans. Walter Jackson Bate (New York: Harcourt Brace Jovanovich, 1970), in *Critical Theory Since Plato*, ed. Hazard Adams (New York: Harcourt Brace Jovanovich, 1972), 67–74, 72.

2. See chapter 22 in E. M. Forster, *Howards End* (New York: Random House, 1921), 186–87.

3. This chapter adapts previously published material from Carol Colatrella, "The Innocent Convict: Character, Reader Sympathy, and the Nineteenth-Century Prison in *Little Dorrit*," in *In the Grip of the Law: Prisons, Trials, and the Space in Between*, ed. Monika Fludernik and Greta Olson (Frankfurt am Main: Peter Lang, 2004), 185–204, and Carol Colatrella, "Information in the Novel and the Novel as Information System: Charles Dickens's *Little Dorrit* and Margaret Drabble's *Radiant Way* Trilogy," *Information and Culture: A Journal of History* 50, no. 3 (2015): 339–71.

4. Geoffrey Nunberg, "James Gleick's "History of Information," *New York Times*, March 18, 2011, https://www.nytimes.com/2011/03/20/books/review/book-review-the-information-by-james-gleick.html.

5. Ian Watt, *The Rise of the Novel: Studies in Defoe, Richardson and Fielding* (Berkeley: University of California Press, 1957). Also see Margaret Anne Doody, *The True Story of the Novel* (New Brunswick: Rutgers University Press, 1997).

6. Marie-Christine Leps, *Apprehending the Criminal: The Production of Deviance in Nineteenth-Century Discourse* (Durham: Duke University Press, 1992).

7. Jill Lepore, "Just the Facts, Ma'am: Fake Memoirs, Factual Fictions, the History of History," *New Yorker*, March 17, 2008, https://www.newyorker.com/magazine/2008/03/24/just-the-facts-maam.

8. Lisa Zunshine, *Why We Read Fiction: Theory of Mind and the Novel* (Columbus: Ohio State University Press, 2006), 36.

9. Zunshine, *Why We Read Fiction,* 13.

10. Zunshine, *Why We Read Fiction,* 47.

11. Roland Barthes, trans. Richard Miller, *S/Z: An Essay* (New York: Hill and Wang, 1974).

12. Richard Menke, *Telegraphic Realism: Victorian Fiction and Other Information Systems* (Stanford: Stanford University Press, 2007).

13. Paula M. L. Moya, "Multifocal Decolonial Novels." Talk presented at Narrative 2020 meeting of the International Society for the Study of Narrative, New Orleans, LA, March 6, 2020.

14. Moya, "Multifocal Decolonial Novels."

15. Moya, "Multifocal Decolonial Novels."

16. Christopher Bode, *The Novel,* trans. James Vigus (Wiley-Blackwell, 2011), xi.

17. Megan Ward, "Our Posthuman Past: Victorian Realism, Cybernetics, and the Problem of Information," *Configurations* 20, no. 3 (Fall 2012): 279–97, 288.

18. Donald O. Case, *Looking for Information: A Survey of Research on Information Seeking, Needs, and Behavior*, 3rd ed. (Bingley, UK: Emerald Group, 2012), 56–57.

19. Case, *Looking for Information,* 56.

20. Case, *Looking for Information,* 56.

21. Case, *Looking for Information,* 57.

22. Case, *Looking for Information,* 57.

23. Michel Foucault, "What Is an Author?," trans. Josué V. Harari in *The Foucault Reader*, ed. Paul Rabinow (New York: Pantheon Books, 1984).

24. Homer, *The Odyssey*, Book XIX, 560–65 cited in Margaret Drabble, *The Gates of Ivory* (New York: Viking, 1991), front matter.

25. Harry Levin, *The Gates of Horn: A Study of Five French Realists* (New York: Oxford University Press, 1963), 49–50.

26. Suzanne Keen, *Empathy and the Novel* (Oxford: Oxford University Press, 2007), 4.

27. Keen, *Empathy and the Novel*, 91.

28. Keen, *Empathy and the Novel*, 91.

29. Claudine Peyre, "Three Interviews with Margaret Drabble," *Cercle* 21 (2011), http://www.cercles.com/n21/peyre.pdf.

30. Janice Carlisle, "*Little Dorrit*: Necessary Fictions," *Studies in the Novel* (1975): 195–214.

31. Sambudha Sen, "*Bleak House* and *Little Dorrit*: The Radical Heritage," *ELH* 65, no. 4 (1998): 945–70.

32. Charles Dickens, *Little Dorrit*, ed. John Holloway (Harmondsworth: Penguin, 1975).

33. Phillip Collins, *Dickens and Crime* (Bloomington: Indiana University Press, 1968).

34. Trey Philpotts, "The Real Marshalsea," *The Dickensian* 87 (1991), 138.

35. Dickens, *Little Dorrit*, 111.

36. Dickens, *Little Dorrit*, 111.

37. Jonathan H. Grossman. *Charles Dickens's Networks: Public Transport and the Novel* (Oxford: Oxford University Press, 2012), 195.

38. Bode, *The Novel*, 5.

39. Menke, *Telegraphic Realism*, 28.

40. N. Katherine Hayles, *Chaos Bound: Orderly Disorder in Contemporary Literature and Science* (Ithaca: Cornell University Press, 1990), 53.

41. Drabble is also a biographer, a literary scholar who edited *The Oxford Companion to English Literature*, an occasional reviewer, and a writer of opinion pieces; sometimes she includes a bibliography in her novels, as she does in *The Gates of Ivory*.

42. Margaret Drabble, *The Radiant Way* (New York: Alfred A. Knopf, 1987), 91.

43. Drabble, *Radiant Way*, 180.

44. Drabble, *Radiant Way*, 28–29.

45. Drabble, *Radiant Way*, 29–30.

46. Drabble, *Radiant Way*, 235.

47. Drabble, *Radiant Way*, 310.

48. Drabble, *Radiant Way*, 311.

49. Drabble, *Radiant Way*, 394.

50. Drabble, *Radiant Way*, 397.

51. Drabble, *Radiant Way*, 401.

52. Drabble, *Radiant Way*, 401.

53. Drabble, *Radiant Way*, 402.

54. Drabble, *Radiant Way*, 408.

55. "Margaret Drabble," *British Council: Literature*, https://literature.british-council.org/writer/margaret-drabble, accessed August 17, 2022.

56. Margaret Drabble, *The Gates of Ivory* (New York: Viking, 1991), 3.

57. Drabble, *The Gates of Ivory*, 421.

58. Margaret Drabble, *A Natural Curiosity* (New York: Viking, 1989), 94.

59. Erich Auerbach, *Mimesis: The Representation of Reality in Western Literature*, trans. Willard R. Trask (Princeton: Princeton University Press, 1953), 557.

Chapter 2

1. Mary Wollstonecraft, *A Vindication of the Rights of Woman with Strictures on Political and Moral Subjects* (London: J. Johnson, 1792), 241, https://oll.libertyfund.org/titles/wollstonecraft-a-vindication-of-the-rights-of-woman.

2. Harriet A. Jacobs, *Incidents in the Life of a Slave Girl*, ed. L. Maria Child (Cambridge: Harvard University Press, 1987), 19.

3. Laura Curtis Bullard, *Christine: or, Woman's Trials and Triumphs*, ed. Denise M. Kohn (Lincoln: University of Nebraska Press, 2010), 207.

4. David F. Noble, *A World without Women: The Christian Clerical Culture of Western Science* (New York: Knopf, 1992), 244.

5. Moira Ferguson, "Mary Wollstonecraft and the Problematic of Slavery," *Feminist Review* 42 (Autumn 1992): 98, 92, 94.

6. Cora Kaplan, *Sea Changes*, 1986: 48, cited by Ferguson, "Mary Wollstonecraft and the Problematic of Slavery," 93.

7. Ferguson, "Mary Wollstonecraft and the Problematic of Slavery," 82.

8. Amanda Claybaugh, *The Novel of Purpose: Literature and Social Reform in the Anglo-American World* (Ithaca: Cornell University Press, 2006), 6.

9. Claybaugh, *The Novel of Purpose*, 36, 32.

10. This section of the chapter has been adapted from Carol Colatrella, "The Evils of Slavery and Their Legacy in American Literature," in *Evil in American Popular Culture*, vol. 2, ed. Jody Pennington and Sharon Packer (Santa Barbara: Praeger, 2014), 45–61.

11. Helen Burke, "Problematizing American Dissent: The Subject of Phillis Wheatley," in *Cohesion and Dissent in American Literature*, ed. Carol Colatrella and Joseph Alkana (Albany: State University of New York, 199), 198.

12. Eric Sundquist, "Slavery, Revolution, and the American Renaissance," in *The American Renaissance Reconsidered*, ed. Walter Benn Michaels and Donald Pease (Baltimore: Johns Hopkins University Press, 1985), 9.

13. Sundquist, "Slavery, Revolution, and the American Renaissance," 8, 7.

14. Abraham Lincoln, Second Inaugural Address, March 4, 1865, http://www.bartleby.com/124/pres32.html.

15. Stephen Jay Gould, *The Mismeasure of Man* (New York: Norton, 1996), 64, 66.

16. Alexis de Tocqueville, *Democracy in America*, vol. 1, ch. 10, ed. J. P. Mayer, trans. George Lawrence (New York: Doubleday, 1969), 342–43.

17. Tocqueville, *Democracy in America*, 343.

18. Charles Dickens, *American Notes for General Circulation*, ed. John S. Whitley and Arnold Goldman (London: Penguin, 2000), 274–75.

19. By 1944, according to Marion Wilson Starling's count, "*six thousand and six ex-slaves* had narrated the stories of their captivity, through interviews, essays, and books," including many who provided their testimony as part of the

Works Progress Administration (WPA) oral history project. Starling's figures are cited by Henry Louis Gates in "Introduction," *The Classic Slave Narratives*, ed. Henry Louis Gates (New York: New American Library, 1987), ix.

20. Attributed to Henry Louis Gates in Deborah E. McDowell and Arnold Rampersad, "Introduction," *Slavery and the Literary Imagination*, ed. Deborah E. McDowell and Arnold Rampersad (Baltimore: Johns Hopkins University Press, 1989), ix.

21. Gates, "Introduction," *The Classic Slave Narratives*, ix.

22. Gates, "Introduction," *The Classic Slave Narratives*, xiv.

23. Mary Prince, *The History of Mary Prince* in *The Classic Slave Narratives*, 194–95.

24. Jacobs, *Incidents in the Life of a Slave Girl* in *The Classic Slave Narratives*, 372.

25. Frances Smith Foster, *Written by Herself: Literary Production by African American Women, 1746–1892* (Bloomington: Indiana University Press, 1993), 102.

26. David S. Reynolds, *Mightier Than the Sword: Uncle Tom's Cabin and the Battle for America* (New York: Norton, 2011).

27. Jane Tompkins, *Sensational Designs: The Cultural Works of American Fiction, 1790–1860* (New York: Oxford University Press, 1986), 126, 127.

28. Harriet Wilson, *Our Nig, or, Sketches from the Life of a Free Black* (New York: Random House, 1983), xxxvi.

29. Elizabeth Keckley, *Behind the Scenes, or Thirty Years a Slave and Four Years in the White House* (New York: Oxford University Press, 1988), 158–59.

30. Edmund Wilson regarded the poetry of *Battle-Pieces* as "versified journalism" in chronicling the progression of the war. See Wilson, *Patriotic Gore: Studies in the Literature of the American Civil War* (W. W. Norton, 1994), 479.

31. Elizabeth Young's *Disarming the Nation: Women's Writing and the American Civil War* (Chicago: University of Chicago Press, 1999), analyzes gendered aspects of Civil War texts.

32. Amy Murrell Taylor, *The Divided Family in Civil War America* (Chapel Hill: University of North Carolina Press, 2009), notes that by 1862 conflicts between brothers were lamented rather celebrated, 75–77. She points out that divided families approached reunion with anxieties, 165.

33. Drew Gilpin Faust, *This Republic of Suffering: Death and the American Civil War* (New York: Knopf, 2008), 141–42.

34. Daniel Aaron, *The Unwritten War: American Writers and the Civil War* (New York: Knopf, 1973), 6.

35. Herman Melville, *Published Poems: Battle-Pieces, John Marr, Timoleon* (Chicago: Northwestern University Press/The Newberry Library, 2009), 115.

36. Stanton Garner's *The Civil War World of Herman Melville* (Lawrence: University of Kansas Press, 1993) and appendices in Herman Melville's *Published Poems* track the inspirations, observations, and contexts for poems in *Battle-Pieces*, clarifying references and allusions.

37. Carolyn Karcher points out that Melville's collection offers little commentary on issues of race and slavery; see *Shadow over the Promised Land* (Baton Rouge: Louisiana State University, 1980). Daniel Aaron in *The Unwritten War* acknowledges that many works of the period do not focus on race (xviii).

38. William Dean Howells, Review of *Battle-Pieces and Aspects of War*, *Atlantic Monthly*. February 1867, http://www.theatlantic.com/magazine/archive/1867/02/herman-melville/8618/. The editors of *The Atlantic Monthly* before, during, and after the Civil War were James Russell Lowell, 1857–1861; James Thomas Fields, 1861–1871; and William Dean Howells, 1871–1881. The magazine was founded in November 1857 by a group of Bostonians, including Ralph Waldo Emerson, Henry Wadsworth Longfellow, Oliver Wendell Holmes, and James Russell Lowell, an ardent abolitionist.

39. Stanton Garner, *The Civil War World of Herman Melville* (Lawrence: University Press of Kansas, 1993), 68.

40. Shira Wolosky, "Claiming the Bible," *The Cambridge History of American Literature, vol. 4: Nineteenth-Century Poetry, 1800–1910*, ed. Sacvan Bercovitch, 200–247 (Cambridge: Cambridge University Press, 2004), 234.

41. Wolosky, "Claiming the Bible," 240.

42. Melville, "Supplement," *Published Poems*, 183.

43. Melville, "Supplement," *Published Poems*, 185.

44. Melville, "Supplement," *Published Poems*, 185.

45. Melville, "Supplement," *Published Poems*, 185.

46. Rebecca Harding Davis, *Bits of Gossip* (Boston: Houghton Mifflin, 1904), 33–35. See the electronic text of Rebecca Harding Davis, *Bits of Gossip* in *Documenting the American South*, https://docsouth.unc.edu/fpn/davisr/menu.html.

47. Rebecca Harding Davis's "John Lamar" was originally published in *The Atlantic Monthly*, April 1862, 411–23.

48. Rebecca Harding Davis, *Stories of the Civil War Era: Selected Writings from the Borderlands*, ed. Sharon M. Harris and Robin L. Cadwallader (Athens: University of Georgia Press, 2010).

49. Davis, *Stories of the Civil War Era*, 11, 13.

50. Davis, *Stories of the Civil War Era*, 22.

51. Cullen Murphy, "A History of *The Atlantic Monthly*," November 1994, http://www.theatlantic.com/past/docs/about/atlhistf.htm.

52. Alcott's story was originally published in *The Atlantic Monthly*, November 1863: 584–95. Alice Fahs describes Alcott's writing as infantilizing African Americans and expressing ambivalence toward them. See Fahs, "Introduction," *Hospital Sketches* (Boston: Bedford/St. Martin's, 2003), 1–50, 41–42.

53. Louisa May Alcott, "The Brothers," in *Civil War Women: The Civil War Seen through Women's Eyes in Stories by Louisa May Alcott, Kate Chopin, Eudora Welty, and Other Great Women Writers*, ed. Frank McSherry Jr., Charles G. Waugh, and Martin Greenberg (New York: Simon and Schuster, 1988), 12–30, 21.

54. Alcott, "The Brothers," 25.

55. Alcott, "The Brothers," 30.

56. Originally published in *Appletons' Journal: Magazine of General Literature* 15, no. 365 (March 18, 1876). Quotations are from Constance Fenimore Woolson, "Crowder's Cove: A Story of War," in *Civil War Women: The Civil War Seen through Women's Eyes in Stories by Louisa May Alcott, Kate Chopin, Eudora Welty, and Other Great Women Writers*, eds. Frank McSherry, Jr., Charles G. Waugh, and Martin Greenberg (New York: Simon and Schuster, 1988), 72–92.

57. Woolson, "Crowder's Cove: A Story of War," 92.

58. Melville, "Supplement," *Published Poems*, 187.

59. Many expressed disappointment that Revolutionary ideals establishing the federal government were no longer the priority, for many states in the South wanted to retain a political economy based on slave labor.

60. Sherry Lee Linko, "Saints, Sufferers, and 'Strong-minded Sisters': Antisuffrage Rhetoric in Rose Terry Cooke's Fiction," *Legacy* 10, no. 1 (1993): 31–46.

61. Claire Delahaye, " 'A Tract in Fiction': Woman Suffrage Literature and the Struggle for the Vote," *European Journal of American Studies* 11, no. 1 (2016): 1–20, 3 and 4, http://ejas.revues.org/11421.

62. Delahaye, "A Tract," 13.

63. Leslie Petty, *Romancing the Vote: Feminist Activism in American Fiction 1870–1920* (Athens: University of Georgia Press, 2006), 63.

64. Petty, *Romancing the Vote*, 66–67, 63.

65. Elizabeth Clark Neidenbach, "Rethinking Reconstruction," review of Daniel Brook, *The Accident of Color: A Story of Race in Reconstruction* (W. W. Norton, 2019), *64 Parishes*. https://64parishes.org/rethinking-reconstruction.

66. Sarah Elbert, *A Hunger for Home: Louisa May Alcott's Place in American Culture* (New Brunswick: Rutgers University Press, 1987), 200.

67. Anthony Lane considers how different film versions emphasize various dimensions of characters in "Greta Gerwig's Raw, Startling *Little Women*," *New Yorker*, December 25, 2019, https://www.newyorker.com/magazine/2020/01/06/greta-gerwigs-raw-startling-little-women.

68. Anne Hollander, "Portraying Little Women through the Ages," in *Little Women and the Feminist Imagination: Criticism, Controversy, Personal Essays*, ed. Janice M. Alberghene and Beverly Lyon Clark (New York: Garland, 1999), 97–101.

69. Hollander, "Portraying Little Women," 97.

70. Hollander, "Portraying Little Women," 98.

71. Hollander, "Portraying Little Women," 99.

72. Richard Brody, "The Compromises of Greta Gerwig's *Little Women*," *New Yorker*, December 31, 2019, https://www.newyorker.com/culture/the-front-row/the-compromises-of-greta-gerwigs-little-women.

73. Jessica Bennett, "This Is 'Little Women' for a New Era," *New York Times*, January 8, 2020, https://www.nytimes.com/2020/01/02/books/little-women-feminism-2019-movie.html.

74. Wendy Ide, "Little Women Review: The Freshest Literary Adaptation of the Year," *The Guardian*, December 29, 2019, https://www.theguardian.com/film/2019/dec/29/little-women-review-greta-gerwig-saoirse-ronan-wendy-ide.

75. Bullard, *Christine*, 244.

76. Bullard, *Christine*, 369.

77. Patricia Ingham, "Introduction, in George Gissing, *The Odd Women* (Oxford: Oxford University Press, 2008), xxiii; Leslie Petty, *Romancing the Vote: Feminist Activism in American Fiction 1870–1920* (Athens: University of Georgia Press, 2006), 168.

78. Petty, *Romancing the Vote*, 169–70.

79. Henry James, *The Bostonians* (New York: New American Library, 1979), 369.

80. Thomas F. Bertonneau, "Like Hypatia before the Mob: Desire, Resentment, and Sacrifice in *The Bostonians* (An Anthropoetics)," *Nineteenth-Century Literature* 53, no. 1 (1998): 56–90.

81. Leslie Petty, "The Political Is Personal: The Feminist Lesson of Henry James's *The Bostonians*," *Women's Studies* 34 (2005): 5, 377–403, considers diverse responses of reformers and their critics to the novel.

82. Horace Elisha Scudder, "*The Bostonians*, by Henry James," *Atlantic* (June 1886) https://www.theatlantic.com/past/docs/unbound/classrev/thebosto.htm.

83. Scudder, "*The Bostonians*, by Henry James."

84. Petty, *Romancing the Vote*, 185.

85. Elaine Showalter, "The Other Bostonians: Gender and Literary Study," *Yale Journal of Criticism* (Spring 1988): 179–87, 180.

86. Roger Ebert, "The Bostonians." *RogerEbert.Com*, January 1, 1984, https://www.rogerebert.com/reviews/the-bostonians-1984.

87. David Sterritt, "'The Bostonians': So Far, the Best Movie of the Year. Merchant; Ivory, Jhabvala (and Henry James) Have Done It Again," *Christian Science Monitor*, August 2, 1984, https://www.csmonitor.com/1984/0802/080209.html.

88. Rita Felski, *Literature after Feminism* (Chicago: University of Chicago Press, 2003), 36–37.

89. George Gissing, *The Odd Women*, ed. Patricia Ingham (Oxford: Oxford University Press, 2000), 139.

90. Gissing, *The Odd Women*, 152.

91. Gissing, *The Odd Women*, 153.

92. Gissing, *The Odd Women*, 153.

93. Gissing, *The Odd Women*, 371.

Chapter 3

1. The quotation from John Donne appears on the title page of Dorothy Sayers, *Gaudy Night* (London: Victor Gollancz, 1936). See John Donne, "Sermon XIV," in *Works*, vol. 1, ed. Henry Alford (London: J. W. Parker, 1839).

2. bell hooks, *Teaching to Transgress* (New York: Routledge, 1994), 207.

3. David Noble, *A World without Women: The Christian Clerical Culture of Western Science* (New York: Knopf, 1992), 244–78.

4. Leslie Garisto Pfaff, "100 Years and Counting." Interview with Jacqueline Littman, *Rutgers Alumni Magazine* (Winter 2018): 52.

5. For a discussion of feminism and romantic love in fictions, see Susan Ostrov Weisser, *The Glass Slipper: Women and Love Stories* (New Brunswick: Rutgers University Press, 2013), esp. 1–16.

6. "Introduction and History," *University of Oxford*, http://www.ox.ac.uk/about/organisation/history.

7. "Women at Oxford," *University of Oxford*, http://www.ox.ac.uk/about/oxford-people/women-at-oxford.

8. Virginia Woolf, *A Room of One's Own* (NY: Harcourt, Brace, World, 1957), 4.

9. Woolf, *A Room of One's Own*, 5–6.

10. Woolf, *A Room of One's Own*, 50.

11. From "Snow, Charles Percy." *Complete Dictionary of Scientific Biography*, 2008, Encyclopedia.com http://www.encyclopedia.com/topic/C.P._Snow.aspx.

12. C. P. Snow, *The Search* (Cornwall: House of Stratus, 2000), 23.

13. Hermione Lee, *Penelope Fitzgerald: A Life* (London: Chatto & Windus, 2013), 30–31.

14. Lee, *Penelope Fitzgerald*, 47.

15. Jacques Rancière, *The Flesh of Words*, trans. Charlotte Mandell (Stanford: Stanford University Press, 2004), 95.

16. Snow, *The Search*, 310–11.

17. Snow, *The Search*, 311.

18. Sayers, *Gaudy Night*, 49.

19. Sayers, *Gaudy Night*, 5.

20. Sayers, *Gaudy Night*, 62.

21. Sayers, *Gaudy Night*, 77.

22. Sayers, *Gaudy Night*, 78.

23. Sayers, *Gaudy Night*, 125.

24. Sayers, *Gaudy Night*, 81.

25. Sayers, *Gaudy Night*, 127.

26. Sayers, *Gaudy Night*, 217.

27. Susan Haack, "After My Own Heart: Dorothy L. Sayers's Feminism," *New Criterion* 19 (May 2001) 9, http://www.newcriterion.com/articles.cfm/sayers-haack-2180.

28. Sayers, *Gaudy Night*, 360.

29. Sayers, *Gaudy Night*, 362.

30. Sayers, *Gaudy Night*, 463.

31. Haack, "After My Own Heart: Dorothy L. Sayers's feminism."

32. Erwin N. Hiebert, "The State of Physics at the Turn of the Century," in *Rutherford and Physics at the Turn of the Century*, eds. Mario Bunge and William R. Shea (NY: Dawson and Science History Publications, 1979), 9.

33. "Early Suffragist Campaigning," UK Parliament, https://www.parliament.uk/about/living-heritage/transformingsociety/electionsvoting/womenvote/overview/earlysuffragist/.

34. "Suffragettes," Wikipedia. http://en.wikipedia.org/wiki/Suffragette. The Wikipedia article cites "SUFFRAGETTES," *Register (Adelaide, SA: 1901–1929)* (Adelaide, SA: National Library of Australia). April 16, 1913, 7, http://trove.nla.gov.au/ndp/del/article/59253869.

35. Penelope Fitzgerald, *The Bookshop, The Gate of Angels, The Blue Flower* (New York: Alfred A. Knopf, 2001), 128–29.

36. Fitzgerald, *The Gate of Angels*, 129.

37. Fitzgerald, *The Gate of Angels*, 129.

38. Fitzgerald, *The Gate of Angels*, 133, 134.

39. "Atomic Theory," *A Dictionary of Science* (Oxford: Oxford University Press, 1999), 60.

40. Stanley Jaki, "The Reality Beneath: The World View of Rutherford," in *Rutherford and Physics at the Turn of the Century*, eds. Mario Bunge and William R. Shea (New York: Dawson and Science History Publications, 1979), 114.

41. Jaki, *The Reality Beneath*, 115.

42. Fitzgerald, *The Gate of Angels*, 132.

43. Fitzgerald, *The Gate of Angels*, 138–39.

44. John Bayley, "Innocents at Home," *New York Review of Books* 39, no. 7 (April 9, 1992): 13–14, does not see a feminist moral in the novel. For him, Fitzgerald "composes with an innocent certainty which avoids any suggestion that she might have a feminist moral in mind, or a dig against science, or a Christian apologetic."

45. Fitzgerald, *The Gate of Angels*, 167.

46. Fitzgerald, *The Gate of Angels*, 169.

47. Fitzgerald, *The Gate of Angels*, 201.

48. Fitzgerald, *The Gate of Angels*, 204.

49. Fitzgerald, *The Gate of Angels*, 204.

50. Fitzgerald, *The Gate of Angels*, 203.

51. Fitzgerald, *The Gate of Angels*, 207.

52. Fitzgerald, *The Gate of Angels*, 221.

53. Fitzgerald, *The Gate of Angels*, 227.

54. Fitzgerald, *The Gate of Angels*, 240.

55. Fitzgerald, *The Gate of Angels*, 241.

56. Fitzgerald, *The Gate of Angels*, 246.

57. Fitzgerald, *The Gate of Angels*, 254.

58. Fitzgerald, *The Gate of Angels*, 259.

59. Fitzgerald, *The Gate of Angels*, 267.

60. Kerry Fried, "High Spirits: The Great Penelope Fitzgerald on Poltergeists, Plots, and Past Masters." *Amazon.com*. Archived on April 3, 2015, in the Internet Archive Wayback Machine, http://www.amazon.com/gp/feature.html?ie=UTF8&docId=10326.

61. Barbara McClintock, a biologist who mostly worked as a sole investigator for decades, received a Nobel Prize in 1983.

62. Jeffrey Eugenides, *The Marriage Plot* (New York: Farrar, Straus, Giroux, 2011), 365.

63. Eugenides, *The Marriage Plot*, 406.

Chapter 4

1. Claudine Hermann, "The Virile System," *Les voleuses de langue* (des femmes, 1976), excerpted in "Claudine Hermann," trans. Marilyn R. Schuster, *New French Feminisms: An Anthology*, ed. Elaine Marks and Isabelle de Courtivron (New York: Schocken, 1980, 1981), 87–89, 87.

2. Rosi Braidotti, "The Subject in Feminism." *Hypatia* 6, no. 2 (Summer 1991): 155–72, 161.

3. This chapter is adapted from Carol Colatrella, "When the Scientist Is a Woman: Novels and Feminist Science Studies," in *Under the Literary Microscope: Science and Society in the Contemporary Novel*, ed. Sina Farzin, Susan M. Gaines, Roslynn D. Haynes (University Park: Pennsylvania State University Press, 2021), 126–47. Also see Margaret Rossiter, *Women Scientists in America: Forging a New World Since 1962*, vol. 3 (Baltimore: Johns Hopkins University Press, 2012); Londa Schiebinger, *Has Feminism Changed Science?* (Cambridge: Harvard University Press, 1999); Banu Subramanian, "Moored Metamorphoses: A Retrospective Essay on Feminist Science Studies," *Signs: A Journal of Woman in Culture and Society* 34, no. 4 (2009): 951–80.

4. Rossiter, *Women Scientists in America*, vol. 3, 42.

5. European Commission, *She-Figures 2015*, 2015, http://ec.europa.eu/research/swafs/pdf/pub_gender_equality/she_figures_2015-final.pdf US National Science Foundation, *Women, Minorities, and Persons with Disabilities in Science and Engineering*, 2017, https://www.nsf.gov/statistics/2017/nsf17310/digest/about-this-report/.

6. *Pathways, Potholes, and the Persistence of Women in Science: Reconsidering the Pipeline*, ed. Enobang Hannah Branch (Lanham: Rowman and Littlefield, 2016); *Why Aren't There More Women in Science?*, ed. by Stephen J. Ceci and Wendy Melissa Williams (Washington, DC: American Psychological

Association, 2007); Alison Coil, "Why Men Don't Believe the Data on Gender Bias in Science," *Wired* (August 25, 2017), https://www.wired.com/story/why-men-dont-believe-the-data-on-gender-bias-in-science/.

7. Jocelyn Steinke, "Connecting Theory and Practice: Using Televised Images of Women Scientist Role Models in Television Programming," *Journal of Broadcasting and Electronic Media* 42, no. 1 (1998): 142–51, and Jenny Kitzinger, Joan Haran, Mwenya Chimba and Tammy Boyce, *Role Models in the Media: An Exploration of the Views and Experiences of Women in Science, Engineering, and Technology*, UK Resource Centre for Women in Science, Engineering, and Technology, Research Report 1 (March 2008), https://orca.cf.ac.uk/17534/1/report_1_kitzinger.pdf.

8. Roslynn D. Haynes, *From Madman to Crime Fighter: The Scientist in Western Culture* (Baltimore: Johns Hopkins University Press, 2017), and Christopher Frayling, *Mad, Bad, and Dangerous: The Scientist and Cinema* (London: Reaktion Books, 2006).

9. Sidney Perkowitz, *Hollywood Science: Movies, Science, and the End of the World* (New York: Columbia University Press, 2007), and David Kirby, *Lab Coats in Hollywood: Science, Scientists, and the Cinema* (Cambridge: MIT Press, 2007).

10. Telegraph Women, "#DistractinglySexy: Female scientists mock Sir Tim Hunt on Twitter," *Telegraph*, June 11, 2015, http://www.telegraph.co.uk/women/womens-life/11667981/Tim-Hunt-Distractinglysexy-female-scientists-post-photos-on-Twitter.html.

11. Suzanne Keen, *Empathy and the Novel* (Oxford: Oxford University Press, 2010), and Lisa Zunshine, *Why We Read Fiction: Theory of Mind and the Novel* (Columbus: Ohio State University Press, 2006).

12. This paragraph adapts a passage from Carol Colatrella, *Toys and Tools in Pink: Cultural Narratives of Gender, Science, and Technology* (Columbus: Ohio State University Press, 2011), 120.

13. Eileen Pollack, "Why Fiction Needs More Women Scientists," *LitHub*, May 10, 2016, https://lithub.com/why-fiction-needs-more-women-scientists/.

14. National Science Foundation, National Center for Science and Engineering Statistics, Women, Minorities, and Persons with Disabilities in Science and Engineering: 2017. Special Report NSF 17-310 (Arlington, VA), 8. www.nsf.gov/statistics/wmpd/.

15. Chapter titles in Schiebinger, *Has Feminism Changed Science?*

16. Elizabeth Gilbert, *The Signature of All Things* (New York: Penguin, 2013).

17. Margaret W. Rossiter, *Women Scientists in America: Struggles and Strategies to 1940*, vol. 1, (Baltimore: Johns Hopkins University Press, 1982).

18. Gilbert, *The Signature of All Things*, 159.

19. Gilbert, *The Signature of All Things*, 162.

20. Gilbert, *The Signature of All Things*, 441.

21. Susan Quinn, *Marie Curie: A Life* (New York: Simon and Schuster, 1995).

22. Brenda Maddox, *Rosalind Franklin: The Dark Lady of DNA* (New York, Harper Collins, 2002), 213.

23. Evelyn Fox Keller, *A Feeling for the Organism: The Life and Work of Barbara McClintock* (New York: W. H. Freeman, 1983), 20, 180.

24. Gilbert, *The Signature of All Things*, 464.

25. Gilbert, *The Signature of All Things*, 497, 496.

26. A. S. Byatt, *A Whistling Woman* (New York: Random House, 2002).

27. Byatt, *A Whistling Woman*, 26.

28. Byatt, *A Whistling Woman*, 56.

29. Byatt, *A Whistling Woman*, 169, 172.

30. Byatt, *A Whistling Woman*, 172.

31. Byatt, *A Whistling Woman*, 188.

32. Byatt, *A Whistling Woman*, 367.

33. Byatt, *A Whistling Woman*, 420.

34. William Boyd, *Brazzaville Beach* (New York: Harper Perennial, 2010).

35. Boyd, *Brazzaville Beach*, 58.

36. Boyd, *Brazzaville Beach*, 87.

37. Schiebinger, *Has Feminism Changed Science?*, 7.

38. W. Faulkner and E. A. Kerr, "On Seeing Brockenspectres: Sex and Gender in Twentieth-Century Science," *Companion to Science in the Twentieth Century*, ed. Dominique Pestre, John Krige (Routledge, 2003), 59–72, 68.

39. Boyd, *Brazzaville Beach*, 196–97, italics in text.

40. Appendix to Boyd, *Brazzaville Beach*, 13.

41. Hilary Rose, *Love, Power and Knowledge: Towards a Feminist Transformation of the Sciences* (Cambridge: Polity Press, 1994), 114.

42. Rose, *Love, Power and Knowledge*, 238.

43. Boyd, *Brazzaville Beach*, 315.

44. Susan M. Gaines, *Carbon Dreams* (Berkeley: Creative Arts Book Company, 2001).

45. Gaines, *Carbon Dreams*, 7.

46. Gaines, *Carbon Dreams*, 9.

47. Gaines, *Carbon Dreams*, 277.

48. Schiebinger, *Has Feminism Changed Science?*, 93.

49. Allegra Goodman, *Intuition* (New York: Random House, 2006), 30.

50. Goodman, *Intuition*, 144.

51. Goodman, *Intuition*, 89.

52. Goodman, *Intuition*, 64.

53. Margaret Rossiter, "The Matthew Matilda Effect in Science," *Social Studies of Science* 23, no. 2 (1993): 325–41.

54. Goodman, *Intuition*, 199.

55. Goodman, *Intuition*, 201.

56. Goodman, *Intuition*, 322.

57. Goodman, *Intuition*, 342.

58. Goodman, *Intuition*, 344.

59. Goodman, *Intuition*, 344.

60. Goodman, *Intuition*, 104.

61. Ann Patchett, *State of Wonder* (New York: Harper Collins, 2011).

62. Patchett, *State of Wonder*, 48.

63. Patchett, *State of Wonder*, 264.

64. Patchett, *State of Wonder*, 224, 232.

65. Patchett, *State of Wonder*, 272.

66. Patchett, *State of Wonder*, 294–95.

67. Patchett, *State of Wonder*, 295.

68. Patchett, *State of Wonder*, 342.

69. Patchett, *State of Wonder*, 322.

70. Lisa Ko, *The Leavers* (Chapel Hill: Algonquin Books, 2017, 2018).

71. Catherine Chung, *The Tenth Muse* (New York: Ecco/HarperCollins, 2019), 9.

72. Chung, *The Tenth Muse*, 59.

73. Chung, *The Tenth Muse*, 60.

74. Chung, *The Tenth Muse*, 38.

75. Chung, *The Tenth Muse*, 65.

76. Chung, *The Tenth Muse*, 277.

77. Sandra Harding, *Whose Science? Whose Knowledge?* (Ithaca: Cornell University Press, 1991), 145.

78. Diana Bilimoria and Abigail Stewart, "'Don't Ask, Don't Tell': The Academic Climate for Lesbian, Gay, Bisexual, and Transgender Faculty in Science and Engineering," *NWSA Journal* 21, no. 2 (2009): 85–103, 92.

79. Evelyn Fox Keller, *Reflections on Gender and Science* (New Haven: Yale University Press, 1985), 6–7.

80. Keller, *Reflections on Gender and Science*, 19.

81. W. Faulkner and E. A. Kerr, "On Seeing Brockenspectres," 59.

82. Donna Haraway, "Situated Knowledges: The Science Question in Feminism and the Partial Perspective." *Feminist Studies* 14, no. 3 (1988): 575–99, 589–90.

83. Schiebinger, *Has Feminism Changed Science?*, 7.

84. Sharon Traweek, *Beamtimes and Lifetimes: The World of High Energy Physics* (Cambridge: Harvard University Press, 1992), 105.

85. Margot Lee Shetterly, *Hidden Figures: The American Dream and the Untold Story of the Black Women Mathematicians Who Helped Win the Space Race* (New York: Harper Collins, 2016), xv.

86. A. O. Scott, "Review: 'Hidden Figures' Honors 3 Black Women Who Helped NASA Soar." *New York Times*, December 22, 2016, https://www.nytimes.com/2016/12/22/movies/hidden-figures-review.html.

87. Paul Byrnes, "Hidden Figures review: These Trailblazing Women Deserve Better," *Sydney Morning Herald*, February 14, 2017, https://www.smh.com.au/entertainment/movies/hidden-figures-review-these-trailblazing-women-deserve-better-20170214-gucbs5.html.

88. Dave McNary, " 'Hidden Figures' Set for Free Screenings in 14 Cities for Black History Month," *Variety*, February 14, 2017, https://variety.com/2017/film/news/hidden-figures-free-screenings-black-history-month-1201988170/.

Chapter 5

1. "Ordination of Women and the Old Testament," *WomenOrdination. Com*, 2010, http://www.womenordination.com/background/ordination-of-women-and-the-old-testament/articletype/articleview/articleid/1094/wasnt-eves-subordina-tion-to-adam-in-genesis-316-a-part-of-the-curse-which-christ-came-to-take-away. Accessed August 3, 2022.

2. Helena Michie and Naomi R. Cahn, *Confinements: Fertility and Infertility in Contemporary Culture* (New Brunswick: Rutgers University Press, 1997), 13.

3. John D. Gibson, "Childbearing and Childrearing: Feminists and Reform," *Virginia Law Review* 73, no. 6 (September 1987): 1145–182: 1145.

4. Barbara Janta, "Britain just expanded free child care. The US should follow its lead," *USA Today*, October 26, 2017, https://www.usatoday.com/story/opinion/2017/10/26/u-k-s-child-care-system-isnt-perfect-but-we-can-still-learn-lot-barbara-janta-column/796324001/.

5. Andrea Tone, *Devices and Desires: A History of Contraceptives in America* (New York: Hill and Wang, 2001).

6. Robin Gregg, *Pregnancy in a High-Tech Age: Paradoxes of Choice* (New York: New York University Press, 1995), 2.

7. Christine Hallett, "The Attempt to Understand Puerperal Fever in the Eighteenth and Early Nineteenth Centuries: The Influence of Inflammation Theory," *Medical History* 49, no. 1 (2005): 1–28: 1.

8. Médecins Sans Frontières, "Medical Guidelines," *Essential Obstetric and Newborn Care: Practical Guide for Midwives, Doctors with Obstetrics Training and Health Care Personnel Who Deal with Obstetric Emergencies*, 2017, https://medicalguidelines.msf.org/viewport/EONC/english/11-4-postpartum-complica-tions-20319320.html.

9. Shelagh Delaney adapted *A Taste of Honey* for the film directed by Tony Richardson.

10. Alfie is played by Michael Caine in the 1966 film directed by Lewis Gilbert.

11. Margaret Drabble, *The Millstone* (Harmondsworth: Penguin, 1968), 94.

12. Drabble, *The Millstone*, 5.

13. Drabble, *The Millstone*, 111.

14. Nancy S. Hardin, "Drabble's *The Millstone*: A Fable for Our Times," *Critique* 15, no. 1 (January 1, 1973): 22–34: 25.

15. Drabble, *The Millstone*, 132.

16. Drabble, *The Millstone*, 139.

17. Drabble, *The Millstone*, 172.

18. Drabble, *The Millstone*, 72.

19. Judy Wajcman, *Feminism Confronts Technology* (University Park: Pennsylvania State University Press, 1991): 54: "reproduction as a natural process, inherent in women alone, and a theory of technology as patriarchal, enabling the male domination of women and nature."

20. Wajcman, *Feminism Confronts Technology*, 73.

21. Rosalind Pollack Petchesky, "Fetal Images: The Power of Visual Culture in the Politics of Reproduction," *Feminist Studies* 13 (1987): 2: 263–92.

22. Bettyann Kevles, *Naked to the Bone: Medical Imaging in the Twentieth Century* (Reading: Helix Books/Addison-Wesley, 1987), 229.

23. Robbie Davis-Floyd, *Birth as An American Rite of Passage* (Berkeley: University of California Press, 2014) and Barbara Katz Rothman, *The Tentative Pregnancy: How Amniocentesis Changes the Experience of Motherhood* (New York: Norton, 1993).

24. Heather Swain, "My Flesh and Blood," *Salon*, May 11, 2003, http://dir.salon.com/story/mwt/feature/2003/03/11/miscarriage/index2.html.

25. Linda L. Layne, "The Child as Gift," in *Transformative Motherhood: On Giving and Getting in a Consumer Culture*, edited by Linda L. Layne (New York: New York University Press, 1999), 1–27.

26. Heather Swain, *Luscious Lemon* (New York: Downtown Press, 2004), 6.

27. Swain, *Luscious Lemon*, 6.

28. Swain, *Luscious Lemon*, 7.

29. Swain, *Luscious Lemon*, 7.

30. Lauren Berlant, "America, 'Fat,' the Fetus," *boundary 2* 21 (1994): 3: 145–195, 150.

31. Berlant, "America, 'Fat,' the Fetus," 184.

32. Fetal narration appears in other texts, often as a humorous acknowledgment of the outcome of sexual intercourse when a fetus comments on the foibles of its parents. Tristram Shandy ruminates in the first four chapters of Lawrence Sterne's novel on what his parents were up to when they "begot" him. Lauren Berlant and Lynne Joyrich analyze the "Womb with a View" episodes of *Moonlighting* in which Maddy Hayes miscarries and Bruce Willis's fetal voice-over in Amy Heckerling's *Look Who's Talking* films as fetal narratives constraining women. Berlant remarks that "The [*Look Who's Talking*] films are caught in a cluster of contradictions organized around questions of *survival*," of fetus and of mother (225). Joyrich footnotes Hope's miscarriage in a 1999 episode of *Thirtysomething*. See Berlant, "America, 'Fat,' The Fetus," in *Gendered Agents: Women*

and Institutional Knowledge, ed. Silvestra Mariniello and Paul A. Bové (Durham: Duke University Press, 1998), and Joyrich, "Tube Tied: Television, Reproductive Politics, and *Moonlighting*'s Family Politics," in *Re-viewing Reception: Television, Gender, and Postmodern Culture* (Bloomington: Indiana University Press, 1996).

33. Swain, *Luscious Lemon*, 103.

34. Barbara Katz Rothman, *The Tentative Pregnancy: How Amniocentesis Changes the Experience of Motherhood* (W. W. Norton, 1993), 2, and Robin Gregg, *Pregnancy in a High-Tech Age: Paradoxes of Choice* (New York: New York University Press, 1995), 22.

35. Swain, *Luscious Lemon*, 79.

36. Swain, *Luscious Lemon*, 108–9.

37. Swain, *Luscious Lemon*, 109.

38. Swain, *Luscious Lemon*, 110. Looking at how visual technology structures hospitalized childbirth as cultural rituals, Robbie Davis-Floyd points out that the visualization of the fetus enabled by ultrasound and fetal heart monitors shapes how mothers engage in labor. Deborah Wilson Lowrey describes such reproductive technologies as "fluid networks of surveillance that promote abstraction, fetishism, transformation of bodies into commodified information, and perceptions of reduced risk." Robbie E. Davis-Floyd, "Birth as an American Rite of Passage," *Childbirth in America*, ed. Karen L. Michaelson (South Hadley: Bergin and Garvey, 1998), 153–72, and Deborah Lowrey, "Understanding Reproductive Technologies as a Surveillant Assemblage: Revisions of Power and Technoscience," *Sociological Perspectives* 47, no. 4 (Winter 2004): 357–70.

39. Petchesky, "Fetal Images," 280, 281–82.

40. Swain, *Luscious Lemon*, 185–86.

41. Swain, *Luscious Lemon*, 188.

42. Swain, *Luscious Lemon*, 190.

43. Barbara Katz Rothman, *Genetic Maps and Human Imaginations: The Limits of Science in Understanding Who We Are* (New York: W. W. Norton, 1998), 183.

44. According to the American Pregnancy Association, waiting for the fetus to be expelled qualifies as a "spontaneous abortion" or a "natural miscarriage," a non-surgical option. American Pregnancy Association, "Blighted Ovum," https://americanpregnancy.org/healthy-pregnancy/pregnancy-complications/blighted-ovum/. Accessed August 3, 2022.

45. Swain, *Luscious Lemon*, 272.

46. Swain, *Luscious Lemon*, 273. See Peggy Orenstein, "Mourning My Miscarriage, *New York Times*, April 21, 2002, https://www.nytimes.com/2002/04/21/magazine/mourning-my-miscarriage.html.

47. Layne, "The Child as Gift," 1–27.

48. John Irving, *The Cider House Rules* (1985) (New York: Bantam Books, 1989), 60.

49. Irving, *The Cider House Rules*, 67.

50. Irving, *The Cider House Rules*, 73.

51. Irving, *The Cider House Rules*, 74.

52. Irving, *The Cider House Rules*, 169.

53. Kristen Luker, "Introduction," *Abortion and the Politics of Motherhood* (Berkeley: University of California Press, 1984), 1–10.

54. Irving, *The Cider House Rules*, 188.

55. Irving, *The Cider House Rules*, 193.

56. Irving, *The Cider House Rules*, 518.

57. Irving, *The Cider House Rules*, 532.

58. Irving, *The Cider House Rules*, 562.

59. Irving, *The Cider House Rules*, 568.

60. Helena Wahlström, "Reproduction, Politics, and John Irving's The Cider House Rules: Women's Rights or 'Fetal Rights,'" *Culture Unbound* 5 (2013): 251.

61. Janet L. Engstrom and Ramona G. Hunter, "Teaching Reproductive Options through the Use of Fiction: The Cider House Rules Project," *Journal of Obstetric, Gynecologic, and Neonatal Nursing* 36 (2007), 464–70: 469.

62. Jennifer Worth, *Call the Midwife: A True Story of the East End in the 1950s* (London: Orion Books, 2012).

63. "*Call the Midwife*," *Wikipedia*, https://en.wikipedia.org/wiki/Call_the_Midwife. Accessed August 16, 2022.

64. See chapter 4 in Carol Colatrella, *Toys and Tools in Pink: Cultural Narratives of Gender, Science, and Technology* (Columbus: Ohio State University Press, 2011).

65. "*Call the Midwife*," *Wikipedia*.

66. The series has been filmed through season 11, while season 12 is in production and season 13 has been confirmed. Lauren Hubbard, "Everything We Know so far about *Call the Midwife* Season 10," *Town and Country Magazine*, February 16, 2020, https://www.townandcountrymag.com/leisure/arts-and-culture/a30753289/call-the-midwife-season-10/, and Lauren Hubbard, "Everything We Know so far about *Call the Midwife* Season 12," *Town and Country Magazine*, August 2, 2022, https://www.townandcountrymag.com/leisure/arts-and-culture/a39465884/call-the-midwife-season-12/.

67. U.K. National Health Service, "The government's 2022 to 2023 mandate to NHS England." March 31, 2002, 25, https://assets.publishing.service.gov.uk/government/uploads/system/uploads/attachment_data/file/1065713/2022-to-2023-nhs-england-mandate.pdf.

68. US Centers for Disease Control, "Racial and Ethnic Disparities Continue in Pregnancy-Related Deaths," September 5, 2019, https://www.cdc.gov/media/releases/2019/p0905-racial-ethnic-disparities-pregnancy-deaths.html: "Black, American Indian, and Alaska Native (AI/AN) women are two to three times

more likely to die from pregnancy-related causes than white women—and this disparity increases with age."

69. Brit Bennett, *The Mothers* (New York: Riverhead Books, 2016).

70. Alexandra Alter, "'The Mothers,' a Debut Novel, Is Already Creating a Stir," *New York Times* October 9, 2016, https://www.nytimes.com/2016/10/10/books/the-mothers-brit-bennett.html.

71. Dorothy Roberts, *Killing the Black Body: Race, Reproduction, and the Meaning of Liberty* (London: Virago, 1998), 246.

72. Roberts, *Killing the Black Body*, 291.

73. Linda Villarosa, "Why America's Black Mothers and Babies Are in a Life-or-Death Crisis," *New York Times*, April 11, 2018, https://www.nytimes.com/2018/04/11/magazine/black-mothers-babies-death-maternal-mortality.html.

74. "Gabrielle Union on the Condition That Caused Her Infertility" (Oprah Winfrey interview with Gabrielle Union), SuperSoul Sunday, OWNTV, You Tube, December 7, 2018, https://www.youtube.com/watch?v=6XJMHhd-a3E.

75. Gabrielle Union, "The Hard Truth about My Surrogacy Journey," *Time*, September 10, 2021. https://time.com/6096588/gabrielle-union-surrogacy/.

76. Serena Williams, "I didn't expect that sharing our family's story of Olympia's birth and all of complications after giving birth would start such an outpouring," Facebook, https://www.facebook.com/watch/?v=10156086135726834. Accessed August 3, 2022.

77. Anne Pollock, *Sickening: Anti-Black Racism and Health Disparities in the United States* (Minneapolis: University of Minnesota Press, 2021), 118.

78. Joyce N. Njoroge and Nisha I. Parikh, "Understanding Health Disparities in Cardiovascular Diseases in Pregnancy among Black Women," *Current Cardiovascular Risk Reports* (2020), 14, 8, https://link.springer.com/content/pdf/10.1007/s12170-020-00641-9.pdf.

79. Bilal G. Morris, "'Sloppy C-Section' That Killed Kira Johnson Prompts Maternal Health Lawsuit Accusing Hospital of Racism," *Newsone*, May 5, 2022. https://newsone.com/4331183/sloppy-c-section-that-killed-kira-johnson-prompts-racism-lawsuit/.

80. S. 1042-117th Congress: Kira Johnson Act, June 24, 2022, https://www.govtrack.us/congress/bills/117/s1042.

81. Nina Martin, Renee Montagne, "Black Mothers Keep Dying after Giving Birth. Shalon Irving's Story Explains Why," *All Things Considered*, December 7, 2017, https://www.npr.org/2017/12/07/568948782/black-mothers-keep-dying-after-giving-birth-shalon-irvings-story-explains-why?t=1655893769720.

82. See Carol Colatrella, "Fear of Reproduction and Desire for Replication in *Dracula*," *Journal of Medical Humanities* 17, no. 3 (Spring 1996): 179–89; Susan Merrill Squier, *Babies in Bottles: Twentieth-Century Visions of Reproductive Technology* (New Brunswick: Rutgers University Press, 1995); and Heather Latimer,

Reproductive Acts: Sexual Politics in North American Fiction and Film (Montreal: McGill-Queens Press, 2013).

83. Phoebe Kolbert, "Status of Abortion Laws, State by State," *Ms.*, July 7, 2022. https://msmagazine.com/2022/07/07/abortion-legal-state-laws/?, and Pam Belluck, "They Had Miscarriages, and New Abortion Laws Obstructed Treatment," *New York Times*, July 17, 2022, https://www.nytimes.com/2022/07/17/health/abortion-miscarriage-treatment.html.

Chapter 6

1. Adrienne Rich, "Notes toward a Politics of Location" (1985), in *Feminist Literary Theory and Criticism*, ed. Sandra M. Gilbert and Susan Gubar (New York: W. W. Norton: 2007), 228–39: 230.

2. Janine DeBaise, "What We Learn," *Body Language* (Charlotte: Main Street Rag, 2019), 15.

3. Carol Colatrella, *Toys and Tools in Pink: Cultural Narratives of Gender, Science, and Technology* (Columbus: Ohio State University Press, 2011), 52–77.

4. Amnesty International, "Violence against Women Is a US Problem, Too," 2019, https://www.amnestyusa.org/violence-against-women-is-a-u-s-problem-too/.

5. Amnesty International, Violence against Women Is a US Problem, Too."

6. Michael Denning, *Mechanic Accents: Dime Novels and Working-Class Culture in America* (London: Verso, 1987), 73.

7. Susan Brownmiller, *Against Our Will: Men, Women, and Rape* (New York: Fawcett, 1975). From Preface to the Early Bird Edition of the ebook: "My takeaway was that rape was a deliberate act of power, dominance, and humiliation committed by men with no moral compass—and that most victims feared their attackers were going to kill them."

8. Michiko Kakutani argues the novel is "a contrived, formulaic book that mechanically pits men against women, old against young, the past against the present." See Kakutani, " 'Paradise': Worthy Women, Unredeemable Men," *New York Times*, January 6, 1998, https://archive.nytimes.com/www.nytimes.com/books/98/01/04/daily/morrison-book-review-art.html.

9. Marni Gauthier, "The Other Side of Paradise: Toni Morrison's (Un) Making of Mythic History," *African American Review* 39, no. 3 (2005): 395–414: 407.

10. Gauthier, "The Other Side of Paradise," 395.

11. Channette Romero, "Creating the Beloved Community: Religion, Race, and Nation in Toni Morrison's *Paradise*," *African American Review* 39, no. 3 (2005): 415–30: 415.

12. Romero, "Creating the Beloved Community," 427.

13. Simone C. Drake, *Critical Appropriations: African American Women and the Construction of Transnational Identity* (Baton Rouge: Louisiana State University Press, 2014), 46.

14. Romero, "Creating the Beloved Community," 416.

15. Gauthier, "The Other Side of Paradise," 398.

16. Gauthier, "The Other Side of Paradise," 397.

17. Toni Morrison, *Paradise* (New York: Penguin, 1999), 306.

18. Morrison, *Paradise*, 297.

19. Morrison, *Paradise*, 308.

20. Romero, "Creating the Beloved Community," 418.

21. "Oliphant v. Suquamish Indian Tribe," *Wikipedia*, http://en.wikipedia.org/wiki/Oliphant_v._Suquamish_Indian_Tribe.

22. "President Obama to sign VAWA with tribal jurisdiction provision," Indianz.com. March 1, 2013, http://www.indianz.com/News/2013/008725.asp. Also see Kathy Dobie, "A Tiny, Little Law," *Harper's Magazine,* February 2011, http://harpers.org/archive/2011/02/tiny-little-laws/.

23. Louise Erdrich, "Rape on the Reservation," *New York Times*, February 26, 2013, https://www.nytimes.com/2013/02/27/opinion/native-americans-and-the-violence-against-women-act.html.

24. Erdrich, "Rape on the Reservation."

25. "President Obama to sign VAWA," Indianz.com.

26. Laura L. Rogers, "The Violence against Women Act: An Ongoing Fixture," U.S. Department of Justice, February 19, 2020, https://www.justice.gov/ovw/blog/violence-against-women-act-ongoing-fixture-nation-s-response-domestic-violence-dating.

27. White House. Fact Sheet: Reauthorization of the Violence against Women Act, March 16, 2022, https://www.whitehouse.gov/briefing-room/statements-releases/2022/03/16/fact-sheet-reauthorization-of-the-violence-against-women-act-vawa/.

28. Louise Erdrich, "Conversation: Louise Erdrich, Author of 'The Round House,'" interview by Jeffrey Brown, *NewsHour*, PBS, October 26, 2012, https://www.pbs.org/video/pbs-newshour-conversation-louise-erdrich-author-of-the-round-house/.

29. Louise Erdrich, *The Round House* (New York: Harper Collins, 2012), 66.

30. In the novel, the 1976 decision in Thomas et al. v. Lark gives the tribal court jurisdiction of a non-Indian business, a grocery store owned by George and Grace Lark and surrounded by tribal land trust property (49), and a 1973 case concerns a man who died near the round house.

31. Erdrich, *The Round House*, 89.

32. Erdrich, *The Round House*, 160.

33. Erdrich, *The Round House*, 223.

34. Erdrich, *The Round House*, 133.

35. Erdrich, *The Round House*, 229–30.

36. This section has been adapted from Carol Colatrella, "Narrative Complexity, Character, and Action: Reconfiguring Gender Norms and Genre Conventions in a Police Procedural," *Signs & Media* 11 (Autumn 2015): 17–39.

37. Jason Mittell, "Narrative Complexity in Contemporary American Television," *Velvet Light Trap* 58, no. 1 (December 2005): 29–40, 32.

38. Brenda's forensic talents are not stereotyped as supernatural, in contradistinction to female profilers in *Profiler* (1996–2000) and *Ghost Whisperer* (2005–2010), who solve crimes based on their unique, somewhat supernatural gifts. In *Profiler* Dr. Sam Waters (Ally Walker) sees through the eyes of others. *Ghost Whisperer*'s Melinda Gordon (Jennifer Love Hewitt) can see and communicate with ghosts.

39. Peter Rabinowitz, *Before Reading: Narrative Conventions and the Politics of Interpretation* (Columbus: Ohio State University Press, 1998), 128.

40. Shlomith Rimmon-Kenan, *Narrative Fiction: Contemporary Poetics* (London: Routledge, 1989), 36.

41. Laura Mulvey, "Visual Pleasure and Narrative Cinema," in *Film Theory and Criticism*, ed. Gerald Mast and Marshall Cohen, 803–16 (New York: Oxford University Press, 1985). Reprinted from *Screen* 16, no. 3.

42. Robert Dale Parker, *How to Interpret Literature: Critical Theory for Literary and Cultural Studies* (New York: Oxford University Press, 2008), 153.

43. Priscilla Walton and Manina Jones, *Detective Agency: Women Rewriting the Hard-Boiled Tradition* (Berkeley and Los Angeles: University of California Press, 1999), 231.

44. James Phelan, *Living to Tell about It: A Rhetoric and Ethics of Character Narration* (Ithaca: Cornell University Press, 2005), 102.

45. Maddy Dychtwald contrasts Brenda Leigh Johnson with other examples of females "in powerful positions" such as Angie Dickinson in *Policewoman* (1974–1978) and the leads in *Cagney & Lacey* (1981–1988), who "were largely token in a sea of dominant males, and most important, strove to be like the men that surrounded them." Gloria Goodale mentions Dychtwald's assertion in "The Closer opened doors for women—and for basic cable," *Christian Science Monitor*, July 12, 2010, http://www.csmonitor.com/USA/2010/0712/The-Closer-opened-doors-for-women-and-for-basic-cable.

46. "Rampart Scandal Timeline," *PBS Frontline*, http://www.pbs.org/wgbh/pages/frontline/shows/lapd/scandal/cron.html.

47. Richard A. Leo, "From Coercion to Deception: The Changing Nature of Police Interrogation in America," in *The Miranda Debate: Law, Justice, and Policing*, ed. Richard A. Leo, George Conner Thomas (Boston: Northeastern University, 1998), 68.

48. Mark A. Godsey, "Shining the Bright Light on Police Interrogation in America" (2009) in *Faculty Articles and Other Publications* 82, https://scholarship.law.uc.edu/fac_pubs/82.

49. A recent version of the approach appears in John E. Reid and Associates, *The Reid Technique of Interviewing and Interrogation* (2014), https://www.iafci.org/app_themes/Docs/2014%20Confernece/Speakers/Reid%202014%20Conference.pdf.

50. Paula A. Bernhard and Rowland S. Miller, "Juror Perceptions of False Confessions versus Witness Recantations," *Psychiatry, Psychology, and Law* 25, no. 4 (2018): 539–49, 539.

51. Walton and Jones, *Detective Agency*, 193, 203.

52. Matt Webb Mitovich, "The Closer Season Finale Recap: The Last Stroh," *TVLine*, August 12, 2012, http://tvline.com/2012/08/13/the-closer-series-finale-recap/.

53. "*The Closer*," *Wikipedia*, http://en.wikipedia.org/wiki/The_Closer#Episodes, accessed August 16, 2022.

54. H. Porter Abbott, *The Cambridge Introduction to Narrative* (Cambridge: Cambridge University Press, 2008), 131.

Chapter 7

1. Sarah Ahmed, "Happy Futures, Perhaps," in *Queer Times, Queer Becomings*, edited by Mikko Tuhkanen, E. L. McCallum (Albany: State University of New York Press, 2011), 159–81, 161.

2. Pelosi delivered the Smith College commencement address on May 17, 2020. See Barbara Solow, "Nancy Pelosi: Smith Graduates Have Power to Shape the Future," *Notes from Paradise*. May 20, 2020, https://www.smith.edu/news/2020-commencement-pelosi.

3. Nancy Armstrong, *Desire and Domestic Fiction: A Political History of the Novel* (Oxford: Oxford University Press, 1987), 38.

4. Armstrong, *Desire and Domestic Fiction*, 38.

5. The reference in Armstrong, *Desire and Domestic Fiction*, 56, is to Showalter's *A Literature of Their Own* (Princeton: Princeton University Press, 1977), 182ff.

6. Corey Greer, "The US Needs a Feminist Federal Budget," *Ms.*, July 17, 2019, https://msmagazine.com/2019/07/17/the-u-s-needs-a-feminist-federal-budget/.

7. "List of Transgender Political Office Holders," *Wikipedia*, https://en.wikipedia.org/wiki/List_of_transgender_political_office-holders. Accessed August 2, 2022.

8. UN Women, "Facts and figures: Leadership and political participation," http://www.unwomen.org/en/what-we-do/leadership-and-political-participation/facts-and-figures. Accessed August 16, 2022.

9. UN Women, "Press Release: To Accelerate Gender Equality, UN Women Launches a Call to Action to Parliamentarians," June 27, 2019, http://www.unwomen. org/en/news/stories/2019/6/press-release-un-women-launches-a-call-to-action-to-parliamentarians. Accessed August 16, 2022. See also Inter-Parliamentary Union, "Women in Parliament," https://www.ipu.org/our-impact/gender-equality/women-in-parliament, accessed August 17, 2022.

10. UN Women, "Press Release: To Accelerate Gender Equality."

11. I have identified only one realist fiction about a non-cis-gendered individual in politics, Austin Chant's 2016 novel *Coffee Boy*: https://www.google.com/books/edition/Coffee_Boy/HMF8zgEACAAJ?hl=en. Accessed August 16, 2022.

12. Zachary Baqué, "Madam President: The Representation of Female Political and Military Power in *Commander in Chief* and in Season 7 of *24*," *Caliban: French Journal of English Studies* 27 (2010): 285–94, https://journals.openedition. org/caliban/2191.

13. US examples include the films *Dave* (1993), *The American President* (1995), and *Air Force One* (1997) and television shows *West Wing* (1999–2006), *24* (2001–2010), and *The Good Wife* (2009–2016). British television shows include *Yes Minister* (1980–1984), *Yes, Prime Minister* (1986–1987), *The Thick of It* (2005, 2007, 2009, 2012), and *The Politician's Wife* (1995).

14. *Kisses for My President*, Internet Movie Database, https://www.imdb. com/title/tt0058266/.

15. For a description of Mrs. Kennedy's preservation and restoration work and publications related to it while she was First Lady, see "Jacqueline Kennedy in the White House," John F. Kennedy Presidential Library and Museum. https://www.jfklibrary.org/learn/about-jfk/jfk-in-history/jacqueline-kennedy-in-the-white-house, accessed December 30, 2022.

16. Elizabeth Ann Haas explains female politicians on screen have "to prove themselves both competent and still somehow 'all woman'" (272); see Haas, "Women, Politics, and Film: All About Eve?," Terry Christensen and Peter J. Haas eds., *Projecting Politics: Political Messages in American Films* (Armonk: M. E. Sharpe, 2005), cited by Zachary Baqué, "Madam President."

17. Charles Brumesco, "Goodbye Veep: the nastiest, sweariest, funniest show on TV is over," *Guardian*, May 13, 2019. https://www.theguardian.com/tv-and-radio/2019/may/13/veep-series-finale-julia-louis-dreyfus.

18. This definition applies to the media representation of feminism in the television shows discussed here, but it does not do justice to the diverse types of feminism, nor does it acknowledge debates between essentialists and social constructionists.

19. Toril Moi, "Feminism, Postmodernism, and Style: Recent Feminist Criticism in the United States." *Cultural Critique* 9 (1988): 3–22, 3. Moi points to Alison Jaggar's "excellent book *Feminist Politics and Human Nature*," to iden-

tify "an agonistic definition of feminism, which I see as the struggle against all forms of patriarchal and sexist oppression. Such an oppositional definition posits feminism as the necessary resistance to patriarchal power. Logically, then, the aim of feminism, like that of any emancipatory theory, is to abolish itself along with its opponent. In a non-sexist, non-patriarchal society, feminism will no longer exist." See Alison Jaggar, *Feminist Politics and Human Nature* (Lanham: Rowman and Littlefield, 1988).

20. Henrietta L. Moore, *Feminism and Anthropology* (Minneapolis: University of Minnesota Press, 1988), 10.

21. This ending is reported in an addendum included in the DVD of the series, although the ending of the US television broadcast is more ambiguous in leaving Ros's decision unresolved.

22. See Jake Kanter, "Netflix Teams with Denmark's DR to Revive Political Drama 'Borgen,'" *Deadline*, April 29, 2020, https://deadline.com/2020/04/netflix-dr-to-revive-borgen-1202920807/, and Lisa Abend, "Danish Political Drama *Borgen* Is Back at Last, with a Fresh Take on Female Power," *Time*, June 3, 2022, https://time.com/6183816/borgen-season-4-netflix/.

23. The official Danish government website explains "In Denmark, politics are about consensus. There are representatives of fourteen parties in the Danish parliament, and since 1909 no party has had enough representatives to rule entirely on its own. Instead, multiple parties put together a ruling coalition." *Denmark: The Official Website of Denmark*, https://denmark.dk/society-and-business/government-and-politics. Accessed August 17, 2022.

24. John Powers, "'Borgen' Is Denmark's 'West Wing' (but Even Better)," *npr.org*, February 5, 2014, http://www.npr.org/2014/02/04/271525839borgen-is-denmarks-west-wing-but-even-better.

25. Serena Davies, "Borgen: series three finale, BBC Four, review," *Telegraph*, December 14, 2013, http://www.telegraph.co.uk/culture/tvandradio/tv-and-radio-reviews/10516591/Borgen-series-three-finale-BBC-Four-review.html.

26. Abend, "Danish Political Drama *Borgen* Is Back at Last."

27. Abend, "Danish Political Drama *Borgen* Is Back at Last."

28. Meredith Blake, "On Location: 'Madam Secretary' puts women in the spotlight—and at a podium in the U.N.," *Los Angeles Times*, April 17, 2016, https://www.latimes.com/entertainment/tv/showtracker/la-et-st-madam-secretary-united-nations-episode-women-20160415-story.html.

29. William Shakespeare, *Macbeth*, act 5, scene 5: "Out, out, brief candle! Life's but a walking shadow, a poor player that struts and frets his hour upon the stage and is heard no more. It is a tale told by an idiot, full of sound and fury, signifying nothing."

30. Brian Lowrey, "'Madam Secretary' Explores 25th Amendment Episode," *CNN Entertainment*, January 11, 2018, https://edition.cnn.com/2018/01/11/enter-

tainment/madam-secretary-preview/index.html: "Specifically, President Dalton is convinced the attack was perpetrated by the Russians, and threatens a response of 'overwhelming force and ferocity.' "

31. Chris Eggertson, "Inside 'Madam Secretary's Trump-Like Impeachment Episode." *Hollywood Reporter*, January 15, 2018, https://www.hollywoodreporter. com/live-feed/inside-madam-secretarys-trump-like-impeachment-episode-107465.

32. Mary Jane, "Who Plays the Vice President on Madam Secretary Cast?" *Monsters and Critics*, November 19, 2018, https://www.monstersandcritics.com/ smallscreen/who-plays-the-vice-president-on-madam-secretary-cast/.

33. Robert Balkovich, "The Real Reason Madam Secretary Was Canceled," *The Looper* June 2, 2020. https://www.looper.com/214030/the-real-reason-madam-secretary-was-canceled/

34. The Hulu series *Mrs. America*, created by Dahvi Waller and produced in 2020 by FXP for showing on FX offers a fictionalized version of 1970s events concerning the ERA.

35. Brooks Barnes, "Networking in the Girls' Lounge," *New York Times*, March 5, 2016, https://www.nytimes.com/2016/03/05/fashion/girls-lounge-busi-nesswomen.html.

36. Georgia politician Stacey Abrams notes that foundational period: "What I see happening right now is the fruition of what was begun with Bella Abzug, Shirley Chisholm and Barbara Jordan—founders of the National Women's Political Caucus in 1971—and others, and I believe it will continue." Interview with Gitika Bhardwaj, "The Rise of Women in US Politics," Chatham House: The Royal Institute of International Affairs, March 8, 2019, https://www.chathamhouse.org/ expert/comment/rise-women-us-politics.

37. *First Lady* (Dir. Stanley Logan) Warner Brothers, 1937.

38. *The First Lady* (Dir. Susanne Bier) Created by Aaron Cooley, Showtime, Lionsgate, 2022, and *Gaslit* (Dir. Matt Ross) Created by Robbie Pickering, Starz, Lionsgate, 2022.

39. *The First Lady*. Show Time, https://www.sho.com/the-first-lady. Accessed August 8, 2022.

40. Jake Tapper, Sunlen Miller, and Devin Dwyer, "Obama Administration Drops 'Marriage Act,' " *ABC News*, February 23, 2011, https://abcnews. go.com/Politics/obama-administration-drops-legal-defense-marriage-act/story?id= 12981242.

41. David Martindale, "A Conversation with Cherry Jones of '24,' " *The Star Telegram*, February 20, 2009, and Justin Ravitz, " '24' Star Cherry Jones on Playing the President and What She Thinks of Meryl Streep in 'Doubt,' " *Vulture*, November 21, 2008. https://www.vulture.com/2008/11/cherry_jones. html. Both articles are cited in "Allison Taylor," *Wikipedia* https://en.wikipedia. org/wiki/Allison_Taylor.

42. Tim Baysinger, "Elizabeth Marvel on Why It's Good Her 'Homeland' President Wasn't a 'Noble Virtuous Hero,' " *Wrap*, May 29, 2018, https://www.thewrap.com/elizabeth-marvel-good-homeland-president-wasnt-noble-virtuous-hero/.

43. Sonia Saraiya, "Review: *House of Cards* Collapses, Finally." *Vanity Fair,* November 2, 2018, https://www.vanityfair.com/hollywood/2018/11/house-of-cards-final-season-review.

44. Inside front flap of book cover of *The Female Persuasion*.

45. Meg Wolitzer, *The Female Persuasion* (New York: Riverhead Books, 2018), 29.

46. Wolitzer, *The Female Persuasion*, 34.

47. Wolitzer, *The Female Persuasion*, 38.

48. Wolitzer, *The Female Persuasion*, 129.

49. Wolitzer, *The Female Persuasion*, 338.

50. Wolitzer, *The Female Persuasion*, 303.

51. Wolitzer, *The Female Persuasion*, 376.

52. Wolitzer, *The Female Persuasion*, 377.

53. Wolitzer, *The Female Persuasion*, 437.

54. Wolitzer, *The Female Persuasion*, 442.

55. Wolitzer, *The Female Persuasion*, 442.

56. Richard O. Prum, *The Evolution of Beauty: How Darwin's Forgotten Theory of Mate Choice Shapes the Animal World—and Us* (New York: Penguin, 2017), 333.

57. Prum, *The Evolution of Beauty*, 332, 334.

58. Prum, *The Evolution of Beauty*, 334.

59. Elizabeth Grosz, *The Nick of Time: Politics, Evolution, and the Untimely* (Durham: Duke University Press, 2004), 119.

60. Nicole Rudick, "A Universe of One's Own," *New York Review of Books*, July 18, 2019, https://www.nybooks.com/articles/2019/07/18/universe-of-ones-own-women-science-fiction/. Rudick's review considers *The Future Is Female!: 25 Classic Science Fiction Stories by Women, from Pulp Pioneers to Ursula K. Le Guin*, edited by Lisa Yaszek (Library of America, 2019).

61. Kaitlin Gow, "How Fiction Impacts Fact: The Social Impact of Books," *Fast Company*, July 12, 2012, https://www.fastcompany.com/1842370/how-fiction-impacts-fact-social-impact-books.

Epilogue

1. Vivian Gornick, "On the Progress of Feminism," *Village Voice*, December 10, 1970, https://www.villagevoice.com/2020/09/28/on-the-progress-of-feminism/.

2. Pope Francis, "A Crisis Reveals What Is in Our Hearts," *New York Times*, November 29, 2020, https://www.nytimes.com/2020/11/26/opinion/pope-francis-covid.html.

3. Jeremy Scahill, "Hope is a discipline: An Interview with Mariame Kaba on the Carceral State." *Intercept*, March 17, 2021, https://theintercept.com/2021/03/17/intercepted-mariame-kaba-abolitionist-organizing/.

4. "Stacey Abrams in Conversation with Charlayne Hunter-Gault." *Bitter Southerner*, August 31, 2021, https://bittersoutherner.com/summer-voices-guest-editor/charlayne-hunter-gault/stacey-abrams.

5. Raffaella Baritono and Valeria Gennero "Introduction," *RSA Journal* 27 (2016), https://www.academia.edu/36663513/Gender_Women_s_and_American_Studies.

6. See Arlin Cuncic, "What Is Homophobia?," Verywell Mind, February 8, 2022, https://www.verywellmind.com/what-is-homophobia: "While homophobia might traditionally have been applied only to those considered to be lesbian or gay, the term also extends to bisexual individuals and transgender and transsexual individuals." Also, see the *World Population Review*: "Atlanta is home to one of the highest LGBT populations per capita, which is 19th among major US metropolitan areas. An estimated 4.2% of Atlanta's metro population is gay, lesbian or bisexual. Atlanta is also the 2nd largest majority black metro area in the country. Still, African Americans in the city have been moving to the suburbs over the last ten years, and the city's black population shrank from 61.4% in 2000 to 54% in 2010." https://worldpopulationreview.com/us-cities/atlanta-ga-population. Accessed July 16, 2022.

7. Susan Faludi. *Backlash: The Undeclared War against Women* (New York: Vintage, 1993), 494.

8. Worldometer, "Covid Live" noted 561,860,061 Coronavirus Cases as of July 12, 2022. https://www.worldometers.info/coronavirus/; Madeline Halpert, "War Has Displaced More Than Eight Million in Ukraine," *Forbes*, May 10, 2022, https://www.forbes.com/sites/madelinehalpert/2022/05/10/war-has-displaced-more-than-8-million-in-ukraine-un-says/?sh=7a9eceb8c44b; Christine Hauser, "A Partial List of Mass Shootings in the United States in 2022," *New York Times*, May 18, 2022, https://www.nytimes.com/article/mass-shootings-2022.html.

9. Maria Cramer, "Here Are Key Passages from the Leaked Supreme Court Draft Opinion," *New York Times*, May 3, 2022, https://www.nytimes.com/2022/05/03/us/supreme-court-abortion-opinion-draft.html; Joan Biskupic, "Leaked Supreme Court Draft Opinion in Abortion Case Leaves Questions about Shape of Final Ruling," *CNN Politics*, May 12, 2022, https://www.cnn.com/2022/05/12/politics/supreme-court-draft-opinion/index.html.

10. Phoebe Kolbert, "Status of Abortion Laws, State by State," *Ms.*, July 7, 2022, https://msmagazine.com/2022/07/07/abortion-legal-state-laws/?.

11. New information appears every day, but here is the latest as of mid-July 2022: US Department of Health and Human Services, "Following President Biden's Executive Order to Protect Access to Reproductive Health Care, HHS Announces

Guidance to Clarify that Emergency Medical Care Includes Abortion Services," July 11, 2022, https://www.hhs.gov/about/news/2022/07/11/following-president-bidens-executive-order-protect-access-reproductive-health-care-hhs-announces-guidance-clarify-that-emergency-medical-care-includes-abortion-services.html; Carrie N. Baker, "President Biden Mobilizes Federal Resources to Support Abortion Access for All," *Ms.*, July 11, 2022, https://msmagazine.com/2022/07/11/biden-abortion-2/; Michelle Goldberg, "A 10-Year-Old Endures the Predictable Result of an Abortion Ban," *New York Times*, July 14, 2022, https://www.nytimes.com/2022/07/14/opinion/10-year-old-abortion.html.

12. "The Ezra Klein Show Transcript: Ezra Klein Interviews Michelle Goldberg," *New York Times*, July 8, 2022, https://www.nytimes.com/2022/07/08/podcasts/transcript-ezra-klein-interviews-michelle-goldberg.html.

13. Ben Parker, Stephanie Steinbrecher, Kelsey Ronan, John McMurtrie, Sophia DuRose, Rachel Villa, and Amy Sumerton. "Lest We Forget the Horrors: A Catalog of Trump's Worst Cruelties, Collusions, Corruptions, and Crimes," *McSweeney's* (January 20, 2021), https://www.mcsweeneys.net/articles/the-complete-listing-atrocities-1-1-056.

14. Anne Sraders and Lance Lambert, "Nearly 100,000 Establishments that Temporarily Shut Down Due to the Pandemic Are Now Out of Business," *Fortune*, September 28, 2020, https://fortune.com/2020/09/28/covid-buisnesses-shut-down-closed/.

15. Samantha Schmidt, "Women Have Been Hit Hardest by Job Losses in the Pandemic. And It May Only Get Worse," *Washington Post*, May 9, 2020, https://www.washingtonpost.com/dc-md-va/2020/05/09/women-unemployment-jobless-coronavirus/.

16. Helen Lewis, "The Coronavirus Is a Disaster for Feminism: Pandemics Affect Men and Women Differently," *Atlantic*, March 19, 2020, https://www.the-atlantic.com/international/archive/2020/03/feminism-womens-rights-coronavirus-Covid-19/608302/.

17. Lewis, "The Coronavirus Is a Disaster for Feminism."

18. Heather Long, "Virtual Schooling Has Largely Forced Moms, Not Dads, to Quit Work. It Will Hurt the Economy for Years," *Washington Post*, November 6, 2020, https://www.washingtonpost.com/road-to-recovery/2020/11/06/women-workforce-jobs-report/. See also Carrie N. Baker, "The Economic Impact of the COVID-19 Pandemic on Women," *Smith Alumnae Quarterly* (Summer 2021): 32–35, https://saqonline.smith.edu/publication/?m=45764&i=712711.

19. Terry Gross interview with Angela Garbes, "Raising Kids Is 'Essential Labor.' It's Also Lonely, Exhausting and Expensive," *NPR Fresh Air*, June 21, 2022, https://www.npr.org/sections/health-shots/2022/06/21/1105849291/essential-labor-angela-garbes-child-care-pandemic-mothering.

20. Sam Smethers, "We're at a Gender Equality Crossroads: Which Path Will the Government Take?" *Guardian* (November 20, 2020), https://www.theguardian.com/commentisfree/2020/nov/20/gender-equality-disruption-covid-19-inequalities#_=_.

21. Elise Gould and Valerie Wilson, "Black Workers Face Two of the Most Lethal Preexisting Conditions for Coronavirus—Racism and Economic Inequality," *Economic Policy Institute*, June 1, 2020, https://www.epi.org/publication/black-workers-covid/.

22. Mark Miller, "Female Workers Could Take Another Pandemic Hit: To Their Retirements," *New York Times*, December 11, 2020, https://www.nytimes.com/2020/12/11/business/women-retirement-covid-social-security.html.

23. NewsOne Staff, "Rest In Power: Notable Black Folks We Lost In 2020," *NewsOne*, November 24, 2020, https://newsone.com/playlist/notable-deaths-2020/.

24. Tucker Higgins and John W. Schoen, "These 4 Charts Describe Police Violence in America," *CNBC* (June 1, 2020), https://www.cnbc.com/2020/06/01/george-floyd-death-police-violence-in-the-us-in-4-charts.html: "Last year, more than 1,000 people were killed by police, according to Mapping Police Violence, one research group. Black people were disproportionately among those killed, the group found. Black people accounted for 24% of those killed, despite making up only about 13% of the population."

25. Evan Hill, Ainara Tiefenthäler, Christiaan Triebert, Drew Jordan, Haley Willis, and Robin Stein, "How George Floyd Was Killed in Police Custody," *New York Times*, May 31, 2020, https://www.nytimes.com/2020/05/31/us/george-floyd-investigation.html.

26. "George Floyd: What Happened in the Final Moments of His Life," *BBC News*, July 16, 2020, https://www.bbc.com/news/world-us-canada-52861726. Citizen journalist Darnella Frazier received a Pulitzer Prize for the video: "Teen Who Shot Video of Floyd's Death Receives Pulitzer Honour," *Al Jazeera*, June 11, 2021, https://www.aljazeera.com/news/2021/6/11/teen-who-shot-video-of-floyds-death-receives-pulitzer-honor.

27. "George Floyd: What Happened."

28. Zamira Rahim and Rob Picheta, "Thousands Around the World Protest George Floyd's Death in Global Display of Solidarity," *CNN World*, June 1, 2020, https://www.cnn.com/2020/06/01/world/george-floyd-global-protests-intl/index.html.

29. Scott Gleeson reported that the Portland and North Carolina teams issued a joint statement: "We took a knee today to protest racial injustice, police brutality and systemic racism against Black people of color in America. We love our country and we have taken this opportunity to hold it to a higher standard. It is our duty to demand that the liberties and freedoms this nation was founded upon are extended to everyone." See "NWSL Players Wear 'Black Lives Matter' Shirts, Kneel before First Game of Challenge Cup," *USA Today*, June 27, 2020, https://www.usatoday.com/story/sports/soccer/2020/06/27/challenge-cup-nwsl-players-wear-black-lives-matter-shirts-kneel/3270385001/.

30. Michele L. Norris, "How a WNBA Assist Helped Raphael Warnock Win a Senate Seat," *Washington Post*, January 6, 2021, https://www.washingtonpost.com/opinions/how-a-wnba-assist-helped-raphael-warnock-win-a-senate-seat/2021/01/06/59368f8c-5067-11eb-bda4-615aaefd0555_story.html.

31. Dan Balz, "The Politics of Race Are Shifting and Politicians Are Struggling to Keep Pace." *Washington Post*, July 5, 2020, https://www.washingtonpost.com/graphics/2020/politics/race-reckoning/.

32. TIME'S UP Guide to Equity and Inclusion during Crisis, "Building an Anti-Racist Workplace," https://timesupfoundation.org/work/equity/guide-equity-inclusion-during-crisis/building-an-anti-racist-workplace/.

33. See Ellise Schaffer, "H.E.R. Performs New Song 'I Can't Breathe,'" *Variety*, https://variety.com/video/h-e-r-debuts-song-inspired-by-george-floyd-i-cant-breathe/. Accessed August 16, 2022.

34. Gabriella Wilson (HER), "I Can't Breathe," 2020, https://genius.com/Her-i-cant-breathe-lyrics. YouTube video: https://www.youtube.com/watch?v=E-1Bf_XWaPE.

35. Chloe Melas, "Demi Lovato Has a Few Words for President Trump," *CNN*, October 14, 2020, https://www.cnn.com/2020/10/14/entertainment/demi-lovato-commander-in-chief-song-interview/index.html. See also Latesha Harris, "Demi Lovato Addresses Trump," *NPR*, October 15, 2020, https://www.npr.org/2020/10/15/923945417/demi-lovato-addresses-trump-with-commander-in-chief-during-billboard-music-award: "Lovato, a queer Hispanic woman, responded to criticism of her politics on Instagram, sharing that she is more interested in voicing her beliefs as an American than pleasing her fans. 'I literally don't care if this ruins my career,' she wrote Wednesday in a time-limited story post. 'This isn't about that. My career isn't about that. I made a piece of art that stands for something I believe in. And I'm putting it out even at the risk of losing fans. I'll take integrity in my work over sales any day.'"

36. The Billboard website publicizing the ceremony pointed to Lovato's motivation in crafting an explicitly political song: "The track, which condemns President Trump, arrived earlier today and features production from Finneas. The singer-songwriter-producer captioned Lovato's single art on Instagram: 'I think people underestimate the bravery it takes to put out a song like this when your platform is as large as Demi's is. But I'm sure if you asked her, she'd tell you it was her responsibility.'" See Lyndsey Havens, "Demi Lovato Live-Debuts Powerful 'Commander in Chief' at 2020 Billboard Music Awards," *Billboard*, October 14, 2020, https://www.billboard.com/articles/awards/bbmas/9466083/demi-lovato-commander-in-chief-2020-billboard-music-awards-video.

37. Demi Lovato, Julia Michaels, Finneas, Justin Tranter and Eren Cannata, "Commander in Chief," 2020, https://genius.com/Demi-lovato-commander-in-chief-lyrics.

38. Dorian Lyskey, "Demi Lovato Has Made the Most Damning Protest song of the Trump Era," *Guardian*, October 15, 2020, https//www.theguardian.com/music/2020/oct/15/demi-lovato-has-made-the-most-damning-protest-song-of-the-trump-era-commander-in-chief.

39. Demi Lovato, "Commander in Chief," *YouTube*, October 14, 2020, https://www.youtube.com/watch?v=n9Y-lS1trhw.

40. "Timeline: Our Fight against Opportunistic Abortion Bans during the COVID-19 Pandemic," *Planned Parenthood,* https://www.plannedparenthood action.org/issues/abortion/state-of-emergency/timeline-our-fight-against-abortion-bans-during-covid19.

41. Nina Totenberg, "Justice Ruth Bader Ginsburg, Champion of Gender Equality, Dies at 87," *NPR,* September 18, 2020, https://www.npr.org/2020/09/18/100306972/justice-ruth-bader-ginsburg-champion-of-gender-equality-dies-at-87: "Just days before her death, as her strength waned, Ginsburg dictated this statement to her granddaughter Clara Spera: 'My most fervent wish is that I will not be replaced until a new president is installed.'"

42. Michelle Goldberg, "Four Wasted Years Thinking about Donald Trump," *New York Times*, October 29, 2020, https://www.nytimes.com/2020/10/29/opinion/trump-arts-culture.html.

43. Goldberg, "Four Wasted Years Thinking about Donald Trump."

44. Michael Lee, "How Athletes Built a Voter-Turnout Machine, for 2020 and Beyond," *Washington Post,* December 3, 2020, https://www.washingtonpost.com/sports/2020/12/03/nba-wnba-turnout-georgia-primary/.

45. In 2018, in an election supervised by Brian Kemp, the Republican candidate for governor, Stacey Abrams lost the governorship of Georgia by 55,000 votes. Carol Anderson asserted that "If the governor's race had taken place in another country, the State Department would have questioned its legitimacy"; see Anderson, "Brian Kemp's Lead in Georgia Needs an Asterisk," *Atlantic*, November 7, 2018, https://www.theatlantic.com/ideas/archive/2018/11/georgia-governor-kemp-abrams/575095/; and Ella Lee, "Fact Check: Post Online about Stacey Abrams' 2018 Run for Georgia Governor Is Partly False," *USA Today*, November 18, 2020, https://www.usatoday.com/story/news/factcheck/2020/11/18/fact-check-partly-false-claim-stacey-abrams-2018-race/6318836002/: "The US House of Representatives Oversight Committee opened an investigation in March 2019 into concerns over voter registration and voter access during the 2018 gubernatorial election and Kemp's tenure as secretary of state, citing a particular concern of reports that Georgians, particularly people of color, 'faced unprecedented challenges with registering to vote and significant barriers to casting their votes' during that election." For more information about the purge of voters in Georgia, see Angela Caputo, Geoff Hing, and Johnny Kauffman, "After the Purge: How a Massive Voter Purge in Georgia Affected the 2018 Election," *APM Reports*, October 29, 2019, https://www.apmreports.org/story/2019/10/29/georgia-voting-registration-records-removed: "On a single day in late July 2017, Kemp's office [Secretary of State in Georgia] had removed from the rolls 560,000 Georgians who had been flagged because they'd skipped one too many elections. Abrams would later call the purge the 'use-it-or-lose-it scheme.' An APM Reports investigation last year estimated 107,000 of the people purged under the policy would otherwise

have been eligible to vote last year." Also, see Maya King, "How Stacey Abrams and Her Band of Believers Turned Georgia Blue," *Politico*, November 8, 2020, https://www.politico.com/news/2020/11/08/stacey-abrams-believers-georgia-blue-434985.

46. "About Stacey Abrams," Fair Fight. https://fairfight.com/about-stacey-abrams/.

47. Erin Delmore, "This Is How Women Voters Decided the 2020 Election," *NBC News*, November 13, 2020, https://www.nbcnews.com/know-your-value/feature/how-women-voters-decided-2020-election-ncna1247746.

48. Delmore, "This Is How Women Voters Decided the 2020 Election."

49. Stacie Taranto and Leandra Zarnow, "Mixed 2020 Election Results Show That Women Still Face a Sexist Political Culture," *Washington* Post, November 6, 2020, https://www.washingtonpost.com/outlook/2020/11/06/mixed-2020-election-results-show-that-women-still-face-sexist-political-culture/.

50. *The Biden Agenda for Women*, https://joebiden.com/womens-agenda/#.

51. Carrie Mihalcik, "First COVID-19 Vaccines Given in the US," *CNET*, December 14, 2020, https://www.cnet.com/science/first-covid-19-vaccines-given-in-the-us/; Samantha Power, "The Can-Do Power: America's Advantage and Biden's Chance," *Foreign Affairs* 100, no. 1 (January/February 2021): 10–24, 17–19.

52. Ryan Goodman, Mari Dugas, and Nicholas Tonckens, "Incitement Timeline: Year of Trump's Actions Leading to the Attack on the Capitol," Just Security. January 11, 2021, https://www.justsecurity.org/74138/incitement-timeline-year-of-trumps-actions-leading-to-the-attack-on-the-capitol/.

53. *Wikipedia*'s crowdsourced compilation of information about the January 6 insurrection includes more than 500 references to news reports and other accounts of the event; see "United States Capitol Attack," *Wikipedia*, https://en.wikipedia.org/wiki/2021_United_States_Capitol_attack. Jackson Katz notes the sociologist Michael Kimmel's work on white men who feel emasculated and deprived of the historic privilege of their fathers and grandfathers. See Jackson Katz and Jeremy Earp, "The Ms. Q&A: Jackson Katz on Performative Patriotism, White Masculinity, and the Future of the Republican Party," *Ms.*, January 8, 2021, https://msmagazine.com/2021/01/08/the-ms-qa-jackson-katz-on-performative-patriotism-white-masculinity-and-the-future-of-the-republican-party/; Nik Popli and Julia Zorthian, "What Happened to Jan. 6 Insurrectionists Arrested in the Year Since the Capitol Riot," *Time*, June 15, 2022, https://time.com/6133336/jan-6-capitol-riot-arrests-sentences/.

54. Marianne Levine, Holly Otterbein, and Burgess Everett, "Election Gambit Blows Up on Hawley and Cruz," *Politico*, January 9, 2021, https://www.politico.com/news/2021/01/09/hawley-cruz-2024-capitol-riots-456671.

55. John Eligon and Thomas Kaplan, "These Are the Republicans Who Supported Impeaching Trump," *New York Times*, January 13, 2021, https://www.nytimes.com/article/republicans-impeaching-donald-trump.html.

56. "Group of House Republicans, Led by Pa. Rep. Brian Fitzpatrick, Wants Trump Censured." *Pittsburgh Tribune-Review*. Associated Press, January 12, 2021, https://triblive.com/news/politics-election/group-of-house-republicans-led-by-pa-rep-brian-fitzpatrick-wants-trump-censured/.

57. For example, see "How Some Members of the Republican Party Have Normalized the Use of Violent Rhetoric," *PBS NewHour*, July 18, 2022, https://www.pbs.org/newshour/show/how-some-members-of-the-republican-party-have-normalized-the-use-of-violent-rhetoric.

58. Information is posted at Congress.gov, https://www.congress.gov/committee/house-select-committee-to-investigate-the-january-6th-attack-on-the-united-states-capitol/hlij00.

59. Roxane Gay, "Ugly Truths about America," *New York Times*, January 10, 2021, https://www.nytimes.com/2021/01/07/opinion/capitol-riot-trump-america.html.

60. See Julie Zeilinger, "Student Loan Debt Is a Feminist Issue," *WMC FBomb*, Women's Media Center, June 25, 2017, https://www.womensmediacenter.com/fbomb/student-loan-debt-is-a-feminist-issue; Morgan Moone, "Voter Suppression Is a Feminist Issue: Lessons for Future Elections," *Queens Daily Eagle*, November 7, 2018, https://queenseagle.com/all/2018/11/7/voter-suppression-is-a-feminist-issue-lessons-for-future-elections; InHerSight, "Why the Fight for $15 is a Feminist Issue," *InHerSight*, August 6, 2018, https://www.inhersight.com/blog/insight-commentary/why-fight-15-dollar-minumum-wage-feminist-issue; "Immigration as a Feminist Issue," National Organization for Women, 2021, https://now.org/resource/immigration-as-a-feminist-issue/; Ampson Hagan, "How Medicare for All Challenges Our Ideas of Black Deservingness," May 27, 2019, http://somatosphere.net/2019/how-medicare-for-all-challenges-our-ideas-of-black-deservingness.html/. All accessed January 16, 2021.

61. Michael D. Shear and Lisa Friedman, "Biden Could Roll Back Trump Agenda with Blitz of Executive Actions," *New York Times*, November 8, 2020, https://www.nytimes.com/2020/11/08/us/politics/biden-trump-executive-action.html; and Michael D. Shear and Peter Baker, "Biden Seeks Quick Start with Executive Actions and Aggressive Legislation," *New York Times*, January 16, 2021, https://www.nytimes.com/2021/01/16/us/politics/biden-administration-executive-action-legislation.html.

62. Julia Barajas, "The Hill We Climb," *LA* Times, January 20, 2021, https://www.latimes.com/world-nation/story/2021-01-20/watch-and-read-amanda-gormans-inauguration-day-poem.

63. "Inaugural Address by President Joseph R. Biden, Jr.," the White House https://www.whitehouse.gov/briefing-room/speeches-remarks/2021/01/20/inaugural-address-by-president-joseph-r-biden-jr/.

64. Aishvarya Kavi, "Biden's 17 Executive Orders and Other Directives in Detail," *New York Times*, January 21, 2021, https://www.nytimes.com/2021/01/20/us/biden-executive-orders.html.

65. Faludi, *Backlash*, 498. Also see the U.N. report *The World's Women 1970–1990: Trends and Statistics* (New York, 1991), which evaluated women's gains and losses and noted in its foreword its status as "a pioneering effort in the study of social trends and statistics to collect and compile statistics by gender." https://unstats.un.org/unsd/demographicsocial/products/worldswomen/documents/ww1990.pdf.

66. Katharine M. Marino and Susan Ware, "Rethinking 'First Wave' Feminisms: An Introduction," *Signs: A Journal of Women in Culture and Society* 47, no.4 (Summer 2022): 811–816, 815.

67. US House of Representatives. Select Committee to Investigate the January 6 Attack on the U.S. Capitol. https://january6th.house.gov/. Accessed July 24, 2022.

68. See Annie Karni and Maggie Haberman, "In Jan. 6 Hearings, Gender Divide Has Been Strong Undercurrent," *New York Times*, July 23, 2022, https://www.nytimes.com/2022/07/23/us/politics/jan-6-hearings-women-witnesses-committee.html: Cheney "was referring to Ms. Matthews as well as Cassidy Hutchinson, another White House aide who appeared at one of the committee's hearings; Caroline Edwards, a Capitol Police officer who testified about how she was assaulted by the rioters, sustained a concussion and continued to fight them off; and Wandrea Moss and her mother, Ruby Freeman, election workers from Georgia who told the panel about how they endured harassment and death threats after Mr. Trump named them in a false conspiracy theory about voter fraud."

69. Shauneen Miranda, "Rep. Cheney Pays Tribute to the Women's Suffrage Movement in Closing Jan. 6 Remarks," *NPR*, July 22, 2022, https://www.npr.org/2022/07/22/1112992409/rep-cheney-jan-6-suffrage-hearing.

70. Jim Russell, "Smith College Commencement Speaker Urges Grads 'to Cast Out Fear and Replace It with Hope.'" See *Mass Live*, May 15, 2022, https://www.masslive.com/news/2022/05/smith-college-commencement-speaker-urges-grads-to-cast-out-fear-and-replace-it-with-hope.html.

71. Beverly Daniel Tatum, "Smith College Commencement Address," May 15, 2022, https://www.smith.edu/about-smith/college-events/commencement/speakers-and-honorary-degrees/dr-beverly-daniel-tatum.

72. Tatum, "Smith College Commencement Address."

73. Silvia Moreno-Garcia, *Mexican Gothic* (New York: Del Rey, 2021), 301.

Bibliography

Aaron, Daniel. *The Unwritten War*. New York: Knopf, 1973.

Abbott, H. Porter. *The Cambridge Introduction to Narrative*. Cambridge, UK: Cambridge University Press, 2008.

Abend, Lisa. "Danish Political Drama *Borgen* Is Back at Last, with a Fresh Take on Female Power." *Time*, June 3, 2022. https://time.com/6183816/borgen-season-4-netflix/.

Abrams, Stacey. "The Rise of Women in US Politics." Interview by Gitika Bhardwaj, London: Chatham House, Royal Institute of International Affairs, March 8, 2019. https://www.chathamhouse.org/expert/comment/rise-women-us-politics.

———. "Stacey Abrams in Conversation with Charlayne Hunter-Gault." *Bitter Southerner*, August 31, 2021. https://bittersoutherner.com/summer-voices-guest-editor/charlayne-hunter-gault/stacey-abrams.

Adichie, Chimamanda Ngozi. "We Should All Be Feminists." Ted Talk delivered December 2012. *YouTube*. https://www.ted.com/talks/chimamanda_ngozi_adichie_we_should_all_be_feminists.

Agulhon, Maurice. *Marianne into Battle: Republican Imagery and Symbolism in France, 1789–1880*. Translated by Janet Lloyd. Cambridge, UK: Cambridge University Press, 1981.

Ahmed, Sarah. "Happy Futures, Perhaps." In *Queer Times, Queer Becomings*. Edited by Mikko Tuhkanen and E. L. McCallum, 159–81. Albany: State University of New York Press, 2011.

Alcott, Louisa May. "The Brothers." In *Civil War Women: The Civil War Seen through Women's Eyes in Stories by Louisa May Alcott, Kate Chopin, Eudora Welty, and Other Great Women Writers*. Edited by Frank McSherry Jr., Charles G. Waugh, and Martin Greenberg. New York: Simon and Schuster, 1988.

———. *Hospital Sketches*. Boston, MA: Bedford/St. Martin's, 2003.

———. *Little Women*. Boston, MA: Little Brown, 1868. Project Gutenberg. https://www.gutenberg.org/files/37106/37106-h/37106-h.htm.

Allen, Virginia, and Douglas K. Blair. "What We Saw at Protest outside Justice Amy Coney Barrett's House." *Daily Signal*, May 11, 2022. https://www.dailysignal.com/2022/05/11/what-we-saw-at-protest-outside-justice-amy-coney-barretts-house/.

"Allison Taylor." *Wikipedia*. https://en.wikipedia.org/wiki/Allison_Taylor.

Alter, Alexandra. "How Feminist Dystopian Fiction Is Channeling Women's Anger and Anxiety." *New York Times*, October 10, 2018. https://www.nytimes.com/2018/10/08/books/feminist-dystopian-fiction-margaret-atwood-women-metoo.html.

———. " 'The Mothers,' a Debut Novel, Is Already Creating a Stir." *New York Times*, October 9, 2016. https://www.nytimes.com/2016/10/10/books/the-mothers-brit-bennett.html.

The Amazing Mrs. Pritchard. Created by Jane Featherstone. BBC One, 2006. https://www.bbc.co.uk/programmes/b006mg4s.

American Pregnancy Association. "Blighted Ovum." Accessed August 3, 2022. https://americanpregnancy.org/healthy-pregnancy/pregnancy-complications/blighted-ovum/.

Amnesty International. "Violence against Women Is a US Problem, Too," June 11, 2011. https://www.amnestyusa.org/violence-against-women-is-a-u-s-problem-too/.

Anderson, Carol. "Brian Kemp's Lead in Georgia Needs an Asterisk." *Atlantic*, November 7, 2018. https://www.theatlantic.com/ideas/archive/2018/11/georgia-governor-kemp-abrams/575095/.

Anzaldúa, Gloria. *Borderlands/La Frontera*. San Francisco: Aunt Lute Books, 1989.

"The Arc of the Moral Universe Is Long, but It Bends toward Justice." Quote Investigator https://quoteinvestigator.com/2012/11/15/arc-of-universe/.

Ardis, Ann. *New Women, New Novels: Feminism and Early Modernism*. New Brunswick, NJ: Rutgers University Press, 1990.

Aristophanes. *The Complete Plays of Aristophanes*. Edited by Moses Hadas. New York: Bantam, 1962.

Armstrong, Nancy. *Desire and Domestic Fiction: A Political History of the Novel*. Oxford: Oxford University Press, 1987.

Atwood, Margaret. "Handmaid's Relevance after Election." *YouTube*, May 22, 2017. https://www.youtube.com/watch?v=BvIpWyWVTdE.

———. "*The Handmaid's Tale* Is Being Read Differently." *YouTube*, May 14, 2018. https://www.youtube.com/watch?v=7a8LnKCzsBw.

———. "Introduction." *The Handmaid's Tale*. New York: Doubleday, 2017.

———. *The Testaments*. New York: Doubleday, 2019.

Auerbach, Erich. *Mimesis: The Representation of Reality in Western Literature*. Trans. Willard R. Trask. Princeton, NJ: Princeton University Press, 1953.

Austen, Jane. *Mansfield Park*. New York: W. W. Norton, 1998.

———. *Pride and Prejudice*. New York: Penguin, 2003.

Baker, Carrie N. "The Economic Impact of the COVID-19 Pandemic on Women." *Smith Alumnae Quarterly* (Summer 2021): 32–35. https://saqonline.smith. edu/publication/?i=712711.

———. "President Biden Mobilizes Federal Resources to Support Abortion Access for All." *Ms.* July 11, 2022. https://msmagazine.com/2022/07/11/ biden-abortion-2/.

Balkovich, Robert. "The Real Reason Madam Secretary Was Canceled." *The Looper* June 2, 2020. https://www.looper.com/214030/the-real-reason-madam-secretary-was-canceled/.

Balz, Dan. "The Politics of Race Are Shifting, and Politicians Are Struggling to Keep Pace." *Washington Post*, July 5, 2020. https://www.washingtonpost. com/graphics/2020/politics/race-reckoning/.

Baqué, Zachary. "Madam President: The Representation of Female Political and Military Power in *Commander in Chief* and in Season 7 of *24*." *Caliban: French Journal of English Studies* 27 (2010): 285–94. https://journals.openedi-tion.org/caliban/2191.

Barajas, Julia. "The Hill We Climb." *LA Times*, January 20, 2021. https://www.latimes. com/world-nation/story/2021-01-20/watch-and-read-amanda-gormans-inauguration-day-poem.

Baritono, Raffaella, and Valeria Gennero. "Introduction." *RSA Journal* 27 (2016). https://www.academia.edu/36663513/Gender_Women_s_and_American_Studies.

Barnes, Brooks. "Networking in the Girls' Lounge." *New York Times*, March 5, 2016. https://www.nytimes.com/2016/03/06/fashion/girls-lounge-business-women.html.

Barthes, Roland. *S/Z: An Essay*. Translated by Richard Miller. New York: Hill and Wang, 1974.

Bayley, John. "Innocents at Home." *New York Review of Books* 39, no. 7 (April 9, 1992): 13–14.

Baysinger, Tim. "Elizabeth Marvel on Why It's Good Her 'Homeland' President Wasn't a 'Noble Virtuous Hero.'" *Wrap*, May 29, 2018. https://www.thewrap.com/ elizabeth-marvel-good-homeland-president-wasnt-noble-virtuous-hero/.

Beard, Mary. *Women and Power: A Manifesto*. New York: Liveright, 2017.

Belluck, Pam. "They Had Miscarriages, and New Abortion Laws Obstructed Treat-ment." *New York Times*, July 17, 2022. https://www.nytimes.com/2022/07/17/ health/abortion-miscarriage-treatment.html.

Beauvoir, Simone de. *The Second Sex* (1952). Translated and edited by H. M. Parshley. New York: Random House/Vintage, 1974.

Belsey, Catherine. "Constructing the Subject." In *Feminisms: An Anthology of Literary Theory and Criticism*, 2nd ed. Edited by Robyn Warhol and Diane Price Herndl. New Brunswick, NJ: Rutgers University Press, 1997.

Bennett, Britt. *The Mothers*. New York: Riverhead Books, 2016.

Bennett, Jessica. "This Is 'Little Women' for a New Era." *New York Times*. January 8, 2020. https://www.nytimes.com/2020/01/02/books/little-women-feminism-2019-movie.html.

Berlant, Lauren. "America, 'Fat,' the Fetus." *boundary 2*, no. 21 (1994): 3: 145–95.

———. "America, 'Fat,' The Fetus." In *Gendered Agents: Women and Institutional Knowledge*. Edited by Silvestra Mariniello and Paul A. Bové, 192–244. Durham, NC: Duke University Press, 1998.

———. *Cruel Optimism*. Durham, NC: Duke University Press, 2011.

Bernhard, Paula A., and Rowland S. Miller, "Juror Perceptions of False Confessions versus Witness Recantations." *Psychiatry, Psychology, and Law* 25, no. 4 (2018): 539–49.

Bertonneau, Thomas F. "Like Hypatia before the Mob: Desire, Resentment, and Sacrifice in *The Bostonians* (An Anthropoetics)." *Nineteenth-Century Literature* 53, no. 1 (1998): 56–90.

The Biden Agenda for Women. https://joebiden.com/womens-agenda/#.

Bilimoria, Diana, and Abigail Stewart. " 'Don't Ask, Don't Tell': The Academic Climate for Lesbian, Gay, Bisexual, and Transgender Faculty in Science and Engineering." *NWSA Journal* 21, no. 2 (2009): 85–103.

Biskupic, Joan. "Leaked Supreme Court Draft Opinion in Abortion Case Leaves Questions about Shape of Final Ruling." *CNN Politics*, May 12, 2022. https://www.cnn.com/2022/05/12/politics/supreme-court-draft-opinion/index.html.

Blake, Meredith. "On Location: 'Madam Secretary' Puts Women in the Spotlight—and at a Podium in the U.N." *Los Angeles Times*, April 17, 2016. https://www.latimes.com/entertainment/tv/showtracker/la-et-st-madam-secretary-united-nations-episode-women-20160415-story.html.

Bode, Christopher. *The Novel*. Translated by James Vigus. Hoboken: Wiley-Blackwell, 2011.

Borgen. Created by Adam Price. DR1, 2010–2022. Netflix. https://www.netflix.com/title/70302482.

Borgen: Power and Glory. Created by Adam Price. 2021–2022. Netflix. https://www.netflix.com/title/81282868.

The Bostonians. Directed by James Ivory. Merchant Ivory Productions, 1984.

Boyd, William. *Brazzaville Beach*. New York: Harper Perennial, 2010.

Braidotti, Rosi. "The Subject in Feminism." *Hypatia* 6, no. 2 (Summer 1991): 155–72.

Branch, Enobang Hannah, ed. *Pathways, Potholes, and the Persistence of Women in Science: Reconsidering the Pipeline*. Lanham, MD: Rowman and Littlefield, 2016.

Brownmiller, Susan. *Against Our Will: Men, Women, and Rape*. New York: Fawcett, 1975.

Brody, Richard. "The Compromises of Greta Gerwig's *Little Women*." *New Yorker*, December 31, 2019. https://www.newyorker.com/culture/the-front-row/the-compromises-of-greta-gerwigs-little-women.

Brumesco, Charles. "Goodbye Veep: The Nastiest, Sweariest, Funniest Show on TV Is Over." *Guardian*. May 13, 2019, https://www.theguardian.com/tv-and-radio/2019/may/13/veep-series-finale-julia-louis-dreyfus.

Bullard, Laura Curtis. *Christine, or Woman's Trials and Triumphs*. Edited by Denise M. Kohn. Lincoln: University of Nebraska, 2010.

Burke, Helen. "Problematizing American Dissent: The Subject of Phillis Wheatley." In *Cohesion and Dissent in American Literature*. Edited by Carol Colatrella and Joseph Alkana, 193–209. Albany: State University of New York, 1994.

Butler, Judith. "A Dissenting View from the Humanities on the AAUP's Statement on Knowledge: In Defense of Critical Inquiry." *Academe* 106, no. 2 (Spring 2020). https://www.aaup.org/article/dissenting-view-humanities-aaup%E2%80%99s-statement-knowledge#.

———. "Imitation and Gender Insubordination." In *Feminist Theory and Criticism*. Edited by Sandra M. Gilbert and Susan Gubar, 708–22. New York: Norton, 2007.

Byatt, A. S. *A Whistling Woman*. New York: Random House, 2002.

Byrnes, Paul. "Hidden Figures Review: These Trailblazing Women Deserve Better." *Sydney Morning Herald*, February 14, 2017. https://www.smh.com.au/entertainment/movies/hidden-figures-review-these-trailblazing-women-deserve-better-20170214-gucbs5.html.

Cai, Weiyi, and Scott Clement. "What Americans Think about Feminism Today." *Washington Post*, January 27, 2016. https://www.washingtonpost.com/graphics/national/feminism-project/poll/.

Call the Midwife. Created by Heidi Thomas. Neil Street Productions. BBC One. https://www.bbc.co.uk/programmes/p0118t80.

———. *Wikipedia*. https://en.wikipedia.org/wiki/Call_the_Midwife.

Captidis, Christine. "Hillary Wears White Pants Suit to Debate, Internet Goes Crazy." *CBS News*, October 20, 2016. https://www.cbsnews.com/news hillary-wears-white-pants-suit-to-debate-internet-goes-crazy/.

Caputo, Angela, Geoff Hing, and Johnny Kauffman. "After the Purge: How a Massive VoterPurge in Georgia Affected the 2018 Election." *APM Reports*, October 29, 2019. https://www.apmreports.org/story/2019/10/29/georgia-voting-registration-records-removed.

Carlisle, Janice. "*Little Dorrit*: Necessary Fictions." *Studies in the Novel* 7, no. 2 (Summer 1975): 195–214.

Case, Donald O. *Looking for Information: A Survey of Research on Information Seeking, Needs, and Behavior*, 3rd ed. Bingley, UK: Emerald Group, 2012.

Case, Sue-Ellen. *Feminism and Theatre*. New York: Methuen, 1988.

Ceci, Stephen J., and Wendy Melissa Williams, eds. *Why Aren't There More Women in Science?* Washington, DC: American Psychological Association, 2007.

Christian, Barbara. "The Race for Theory." *Feminist Studies* 14, no. 1 (Spring 1988): 67–79.

Chung, Catherine. *The Tenth Muse*. New York: Harper Collins, 2019.

Claybaugh, Amanda. *The Novel of Purpose: Literature and Social Reform in the Anglo-American World*. Ithaca, NY: Cornell University Press, 2006.

The Closer. Created by James Duff, Michael M. Robin, and Greer Shephard. Warner Brothers Television, 2005–2012. https://www.starttv.com/shows/the-closer.

"*The Closer*," *Wikipedia*. Accessed June 15, 2022. https://en.wikipedia.org/wiki/List_of_The_Closer_episodes.

Cohen, Travis. "This Is What Righteousness Sounds Like: The Importance of Emma González." *Miami New Times*, February 19, 2018. https://www.miaminewtimes.com/arts/emma-gonzalez-stoneman-douglas-survivor-makes-righteous-speech-10100848.

Coil, Alison. "Why Men Don't Believe the Data on Gender Bias in Science." *Wired*, August 25, 2017. https://www.wired.com/story/why-men-dont-believe-the-data-on-gender-bias-in-science/.

Colatrella, Carol. "The Evils of Slavery and Their Legacy in American Literature." In *Evil in American Popular Culture*, vol. 2. Edited by Jody Pennington and Sharon Packer, 45–61. Santa Barbara, CA: Praeger, 2014.

———. "Fear of Reproduction and Desire for Replication in *Dracula*." *Journal of Medical Humanities* 17, no. 3 (Spring 1996): 179–89

———. "Information in the Novel and the Novel as Information System: Charles Dickens's *Little Dorrit* and Margaret Drabble's *Radiant Way* Trilogy. *Information and Culture: A Journal of History* 50, no. 3 (2015): 339–71.

———. "The Innocent Convict: Character, Reader Sympathy, and the Nineteenth-Century Prison in *Little Dorrit*." In *In the Grip of the Law: Prisons, Trials, and the Space in Between*. Edited by Monika Fludernik and Greta Olson, 185–204. Frankfurt am Main, Germany: Peter Lang, 2004.

———. "Narrative Complexity, Character, and Action: Reconfiguring Gender Norms and Genre Conventions in a Police Procedural." *Signs & Media* 11 (Autumn 2015): 17–39.

———. "Review of Christopher F. Karpowitz and Tali Mendelberg, *The Silent Sex: Gender, Deliberation, and Institutions*." *International Journal of Gender, Science, and Technology* 8, no. 2 (2016): 313–16. http://genderandset.open.ac.uk/index.php/genderandset/article/view/453.

———. *Toys and Tools in Pink: Cultural Narratives of Gender, Science, and Technology*. Columbus: Ohio State University Press, 2011.

———. "Work for Women: Recuperating Charlotte Perkins Gilman's Reform Fiction." *Research in Science and Technology Studies* (*Knowledge and Society*, vol. 12). Edited by Shirley Gorenstein, 53–76. Stamford, CT: JAI Press, 2000.

Coleman, Rebecca, and Debra Ferreday. "Introduction: Hope and Feminist Theory." In *Hope and Feminist Theory*. Edited by Rebecca Coleman and Debra Ferreday, 1–10. New York: Routledge, 2018.

Collins, Phillip. *Dickens and Crime*. Bloomington: Indiana University Press, 1968.

"The Colors of Women's Suffrage." *Recollections*, June 17, 2019. https://recollections. biz/blog/colors-womens-suffrage.

"The Colours of the Suffragettes." *Women's History Bites*, November 25, 2014. https://irishwomenshistory.blogspot.com/2014/11/the-colours-of-suffragettes. html.

"The Combahee River Collective Statement," November 6, 2020. https://combahee rivercollective.weebly.com/the-combahee-river-collective-statement.html.

Commander in Chief. Created by Rod Lurie. Touchstone Television, 2005–2006. Prime Video. https://www.amazon.com/Commander-In-Chief-Season-1/ dp/B003YDLSCE.

Connell, R. W. *Masculinities*. Berkeley: University of California Press, 2005.

Cooper, Anna Julia. *A Voice from the South*. New York: Oxford University Press, 1988.

Cramer, Maria. "Here Are Key Passages from the Leaked Supreme Court Draft Opinion." *New York Times*, May 3, 2022. https://www.nytimes.com/2022/05/03/ us/supreme-court-abortion-opinion-draft.html.

Crenshaw, Kimberlé Williams. "Mapping the Margins: Intersectionality, Identity Politics, and Violence against Women of Color. https://www.racialequitytools. org/resourcefiles/mapping-margins.pdf. Accessed June 15, 2022.

Cuncic, Arlin. "What Is Homophobia?" Verywell Mind, February 8, 2022. https:// www.verywellmind.com/what-is-homophobia.

Davidow, Ellen Messer. "The Philosophical Bases of Feminist Literary Criticisms." *New Literary History* 19, no. 1 (Autumn 1987): 65–103.

Davies, Serena. "Borgen: Series Three Finale, BBC Four, Review." *Telegraph*, December 14, 2013. http://www.telegraph.co.uk/culture/tvandradio/tv-and-radio-reviews/10516591/Borgen-series-three-finale-BBC-Four-review.html.

Davis, Rebecca Harding. *Bits of Gossip*. Boston, MA: Houghton Mifflin, 1904.

———. *Bits of Gossip*. In *Documenting the American South*. https://docsouth.unc. edu/fpn/davisr/menu.html.

———. "John Lamar." In *Stories of the Civil War Era: Selected Writings from the Borderlands*. Edited Sharon M. Harris and Robin L. Cadwallader, 1–23. Athens: University of Georgia Press, 2010.

Davis-Floyd, Robbie E. "Birth as an American Rite of Passage." In *Childbirth in America*, edited by Karen L. Michaelson, 153–72. South Hadley, MA: Bergin and Garvey, 1998.

———. *Birth as an American Rite of Passage*. Berkeley: University of California Press, 2014.

DeBaise, Janine. "What We Learn." In *Body Language*. Charlotte NC: Main Street Rag Publishing Company, 2019.

Delahaye, Claire. "'A Tract in Fiction': Woman Suffrage Literature and the Struggle for the Vote." *European Journal of American Studies* 11, no. 1 (2016): 1–20. http://ejas.revues.org/11421.

Delmore, Erin. "This Is How Women Voters Decided the 2020 Election." *NBC News*, November 13, 2020. https://www.nbcnews.com/know-your-value/feature/how-women-voters-decided-2020-election-ncna1247746.

Denmark: The Official Website of Denmark. https://denmark.dk/society-and-business/government-and-politics. Accessed August 17, 2022.

Denning, Michael. *Mechanic Accents: Dime Novels and Working-Class Culture in America.* London: Verso, 1987.

Dickens, Charles. *American Notes for General Circulation* (1842). Edited by John S. Whitley and Arnold Goldman. London: Penguin, 2000.

———. *Hard Times.* London: Penguin, 1978.

———. *Little Dorrit.* Harmondsworth: Penguin, 1975.

Dobie, Kathy. "A Tiny, Little Law." *Harper's Magazine*, February 2011. http://harpers.org/archive/2011/02/tiny-little-laws/.

Doody, Margaret Anne. *The True Story of the Novel.* New Brunswick, NJ: Rutgers University Press, 1997.

Douglas, Susan. *Where the Girls Are: Growing Up Female with Mass Media.* New York: Random House, 1995.

Dow, Bonnie. *Prime Time Feminism: Television, Media Culture, and the Women's Movement Since 1970.* Philadelphia: University of Pennsylvania Press, 1996.

Drabble, Margaret. *The Gates of Ivory.* New York: Viking, 1991.

———. *The Millstone.* Harmondsworth, UK: Penguin, 1968.

———. *A Natural Curiosity.* New York: Viking, 1989.

———. *The Radiant Way.* New York: Alfred A. Knopf, 1987.

Drake, Simone C. *Critical Appropriations: African American Women and the Construction of Transnational Identity.* Baton Rouge: Louisiana State University Press, 2014.

DuPlessis, Rachel Blau. Interview by Kirsten Grogan. *The Oxonian* 29, no. 4 (December 5, 2015). http://www.oxonianreview.org/wp/an-interview-with-rachel-blau-duplessis/.

Ebert, Roger. "The Bostonians." *Rogert Ebert.Com*, January 1, 1984. https://www.rogerebert.com/reviews/the-bostonians-1984.

Eggertson, Chris. "Inside 'Madam Secretary's' Trump-Like Impeachment Episode." *Hollywood Reporter*, January 15, 2018. https://www.hollywoodreporter.com/live-feed/inside-madam-secretarys-trump-like-impeachment-episode-107465.

Elbert, Sarah. *A Hunger for Home: Louisa May Alcott's Place in American Culture.* New Brunswick, NJ: Rutgers University Press, 1987.

Eligon, John, and Thomas Kaplan. "These Are the Republicans Who Supported Impeaching Trump." *New York Times*, January 13, 2021. https://www.nytimes.com/article/republicans-impeaching-donald-trump.html.

Eliot, George. *Middlemarch: A Study of Provincial Life.* New York: New American Library, 1964.

Ellmann, Mary. *Thinking about Women*. New York: Harcourt Brace Jovanovich, 1968.

Engstrom, Janet L., and Ramona G. Hunter. "Teaching Reproductive Options through the Use of Fiction: *The Cider House Rules* Project." *Journal of Obstetric, Gynecologic, and Neonatal Nursing* 36, no. 5 (2007): 464–70.

Erdrich, Louise. "Conversation: Louise Erdrich, Author of 'The Round House.'" Interview by Jeffrey Brown. *PBS NewsHour*. October 26, 2012. https://www.pbs.org/video/pbs-newshour-conversation-louise-erdrich-author-of-the-round-house/.

———. "Rape on the Reservation." *New York Times*, February 26, 2013. https://www.nytimes.com/2013/02/27/opinion/native-americans-and-the-violence-against-women-act.html.

———. *The Round House*. New York: Harper Collins, 2012.

Eugenides, Jeffrey. *The Marriage Plot*. New York: Farrar, Straus, Giroux, 2011.

European Commission. *She-Figures 2015*. 2015. http://ec.europa.eu/research/swafs/pdf/pub_gender_equality/she_figures_2015-final.pdf.

Evans, Elizabeth. "What Makes a (Third) Wave?" *International Feminist Journal of Politics* 18, no. 3 (2016): 409–28.

Eve, Martin. *Literature against Criticism: University English and Contemporary Fiction in Conflict*. Cambridge, UK: Open Book Publishers, 2016.

Fahs, Alice. "Introduction." In *Hospital Sketches*, by Louisa May Alcott. 1–50. Boston, MA: Bedford/St. Martin's, 2003.

Fair Fight. "About Stacey Abrams." https://fairfight.com/about-stacey-abrams/. Accessed June 15, 2022.

Faludi, Susan. *Backlash: The Undeclared War against Women*. New York: Vintage, 1993.

Faulkner, W., and E. A. Kerr, "On Seeing Brockenspectres: Sex and Gender in Twentieth-Century Science." In *Companion to Science in the Twentieth Century*. Edited by Dominique Pestre and John Krige, 59–72. London: Routledge, 2003.

Felski, Rita. *Literature after Feminism*. Chicago: University of Chicago Press, 2003.

"Feminist Resources for #TheResistance." *Signs (Virtual Issue)*. http://signsjournal.org/features/virtual-issues/feminist-resources-for-theresistance/#models. Accessed August 17, 2022.

Ferguson, Moira, ed. *First Feminists: British Women Writers, 1578–1799*. Bloomington: Indiana University Press, 1985.

———. "Mary Wollstonecraft and the Problematic of Slavery." *Feminist Review* 42, no. 1 (Autumn 1992): 82–102.

Fetterley, Judith. *The Resisting Reader: A Feminist Approach to American Fiction*. Bloomington: Indiana University Press, 1978.

Finke, Laurie. *Feminist Theory, Women's Writing*. Ithaca, NY: Cornell University Press, 2018.

First Lady. Directed by Stanley Logan. Warner Brothers, 1937.

The First Lady. Created by Aaron Cooley. Directed by Susanne Bier. Lionsgate Television, 2022.

Fisher, Laura R. *Reading for Reform: The Social Work of Literature in the Progressive Era*. Minneapolis: University of Minnesota Press, 2019.

Fitzgerald, Penelope. *The Bookshop, The Gate of Angels, The Blue Flower*. New York: Alfred A. Knopf, 2001.

Flexner, Eleanor. *Century of Struggle*. Cambridge, MA: Harvard University Press, 1975.

Forster, E. M. *Howards End*. New York: Random House, 1921.

Foster, Frances Smith. *Written by Herself: Literary Production by African American Women, 1746–1892*. Bloomington: Indiana University Press, 1993.

Foucault, Michel. *The Foucault Reader*. Edited by Paul Rabinow. New York: Pantheon Books, 1984.

Fourteenth Amendment," *Legal Information Institute*. Cornell Law School. https://www.law.cornell.edu/constitution/amendmentxiv.

Frankel, Laurie. " 'This Is How It Always Is' Was Inspired by Its Author's Transgender Child," Interview by NPR Staff. NPR January 30, 2017. https://www.npr.org/2017/01/30/512030431/this-is-how-it-always-is-was-inspired-by-its-authors-transgender-child.

———. *This Is How It Always Is*. New York: Flatiron Books, 2017.

Frayling, Christopher. *Mad, Bad, and Dangerous: The Scientist and Cinema*. London: Reaktion Books, 2006.

Freeman, Elizabeth. *Time Binds: Queer Temporalities, Queer Histories*. Durham, NC: Duke University Press, 2010.

Fried, Kerry. "High Spirits: The Great Penelope Fitzgerald on Poltergeists, Plots, and Past Masters." *Amazon.com*. Archived on April 3, 2015, in the Internet Archive Wayback Machine. http://www.amazon.com/gp/feature.html?ie=UTF8&docId=10326.

Friedman, Vanessa. "Kamala Harris in a White Suit: Dressing for History." *New York Times*, November 8, 2020. https://www.nytimes.com/2020/11/08/fashion/kamala-harris-speech-suffrage.html.

Fuss, Diana. *Essentially Speaking: Feminism, Nature and Difference*. New York: Routledge, 1989.

Gaines, Susan M. *Carbon Dreams*. Berkeley, CA: Creative Arts Book Company, 2001.

Ganobcsik-Williams, Lisa. "Charlotte Perkins Gilman and *The Forerunner*: A New Woman's Changing Perspective on American Immigration." In *Feminist Forerunners: New Womanism and Feminism in the Early Twentieth Century*. Edited by Ann Heilman, 44–56. London: Pandora, 2003.

Garfield, Leanna. "Thousands of Women Will Wear Pink 'Pussy Hats' the Day after Trump's Inauguration." *Business Insider*, January 18, 2017. http://www.businessinsider.com/pussy-hats-womens-march-washington-trump-inauguration-2017-1.

Garner, Stanton. *The Civil War World of Herman Melville*. Lawrence: University of Kansas Press, 1993.

Gaslit. Created by Robbie Pickering. Directed by Matt Ross. Starz, Lionsgate Television, 2022.

Gates, Henry Louis, ed. *The Classic Slave Narratives*. New American Library, 1987.

Gauthier, Marni. "The Other Side of Paradise: Toni Morrison's (Un)Making of Mythic History." *African American Review* 39, no. 3 (2005): 395–414.

Gay, Roxane. *Bad Feminist: Essays*. New York: Harper, 2014.

———. "Ugly Truths about America." *New York Times*, January 10, 2021. https://www.nytimes.com/2021/01/07/opinion/capitol-riot-trump-america.html.

"George Floyd: What Happened in the Final Moments of His Life." *BBC News*, July 16, 2020. https://www.bbc.com/news/world-us-canada-52861726.

Gerstein, Josh, and Alexander Ward, "Supreme Court Has Voted to Overturn Abortion Rights, Draft Opinion Shows." *Politico*. May 2, 2022. https://www.politico.com/news/2022/05/02/supreme-court-abortion-draft-opinion-00029473.

Gibson, John D. "Childbearing and Childrearing: Feminists and Reform." *Virginia Law Review* 73, no. 6 (September 1987): 1145–182.

Gilbert, Elizabeth. *The Signature of All Things*. New York: Penguin, 2013.

Gilbert, Sophie. "The Remarkable Rise of the Feminist Dystopia." *Atlantic*, October 4, 2018. https://www.theatlantic.com/entertainment/archive/2018/10/feminist-speculative-fiction-2018/571822/.

Gill, Rosalind. *Gender and the Media*. Cambridge UK: Polity, 2007.

Gill-Peterson, Julian. *Histories of the Transgender Child*. Minneapolis: University of Minnesota Press, 2018.

Gilman, Charlotte Perkins. *Suffrage Songs and Verses*. New York: Charlton Company, 2011. Posted at *A Celebration of Women Writers*. http://digital.library.upenn.edu/women/gilman/suffrage/suffrage.html.

———. *What Diantha Did*. Middlesex, UK: Echo Library, 2009.

Gissing, George. *The Odd Women*. Edited by Patricia Ingham. Oxford, UK: Oxford University Press, 2000.

Gleeson, Scott. "NWSL Players Wear 'Black Lives Matter' Shirts, Kneel Before First Game of Challenge Cup." *USA Today*, June 27, 2020. https://www.usatoday.com/story/sports/soccer/2020/06/27/challenge-cup-nwsl-players-wear-black-lives-matter-shirts-kneel/3270385001/.

Godsey, Mark A. "Shining the Bright Light on Police Interrogation in America." *Faculty Articles and Other Publications* 82 (2009): 711–735. https://scholarship.law.uc.edu/fac_pubs/82.

Goldberg, Michelle. "The Ezra Klein Show Transcript: Ezra Klein Interviews Michelle Goldberg." *New York Times*, July 8, 2022. https://www.nytimes.com/2022/07/08/podcasts/transcript-ezra-klein-interviews-michelle-goldberg.html.

———. "Four Wasted Years Thinking about Donald Trump." *New York Times*, October 29, 2020. https://www.nytimes.com/2020/10/29/opinion/trump-arts-culture.html?

———. "Margaret Atwood's Dystopia, and Ours." *New York Times*, September 14, 2019. testaments-handmaids-tale.html.

Good Girls Revolt. Created by Dana Calvo. Tristar Television, 2015–16. https://www.amazon.com/Good-Girls-Revolt-Season-1/dp/B086HVRRH5.

Goodale, Gloria. "The Closer Opened Doors for Women—and for Basic Cable." *Christian Science Monitor*, July 12, 2010. http://www.csmonitor.com/USA/2010/0712/The-Closer-opened-doors-for-women-and-for-basic-cable.

Goodman, Allegra. *Intuition*. New York: Random House, 2006.

Goodman, Robin Truth. "Introduction." In *The Bloomsbury Handbook of 21st-Century Feminist Theory*. Edited by Robin Truth Goodman, 1–18. London: Bloomsbury, 2019.

Goodman, Ryan, Mari Dugas, and Nicholas Tonckens, "Incitement Timeline: Year of Trump's Actions Leading to the Attack on the Capitol." *Just Security*, January 11, 2021. https://www.justsecurity.org/74138/incitement-timeline-year-of-trumps-actions-leading-to-the-attack-on-the-capitol/.

Gornick, Vivian. "On the Progress of Feminism." *Village Voice*. December 10, 1970. https://www.villagevoice.com/2020/09/28/on-the-progress-of-feminism/.

Gould, Elise, and Valerie Wilson. "Black Workers Face Two of the Most Lethal Preexisting Conditions for Coronavirus—Racism and Economic Inequality." *Economic Policy Institute*, June 1, 2020. https://www.epi.org/publication/black-workers-covid/.

Gould, Stephen Jay. *The Mismeasure of Man*. New York: Norton, 1996.

Gow, Kaitlin. "How Fiction Impacts Fact: The Social Impact of Books." *Fast Company*, July 12, 2012. https://www.fastcompany.com/1842370/how-fiction-impacts-fact-social-impact-books.

Greer, Corey. "The US Needs a Feminist Federal Budget." *Ms.*, July 17, 2019. https://msmagazine.com/2019/07/17/the-u-s-needs-a-feminist-federal-budget/.

Gregg, Robin. *Pregnancy in a High-Tech Age: Paradoxes of Choice*. New York: New York University Press, 1995.

Grossman, Jonathan H. *Charles Dickens's Networks: Public Transport and the Novel*. Oxford, UK: Oxford University Press, 2012.

Grosz, Elizabeth. *The Nick of Time: Politics, Evolution, and the Untimely*. Durham, NC: Duke University Press, 2004.

Haack, Susan. "After My Own Heart: Dorothy L. Sayers's Feminism." *New Criterion* 19 (May 2001): 9. http://www.newcriterion.com/articles.cfm/sayers-haack-2180.

Haas, Elizabeth Ann. "Women, Politics, and Film: All about Eve?" *Projecting Politics: Political Messages in American Films*. Edited by Terry Christensen and Peter J. Haas. Armonk: M. E. Sharpe, 2005.

Hagan, Ampson. "How Medicare for All Challenges Our Ideas of Black Deservingness," May 27, 2019. http://somatosphere.net/2019/how-medicare-for-all-challenges-our-ideas-of-black-deservingness.html/.

Hallett, Christine. "The Attempt to Understand Puerperal Fever in the Eighteenth and Early Nineteenth Centuries: The Influence of Inflammation Theory." *Medical History* 49, no. 1 (2005): 1–28.

Halpert, Madeleine. "War Has Displaced More Than Eight Million in Ukraine." *Forbes*, May 10, 2022. https://www.forbes.com/sites/madelinehalpert/2022/05/10/war-has-displaced-more-than-8-million-in-ukraine-un-says/?

The Handmaid's Tale. Created by Bruce Miller. MGM Television. 2017. Hulu. https://www.hulu.com/series/the-handmaids-tale-565d8976-9d26-4e63-866c-40f8a137ce5f.

The Handmaid's Tale. Directed by Volker Schlöndorff. Cinecom Pictures, 1990.

Hardin, Nancy S. "Drabble's *The Millstone*: A Fable for Our Times." *Critique* 15, no. 1 (January 1, 1973): 22–34.

Harding, Sandra. *Whose Science? Whose Knowledge?* Ithaca, NY: Cornell University Press, 1991.

Harper, Frances E. W. *Iola Leroy, or Shadows Uplifted.* New York: Oxford University Press, 1988.

Harris, Latesha. "Demi Lovato Addresses Trump." *NPR.* October 15, 2020. https://www.npr.org/2020/10/15/923945417/demi-lovato-addresses-trump-with-commander-in-chief-during-billboard-music-award.

Hauser, Christine. "A Partial List of Mass Shootings in the United States in 2022." *New York Times*, May 18, 2022. https://www.nytimes.com/article/mass-shootings-2022.html.

Harvey, Alison. *Feminist Media Studies.* Cambridge, UK: Polity, 2019.

Havens, Lyndsey. "Demi Lovato Live-Debuts Powerful 'Commander in Chief' at 2020 Billboard Music Awards." *Billboard*, October 14, 2020. https://www.billboard.com/articles/awards/bbmas/9466083/demi-lovato-commander-in-chief-2020-billboard-music-awards-video.

Hayden, Dolores. *The Grand Domestic Revolution: A History of Feminist Designs for American Homes, Neighborhoods, and Cities.* Cambridge, MA: MIT Press, 1985.

Hayles, N. Katherine. *Chaos Bound: Orderly Disorder in Contemporary Literature and Science.* Ithaca, NY: Cornell University Press, 1990.

Haynes, Roslynn D. *From Madman to Crime Fighter: The Scientist in Western Culture.* Baltimore, MD: Johns Hopkins University Press, 2017.

Heilman, Ann. "Introduction." In *Feminist Forerunners: New Womanism and Feminism in the Early Twentieth Century.* Edited by Ann Heilman, 1–14. London: Pandora, 2003.

Hekman, Susan. "Subject." In *The Bloomsbury Handbook of 21st-Century Feminist Theory.* Edited by Robin Truth Goodman, 21–31. London: Bloomsbury, 2019.

Henry, Rachael. "Attitudes to Gender in 2016 Britain: 8,000 Sample Study for Fawcett Society." *Survation.* http://survation.com/uk-attitudes-to-gender-in-2016-survation-for-fawcett-society/.

Hermann, Claudine. "The Virile System." Translated by Marilyn R. Schuster. In *New French Feminisms: An Anthology.* Edited by Elaine Marks and Isabelle de Courtivron, 87–89. New York: Schocken, 1981.

Hidden Figures. Directed by Theodore Melfi. 20th-Century Fox, 2016.

Hiebert, Erwin N. "The State of Physics at the Turn of the Century." *Rutherford and Physics at the Turn of the Century.* Edited by Mario Bunge and William R. Shea. New York: Dawson and Science History Publications, 1979.

Higgins, Tucker, and John W. Schoen. "These 4 Charts Describe Police Violence in America." *CNBC.* June 1, 2020. https://www.cnbc.com/2020/06/01/george-floyd-death-police-violence-in-the-us-in-4-charts.html.

Hill, Evan, Ainara Tiefenthäler, Christiaan Triebert, Drew Jordan, Haley Willis, and Robin Stein. "How George Floyd Was Killed in Police Custody." *New York Times,* May 31, 2020. https://www.nytimes.com/2020/05/31/us/george-floyd-investigation.html.

Hollander, Anne. "Portraying Little Women through the Ages." In *Little Women and the Feminist Imagination: Criticism, Controversy, Personal Essays.* Edited by Janice M. Alberghene and Beverly Lyon Clark, 97–101. New York: Garland, 1999.

hooks, bell. *Feminism Is for Everybody: Passionate Politics.* New York: Routledge, 2014.

———. *Teaching to Transgress.* New York: Routledge, 1994.

Horace, "The Art of Poetry." Edited and translated by Walter Jackson Bate. In *Critical Theory Since Plato.* Edited by Hazard Adams, 67–74. New York: Harcourt Brace Jovanovich, 1972.

"How Some Members of the Republican Party Have Normalized the Use of Violent Rhetoric." *PBS NewHour.* July 18, 2022. https://www.pbs.org/newshour/show/how-some-members-of-the-republican-party-have-normalized-the-use-of-violent-rhetoric.

Howells, William Dean. [Review of *Battle-Pieces and Aspects of War.*] *Atlantic Monthly,* February 1867. http://www.theatlantic.com/magazine/archive/1867/02/herman-melville/8618/.

Hubbard, Lauren. "Everything We Know so Far about *Call the Midwife* Season 10." *Town and Country Magazine,* February 16, 2020. https://www.townandcountrymag.com/leisure/arts-and-culture/a30753289/call-the-midwife-season-10/.

———. "Everything We Know so Far about *Call the Midwife* Season 12." *Town and Country Magazine,* August 2, 2022. https://www.townandcountrymag.com/leisure/arts-and-culture/a39465884/call-the-midwife-season-12/.

Ide, Wendy. "Little Women Review: The Freshest Literary Adaptation of the Year." *Guardian,* December 29, 2019. https://www.theguardian.com/film/2019/dec/29/little-women-review-greta-gerwig-saoirse-ronan-wendy-ide.

Ingham, Patricia "Introduction." In George Gissing, *The Odd Women*, vii–xxv. Oxford, UK: Oxford University Press, 2008.

InHerSight. "Why the Fight for $15 Is a Feminist Issue," August 6, 2018. https://www.inhersight.com/blog/insight-commentary/why-fight-15-dollar-minumum-wage-feminist-issue.

Inter-Parliamentary Union. "Women in Parliament." https://www.ipu.org/our-impact/gender-equality/women-in-parliament. Accessed August 17, 2022.

Irving, John. *The Cider House Rules*. New York: Bantam, (1985) 1989.

Jacobs, Harriet A. *Incidents in the Life of a Slave Girl*. Edited by Jean Fagan Yellin. Cambridge, MA: Harvard University Press, (1861) 1987.

"Jacqueline Kennedy in the White House," John F. Kennedy Presidential Library and Museum. https://www.jfklibrary.org/learn/about-jfk/jfk-in-history/jacqueline-kennedy-in-the-white-house. Accessed December 30, 2022.

Jaggar, Alison. *Feminist Politics and Human Nature*. Rowman & Littlefield Publishers, 1988.

Jaki, Stanley. "The Reality Beneath: The World View of Rutherford." In *Rutherford and Physics at the Turn of the Century*. Edited by Mario Bunge and William R. Shea. New York: Dawson and Science History, 1979.

James, Henry. *The Bostonians*. New York: New American Library, 1979.

———. *Novels 1881–1886: Washington Square, The Portrait of a Lady, The Bostonians*. New York: Library of America, 1985.

Jane, Mary. "Who Plays the Vice President on Madam Secretary Cast?" *Monsters and Critics*, November 19, 2018. https://www.monstersandcritics.com/smallscreen/who-plays-the-vice-president-on-madam-secretary-cast/.

Janta, Barbara. "Britain Just Expanded Free Child Care. The US Should Follow Its Lead." *USA Today*, October 26, 2017. https://www.usatoday.com/story/opinion/2017/10/26/u-k-s-child-care-system-isnt-perfect-but-we-can-still-learn-lot-barbara-janta-column/796324001/.

Joyrich, Lynn. *Re-viewing Reception: Television, Gender, and Postmodern Culture*. Bloomington: Indiana University Press, 1996.

Kaba, Mariame. "Hope Is a Discipline: An Interview with Mariame Kaba on the Carceral State." Interview by Jeremy Scahill. *The Intercept*, March 17, 2021. https://theintercept.com/2021/03/17/intercepted-mariame-kaba-abolitionist-organizing/.

Kakutani, Michiko. " 'Paradise': Worthy Women, Unredeemable Men." *New York Times*, January 6, 1998. https://archive.nytimes.com/www.nytimes.com/books/98/01/04/daily/morrison-book-review-art.html.

Kanter, Jake. "Netflix Teams with Denmark's DR to Revive Political Drama 'Borgen.' " *Deadline*, April 29, 2020. https://deadline.com/2020/04/netflix-dr-to-revive-borgen-1202920807/.

Karcher, Carolyn. *Shadow over the Promised Land*. Baton Rouge: Louisiana State University, 1980.

Karni, Annie. and Maggie Haberman, "In Jan. 6 Hearings, Gender Divide Has Been Strong Undercurrent." *New York Times*, July 23, 2022. https://www.

nytimes.com/2022/07/23/us/politics/jan-6-hearings-women-witnesses-committee.html.

Karpowitz, Christopher F., and Tali Mendelberg. *The Silent Sex: Gender, Deliberation, and Institutions.* Princeton, NJ: Princeton University Press, 2014.

"Kathoey," *Wikipedia.* https://en.wikipedia.org/wiki/Kathoey.

Katz, Jeremy, and Jeremy Earp. "The Ms. Q&A: Jackson Katz on Performative Patriotism, White Masculinity, and the Future of the Republican Party." *Ms.*, January 8, 2021. https://msmagazine.com/2021/01/08/the-ms-qa-jackson-katz-on-performative-patriotism-white-masculinity-and-the-future-of-the-republican-party/.

Kavi, Aishvarya. "Biden's 17 Executive Orders and Other Directives in Detail." *New York Times*, January 21, 2021. https://www.nytimes.com/2021/01/20/us/biden-executive-orders.html.

Keckley, Elizabeth. *Behind the Scenes, or Thirty Years a Slave and Four Years in the White House.* New York: Oxford University Press, 1988.

Keen, Suzanne. *Empathy and the Novel.* Oxford: Oxford University Press, 2007.

Keller, Evelyn Fox. *A Feeling for the Organism: The Life and Work of Barbara McClintock.* New York: W. H. Freeman, 1983.

———. *Reflections on Gender and Science.* New Haven, CT: Yale University Press, 1985.

Kevles, Bettyann. *Naked to the Bone: Medical Imaging in the Twentieth Century.* Reading, MA: Helix Books/Addison-Wesley, 1987.

King, Maya. "How Stacey Abrams and Her Band of Believers Turned Georgia Blue." *Politico*, November 8, 2020. https://www.politico.com/news/2020/11/08/stacey-abrams-believers-georgia-blue-434985.

"The King Philosophy." The King Center. http://www.thekingcenter.org/king-philosophy.

Kirby, David. *Lab Coats in Hollywood: Science, Scientists, and the Cinema.* Cambridge, MA: MIT Press, 2007.

Kisses for My President. Internet Movie Database. https://www.imdb.com/title/tt0058266/.

Kitzinger, Jenny, Joan Haran, Mwenya Chimba, and Tammy Boyce. *Role Models in the Media: An Exploration of the Views and Experiences of Women in Science, Engineering, and Technology.* UK Resource Centre for Women in Science, Engineering, and Technology. Research Report 1 (March 2008). https://orca.cf.ac.uk/17534/1/report_1_kitzinger.pdf.

Ko, Lisa. *The Leavers.* Chapel Hill, NC: Algonquin Books, 2017.

Kolbert, Phoebe. "Status of Abortion Laws, State by State," *Ms.*, July 7, 2022. https://msmagazine.com/2022/07/07/abortion-legal-state-laws/?

Kolodny, Annette. "Dancing through the Minefield." *Feminist Studies* 6, no. 1 (Spring 1980): 1–25.

Kraditor, Aileen S. *The Ideas of the Women's Suffrage Movement, 1890–1920.* New York: Norton, 1981.

Lane, Anthony. "Greta Gerwig's Raw, Startling *Little Women*." *New Yorker*, December 25, 2019. https://www.newyorker.com/magazine/2020/01/06/greta-gerwigs-raw-startling-little-women.

Lanser, Susan S. "The (Ir)relevance of Narratology." In *Relevance and Narrative Research*. Edited by Matei Chihaia and Katharina Rennhak, 3–17. Lanham, MD: Lexington Books, 2019.

Larsen, Nella. *Quicksand*. New York: Penguin, 2002.

Latimer, Heather. *Reproductive Acts: Sexual Politics in North American Fiction and Film* Montreal, QC: McGill-Queens Press, 2013.

Layne, Linda L. "The Child as Gift." In *Transformative Motherhood: On Giving and Getting in a Consumer Culture*. Edited by Linda L. Layne, 1–27. New York: New York University Press, 1999.

Ledger, Sally. *The New Woman: Fiction and Feminism at the Fin de Siècle*. Manchester, UK: Manchester University Press, 1997.

Lee, Ella. "Fact Check: Post Online about Stacey Abrams' 2018 Run for Georgia Governor Is Partly False." *USA Today*, November 18, 2020. https://www.usatoday.com/story/news/factcheck/2020/11/18/fact-check-partly-false-claim-stacey-abrams-2018-race/6318836002.

Lee, Hermione. *Penelope Fitzgerald: A Life*. London: Chatto & Windus, 2013.

Lee, Michael. "How Athletes Built a Voter-Turnout Machine, for 2020 and Beyond." *Washington Post*, December 3, 2020. https://www.washingtonpost.com/sports/2020/12/03/nba-wnba-turnout-georgia-primary/.

Leo, Richard A. "From Coercion to Deception: The Changing Nature of Police Interrogation in America." In *The Miranda Debate: Law, Justice, and Policing*. Edited by Richard A. Leo and George Conner Thomas, 65–74. Boston, MA: Northeastern University, 1998.

Lepore, Jill. "Just the Facts, Ma'am: Fake Memoirs, Factual Fictions, the History of History." *New Yorker*, March 17, 2008. https://www.newyorker.com/magazine/2008/03/24/just-the-facts-maam.

Leps, Marie-Christine. *Apprehending the Criminal: The Production of Deviance in Nineteenth-Century Discourse*. Durham, NC: Duke University Press, 1992.

Levin, Harry. *The Gates of Horn: A Study of Five French Realists*. New York: Oxford University Press, 1963.

Levine, Marianne, Holly Otterbein, and Burgess Everett. "Election Gambit Blows Up on Hawley and Cruz." *Politico*. January 9, 2021. https://www.politico.com/news/2021/01/09/hawley-cruz-2024-capitol-riots-456671.

Lewis, Helen. "The Coronavirus Is a Disaster for Feminism: Pandemics Affect Men and Women Differently." *Atlantic*. March 19, 2020. https://www.theatlantic.com/international/archive/2020/03/feminism-womens-rights-coronavirus-covid19/608302/.

Lincoln, Abraham. Second Inaugural Address, March 4, 1865. http://www.bartleby.com/124/pres32.html.

Linko, Sherry Lee. "Saints, Sufferers, and 'Strong-minded Sisters': Anti-suffrage Rhetoric in Rose Terry Cooke's Fiction." *Legacy* 10, no. 1 (1993): 31–46.

"List of Transgender Political Office Holders." *Wikipedia*. https://en.wikipedia.org/wiki/List_of_transgender_political_office-holders.

Little Women. Directed by Greta Gerwig. Columbia Pictures, 2019.

Long, Heather. "Virtual Schooling Has Largely Forced Moms, Not Dads, to Quit Work." *Washington Post*, November 6, 2020. https://www.washingtonpost.com/road-to-recovery/2020/11/06/women-workforce-jobs-report/.

Lorber, Judith. *Gender Inequality: Feminist Theories and Politics*. Los Angeles: Roxbury, 2005.

Lorde, Audre. "The Transformation of Silence into Language and Action" from *Sister Outsider* (1984). In *Feminist Literary Theory and Criticism*. Edited by Sandra M. Gilbert and Susan Gubar, 225–28. New York: W. W. Norton, 2007.

Lovato, Demi. "Commander in Chief." *YouTube*, October 14, 2020. https://www.youtube.com/watch?v=n9Y-lS1trhw.

Lovato, Demi, Julia Michaels, Finneas, Justin Tranter, and Eren Cannata, "Commander in Chief," 2020. https://genius.com/Demi-lovato-commander-in-chief-lyrics.

Lowrey, Brian. "'Madam Secretary' Explores 25th Amendment Episode." *CNN Entertainment*, January 11, 2018. https://edition.cnn.com/2018/01/11/entertainment/madam-secretary-preview/index.html.

Lowrey, Deborah. "Understanding Reproductive Technologies as a Surveillant Assemblage: Revisions of Power and Technoscience." *Sociological Perspectives* 47, no. 4 (Winter 2004): 357–70.

Luker, Kristen. *Abortion and the Politics of Motherhood*. Berkeley: University of California Press, 1984.

Lynskey, Dorian. "Demi Lovato Has Made the Most Damning Protest Song of the Trump Era." *Guardian*, October 15, 2020. https://www.theguardian.com/music/2020/oct/15/demi-lovato-has-made-the-most-damning-protest-song-of-the-trump-era-commander-in-chief.

Madam Secretary. Created by Barbara Hall. CBS Television Studios, 2014–2019. Netflix. https://www.netflix.com/title/80024232.

Maddox, Brenda. *Rosalind Franklin: The Dark Lady of DNA*. New York, Harper Collins, 2002.

"Margaret Drabble." *British Council: Literature*. https://literature.britishcouncil.org/writer/margaret-drabble. Accessed August 17, 2022.

Marino, Katharine M., and Susan Ware. "Rethinking 'First Wave' Feminisms: An Introduction." *Signs: A Journal of Women in Culture and Society* 47, no. 4 (Summer 2022): 811–16.

Martin, Nina, and Renee Montagne. "Black Mothers Keep Dying after Giving Birth, Shalon Irving's Story Explains Why." *All Things Considered*, December 7, 2017. https://www.npr.org/2017/12/07/568948782/black-mothers-keep-dying-after-giving-birth-shalon-irvings-story-explains-why?t=1655893769720.

McArdle, Terence. "How Women Got the Vote." *Washington Post*, November 10, 2017. https://www.washingtonpost.com/news/retropolis/wp/2017/11/10/night-of-terror-the-suffragists-who-were-beaten-and-tortured-for-seeking-the-vote/.

McNary, Dave. " 'Hidden Figures' Set for Free Screenings in 14 Cities for Black History Month." *Variety*, February 14, 2017. https://variety.com/2017/film/news/hidden-figures-free-screenings-black-history-month-1201988170/.

Médecins Sans Frontières. *Medical Guidelines: Essential Obstetric and Newborn Care: Practical Guide for Midwives, Doctors with Obstetrics Training and Health Care Personnel Who Deal with Obstetric Emergencies*, 2017. https://medicalguidelines.msf.org/en/viewport/ONC/english/essential-obstetric-and-newborn-care-51415817.html.

Melas, Chloe. "Demi Lovato Has a Few Words for President Trump." *CNN*, October 14, 2020. https://www.cnn.com/2020/10/14/entertainment/demi-lovato-commander-in-chief-song-interview/index.html.

Melville, Herman. *Published Poems: Battle-Pieces, John Marr, Timoleon*. Chicago, IL: Northwestern University Press/The Newberry Library, 2009.

Menke, Richard. *Telegraphic Realism: Victorian Fiction and Other Information Systems*. Stanford, CA: Stanford University Press, 2007.

Michie, Helena, and Naomi R. Cahn. *Confinements: Fertility and Infertility in Contemporary Culture*. New Brunswick, NJ: Rutgers University Press, 1997.

Mihalcik, Carrie. "First COVID-19 Vaccines Given in the US." *CNET*, December 14, 2020. https://www.cnet.com/science/first-covid-19-vaccines-given-in-the-us/.

Miller, Mark. "Female Workers Could Take Another Pandemic Hit: To Their Retirements." *New York Times*, December 11, 2020. https://nyti.ms/2W1bWFg.

Miranda, Shauneen. "Rep. Cheney Pays Tribute to the Women's Suffrage Movement in Closing Jan. 6 Remarks." *NPR*, July 22, 2022. https://www.npr.org/2022/07/22/1112992409/rep-cheney-jan-6-suffrage-hearing.

"Mission Statement." *Trans Book Review*. https://transbookreviews.wordpress.com/.

Mitovich, Matt Webb. "The Closer Season Finale Recap: The Last Stroh." *TVLine*, August 12, 2012. http://tvline.com/2012/08/13/the-closer-series-finale-recap/.

Mittell, Jason. "Narrative Complexity in Contemporary American Television." *Velvet Light Trap* 58, no. 1 (December 2005): 29–40.

Moi, Toril. "Feminism, Postmodernism, and Style: Recent Feminist Criticism in the United States." *Cultural Critique* 9 (1988): 3–22.

Moone, Morgan. "Voter Suppression Is a Feminist Issue: Lessons for Future Elections." *Queens Daily Eagle*, November 7, 2018. https://queenseagle.com/all/2018/11/7/voter-suppression-is-a-feminist-issue-lessons-for-future-elections.

Moore, Henrietta L. *Feminism and Anthropology*. Minneapolis: University of Minnesota Press, 1988.

Moreno-Garcia, Silvia. *Mexican Gothic*. New York: Del Rey, 2020.

Morris, Bilal G. " 'Sloppy C-Section' That Killed Kira Johnson Prompts Maternal Health Lawsuit Accusing Hospital of Racism." *Newsone*, May 5, 2022. https://

newsone.com/4331183/sloppy-c-section-that-killed-kira-johnson-prompts-racism-lawsuit/.

Morrison, Toni. *Paradise*. New York: Penguin, 1999.

Mouly, Françoise. "Cover Story: Abigail Gray Swartz's 'The March.'" *New Yorker*, January 27, 2017. https://www.newyorker.com/culture/culture-desk/cover-story-2017-02-06.

Moya, Paula M. L. "Multifocal Decolonial Novels." Talk presented at Narrative 2020 meeting of the International Society for the Study of Narrative. New Orleans, LA, March 6, 2020.

Mrs. America. Created by Dahvi Waller. Hulu/FXP. 2020.

Mukhopadhyay, Samhita, and Kate Harding (eds.). *Nasty Women: Feminism, Resistance, and Revolution in Trump's America*. New York: Picador, 2017.

Mulvey, Laura. "Visual Pleasure and Narrative Cinema." In *Film Theory and Criticism*, edited by Gerald Mast and Marshall Cohen, 803–16. New York: Oxford University Press, 1985.

Murphy, Cullen. "A History of *The Atlantic Monthly*," November 1994. http://www.theatlantic.com/past/docs/about/atlhistf.htm.

Murray, Oswyn. "Life and Society in Classical Greece." *The Oxford History of the Classical World*. Edited by John Boardman, Jasper Griffin, and Oswyn Murray, 205–33. Oxford, UK: Oxford University Press, 1986.

"Nancy Pelosi Offers Election Night Predictions." *PBS NewsHour*, November 8, 2016. https://www.pbs.org/video/nancy-pelosi-offers-election-night-predictions-1485909178/.

National Organization for Women. "Immigration as a Feminist Issue." https://now.org/resource/immigration-as-a-feminist-issue/. Accessed January 16, 2021.

National Science Foundation, National Center for Science and Engineering Statistics, 2017. *Women, Minorities, and Persons with Disabilities in Science and Engineering: 2017*. Special Report NSF 17-310. Arlington, VA. www.nsf.gov/statistics/wmpd/.

Neidenbach, Elizabeth Clark. "Rethinking Reconstruction." Review of Daniel Brook, *The Accident of Color: A Story of Race in Reconstruction*. *64 Parishes*. https://64parishes.org/rethinking-reconstruction.

"New Yorker Celebrates Intersectional Feminism with New 'Rosie the Riveter' Cover." *The Griot*, January 28, 2017. https://thegrio.com/2017/01/28/new-yorker-celebrates-intersectional-feminism-with-new-rosie-the-riveter-cover/.

NewsOne Staff. "Rest in Power: Notable Black Folks We Lost in 2020." *NewsOne*, November 24, 2020. https://newsone.com/playlist/notable-deaths-2020/.

Njoroge, Joyce N., and Nisha I. Parikh. "Understanding Health Disparities in Cardiovascular Diseases in Pregnancy among Black Women: Prevalence, Preventive Care, and Peripartum Support Networks." *Current Cardiovascular Risk Reports* 14, no. 8 (2020). https://link.springer.com/content/pdf/10.1007/s12170-020-00641-9.pdf.

Noble, David F. *A World without Women: The Christian Clerical Culture of Western Science*. New York: Knopf, 1992.

Norris, Michele L. "How a WNBA Assist Helped Raphael Warnock Win a Senate Seat." *Washington Post*, January 6, 2021. https://www.washingtonpost.com/opinions/how-a-wnba-assist-helped-raphael-warnock-win-a-senate-seat/2021/01/06/59368f8c-5067-11eb-bda4-615aaefd0555_story.html.

"Oliphant v. Suquamish Indian Tribe," *Wikipedia*. http://en.wikipedia.org/wiki/Oliphant_v._Suquamish_Indian_Tribe.

"Ordination of Women and the Old Testament," 2010. *WomenOrdination.Com*. http://www.womenordination.com/background/ordination-of-women-and-the-old-testament/articletype/articleview/articleid/1094/wasnt-eves-subordination-to-adam-in-genesis-316-a-part-of-the-curse-which-christ-came-to-take-away.

Orenstein, Peggy. "Mourning My Miscarriage." *New York Times Magazine*, April 21, 2002. https://www.nytimes.com/2002/04/21/magazine/mourning-my-miscarriage.html.

Parker, Ben, Stephanie Steinbrecher, Kelsey Ronan, John McMurtrie, Sophia DuRose, Rachel Villa, and Amy Sumerton. "Lest We Forget the Horrors: A Catalog of Trump's Worst Cruelties, Collusions, Corruptions, and Crimes." *McSweeney's*. January 20, 2021. https://www.mcsweeneys.net/articles/the-complete-listing-atrocities-1-1-056.

Parker, Robert Dale. *How to Interpret Literature: Critical Theory for Literary and Cultural Studies*. New York: Oxford University Press, 2008.

Patchett, Ann. *State of Wonder*. New York: Harper Collins, 2011.

Pearl, Diana. " 'Pussyhats' Galore: Inside the Pink Toppers Thousands Will Wear to the Women's March on Washington." *People Politics*. January 21, 2017. http://people.com/politics/pussyhats-galore-inside-the-pink-toppers-thousands-will-wear-to-the-womens-march-on-washington/.

Perkowitz, Sidney. *Hollywood Science: Movies, Science, and the End of the World*. New York: Columbia University Press, 2007.

Petchesky, Rosalind Pollack. "Fetal Images: The Power of Visual Culture in the Politics of Reproduction." *Feminist Studies* 13, no. 2 (1987): 263–92.

Petty, Leslie. "The Political Is Personal: The Feminist Lesson of Henry James's *The Bostonians*," *Women's Studies* 34, no. 5 (2005): 377–403.

———. *Romancing the Vote: Feminist Activism in American Fiction 1870–1920*. Athens: University of Georgia Press, 2006.

Peyre, Claudine. "Three Interviews with Margaret Drabble." *Cercle* 21 (2011). http://www.cercles.com/n21/peyre.pdf.

Pfaff, Leslie Garisto, "100 Years and Counting." Interview with Jacqueline Littman, *Rutgers Alumni Magazine* (Winter 2018): 51–53.

Phelan, James. *Living to Tell about It: A Rhetoric and Ethics of Character Narration*. Ithaca, NY: Cornell University Press, 2005.

Phelps, Elizabeth Stuart. *Doctor Zay*. New York: Feminist Press, 1987.

————. *The Silent Partner*. New York: Feminist Press, 1983.

Philpotts, Trey. "The Real Marshalsea." *The Dickensian* 87 (1991): 130–45.

Pollack, Eileen. "Why Fiction Needs More Women Scientists." *LitHub*, May 10, 2016. https://lithub.com/why-fiction-needs-more-women-scientists/.

Pollock, Anne. *Sickening: Anti-Black Racism and Health Disparities in the United States*. Minneapolis: University of Minnesota Press, 2021.

Pope Francis. "A Crisis Reveals What Is in Our Hearts." *New York Times*. November 29, 2020. https://www.nytimes.com/2020/11/26/opinion/pope-francis-covid.html.

Popli, Nik, and Julia Zorthian. "What Happened to Jan. 6 Insurrectionists Arrested in the Year since the Capitol Riot." *Time*. June 15, 2022. https://time.com/6133336/jan-6-capitol-riot-arrests-sentences/.

Povich, Lynn. *The Good Girls Revolt: How the Women of Newsweek Sued their Bosses and Changed the Workplace*. New York: Public Affairs, 2012.

Power, Samantha. "The Can-Do Power: America's Advantage and Biden's Chance," *Foreign Affairs* 100, no. 1 (January/February 2021): 10–24, 17–19.

Powers, John. " 'Borgen' Is Denmark's 'West Wing' (but Even Better)." *NPR*, February 5, 2014. http://www.npr.org/2014/02/04/271525839/borgen-is-denmarks-west-wing-but-even-better.

"President Obama to Sign VAWA with Tribal Jurisdiction Provision." Indianz.com. March 1, 2013. http://www.indianz.com/News/2013/008725.asp. Accessed January 9, 2021.

Prum, Richard O. *The Evolution of Beauty: How Darwin's Forgotten Theory of Mate Choice Shapes the Animal World—and Us*. New York: Penguin, 2017.

Pussyhat Project, "Design Interventions for Social Change." https://www.pussy-hatproject.com/our-story/. Accessed August 17, 2022.

Quinn, Susan. *Marie Curie: A Life*. New York: Simon and Schuster, 1995.

Rabinowitz, Nancy Sorkin. *Anxiety Veiled: Euripides and the Traffic in Women*. Ithaca, NY: Cornell University Press, 1993.

Rabinowitz, Peter. *Before Reading: Narrative Conventions and the Politics of Interpretation*. Columbus: Ohio State University Press, 1998.

Rahim, Zamira, and Rob Picheta, "Thousands around the World Protest George Floyd's Death in Global Display of Solidarity." *CNN World*, June 1, 2020. https://www.cnn.com/2020/06/01/world/george-floyd-global-protests-intl/index.html.

"Rampart Scandal Timeline." *PBS Frontline*. Accessed August 6, 2022. http://www.pbs.org/wgbh/pages/frontline/shows/lapd/scandal/cron.html.

Rancière, Jacques. *The Flesh of Words*. Translated by Charlotte Mandell. Stanford, CA: Stanford University Press, 2004.

Rappaport, Scott. "Literature Professor Links Santa Cruz to International Theater Event for Peace." *UC Currents Online*. February 17, 2003. https://currents.ucsc.edu/02-03/02-17/play.html.

Rappoport, Jill. *Giving Women: Alliance and Exchange in Victorian Culture*. Oxford, UK: Oxford University Press, 2012.

Reynolds, David S. *Mightier than the Sword: Uncle Tom's Cabin and the Battle for America*. New York: Norton, 2011.

Rich, Adrienne. "Notes toward a Politics of Location," originally published in *Arts of the Possible: Essays and Conversations*. New York: W. W. Norton, 2001. In *Feminist Literary Theory and Criticism*, edited by Sandra M. Gilbert and Susan Gubar. 228–39. W. W. Norton: 2007.

Rimmon-Kenan, Shlomith. *Narrative Fiction: Contemporary Poetics*. London: Routledge, 1989.

Roberts, Dorothy. *Killing the Black Body: Race, Reproduction, and the Meaning of Liberty*. London: Virago, 1998.

Rogers, Laura L. "The Violence against Women Act: An Ongoing Fixture." U.S. Department of Justice. February 19, 2020. https://www.justice.gov/ovw/blog/violence-against-women-act-ongoing-fixture-nation-s-response-domestic-violence-dating. Accessed January 9, 2021.

Romero, Channette. "Creating the Beloved Community: Religion, Race, and Nation in Toni Morrison's *Paradise*." *African American Review* 39, no. 3 (2005): 415–30.

Rooney, Ellen. "The Literary Politics of Feminist Theory." In *The Cambridge Companion to Feminist Literary Theory*. Edited by Ellen Rooney, 73–95. Cambridge, UK: Cambridge University Press, 2006.

Rose, Hilary. *Love, Power and Knowledge: Towards a Feminist Transformation of the Sciences*. Cambridge, UK: Polity Press, 1994.

Rossiter, Margaret W. "The Matthew Matilda Effect in Science." *Social Studies of Science* 23, no. 2 (1993): 325–41.

———. *Women Scientists in America: Struggles and Strategies to 1940*, vol. 1. Baltimore, MD: Johns Hopkins University Press, 1982.

———. *Women Scientists in America: Forging a New World Since 1962*, vol. 3. Baltimore, MD: Johns Hopkins University Press, 2012.

Rothman, Barbara Katz. *Genetic Maps and Human Imaginations: The Limits of Science in Understanding Who We Are*. New York: W. W. Norton, 1998.

———. *The Tentative Pregnancy: How Amniocentesis Changes the Experience of Motherhood*. New York: W. W. Norton, 1993.

Rothstein, Mervyn. "No Balm in Gilead for Margaret Atwood." *New York Times*, February 17, 1986. https://www.nytimes.com/books/00/09/03/specials/atwood-gilead.html.

Rudick, Nicole. "A Universe of One's Own." *New York Review of Books*. July 18, 2019. https://www.nybooks.com/articles/2019/07/18/universe-of-ones-own-women-science-fiction/.

Russell, Jim. "Smith College Commencement Speaker Urges Grads 'To Cast Out Fear and Replace It with Hope.'" *Mass Live*, May 15, 2022. https://www.

masslive.com/news/2022/05/smith-college-commencement-speaker-urges-grads-to-cast-out-fear-and-replace-it-with-hope.html.

Sandberg, Sheryl. "Why We Have Too Few Women Leaders." Ted talk delivered in December 2010. https://www.ted.com/talks/sheryl_sandberg_why_we_have_too_few_women_leaders.

Saraiya, Sonia. "Review: *House of Cards* Collapses, Finally." *Vanity Fair.* November 2, 2018. https://www.vanityfair.com/hollywood/2018/11/house-of-cards-final-season-review.

Sawdey, Evan. [Review] "Beyonce: Lemonade." *Pop Matters.* April 27, 2016. https://www.popmatters.com/beyonce-lemonade-2495435666.html.

Sayers, Dorothy, *Gaudy Night.* London: Victor Gollancz, 1936.

Schaffer, Elise. "H.E.R. Performs New Song 'I Can't Breathe.'" *Variety.* https://variety.com/video/h-e-r-debuts-song-inspired-by-george-floyd-i-cant-breathe/. Accessed January 16, 2021.

Schiebinger, Londa. *Has Feminism Changed Science?* Cambridge, MA: Harvard University Press, 2001.

Schmidt, Samantha. "Women Have Been Hit Hardest by Job Losses in the Pandemic. And It May Only Get Worse." *Washington Post*, May 9, 2020. https://www.washingtonpost.com/dc-md-va/2020/05/09/women-unemployment-jobless-coronavirus/.

Scott, A. O. "Review: 'Hidden Figures' Honors 3 Black Women Who Helped NASA Soar." *New York Times.* December 22, 2016. https://www.nytimes.com/2016/12/22/movies/hidden-figures-review.html?referrer=google_kp.

Scudder, Horace Elisha. "*The Bostonians*, by Henry James." *Atlantic*, June 1886. https://www.theatlantic.com/past/docs/unbound/classrev/thebosto.htm.

Sen, Sambudha. "*Bleak House* and *Little Dorrit*: The Radical Heritage." *ELH* 65, no. 4 (1998): 945–70.

Shear, Michael D., and Peter Baker. "Biden Seeks Quick Start with Executive Actions and Aggressive Legislation." *New York Times.* January 16, 2021. https://www.nytimes.com/2021/01/16/us/politics/biden-administration-executive-action-legislation.html.

Shear, Michael D., and Lisa Friedman. "Biden Could Roll Back Trump Agenda with Blitz of Executive Actions." *New York Times*, November 8, 2020. https://www.nytimes.com/2020/11/08/us/politics/biden-trump-executive-action.html.

Shetterly, Margot Lee. *Hidden Figures: The American Dream and the Untold Story of the Black Women Mathematicians Who Helped Win the Space Race.* New York: Harper Collins, 2016.

Showalter, Elaine. "The Other Bostonians: Gender and Literary Study." *Yale Journal of Criticism* 1, no. 2 (Spring 1988): 179–87.

Shulman, Robert. "Introduction." *The Yellow Wallpaper and Other Stories.* Oxford, UK: Oxford University Press, 1995.

"Sit in a Drizzle to See Greek Play: Courageous Suffragists in Outdoor Theatre Hear Aristophanes Plead Their Cause." *New York Times.* September 20, 1912.

https://www.nytimes.com/1912/09/20/archives/sit-in-a-drizzle-to-see-greek-play-courageous-suffragists-in.html.

Slavery and the Literary Imagination. Edited by Deborah E. McDowell and Arnold Rampersad. Baltimore, MD: Johns Hopkins University Press, 1989.

Smethers, Sam. "We're at a Gender Equality Crossroads: Which Path Will the Government Take?" *Guardian.* November 20, 2020. https://www.theguardian.com/commentisfree/2020/nov/20/gender-equality-disruption-covid-19-inequalities#_=_.

"Snow, Charles Percy." *Complete Dictionary of Scientific Biography.* Encyclopedia.com. 2008. http://www.encyclopedia.com/topic/C.P._Snow.aspx.

Snow, C. P. *The Search.* Cornwall, UK: House of Stratus, 2000.

Solow, Barbara. "Nancy Pelosi: Smith Graduates Have Power to Shape the Future." *Notes from Paradise.* May 20, 2020. https://www.smith.edu/news/2020-commencement-pelosi.

Sottile, Alexis. "'Good Girls Revolt': Inside Landmark Lawsuit behind New Feminist Series: Fact-checking the Fictionalized Account of the 1970 Female Uprising at 'Newsweek.'" *Rolling Stone,* November 3, 2016. https://www.rollingstone.com/culture/news/good-girls-revolt-inside-lawsuit-that-inspired-amazon-show-w447701.

Squier, Susan Merrill. *Babies in Bottles: Twentieth-Century Visions of Reproductive Technology.* New Brunswick, NJ: Rutgers University Press, 1995.

Sraders, Anne, and Lance Lambert. "Nearly 100,000 Establishments That Temporarily Shut Down Due to the Pandemic Are Now Out of Business." *Fortune,* September 28, 2020. https://fortune.com/2020/09/28/covid-buisnesses-shut-down-closed/.

Stansell, Christine. "Elizabeth Stuart Phelps: A Study in Female Rebellion." *Massachusetts Review* 13, no. 1/2 (Winter-Spring, 1972): 239–56.

———. *The Feminist Promise: 1792 to the Present.* New York: Modern Library, 2011.

Steinke, Jocelyn. "Connecting Theory and Practice: Using Televised Images of Women Scientist Role Models in Television Programming." *Journal of Broadcasting and Electronic Media* 42, no. 1 (1998): 142–51.

Sterritt, David. "'The Bostonians': So far, the Best Movie of the Year. Merchant, Ivory, Jhabvala (and Henry James) Have Done It Again." *Christian Science Monitor,* August 2, 1984. https://www.csmonitor.com/1984/0802/080209.html.

Stewart, Noah. "Toward a Definition of the Police Procedural." *Noah's Archives: Curating Genre Fiction since 1972,* March 30, 2014. http://noah-stewart.com/2014/03/30/toward-a-definition-of-the-police-procedural/.

Stimpson, Catherine. "Reading for Love: Canons, Paracanons, and Whistling Jo March." In *Little Women and the Feminist Imagination: Criticism, Controversy, Personal Essay.* Edited by Janice M. Alberghene and Beverly Lyon Clark, 62–81. New York and London: Garland, 1999.

Stowe, Harriet Beecher. *Uncle Tom's Cabin or, Life among the Lowly.* New York: Penguin, 1981.

Subramanian, Banu. "Moored Metamorphoses: A Retrospective Essay on Feminist Science Studies." *Signs: A Journal of Woman in Culture and Society* 34, no. 4 (2009): 951–80.

"Suffragettes." *Wikipedia.* http://en.wikipedia.org/wiki/Suffragette.

Sundquist, Eric. "Slavery, Revolution, and the American Renaissance." In *The American Renaissance Reconsidered.* Edited by Walter Benn Michaels and Donald Pease, 1–33. Baltimore, MD: Johns Hopkins University Press, 1985.

Swain, Heather. *Luscious Lemon.* New York: Downtown Press, 2004.

———. "My Flesh and Blood." *Salon,* May 11, 2003. http://dir.salon.com/story/mwt/feature/2003/03/11/miscarriage/index2.html.

Tapper, Jake, Sunlen Miller, and Devin Dwyer. "Obama Administration Drops 'Marriage Act.'" *ABC News,* February 23, 2011. https://abcnews.go.com/Politics/obama-administration-drops-legal-defense-marriage-act/story?id=12981242.

Taranto, Stacie, and Leandra Zarnow. "Mixed 2020 Election Results Show that Women still Face a Sexist Political Culture." *Washington Post,* November 6, 2020. https://www.washingtonpost.com/outlook/2020/11/06/mixed-2020-election-results-show-that-women-still-face-sexist-political-culture/.

"A Taste of Honey." *BFI Screen Online.* http://www.screenonline.org.uk/film/id/439975/.

Tatum, Beverly Daniel. "Smith College Commencement Address," May 15, 2022. https://www.smith.edu/about-smith/college-events/commencement/speakers-and-honorary-degrees/dr-beverly-daniel-tatum.

Taub, Amanda. "On Social Media's Fringes, Growing Extremism Targets Women." *New York Times,* May 9, 2018. https://www.nytimes.com/2018/05/09/world/americas/incels-toronto-attack.html.

Taylor, Alan. "Photos of the Women's Marches around the World." *Atlantic,* January 21, 2017. https://www.theatlantic.com/photo/2017/01/photos-of-the-womens-marches-around-the-world/514049/.

Taylor, Amy Murrell. *The Divided Family in Civil War America.* Chapel Hill: University of North Carolina Press, 2009.

Taylor, Mary. *Miss Miles: A Tale of Yorkshire Life Sixty Years Ago.* New York: Oxford University Press, 1990.

Technology and Humanity. Edited by Carol Colatrella. Ipswich, MA: Salem Press, 2013.

"Teen Who Shot Video of Floyd's Death Receives Pulitzer Honour." *Al Jazeera,* June 11, 2021. https://www.aljazeera.com/news/2021/6/11/teen-who-shot-video-of-floyds-death-receives-pulitzer-honor.

Telegraph Women. "#DistractinglySexy: Female Scientists Mock Sir Tim Hunt on Twitter." *Telegraph.* June 11, 2015. http://www.telegraph.co.uk/women/womens-life/11667981/Tim-Hunt-Distractinglysexy-female-scientists-post-photos-on-Twitter.html.

"Theodore Parker and the 'Moral Universe.'" *NPR,* September 2, 2010. http://www.npr.org/templates/story/story.php?storyId=129609461.

Thomas III, William G. "Television News and the Civil Rights Struggle: The Views in Virginia and Mississippi." *Southern Spaces*, November 3, 2004. https://southernspaces.org/2004/television-news-and-civil-rights-struggle-views-virginia-and-mississippi/.

TIME'S UP Guide to Equity and Inclusion during Crisis. "Building an Anti-Racist Workplace." https://timesupfoundation.org/work/equity/guide-equity-inclusion-during-crisis/building-an-anti-racist-workplace/.

"Timeline: Our Fight against Opportunistic Abortion Bans during the COVID-19 Pandemic." *Planned Parenthood*. https://www.plannedparenthoodaction.org/issues/abortion/timeline-our-fight-against-abortion-bans-during-covid19.

Tocqueville, Alexis de. *Democracy in America*. Edited by J. P. Mayer. Translated by George Lawrence. New York: Doubleday, 1969.

Todd, Janet. *Feminist Literary History: A Defence*. Cambridge, UK: Polity Press, 2007.

Tompkins, Jane. *Sensational Designs: The Cultural Works of American Fiction, 1790–1860*. New York: Oxford University Press, 1986.

Tone, Andrea. *Devices and Desires: A History of Contraceptives in America*. New York: Hill and Wang, 2001.

Totenberg, Nina. "Justice Ruth Bader Ginsburg, Champion of Gender Equality, Dies at 87." *NPR*, September 18, 2020. https://www.npr.org/2020/09/18/100306972/justice-ruth-bader-ginsburg-champion-of-gender-equality-dies-at-87.

Traister, Rebecca. *Good and Mad: The Revolutionary Power of Women's Anger*. New York: Simon and Schuster, 2018.

"Transcript: Donald Trump's Taped Comments about Women." *New York Times*, October 8, 2016. https://www.nytimes.com/2016/10/08/us/donald-trump-tape-transcript.html.

Traweek, Sharon. *Beamtimes and Lifetimes: The World of High Energy Physics*. Cambridge, MA: Harvard University Press, 1992.

Union, Gabrielle. "The Hard Truth about My Surrogacy Journey." *Time*. September 10, 2021. https://time.com/6096588/gabrielle-union-surrogacy/.

———. "Gabrielle Union on the Condition That Caused Her Infertility." Interview by Oprah Winfrey. SuperSoul Sunday, OWNTV, *YouTube*, December 7, 2018. https://www.youtube.com/watch?v=6XJMHhd-a3E.

United Kingdom. National Health Service. "The Government's 2022 to 2023 Mandate to NHS England." March 31, 2002. https://assets.publishing.service.gov.uk/government/uploads/system/uploads/attachment_data/file/1065713/2022-to-2023-nhs-england-mandate.pdf.

———. Parliament. "Early Suffragist Campaigning." https://www.parliament.uk/about/livingheritage/transformingsociety/electionsvoting/womenvote/overview/earlysuffragist/. Accessed August 3, 2022.

———. Public General Acts. Equality Act 2010. https://www.legislation.gov.uk/ukpga/2010/15/contents.

United Nations. *The World's Women 1970–1990: Trends and Statistics.* New York, 1991. https://unstats.un.org/unsd/demographicsocial/products/worlds-women/documents/ww1990.pdf.

United Nations Women. "Emma Watson: Gender Equality Is Your Issue Too." September 20, 2014. https://www.unwomen.org/en/news/stories/2014/9/emma-watson-gender-equality-is-your-issue-too.

———. "Facts and Figures: Leadership and Political Participation." September 1, 2021. http://www.unwomen.org/en/what-we-do/leadership-and-political-participation/facts-and-figures.

———. Meghan Markle Speech at UN Women 2015. *YouTube,* November 17, 2016. https://www.youtube.com/watch?v=EDvV-xfrqIM.

———. "Press Release: To Accelerate Gender Equality, UN Women Launches a Call to Action to parliamentarians." June 27, 2019, Phttp://www.unwomen.org/en/news/stories/2019/6/press-release-un-women-launches-a-call-to-action-to-parliamentarians.

US Centers for Disease Control, "Racial and Ethnic Disparities Continue in Pregnancy-Related Deaths," September 5, 2019. https://www.cdc.gov/media/releases/2019/p0905-racial-ethnic-disparities-pregnancy-deaths.html.

US Congress. S. 1042-117th Congress: Kira Johnson Act, June 24, 2022. https://www.govtrack.us/congress/bills/117/s1042

US Department of Health and Human Services. "Following President Biden's Executive Order to Protect Access to Reproductive Health Care, HHS Announces Guidance to Clarify that Emergency Medical Care Includes Abortion Services," July 11, 2022. https://www.hhs.gov/about/news/2022/07/11/following-president-bidens-executive-order-protect-access-reproductive-health-care-hhs-announces-guidance-clarify-that-emergency-medical-care-includes-abortion-services.html.

US Department of Labor. "DOL Policies on Gender Identity: Rights and Responsibilities." https://www.dol.gov/agencies/oasam/centers-offices/civil-rights-center/internal/policies/gender-identity.

US House of Representatives. Select Committee to Investigate the January 6th Attack on the US Capitol. https://january6th.house.gov/. Accessed July 24, 2022.

US Library of Congress. "Sailors Attacking Pickets, 1917." Library of Congress. https://www.loc.gov/item/mnwp000210/.

US National Science Foundation. *Women, Minorities, and Persons with Disabilities in Science and Engineering,* 2017. https://www.nsf.gov/statistics/2017/nsf17310/digest/about-this-report/.

Veep. Created by Armando Iannuci, 2012–2019. HBO Entertainment. Hulu. https://www.hulu.com/series/veep-cbb72a65-7727-4959-ad0c-de60c0546e1f.

Victor, Daniel. "Access Hollywood' Reminds Trump: 'The Tape Is Very Real.' " *New York Times,* November 28, 2017, https://www.nytimes.com/2017/11/28/us/politics/donald-trump-tape.html.

Villarosa, Linda. "Why America's Black Mothers and Babies Are in a Life-or-Death Crisis." *New York Times*, April 11, 2018. https://www.nytimes.com/2018/04/11/magazine/black-mothers-babies-death-maternal-mortality.html.

Wagner, John. "Bernie Sanders Wins Backing of African American Group in Nevada's Largest County." *Washington Post*, February 19, 2016.

Wahlström, Helena. "Reproduction, Politics, and John Irving's The Cider House Rules: Women's Rights or 'Fetal Rights.'" *Culture Unbound* 5, no. 2 (2013): 251–71.

Wajcman, Judy. *Feminism Confronts Technology*. University Park, PA: Pennsylvania State University Press, 1991.

Walezak, Emilie. *Rethinking Contemporary British Women's Writing: Realism, Feminism, Materialism*. London: Bloomsbury, 2021.

Walton, Priscilla, and Manina Jones. *Detective Agency: Women Rewriting the Hard-Boiled Tradition*. Berkeley and Los Angeles: University of California Press, 1999.

Ward, Megan. "Our Posthuman Past: Victorian Realism, Cybernetics, and the Problem of Information." *Configurations* 20, no. 3 (2012): 279–97.

Watt, Ian. *The Rise of the Novel: Studies in Defoe, Richardson and Fielding*. Berkeley, CA: University of California Press, 1957.

Weiner, Jennifer. "How Do I Explain Kavanaugh to My Daughters?" *New York Times*. October 9, 2018. https://www.nytimes.com/2018/10/09/opinion/kavanaugh-justice-princeton-women.html.

Weisser, Susan Ostrov. *The Glass Slipper: Women and Love Stories*. New Brunswick, NJ: Rutgers University Press, 2013.

Wharton, Edith. *The House of Mirth*. London: Virago, 2007.

Wilson, Edmund. *Patriotic Gore: Studies in the Literature of the American Civil War*. W. W. Norton, 1994.

Wilson, Gabriella. (H.E.R.). "I Can't Breathe." 2020. https://genius.com/Her-i-cant-breathe-lyrics.

Wilson, Harriet. *Our Nig, or, Sketches from the Life of a Free Black*. New York: Random House, 1983.

Wolitzer, Meg. *The Female Persuasion*. New York: Riverhead Books, 2018.

Wollstonecraft, Mary. *A Vindication of the Rights of Woman with Strictures on Political and Moral Subjects*. London: J. Johnson, 1792. https://oll.libertyfund.org/titles/wollstonecraft-a-vindication-of-the-rights-of-woman.

Wolosky, Shira. "Claiming the Bible." In *The Cambridge History of American Literature, vol.4: Nineteenth-Century Poetry, 1800–1910*. Edited by Sacvan Bercovitch, 200–47. Cambridge, UK: Cambridge University Press, 2004.

Woolf, Virginia. *A Room of One's Own*. New York: Harcourt, Brace, World, 1957.

Woolson, Constance Fenimore "Crowder's Cove: A Story of War." In *Civil War Women: The Civil War Seen through Women's Eyes in Stories by Louisa May Alcott, Kate Chopin, Eudora Welty, and Other Great Women Writers*. Edited by Frank McSherry Jr., Charles G. Waugh, and Martin Greenberg, 72–92. New York: Simon and Schuster, 1988.

World Population Review. Accessed August 6, 2022. https://worldpopulationreview. com/us-cities/atlanta-ga-population.

Worldometer, "Covid Live." https://www.worldometers.info/coronavirus/. Accessed July 12, 2022.

Worth, Jennifer. *Call the Midwife: A True Story of the East End in the 1950s.* London: Orion Books, 2012.

Young, Elizabeth. *Disarming the Nation: Women's Writing and the American Civil War.* Chicago: University of Chicago Press, 1999.

Zeilinger, Julie. "Student Loan Debt Is a Feminist Issue." *WMC FBomb.* Women's Media Center. June 25, 2017. https://www.womensmediacenter.com/fbomb/ student-loan-debt-is-a-feminist-issue.

Zimmerman, Jess. "The Myth of the Well-Behaved Women's March." *New Republic.* January 24, 2017. https://newrepublic.com/article/140065/myth-well-behaved-womens-march.

Zunshine, Lisa. *Why We Read Fiction: Theory of Mind and the Novel.* Columbus: Ohio State University Press, 2006.

Index